AFPC®

STUDY TEXT

Paper G20

Personal Investment Planning

IN THIS JULY 2005 EDITION

- Comprehensive coverage based on the **2005 syllabus**, reflecting all syllabus changes

- Coverage of changes introduced in **the tax year 2005/06**

UPDATES ARE AVAILABLE ON OUR WEBSITE AT:

www.bpp.com/afpc

(see page (v) for more details)

BPP Professional Education
July 2005

First edition 1996
Tenth edition July 2005

ISBN 0 7517 2338 X (previous edition 0 7517 1698 7)

British Library Cataloguing-in-Publication Data
A catalogue record for this book
is available from the British Library

Published by

BPP Professional Education
Aldine House, Aldine Place
London W12 8AW

www.bpp.com

Printed in Great Britain by WM Print

We are grateful to the Chartered Insurance Institute® for permission to reproduce in this text the syllabus of which the Institute holds the copyright.

AFPC® is a registered trademark of the Chartered Insurance Institute®. The CII® does not endorse, promote, review or warrant the accuracy of the products or services offered by BPP Professional Education.

CONTENTS

Page

INTRODUCTION

(v)

Preface - How to use this Study Text - Syllabus - The examination paper

TAX TABLES

ANSWERS

PRACTICE EXAMINATION

ANSWERS TO PRACTICE EXAMINATION

INDEX

REVIEW FORM & FREE PRIZE DRAW

ORDER FORM

PREFACE

The examination syllabus of the Advanced Financial Planning Certificate is a demanding test of each candidate's knowledge and skills.

Thorough, up-to-date and effective learning and practice material is crucial for busy professionals preparing for qualifying exams. In our many years of publishing for professional exams, we have learnt this lesson well. All our Study Texts are written by qualified professionals. The resulting material is *comprehensive* - covering the *whole* syllabus - *on target* - covering *only* the syllabus - and *up-to-date* at the month of publication.

This Study Text has been written specifically for the Advanced Financial Planning Certificate Paper G20 *Personal Investment Planning*. The syllabus is reproduced and has been cross-referenced to the text, so you can be assured that coverage is complete. The syllabus is followed by details of the examination paper format.

The main body of the Study Text takes you through the syllabus in easily managed stages, with plenty of opportunities for skill - and exam question - practice. All examinable topics are covered in full. For a brief guide to the structure of the text, and how it may most effectively be used, see page (vi).

Updates to this Study Text

To cover changes occurring in the twelve months after the publication of this Study Text, we provide free **Updates.**

Possible changes to be covered in Updates are:

- Syllabus changes, which normally take effect from January. (Look out for an Update in November or December.)

- Changes in legislation, which for AFPC may be examined three months after they become legally effective.

To register for your free Updates, go to our website at **www.bpp.com/afpc**. Once you register, you will receive Email Alerts when future Updates are published. If you do not have Internet access, please call our Customer Service Team on 0845 0751 100 to request a free printed copy of Updates.

BPP Professional Education
July 2005

HOW TO USE THIS STUDY TEXT

This Study Text has been designed to help you get to grips as effectively as possible with the content and scope of Paper G20: *Personal Investment Planning.*

Each *chapter* of the Study Text is divided into *sections* and contains:

- A list of topics covered, cross-referenced to the syllabus
- An introduction to put the chapter in context
- Clear, concise topic-by-topic coverage
- Examples and exercises to reinforce learning, confirm understanding and stimulate thought
- A roundup of the key points in the chapter
- A quiz (with answers at the end of the Study Text)
- Answers to the exercises
- A practice question of examination standard (with an answer at the end of the Study Text)

Chapter roundup and quiz

At the end of each chapter, you will find two boxes. The first box is the *Chapter roundup* which summarises key points. The second box is the *Quick Quiz*, which serves a number of purposes.

- It is an essential part of the chapter roundup and can be glanced over quickly to remind yourself of key issues covered by the chapter.

- It is a quiz, pure and simple. Try doing a quiz each morning to revise what you read the night before.

- It is a revision tool. Shortly before your examination sit down with pen and paper and try to answer all the questions fully.

The answers to quiz questions are given at the end of the Study Text.

Practice questions

You can use the practice question at the end of each chapter to make sure that you have learnt the topics covered up to examination standard.

Practice examination

At the end of this Study Text, you will find a full practice examination. You should attempt it under strict examination conditions before you sit the real examination.

SYLLABUS

Objective

The **objective** of G20 is to develop in the candidate:

- A sound knowledge and understanding of investments

- The ability to advise individual clients on the construction of investment portfolios to meet current and foreseeable future needs

- The ability to apply knowledge and skills to practical situations

- The ability to synthesise different aspects of the syllabus and apply them to given scenarios

Assumed knowledge and application skills

It is assumed that the candidate already has the knowledge and application skills gained from study of the relevant elements of **units 1, 2 and 3 of the FPC or equivalent qualification**.

It is also assumed that the candidate can use basic financial mathematics for tasks such as grossing up, projecting future values of current amounts and discounting future amounts into current values.

Notes

The syllabus is examined on the basis of the legislative position in England **three months** prior to the examination date.

The syllabus printed below will be examined in 2005. (See page (v) for details of our free *Updates.*)

		Covered in Chapter
1	**Fundamental principles of portfolio construction**	
1.1	*The factors to consider when building a portfolio* Candidates should be able to *explain* the following factors and the interrelationship between them: the rationale for diversification, the need for a balanced portfolio, the meaning of risk (systematic and non-systematic), effects of inflation and of asset value deflation (eg house prices 1989-91), the relevance of different time periods, accessibility, liquidity, marketability, flexibility, volatility, impact of taxation.	1
1.2	*Terminology and Stock Exchange practice* Candidates should be able to *explain* and *calculate* (where appropriate) the following investment terms: dividends, P/E ratios, EPS ratio, yield, gearing, rights issue, scrip issue, coupon, contract note, equalisation, distributor status, mechanisms for buying and selling, pound-cost averaging, dividend cover, bonus issues.	1

Syllabus

		Covered in Chapter

2 Investments

Candidates should be able to *explain* the structure, features, tax treatment, charging structure, pricing, methods of investment and disposal and uses of:

2.1	**Deposit based investments** Bank accounts, building society accounts (including gross deposits and offshore deposits), money market deposits, National Savings, TOISAs, cash Individual Savings Accounts (ISAs), cash funds.	2, 6
2.2	**Fixed interest securities** Gilts (fixed interest and index-linked), strips, local authority bonds, corporate bonds, debentures and loan stocks, Permanent Interest Bearing Shares (PIBS), Perpetual Subordinated Bonds (PSBs), loan notes.	3
2.3	**Packaged investments** With-profits and unit-linked endowments (including traded endowments), with-profit bonds (including treatment of market value adjustment), guaranteed income bonds, guaranteed growth bonds, guaranteed equity bonds (including the use of derivatives), protected capital equity bonds, high income bonds, cash unit trusts, annuities, (conventional, unitised and with-profits), back-to-back packages, friendly society plans.	4, 5
2.4	**Collective investments (UK and overseas)** Investment bonds, unit trusts (with and without a guarantee element), investment trusts including split-capital trusts, Open Ended Investment Companies (OEICs), Investment Companies with Variable Capital (ICVC), Personal Equity Plans (PEPs), ISAs, Undertakings for Collective Investments in Transferable Securities (UCITS), offshore bonds, SICAV, Exchange Traded Funds, distributor and non-distributor funds, offshore insurance bonds.	5, 6, 8
2.5	**Equities** Ordinary shares, non-voting shares, quoted/unquoted listings on main stock exchanges and AIM, warrants, convertible shares, preference shares, share option schemes (ie company share option plans, unapproved schemes, share incentive plans, SAYE share save schemes).	7, 11
2.6	**Offshore funds** Equities, offshore bonds, foreign currency, foreign government stock.	9
2.7	**Derivatives** Futures, options and their use in investment products with a protected or guaranteed element, covered warrants.	10
2.8	**Collectibles** Works of art, antiques, coins, stamps and other collectibles used for investment purposes.	11

THE EXAMINATION PAPER

The examination is in three sections, which together carry 200 marks.

(a) Section A consists of several short answer questions, which mostly require you to recite factual information.

(b) Section B consists of a single long question. You can expect to be given extensive information about an individual. You will have to analyse the information and make recommendations.

(c) Section C consists of three questions. You must answer any two. The questions are likely to give you information about individuals and then ask you questions about their investments and what changes you would recommend.

LEGISLATION

The AFPC examinations are based on the legislative position in the UK **three months before the date of the examination**. This means that the April examinations will be based on the tax year ending in that same month, and the October examinations will be based on the current tax year. Thus, the October 2005 and April 2006 examinations will both be based on the 2005/06 tax year.

How up-to-date is your BPP study material?

This Study Text is up-to-date as at 1 June 2005. In particular, it has been updated for relevant changes announced in the 2005 Budget for the tax year 2005/06. Legislation which affects AFPC in the twelve months from June 2005 will be covered by our free Updates, available on our website at **www.bpp.com/afpc** (see page (v) for further details).

Chapter 1

FUNDAMENTAL PRINCIPLES OF PORTFOLIO CONSTRUCTION

Chapter topic list		Syllabus reference
1	Introduction to portfolio construction	1.1
2	The rationale for diversification	1.1
3	The need for a balanced portfolio	1.1
4	Risk and its measurement	1.1
5	The effect of inflation and asset deflation	1.1
6	The relevance of different time periods	1.1
7	Accessibility, liquidity, marketability, flexibility and volatility	1.1
8	Impact of taxation	1.1
9	The interrelationship between the factors	1.1
10	Terminology and Stock Exchange practice	1.2

Introduction

Part of the role of any financial adviser is to construct a portfolio to suit a client's needs. In this chapter we will explore the fundamental principles of constructing an investment portfolio.

In this and in following chapters you will learn the constituent parts of portfolio construction so that you will be able to bring all the factors together into a final investment portfolio.

1 INTRODUCTION TO PORTFOLIO CONSTRUCTION

1.1 Before constructing an investment portfolio, an adviser will already have undertaken a considerable amount of work of a fact-finding nature. He will have talked to the client, and above all, listened to the client's needs. He should understand the client's attitude to risk and long-term financial ambitions. The information collection is vital to the construction of a portfolio which will fit the particular client's needs.

1.2 Each client has different needs. Two clients of similar age may live next door to each other and have the same amount of capital to invest. The portfolios which are constructed for them may be completely different, because their financial aims are diverse.

1.3 When all the necessary background information has been collected and collated, the adviser must make an analysis of the facts before putting forward his recommendations.

1.4 Financial planning is not a precise art. There is no single right answer. If two financial advisers are presented with the same factual information relating to a client, it is likely that they will produce two different solutions. Neither will be completely right nor completely wrong. Much of the art of investment planning is based on predictions and assumptions. One investment adviser may consider that the Japanese market must have bottomed out and therefore there is considerable growth potential, and his colleague may think the reverse. Only time and hindsight will prove which one is correct.

1.5 The financial adviser needs a sound knowledge of the investment market. He must know how the market works and the available products at a given time. Some advice will be influenced by what has happened in the past but this is not always an indication of what may happen in the future. The adviser must have an open mind and frequently ask the question 'What if this time the cycle changes?'

1.6 The adviser must always act in an ethical way and within the constraints of the Financial Services and Markets Act 2000 (FSMA 2000). This is particularly relevant if the adviser is a tied agent and can only advise on the contracts of one provider.

1.7 All financial advisers should consider the following factors when constructing a portfolio.

- The rationale for diversification
- The need for a balanced portfolio
- The meaning of risk
- The effect of inflation and asset deflation
- The relevance of different time periods
- Accessibility, liquidity, marketability, flexibility, volatility
- Impact of taxation
- The interrelationship between the factors

We will now consider these factors in turn.

2 THE RATIONALE FOR DIVERSIFICATION

2.1 One of the most difficult areas of portfolio construction is the reduction of risk. Although risk cannot be entirely removed, the extent of risk can be managed by a well diversified portfolio. We will now look at a number of methods of diversification.

(a) Using different **types of investment (asset classes)**

    (i) **Cash** can be used as an emergency fund or for instantly accessible money. At times when the future for interest rates is uncertain, it may be wise to hold some cash in variable rate deposits, in the hope of a rate rise and some in fixed rate deposits as a hedge against a possible fall in the rate.

    (ii) **Fixed interest securities,** such as government bonds, NS&I Savings Certificates or guaranteed income bonds give a secure income and known redemption value at a fixed future date.

    (iii) **Equities** can be used to produce a potentially increasing dividend income and capital growth. For example, a share yielding 3% income plus capital growth of 6% gives an overall return of 9%, compared with a building society deposit account yielding, say, 4%.

    (iv) **Collective investments** such as unit trusts, investment trusts or unit linked insurance products spread the risk still further. In this case the client is participating in a pool of shares. He may chose a fund investing in a number of different economies, thereby reducing risk still further. Pooled investments may be a sensible method of obtaining exposure to some of the less sophisticated world markets where there is a high risk in holding one company's shares.

(v)   The use of **property**, whether residential or commercial and other types of assets such as antiques, coins, stamps etc helps to spread risk.

(b)   Using a **spread of shares** across different sectors of the market. In this way there is a reduced concentration of capital in any one sector. Sometimes a client will have a large holding in one share, perhaps because of an inheritance or as the result of a share option scheme. Such a client should be made aware of the potential risk of such a large holding. For example, £50,000 invested in, say, shares in Vodafone plc is wholly exposed if the company underperforms. If, on the other hand, £50,000 is spread (across a variety of equities, with no more than £5,000 invested in any one share, underperformance by one or two companies means that only 10 to 20 per cent of the portfolio is adversely effected. If the other 80% of the portfolio is performing well this may outweigh the poor performance of the one or two underperforming shares. (Having a spread of shares is known as **diversification**.)

(c)   Using a **spread of UK and international shares**. Although most UK investors will have a portfolio which is predominantly UK stock, the attraction of diversifying into international shares is to take advantage of other economies' financial cycles, interest rates and currency movements. Returns on equities in different international sectors may vary widely.

3   THE NEED FOR A BALANCED PORTFOLIO

3.1   The ideal portfolio is likely to have have a balance between asset classes: cash deposits, fixed interest, equities and property. The percentage in each sector will depend upon the client's need and attitude to risk. The very cautious investor may wish to have 100% investment in cash. The financial adviser may suggest, say, 5% in a pooled investment, such as a fund of funds unit trust or the with profits fund of an investment bond. A reason for this advice would be to aim to achieve a real rate of return over inflation, if only on a very small part of the portfolio. At the other end of the spectrum no investor should be totally invested in equities: he will need some accessible funds and should probably also have an exposure to fixed interest securities.

3.2   The use of cash in a portfolio is obviously to give easy access to funds. There is also a need for fixed interest as well as equities. Although equities should give a real rate of return over inflation over long periods, there are times in the economic cycle when a client would obtain a better short-term return from a fixed interest security. This is a reason to hold both types of investment. The percentage of the holdings will vary depending on the view of what may happen in the market. If the view is that interest rates may fall, it may be time to hold a higher percentage of gilts to take advantage of a capital gain in the holding when the rates reduce.

3.3   If a portfolio has been constructed to produce income, there is also a good argument for having the portfolio balanced between fixed interest and equity investments. The equities will show a lower yield at the outset but over a period the income should increase. It may, however, be more volatile. The income from fixed interest securities may be higher but it is fixed. This income may from time to time look less attractive if interest rates rise. If the client holds a balanced portfolio, he should be able to maintain a smoother income pattern than could be produced from a 100% fixed interest or a 100% equity portfolio. Companies may pay low dividends but make use of share buy-backs or special dividends. This could result in a need for a change in the balance of equities and fixed interest in a portfolio.

4 RISK AND ITS MEASUREMENT

4.1 **Risk** can be described as the possibility of suffering some form of loss. Let us look at the losses which could occur in investments.

Investment risks

4.2 Risk in investment can never be totally eliminated. A client who invests only in the bank or building society may think that she has eliminated risk. This is not so: she runs the following risks.

(a) The institution holding the deposit could go into liquidation (a **default risk** for the investor). The investor may find herself making a claim on the **Financial Services Compensation Scheme** which protects individual bank and building society depositors for 100% of the first £2,000 they have invested, plus 90% of the next £33,000 (ie £31,700 in total).

(b) The rate of interest may be variable and may fall.

(c) The rate of interest may not match inflation.

4.3 The investor in shares is exposed to the following risks.

(a) The risk that the market as a whole will fall, thus affecting the value of the investor's holdings, as for example in 1987 when the stock market fell by around 20% in two days. This is known as **systematic risk**. All assets in an asset class are affected by systematic risk. Systematic risk also occurs when an increase in inflation depresses the price of gilts. All gilts are affected by this.

(b) The risk that a particular company share will fall in price irrespective of the overall performance of the market. This is known as **unsystematic risk** or **non-systematic risk**. The share prices of companies in the food processing sector suffered non-systematic risk following the BSE scare. Unsystematic risk can be reduced by diversifying across individual shares. Systematic risk cannot be diversified away.

4.4 An investor in government securities may feel that he has reduced his investment risk but he, too, is exposed to a risk on interest and capital as follows.

(a) Although he has a known income from his investment, if interest rates rise the yield may cease to be attractive.

(b) If he wishes to sell the stock prior to redemption, if interest rates have risen the underlying capital value will probably have fallen.

4.5 An investor in property suffers from the risk associated with **illiquidity**. A sale can only be made if a buyer can be found and this can prove a great problem. During the early 1990s, with a stagnant housing and property market few buyers could be found, prices fell and some homebuyers found that they had negative equity. If a client invests in property via the medium of a property unit trust or investment bond he may suffer similar, although not such acute, illiquidity. Under the terms of these investments the proceeds of a sale may be delayed for up to six months to allow the managers to realise assets to pay the investor.

Beta factors

4.6 As we saw above, investment-specific (non-systematic) risk can be reduced by diversification, but market (systematic) risk still remains. The **beta factor** measures the **volatility of a security relative to the market** as a whole.

4.7 The higher the value of beta for a security, the greater the movement in its return relative to the market.

- A security with a **beta factor of 1** moves in line with the market. If the market (for example, as indicated by a share price index such as the FTSE-100) moves up 5%, the price of this security is likely to move up 5%.

- A security with a **beta factor greater than 1** varies more widely than the market. If the market moves up 5%, the price of a security with a beta of 2 is likely to move up 10%.

- A security with a **beta factor of less than 1** fluctuates less than the wider market. If the market moves up or down 10%, the price of a security with a beta of 0.5 is likely to move up or down respectively by 5%.

Beta factors for collective funds

4.8 Beta factors are calculated for collective funds as well as for individual securities. The beta factors for funds measure the fund's volatility against a benchmark such as the FT-SE All-Share Index, or some other benchmark appropriate to the fund.

4.9 Betas for fund are generally calculated over a 36-month period, from monthly data.

- A fund with a beta factor of 1 moves in line with its benchmark.
- A fund with a beta factor greater than 1 is more volatile than its benchmark.
- A fund with a beta factor of less than 1 is less volatile than its benchmark.

4.10 Beta factors are calculated from historical data. Changes in the strategy of a fund, or changes resulting from a change in manager, may mean that future performance and volatility differ from the past.

Alpha

4.11 **Alpha** is a measure of the risk-adjusted return of a fund. Alpha measures the difference between the actual return of a fund and its expected performance, given its level of risk as measured by beta.

4.12 A positive alpha indicates the fund has performed better than expected, given its level of risk (beta). A negative alpha indicates the fund has underperformed for a fund with its level of risk.

4.13 In practice, a negative alpha is more likely because of the effect of fund management charges in reducing the overall return.

5 THE EFFECT OF INFLATION AND ASSET DEFLATION

5.1 With **inflation** at its current relatively low levels, it is easy to forget the ravages of inflation on people's investments and savings back in the 1970s, but it is still a relevant factor in the design of investment portfolios.

Exercise 1

Can you give a definition of inflation?

5.2   Inflation is the increase in the price of goods and services over a given time. The increase is calculated by the increase in the price of a basket of goods and services. UK price inflation for the consumer is measured by indices which include the **Consumer Prices Index** (CPI) and the **Retail Prices Index** (RPI).

Exercise 2

If a price index for February was 138.8, while for February in the previous year it was 142.1, calculate the annual rate of inflation.

5.3   The RPI was rebased in January 1987 at 100.0 and the annual increases are calculated from this base. The CPI is a newer measure of inflation calculated on a basis which is harmonised with the inflation measures of other European countries. The CPI excludes most housing costs, while the RPI includes such costs. The CPI is now used as the basis for the UK Government's inflation target. Pensions and benefits, and index-linked gilts, continue to be calculated using the RPI.

5.4   Inflation has an effect on investment planning for two reasons.

(a)   The client will wish to maintain the purchasing power of his capital whether it is held in equities, commodities, property etc. The only way that this can be achieved is by receiving a rate of return in excess of inflation, **a real rate of return**.

(b)   The client will wish to maintain the purchasing power of his income. Therefore, he needs to achieve an increasing income at least in line with inflation.

5.5   A client may able to enhance the purchasing power of his capital and income by investing in asset-backed investments, such as shares or property. Deposit type investments show no capital growth. The original capital invested retains its nominal value at redemption and income fluctuates in line with interest rates.

5.6   As can be seen, clients will seek to achieve a real rate of return over inflation. This does not mean that a very high nominal rate of return has to be achieved. (Nominal interest rate = RPI + Real interest rate.) At the time of writing, a typical return on deposits is up to around 4.5% pa before tax, compared with inflation of around 2%.

5.7   From time to time, real asset values will fall. Property is a good example. In the 1980s there was a boom in house prices. In the early 1990s with the effects of the recession, unemployment and tax changes, demand fell away. Many people could not sell, and if they did, it was at a price below the purchase price. The housing market will also vary depending upon which area of the country you live in. In 2005, a recent house price boom appears to have slowed significantly, and there have been falls in residential property prices.

5.8   In years of poor stock market performance, clients may see the real value of their shares fall. However, if you look at longer periods of investment, the real rate of return on equities is more often positive.

5.9   Inflation has most effect on those living on a fixed income arising from pensions and deposit type investments. In periods of high inflation such people see the purchasing power of their income reduce. They can be adversely affected by a sudden increase in a commodity price, such as oil during the Middle East oil crisis in the 1970s. Such investors can also see the purchasing power of their income reduce if interest rates fall sharply as happened in the early 1990s with low inflation, but also low interest rates.

5.10   Those in employment are less affected by inflation as normally earnings rise faster than inflation. Those in employment are, however, likely to be adversely affected by rising interest rates increasing their mortgage repayments.

5.11   Inflation is not only a phenomenon of the UK. If a client has a portfolio of international shares, unit or investment trusts, the effect of inflation in these economies needs to be taken into account. As we are all aware, in some Latin American countries inflation has often run into double figures and conversely in, say, Switzerland, there has been virtually no inflation for many years. If inflation is very high, governments may seek to increase interest rates which, in turn, could have an adverse effect on the price of equities and consequently upon investment performance.

5.12   Even in a period of low inflation, this factor must still be considered in portfolio construction. A sudden international crisis could create a commodity shortage, which could lead to rising price. Government policy on interest rates can change. Therefore advisers need to continue to be aware of the effects of inflation particularly when planning for the elderly. Such clients need to achieve real returns for many years. In their case they may have need of services, such as nursing and care, where the cost of the service traditionally rises quicker than inflation.

6   THE RELEVANCE OF DIFFERENT TIME PERIODS

6.1   The expression 'timescale of investment' means asking: Does the client need access to his capital, next week, next month, next year? Or does he not know, perhaps? If the client definitely knows that he needs money in three months time, perhaps to pay the next school fees bill, then, however great the potential short-term reward may be from a particular share, the correct solution must generally be to place the available money on deposit at the most competitive short-term interest rate.

6.2   **Accessible cash.** Every portfolio should include some money held on deposit in a bank or building society. This money will be earmarked for known expenditures such as holidays, tax bills or school fees.

6.3   **The emergency fund.** A client should have an emergency fund of easily accessible cash. The amount of this emergency fund will vary from client to client. Some will like the comfort factor of a large fund. Others will see this as 'dead money' because there is no chance of any capital growth on the original investment. The attitude of those in retirement and those in employment may be vastly different. Clients who have retired often want a great deal more capital in deposit type funds because of a fear of needing access to cash. Those still in employment feel they can rely on a continuing income stream to fund emergency outgoings and prefer long term investment.

6.4   There is a skill in the time management of a client's cash deposits. Initially it may appear that he needs liquidity of, say, £20,000, but on further investigation it may be possible to say that only £5,000 needs to be in an account with instant access and the balance invested with a notice period of three or six months. In this way a higher rate of interest can be obtained

Pound cost averaging

6.5 The regular investment of a constant sum gives the advantage of smoothing out the effects of price variations through **pound cost averaging**. In theory, an investor should always buy when prices are low and sell when they are high. This is very difficult to achieve. A regular investor who commits a constant sum of money will, however, always have a lower overall cost to the one who buys a constant number of units because his regular sum buys more units when the price is low and fewer when it is high.

Example

6.6 Two investors are making regular investments in the units of XYZ unit trust. Mr A decides to invest a constant amount of £60 per month. Mr B wishes to buy 20 units per month. The price of the units for the first five months was as follows.

Month	Price per unit (£)
1	3
2	2
3	4
4	3
5	4

Calculate the average price per unit for Mr A and Mr B, and compare the two.

Answer

6.7

Mr A:

Month	Price (£)	Number of units	(=£60 ÷ price)
1	3	20	
2	2	30	
3	4	15	
4	3	20	
5	4	15	
		100	

Total invested: $5 \times £60 = £300$

Average price $= \dfrac{£300}{100} = £3.00$

Mr B:

Mr B will also have bought a total of 100 units but, since he was buying a constant number of units each month, his average price will be the arithmetical mean of the five prices:

Average price $= \dfrac{3+2+4+3+4}{5} = £3.20$

6.8 From the above it can be seen that Mr A's average unit price (and total investment) will be lower than Mr B's. Although both have bought the same number of units, Mr A has benefited from pound cost averaging.

7 ACCESSIBILITY, LIQUIDITY, MARKETABILITY, FLEXIBILITY AND VOLATILITY

7.1 When an adviser is considering an investment to include in a portfolio, he or she should evaluate it under the headings of **accessibility, liquidity, marketability, flexibility and volatility.** We will now look at the main asset classes under these headings.

Deposit investments

7.2 Cash deposits with banks or building societies have either immediate access or only a short notice period, so liquidity is no problem. There is no question of marketability or volatility. The only slight volatility is in changing interest rates. The accounts are not very flexible.

Fixed interest investments

7.3 Most fixed interest securities, such as gilts and loan stock, can be bought and sold easily on the market. It should be possible to dispose of a gilt easily. A corporate loan stock may be more difficult if potential investors are concerned about the security of the company to whom the money had been lent. There can be volatility of the price of fixed interest stocks during their life but the investor has the security of knowing that if the stock is held until redemption he will get a return of a fixed amount.

Other investments

7.4 When a client invests in shares he tends to believe that he will be able to realise his investment easily if there is a desperate need for cash. However, it is important that he appreciates the following disadvantages of equity investments.

(a) Although blue-chip stock has good marketability, there is no guarantee of the price which will be obtained in an emergency sale, particularly in a falling market.

(b) If the client holds shares in smaller companies there can be considerable difficulty in selling particularly in a falling market. There will only be two or three market makers and nobody may want to buy. The performance of these shares may be volatile.

(c) Private company shares are almost unmarketable other than to other members of the family and there can also be a problem over valuation.

(d) Shares in overseas companies may be difficult to sell especially in some of the under-developed overseas stock markets. There can also be considerable price volatility.

(e) Unquoted shares such as holdings under the Enterprise Investment Scheme (EIS) are often unmarketable.

Property investment

7.5 If clients invest directly in property, they must be aware of the relative illiquidity of the asset. A sale can only be made if a buyer can be found and this can prove a great problem. During the early 1990s with a stagnant housing and property market, few buyers could be found and prices fell. If a client invests in property via the medium of a property unit trust or investment bond he may suffer similar, though not so acute illiquidity. Under the terms of these investments, the proceeds of a sale may be delayed, typically for up to six months, to allow the managers to realise assets to pay the investor.

Exercise 3

In order fully to understand the importance of timescale of investment and liquidity, see if you can construct a list of investments using the headings:

Short term	Under three months
Short to medium term	Three months to five years
Medium term	Five years plus
Long term	Ten years plus

Against each investment annotate L for liquid or I for illiquid.

8   IMPACT OF TAXATION

8.1   The client's tax position is very relevant to the design of a portfolio. If the client pays no tax, it will be important to select investments where income is paid gross or, at least, tax can be reclaimed.

8.2   If a client pays the higher rate of tax, he should be guided to maximise all tax-free investments, such as National Savings & Investments (NS&I) Savings Certificates, and ISAs (Individual Savings Accounts). It also makes sense to invest in capital growth rather than income producing assets. Paying tax on income is unavoidable but capital gains tax on growth may be avoided by keeping within the annual exemption (£8,500 for 2005/06).

8.3   From time to time governments offer tax incentives, for example **tax relief on pension contributions** and the tax-free roll up of capital gains in **Individual Savings Accounts (ISAs)**. The tax relief on pension contributions is obviously a real benefit, particularly for a higher rate taxpayer who might be a basic rate taxpayer in retirement when her taxable pension benefits are taken. Similarly, the ability for a higher rate taxpayer with larger sums to invest to build up a portfolio of ISAs without suffering capital gains tax is an advantage. However, for many basic rate taxpayers, an ISA does not offer a great advantage. Only some investors achieve capital gains in excess of their annual exemption. The tax advantage may be outweighed by the charges for investing in the plan. A **corporate bond ISA** may be more attractive to the basic rate taxpayer. A high tax-free income can be achieved and, if the scheme can be packaged to give virtual security of capital, this may be attractive from a tax and investment view.

8.4   Retaining an investment in an existing **TESSA-only ISA** (TOISA) is worth considering for anyone paying tax who in normal circumstances would hold some cash in building society or deposit accounts. The ability to secure a gross rate of interest without risk is attractive. All TESSAs matured by 5 April 2004 and the investor had six months following maturity in which to reinvest the capital in an ISA without affecting annual ISA contribution limits.

8.5   Some schemes which offer tax incentives also carry high risk, for example **Enterprise Investment Scheme (EIS)** investments and **Enterprise Zone Trusts (EZTs)**. In this case the scheme should not be considered solely upon the tax incentive. Capital could be lost.

8.6   Tax incentives should not be allowed to distort a portfolio. A sensible long-term investment giving a real rate of return must be preferable to a dubious investment with a small amount of tax relief.

Exercise 4

(a)   What do the following abbreviations stand for? ISA, EZT, PEP, EIS, TESSA

(b)   Should a higher rate taxpayer aim for capital growth or income producing investments?

(c)   A non-taxpayer can receive 3.6% net from a building society or 4.2% from an insurance company guaranteed income bond. Which is more attractive?

9   THE INTERRELATIONSHIP BETWEEN THE FACTORS

9.1   When constructing a portfolio, an adviser should take into account all the factors we have discussed in this chapter.

9.2   As you have read, there is an interrelationship between the factors. For example, when a client invests in equities, there is a correlation between risk and timescale. If shares are held for a long period, say 10 years, traditionally (but not necessarily for the future) they have outperformed deposit based investments. It is important that if the market suffers a fall, clients should not sell in panic. If they are prepared to hold the shares for a long period they should, over the long term, reap the rewards of increasing dividend income and capital growth. However, if they panic and sell following a fall in the market, they will crystallise a loss.

9.3   In Section 7 of this chapter, we discussed the relationship between accessibility, liquidity, marketability and volatility. Those securities which are less marketable are also more volatile and higher risk.

9.4   At the other end of the risk spectrum, deposits are low risk, have low volatility and are easily accessible.

10   TERMINOLOGY AND STOCK EXCHANGE PRACTICE

10.1   For the G20 paper, you should have a knowledge of investment terms. The most common are listed below in a **glossary of investment terms** below.

GLOSSARY OF INVESTMENT TERMS

AIM. The Alternative Investment Market started in 1995. This market, with less stringent requirements than the main market, is for companies who cannot or do not wish to apply for a full stock market quotation.

Allotment (letter of allotment). A letter of allotment is issued to an investor for a new issue of shares stating how many shares have been allotted to him.

Arbitrage. Profiting from the transfer of funds from one market to another to take advantage of anomalous differences in interest rates, exchange rates, or commodity prices between the two markets.

Asset value. The total value of the assets of a company less its liabilities, divided by the number of ordinary shares in issue.

Bear market. A market in which prices are generally falling or expected to fall.

Bid price. The price at which a market maker will buy shares. He will sell shares at the offer price. The difference between the two prices is known as the bid-offer spread.

Blue chip. Name for any of the ordinary shares in the most highly regarded companies traded on a stock market.

Bond. An 'IOU' issued by a borrower to a lender. Bonds usually take the form of fixed interest securities issued by governments, local authorities or companies.

Bonus issue. The issue of new share certificates to existing shareholders to reflect the accumulation of profits in the reserves of a company's balance sheet. The shareholders do not pay for the new shares.

Bulldogs. Fixed interest securities/loan stock issued and guaranteed by foreign governments and denominated in sterling.

Bull market. A market in which prices are generally rising or expected to rise.

Call. A demand for a payment due on nil or partly-paid stock.

Call option. The right to buy a share or fixed asset at a fixed price within a specified time period.

Cancellation price. The lowest price at which the manager of a unit trust may offer to redeem units on a particular day.

Capital gearing. The ratio of fixed interest loan stock and preference shares to the ordinary share capital in a company.

Clean price. The price of a gilt-edged security excluding the accrued interest since the previous dividend payment.

Contract note. A document sent by a stockbroker or a commodity broker to a client as evidence that the broker has bought or sold securities in accordance with the client's instructions.

Convertible. A security, usually a bond or debenture, which can be converted into the ordinary shares or preference shares of the company at a fixed date in the future at a fixed price.

Coupon. Rate of interest paid by a fixed interest bond.

Cumulative preference share. A type of preference share that entitles the owner to receive any dividends not paid in previous years.

Debenture. A long-term loan taken by a company. It is usually a loan repayable at a fixed date. Most debentures also pay a fixed rate of interest and this interest must be paid before a dividend is paid to shareholders.

Derivative instrument. A financial instrument which is valued according to the expected price movements of an underlying asset which may be a commodity, a currency or a security. Derivatives can be used to hedge a position or establish a synthetic open position eg futures, warrants, options, swaps.

Dividend. A dividend is the distribution of part of the earnings of a company to its shareholders. A dividend is normally expressed as an amount per share on par value, eg 15% on a £1 share would pay 15p.

Dividend yield. The dividend expressed as a percentage of the share price. Thus if the market price of the £1 share (above) is now £5, the dividend yield would be $1/5 \times 15\% = 3\%$.

Dividend cover. The number of times a company's dividends to ordinary shareholders could be paid out of net profit after tax in the same period.

Earnings per share. The earnings of a company over a stated period (usually one year) divided by the number of ordinary shares issued by the company.

Equities. Ordinary shares of companies. In the event of liquidation, ordinary shareholders are entitled to share out the assets remaining after all other creditors have been paid out.

Equity capital. The part of the capital of a company owned by ordinary shareholders.

Eurobond. Fixed interest security issued by either governments or large companies and issued in a currency other than that of the country or market in which it is issued.

Eurosterling. Sterling deposits held by foreign institutions outside the UK.

Fixed interest security. A type of security that gives a fixed stated interest payment.

Floating exchange rate. A rate of exchange between one currency and others that is permitted to float according to market forces.

Floating rate notes. Short-term high interest debt instruments issued by banks which are adjusted periodically and based on the London Inter-Bank Offered Rate (LIBOR).

Flotation. The process of launching a public company for the first time by inviting the public to subscribe for its shares.

Footsie. The Financial Times - Stock Exchange 100 (FTSE 100) share index.

Futures contract. An agreement to buy or sell a fixed quantity of a particular commodity, currency or security for delivery at a fixed date in the future at a fixed price.

Gilt-edged security (gilt). A fixed interest security or stock issued by the British government.

Gross yield. The yield on a security calculated before tax is deducted. The yield after tax is called the net yield.

Hedging. An operation undertaken by a trader or dealer who wishes to protect an open position especially in the sale or purchase of a commodity, currency, security etc. that is likely to fluctuate in price over the period that the position remains open.

Index linked gilts. A type of government stock with a low 'coupon' which is guaranteed to rise in line with the Retail Prices Index. There is also a guarantee that the final redemption price will be linked to the Retail Prices Index.

Index tracking funds. Usually equity-based funds which are constructed to match closely the performance of a market index, eg the FTSE 100 Index or the FTSE All-Share Index.

Initial charge. The charge paid to managers of a unit trust by an investor when units are first purchased. Initial charges can range between 5% and 6%, as set down in the trust deed, but discounts may be offered by brokers.

Interbank market. The part of the London money market in which banks lend to each other and to other financial institutions. The London Interbank Offered Rate (LIBOR) is the rate of interest charged on interbank loans.

Irredeemable securities. Securities such as some government loan stock and some debentures on which there is no date given for the redemption of the capital sum.

Issue by tender. A method of issuing shares on the Stock Exchange in which an issuing house asks investors to tender for them.

Issue price. The price at which a new issue of shares is sold to the public.

Issuing house. A financial institution that specialises in assisting in the flotation of companies on the Stock Exchange.

Listed security. A security which has a quotation on a recognised stock exchange.

Longs. Government stock with more than 15 years to redemption.

Market maker. A dealer in securities on the Stock Exchange who undertakes to buy and sell securities as a principal and is therefore obliged to maintain dealing prices for particular securities.

Mediums. Government stock with redemption dates between five and fifteen years (or, seven and fifteen years).

Mid price. The average of the offer price of a security, commodity or currency and the bid price. It is the mid price that is most often quoted in the financial press.

Money market. The UK market for short term loans in which money brokers arrange for loans between the banks, the government, the discount houses and the accepting houses. Private investors, through their banks, can place deposits in the money market at a higher rate of interest than bank deposit accounts.

Negative equity. A situation where an asset, such as a house, has a market value below the sum of money borrowed to purchase it.

Net asset value. The total assets of an organisation less all liabilities and all capital charges including debentures, loan stocks and preference shares.

Nominal value. The face value of a share or gilt.

Offer price. The price at which a security is offered for sale by a market maker.

Opening prices. The bid prices and offer prices made at the opening of a day's trading on any security or commodity market.

Option. The right to buy or sell a fixed quantity of a commodity, currency or security at a particular date at a particular price.

Ordinary share. A unit of the share capital of a company.

Paid up share. A share in respect of which the par value has been paid in full.

Partly paid share. Shares on which the full nominal or par value has not been paid.

Pound cost averaging. A method of accumulating capital by investing a fixed sum of money in a particular investment every month or other period. When prices fall, the fixed sum will buy correspondingly more shares or units. When prices rise, fewer shares or units are bought.

Preference share. A share in a company yielding a fixed rate of interest.

Participating preference share. These shares carry additional rights to a further share in the profits in the company after the ordinary shareholders have received a stated percentage.

Price/earnings ratio. The current market price of a company share divided by the earnings per share of the company.

Prospectus. A document which gives details of a new issue of shares. It is an invitation to the public to buy shares or debentures in the company.

Put option. The right to sell a share or asset at a fixed price within a specified time period.

Redeemable preference share. This is a preference share but the company reserves the right to redeem the share either out of profits or out of the proceeds of a further issue of shares.

Redemption date. The repayment date or dates for gilts, debentures and similar fixed interest securities.

Redemption yield. Overall return on a gilt to redemption date – including capital gain or loss – annualised over the remaining term.

Rights issue. A method by which companies quoted on a stock exchange raise new capital in exchange for new shares. Existing shareholders must be offered the new shares in proportion to their holdings of old shares eg one for four rights issue.

Running yield. The percentage income paid to an investor in gilts as a percentage of the investment. It is calculated by dividing the yield per £100 of nominal stock by the current market price.

SETS. The Stock Exchange Electronic Trading System. The automated matching mechanism used for trading in large capitalisation stocks on the London Stock Exchange.

Shorts. Government stock with less than five years (or, less than seven years) to redemption.

Spread. The difference between the buying and selling price made by a market maker on the Stock Exchange.

Tap stock. A government security from an issue which has not been fully subscribed, which is released onto the market when the price reaches predetermined levels.

Umbrella fund. An offshore fund consisting of a fund of funds that invests in other offshore funds.

Unquoted company. A company whose securities are not normally available to the public on a stock exchange.

Warrant. A security which offers the owner the right to subscribe for the ordinary shares of a company at a fixed price at a fixed future date.

Yield. The income from an investment.

Yield gap. The difference between the average annual dividend yield on equities and the average annual yield on long dated gilt-edged securities.

Zero coupon bond. A type of bond or preference share which offers no interest payments but which is sold at a lower price than its redemption value.

Chapter roundup

In this chapter we have studied:

- The principles of portfolio construction
- The importance of diversification and a balanced portfolio
- The factors of accessibility, marketability, volatility, time-scale, inflation, risk and the tax implications
- The interaction of all the factors

Quick Quiz

1   What is the likely timescale for a short-term investment?
2   What is negative equity?
3   What is systematic risk?
4   What is a real rate of return?
5   Which of the following people is more likely to be affected by inflation: a retired person or a young person who has just started his first job?
6   If interest rates fall, are share prices likely to rise or fall?
7   Why are overseas equities more risky than UK equities for a UK investor?
8   At what price will a share normally be quoted in the financial pages?

The answers to the quiz can be found at the end of this Study Text. Before checking your own answers against them, you should look back at this chapter and use the information in it to correct your answers.

Answers to exercises

1   Inflation is an increase in the general level of prices in an economy over a period of time. The rate of inflation can be measured by the use of an index which measures the changes in consumer prices.

2   The calculation is:

$$\frac{\text{Index for February (Year X)} - \text{Index for February (Year X - 1)}}{\text{Index for February (Year X - 1)}} \times 100$$

$$\frac{142.1 - 138.8}{138.8} \times 100 = 2.38\%$$

3   Short-term investments   Instant access bank or building society account   L

Short/Medium-term	90 day bank or building society accounts	L
	Short/medium dated gilts	L
	Guaranteed income bonds	I
	Local authority bonds	I

Medium-term	Investment bonds	L
	Unit trusts/OEICs	L
	Investment trusts	L
	Shares in quoted companies	L
	PEPs (started before 6.4.99)	L
	Individual Savings Account	L
	Enterprise Investment Scheme	I

Long-term	Investment bonds	L
	Long term gilts	L
	Shares in quoted companies	L
	Shares in unquoted companies	I
	10 year back to back scheme	I
	Unit trusts/OEICs	L
	Investment trusts	L
	PEPs/ISAs	L

4   (a)   Individual Savings Account, Enterprise Zone Trust, Personal Equity Plan, Enterprise Investment Scheme, Tax Exempt Special Savings Account.

(b)   Higher rate taxpayers should aim for capital growth because there is a greater facility to avoid capital gains tax.

(c)   The building society, because tax can be reclaimed, making a gross return of (3.6 / 0.8 =) 4.5%. Tax cannot be reclaimed from the income payment of an insurance company based guaranteed income bond. (An election on Form R85 can be made to receive building society interest gross.)

PRACTICE QUESTION 1: PORTFOLIO (30 Marks)   *27 mins*

John, aged 40, has just inherited £40,000 from his mother. He wishes to invest for capital growth but he may need access to funds in 12 months time. He is interested in having his money professionally managed. However, he is anxious about certain aspects of the investment process.

(a)   Explain to John the effect inflation could have on his portfolio.   (7 marks)

(b)   John says he may consider buying a small cottage as an investment rather than proceeding with a portfolio. Explain to John the possible pitfalls of property investment.   (8 marks)

(c)   John says he wants long-term growth without undue risk and some funds must be available on easy access. Explain briefly how you would construct a portfolio to meet his needs.

(8 marks)

(d)   John is married to Amy, aged 32. She does not work and is a non-taxpayer. Will this fact have any influence on the construction of the portfolio?   (7 marks)

The answer to the practice question can be found at the end of this Study Text

Chapter 2

DEPOSIT BASED INVESTMENTS

Chapter topic list	Syllabus reference
1 Introduction to low risk investments	2.1
2 Bank and building society accounts	2.1
3 Offshore deposit accounts	2.1
4 Money market deposits	2.1
5 National Savings & Investments	2.1

Introduction

In this chapter, we examine the different types of deposit based investment. These fall into the minimal to low risk category of investment. We will look at their individual features, tax treatment, charging structure, methods of purchase and sale and their uses in the construction of an investment portfolio.

1 INTRODUCTION TO LOW RISK INVESTMENTS

1.1 When deposit based investments are mentioned, you may immediately think of the bank or building society account, either on- or offshore. As we will see in Chapter 6, however, it is possible to use a unit trust for deposits if the cash fund is selected.

1.2 A deposit is a low risk investment. It pays interest but there is no growth on the nominal value of the capital originally deposited. It therefore provides no hedge against inflation.

1.3 The interest paid on such accounts is normally variable and will alter in line with interest rate changes. Higher interest rates can be achieved by the investment of larger sums. The returns are usually tiered with investors receiving increasing rates of interest for deposits in excess of £10,000 and again when the amount exceeds £25,000. It should be noted that higher rates of interest can normally be secured by investing with the smaller banks or building societies or if the client uses a postal account. In order to see for yourself the range of accounts and interest payments currently being offered on different types of account, try Exercise 1 below. Completing this Exercise will make it easier for you to quote examples in the exam.

1.4 Interest is normally credited to deposit accounts once a year. However, a lower rate of interest credited to an account monthly or quarterly may achieve a higher overall return.

1.5 Financial advisers must not overlook the deposit type of investment. It is a useful way for a client to keep money which is needed for a specific reason or as an emergency fund. It can also be used for funds awaiting investment.

1.6 National Savings & Investments (NS&I) offers deposit based investments via its bank accounts. These accounts pay gross interest and are useful for non-taxpayers. NS&I Savings Certificates, which give a tax-free roll up, should form part of a well spread portfolio for a basic or higher rate taxpayer.

1.7 Up to £3,000 per year can be invested in the **cash component of ISAs**. ISAs are covered in Chapter 8 of this Study Text.

Exercise 1

Look in a newspaper or internet source.

(a) Find the best interest rate currently being offered for an investment of £10,000 in a bank or building society account, interest on the account is to be paid annually and access to be 90 days.

(b) If you have £50,000 to invest on the same basis as (a) above can you find a better interest rate?

(c) Find the best interest rate currently being offered if you have £20,000 to invest in a bank or building society account. The account is to pay a monthly income with immediate access.

(d) Find the best interest rate currently being offered by a bank or building society if you have £2,000 to invest. Interest is to be paid annually with instant access.

---

2 BANK AND BUILDING SOCIETY ACCOUNTS

2.1 We will now look at each type of deposit based investment. In the past it may have been appropriate to differentiate between bank and building society accounts but now both types of institution offer similar products, so we will deal with them together.

Types of account

Current account

2.2 Most people would find it difficult to handle their financial affairs without access to a **current account**.

(a) This account gives them the facility to receive payments such as salary. They can set up direct debits for the payment of regular outgoings such as the mortgage and utility bills. A chequebook, debit card, cashpoint and overdraft facility will also be available.

(b) Traditionally, current accounts offered a free banking facility but gave no interest on the deposit. However, in recent years there has been a growth in interest paying cheque accounts offered by banks and building societies. The interest offered increases with the size of the balance on deposit. However, restrictions may apply. Some accounts require a minimum investment or minimum withdrawal amount. There are also a number of institutions offering a 24 hour banking service.

(c) Many banks and building societies now offer incentives to students and it is worth making a thorough search of the market to find the most advantageous incentives available. Students may be offered an interest free overdraft facility for an amount up to, say, £1,000.

Deposit or investment account

2.3 These accounts offer no cheque book facility but interest is paid on the investment. The rates of interest are likely to be relatively low and will be variable and probably tiered according to the balance in the account. Various types of these accounts are noted below.

(a) **Instant access account.** As the name implies, this account allows the investor immediate access to funds.

(b) **Cash ISAs.** Individual Savings Accounts (ISAs) are offered by most major deposit-takers. An individual can invest £3,000 per tax year in either a **cash mini-ISA** or the cash component of a **maxi-ISA**. Interest is tax-free. See Chapter 8 for detailed coverage of ISAs.

(c) **TOISAs.** The Tax Exempt Special Savings Account (TESSA) was a tax free savings plan which could be operated through a bank or building society. TESSAs ran for a five year period with a maximum investment of £9,000. No new TESSA could be opened after 5 April 1999 and so the last TESSAs matured on 5 April 2004. Within six months of maturity the capital component, but not the interest, could be transferred either to the cash component of an ISA, without affecting the ISA annual allowance for that year, or to a special TESSA only ISA (TOISA). Since the investor is given six months to decide, the last possible date for reinvestment was 5 October 2004, for a TESSA maturing on 5 April 2004.

(d) **Notice account.** In this case a higher rate of interest will normally be paid on the account. In order to achieve this, the client must give 30, 60 or 90 days notice of withdrawal unless he wishes to lose interest.

(e) **Monthly interest account.** The interest paid on this account is typically lower than on the instant or notice account because of the increased frequency of payment of interest. Interest rates are usually variable and tiered according to the amount invested. Access can be immediate or with a waiting period depending on the interest rate selected.

(f) **Fixed rate account.** These accounts are usually special offer products. The account runs for a fixed term: 1, 2, 3, 4 or 5 years with little or no access without severe penalty. The interest paid will be guaranteed for the term and the original deposit will be returned at maturity. The interest can be paid annually or monthly.

(g) **Stepped interest account.** These accounts offer a guaranteed rate to the investor. The offer is in two parts: a rate which is acceptable in the current deposit market plus the promise of a guaranteed increase during the term of the bond. For example, a five year step-up bond might offer a gross rate of interest of 3.0% in year one, 3.25% in year two, 3.50% in year three, rising to 4.0% in year four and a final 4.5% in year five.

(h) **Regular savings schemes.** These accounts allow for a savings scheme with regular savings being made each month and some access to funds without penalty.

Exercise 2

A friend says that he is using his building society account to build up capital for the future. He says that as the interest rate is in excess of the Retail Prices Index, he has an inflation-proofed investment for his capital.

Is he correct? If not, why not?

Tax treatment

2.4 The interest on bank and building society accounts is generally paid net of 20% tax. The deposit taker pays the tax deducted to **HMRC** (Her Majesty's Revenue and Customs – the new name for the Inland Revenue). A non-taxpayer can have the interest paid gross by completing a form R85. The relevant tax year is the tax year in which the interest was **received**.

- **Non-taxpayers** can reclaim all tax deducted.

- **Starting rate (10%) taxpayers** can reclaim a partial refund, as their liability is 10%.

- **Basic rate (22%) taxpayers** have no more tax to pay in addition to the 20% deducted at source.

- **Higher rate (40%) taxpayers** pay the additional 20% tax due, through their annual tax assessment.

2.5   As there is no capital appreciation on a deposit investment, there is no charge to capital gains tax.

Charges

2.6   There is no explicit charging structure within a deposit account. However, there is a hidden charge. The institution needs to cover its costs and make a profit. It does this through the difference between the rates of interest given to depositors and charged to borrowers.

Method of purchase and sale

2.7   The method of opening and operating a bank or building society account is one of the simplest of all investments. It can be done in person by visiting a branch of a bank or building society which for most people is in the next street, village or town. Accounts may be operated by **telephone**, by **post** or via the **internet.** Currently, some of the best rates of interest can be found among internet-based accounts.

Risk

2.8   (a)   The risk on a deposit investment is low because the original capital is secure at all times.

       (b)   There is a risk as far as interest rates are concerned. If the account is linked to a variable rate of interest, this may fall. If the investor has selected a fixed rate and fixed term bond, external interest rates may rise, but the guaranteed rate on the bond will, of course, remain unaltered.

       (c)   The other risk for the investor in deposits is the chance that the institution with whom his money is deposited will go into liquidation, as happened with the Bank of Credit and Commerce International, for example. In this event the depositor will have recourse to the **Financial Services Compensation Scheme,** which is administered by the Financial Services Authority (FSA), subject to the limits mentioned earlier.

       (d)   The restriction on compensation does lead some investors to consider spreading their capital between a number of banks and building societies in order to reduce the risk. This may, however, be a disadvantage, as the client may secure a lower rate of interest because he is investing a smaller amount with each institution, thus missing out on the higher rates offered for large deposits.

Exercise 3

Does risk occur when investing in deposit type investments?

If so, what are the risks involved and what can an investor do to reduce them?

Uses

2.9 The adviser should not overlook bank and building society accounts as part of a portfolio construction. They may be used in the following circumstances.

(a) To provide capital available on instant access to pay for day to day living expenses. It is obviously an advantage if an account can be selected which pays some interest, however small, and imposes no charges.

(b) To provide an investment for the highly risk-averse client. In this case, if there is a considerable amount of money to invest, the adviser will need to use a spread of accounts, instant access, notice and fixed term. He will need to ensure that he has invested sufficient in each account to secure advantageous terms.

(c) To provide an investment for the client with a very small amount of capital to invest. In this case it is important that the capital is secure and most probably that there is instant access to funds.

(d) To provide an emergency fund of capital in case a client is made redundant, the roof needs repairing or there is a large repair bill for the car. The obvious investment medium for such cash is the deposit fund where the nominal value of the capital is secure and access is available with little or no penalty. The size of such a fund varies according to each client s individual circumstances and attitude to risk.

(e) To provide a balanced portfolio for those who only want a small percentage of their capital exposed to risk. Investors who are only prepared to take a risk with, say, 10% of their capital may need to place the balance on deposit. In this instance the adviser will attempt to secure the highest interest rate available, possibly a fixed rate if he thinks interest rates will fall. Long notice periods or fixed terms may be acceptable to such clients for part of their portfolio.

(f) To provide an account for non-taxpayers, including children. They may need to use bank or building society accounts if the gross interest rate is attractive. On completion of the R85 payment will be made gross.

(g) To provide a short term home for capital which is earmarked for use in the near future, for example to buy a house, a boat, pay the school fees or take an exotic holiday. In this case it is necessary to select a notice period to fit the access requirement.

(h) To provide a regular income. A monthly interest account may be used for such an investor. A fixed rate monthly bond would be particularly useful for such a client.

(i) To provide a means of regular savings. The bank or building society regular savings plans are useful for small investors. There is typically no fixed term and access to at least some of the capital without penalty.

(j) To provide a temporary deposit for money awaiting investment in the equity market because the timing for entry or re-entry is not currently deemed to be right.

Exercise 4

Deposit based investments should not be overlooked in the construction of a portfolio.

Review the uses of building society and bank accounts listed in Paragraph 2.8 and think of some more examples of your own.

---

3 OFFSHORE DEPOSIT ACCOUNTS

3.1 Overseas bank and building society accounts and cash funds offered by investment houses are open to UK residents and expatriates. The deposits can be held in sterling or other currencies, for example euros or US dollars. UK residents seeking an offshore deposit account will normally use a bank or building society in Jersey, Guernsey or the Isle of Man.

Types of account

3.2 The range of accounts available is similar to that offered onshore. The client can select an instant access, notice or fixed rate, fixed term account. The interest rates offered reflect UK interest rates.

Tax treatment

3.3 The interest is paid gross on all accounts. UK residents must declare this income to HMRC.

Charges

3.4 There is no extra charge or penalty for investing offshore. As with onshore accounts, the deposit taking institution normally covers its costs and profit from the spread between deposit and borrowing rates of interest.

Method of purchase and sale

3.5 The investor in an offshore deposit account will normally conduct all transactions by post or bank credit transfer.

Risk

3.6 The **interest risk** for an offshore deposit held in sterling is the same as for one held onshore and concerns possible interest rate changes. However, if the deposit is held in foreign currency, there is obviously the dual risk of both changes in interest rates and also exchange rates. (Note that Gibraltar's currency is the pound sterling.)

3.7 The other risk to consider is that of possible default by the institution, if it gets into financial difficulties. If the investment is in Jersey or Guernsey, there is no Depositor Protection Scheme. If the investment is deposited in the Isle of Man, a compensation scheme is available which secures 75% of the first £20,000 invested (£15,000 maximum compensation). Gibraltar has a Deposit Protection Scheme providing compensation of 90% of total deposits up to a maximum of £18,000.

Uses

3.8 Offshore bank and building society accounts:

(a) May be useful for investors who need capital outside the UK and will use their interest offshore, for example if they have a property in France or Spain

(b) May be useful to an investor who is planning to move or retire abroad

(c) Have sometimes been used by investors seeking confidentiality in their affairs. However, as mentioned above, income must be declared by UK domiciled taxpayers, and see below on the European Savings Directive

European Savings Directive

3.9 The European Savings Directive came into force at the beginning of 2005 and arises from an agreement between the EU and Switzerland. Under this Directive, most EU states, including the UK, have agreed to automatic exchange of information between their respective tax authorities on most interest-bearing accounts held by individuals. The Directive covers dependent territories such as the Channel Islands, the Isle of Man and Caribbean territories, and Gibraltar.

4 MONEY MARKET DEPOSITS

4.1 Banks and building societies offer the personal investor the opportunity to invest capital in the money market. This is a facility only available to those with sizeable amounts of capital to deposit for a short term. The money can be placed on the market by a UK or offshore branch of a bank or building society. The bank will quote a guaranteed rate for a fixed period, which may be anything between overnight and one year (the maximum). Once the client accepts the rate the money is held for the agreed term. On maturity if the client wants to deposit the money for a further term, a new fixed rate is agreed. The rates quoted are directly linked to the interbank rate. There is, however, no access to the capital until the end of the term.

Tax situation

4.2 The interest on money market deposits is paid net of 20% tax and added to the capital at maturity. Interest on investments over £50,000 can be paid gross and interest paid on sums invested via offshore banks or building societies will be paid gross.

Uses

4.3 The money market facility can be useful for large amounts of capital requiring a short-term home, for example the proceeds of the sale of a business or a house or an inheritance awaiting investment. The trustees of a pension scheme may use the money market as a means of investing capital required for a member of the scheme who is shortly to retire. Liquid funds will be needed to pay out the benefits.

Exercise 5

Assuming that a client has £60,000 to invest for three months, look in the Financial Times and see if you can find the most competitive rate currently available using:

(a) Money market rates
(b) A unit trust cash fund of your choice, or
(c) An instant access building society account

---

5 NATIONAL SAVINGS & INVESTMENTS

5.1 There are banking accounts and fixed term bonds offered by the government via National Savings & Investments (NS&I). NS&I is not a licensed deposit taker and NS&I products are not regulated under the terms of the **Financial Services and Markets Act 2000** (FSMA 2000). However, since NS&I is government-backed, investments in NS&I can be treated as very safe. Most NS&I transactions can be conducted through Post Offices.

5.2 Although NS&I products are primarily aimed at the smaller investor, it is vital that the adviser understands the accounts available and incorporates them into investment portfolios if applicable. Knowledge of NS&I products is required for the G20 exam.

Easy Access Savings Account

5.3 NS&I introduced the **Easy Access Savings Account** in 2004. This instant access account can be operated by telephone, by post, at Post Offices, or at ATMs using a cash card. Interest is variable and is at tiered rates.

(a) **Tax treatment.** Interest is paid gross, but taxable as savings income (therefore at 0%, 10%, 20% or 40% depending on the investor's tax band).

(b) **Uses.** This account can be used for amounts from £100 to £2,000,000. The account can be held by those aged 11 or over, either individually or jointly with another person. The interest rate tiers are reasonably competitive with many retail bank and building society rates.

Investment Account

5.4 This is another NS&I banking account. The variable interest rate is tiered according to the amount invested. The rate of interest for small deposits may be attractive compared with many bank and building society accounts for similar amounts. Access to funds is via Post Offices, having given notice of one month.

(a) **Tax treatment.** Interest is paid gross but is liable to income tax and must be declared.

(b) **Uses.** This account will be useful in the following circumstances.

(i) For an investor with a small amount to deposit. This is because the interest rate is usually competitive for this size of investment.

(ii) For the investment of children's money, because of the competitive interest rate and gross payment of interest. (Remember though that interest on bank and building society accounts can be paid gross to non-taxpayers, including children, if Form R85 is completed.)

(iii) The accounts can be held by trustees.

Income Bonds

5.5 This investment provides the investor with a regular *monthly* income and total security of capital. The interest rate is *variable* but competitive and currently a higher rate can be achieved for investments in excess of £25,000. There is no fixed term to the bond and capital can be withdrawn in whole or part having given three months notice, or without notice at 90 days loss of interest.

(a) **Tax treatment.** The interest from the Income Bond is paid gross but is liable to tax and must be declared to HMRC.

(b) **Uses.** These bonds are useful in the following circumstances.

(i) For investors requiring a monthly income. The interest rate is normally competitive with similar products on the market. The fact that there is no fixed term and reasonable access makes it a flexible arrangement.

(ii) For non-taxpayers who will find the access to gross interest attractive.

(iii) For retired clients who can hold this bond in addition to Pensioners Bonds. They may wish to hold a considerable amount of capital in these income producing investments.

Pensioners Bond

5.6 There are some significant differences between this and the standard Income Bond, not least, of course, being the age restriction. The bond is only available to those over age 60. The other main differences are that the bond runs for a fixed term and offers a guaranteed rate of interest. The Pensioners Bond is currently offered on a term of one, two or five years. Access to the bond can be obtained with or without notice but an interest penalty will be applied.

(a) **Tax treatment**. The interest from the Pensioners Bond is paid gross but is liable to tax and must be declared to HMRC.

(b) **Uses**. Obviously anyone over age 60 requiring a guaranteed income should invest in these bonds so long as the interest rate is competitive (up to the £1,000,000 sole or joint maximum). The return is particularly attractive for non-taxpayers (as interest is paid gross).

NS&I Savings Certificates

5.7 National Savings Certificates have been issued by the Government for many years. They come in two and five year investment terms giving a guaranteed rate of interest which is added to the capital and paid out at maturity. Each issue of certificates has a different declared rate of guaranteed interest. If an investor fails to redeem the certificate at the end of a five year period a **General Extension Rate** of interest will apply. This is low and such certificates should be encashed and the proceeds reinvested. The maximum investment limit of £15,000 per issue can be exceeded if the person is reinvesting maturing certificates.

There are normally two issues of certificate. One (Fixed Interest Certificates) offers a fixed rate of interest to maturity and the other (Index Linked Certificates) gives a return linked to changes in the RPI plus guaranteed extra interest.

(a) **Tax treatment**. The returns from NS&I Savings Certificates are free of income and capital gains tax.

(b) **Uses**. These certificates could suit those in the following circumstances.

(i) For taxpayers whether basic or higher as they give a tax free return.

(ii) For an investor wishing to secure a fixed rate of interest. If it is felt that interest rates may fall, the fixed rate issue may be attractive.

(iii) For an investor who feels that inflation may be about to rise. For such a person, the purchase of the index-linked issue will be sensible. The investor secures a real rate of return on his investment, ie interest on top of the RPI.

(c) There is no limit on reinvestment of matured certificates.

(d) Matured certificates which are not encashed or reinvested earn the low General Extension Rate.

Capital Bonds

5.8 NS&I Capital Bonds do not pay out interest. Interest is added to the original investment over a five year term. The total interest which will be added to the capital is guaranteed but it rises over the investment period.

(a) **Tax treatment**. The interest from the Capital Bond is paid gross on maturity but is liable to tax and must be declared to the HMRC annually.

(b) **Uses**. The Capital Bond is useful in the following circumstances.

    (i) As an investment for the cautious client who wants a guaranteed return on a capital investment. If he is a taxpayer, the ordinary issue of Savings Certificates may give a better return because it pays tax free interest.

    (ii) As an investment for a non-taxpayer who will obtain a better return from the Capital Bond than the current series of Savings Certificates because he will not be liable to tax on the interest.

Fixed Rate Savings Bonds

5.9 NS&I Fixed Rate Savings Bonds bonds pay a fixed rate net of 20% tax. There are currently three issues available for periods of one year, three years and five years. Higher rates are payable for higher sums invested and for longer periods of investment term. A monthly income option is available at slightly lower rates.

Children's Bonus Bonds

5.10 NS&I Children's Bonus Bonds offer a guaranteed rate of interest on the capital invested for a five year period. New fixed rates are notified at the end of each five-year period. The bonds must be encashed by age 21. The maximum investment is £3,000 per child per issue and the bonds can only be purchased for children under 16 years of age by someone over 16.

(a) **Tax treatment**. The returns from the Children's Bonus Bond are tax free (even on parental gifts)

(b) **Uses**. The Children's Bonus Bond is a useful vehicle for parents, grandparents or other relatives who wish to invest for children.

(c) Investment starts at £25. If the bond is repaid before the end of the five year term, a lower rate is paid.

Premium Bonds

5.11 NS&I Premium Bonds are an investment where the monthly 'interest', instead of being paid to the investor, is paid into a prize fund. For every £1 invested, a serial number is allocated to the bond holder. Serial numbers are picked by a machine called ERNIE (Electronic Random Number Indicator Equipment). If the bondholder has a serial number which matches one picked by ERNIE they have won a prize.

(a) Prizes range from £1 million down to £50.

(b) Prizes are free of UK income and capital gains tax.

(c) The maximum holding is £30,000.

(d) The odds of a £1 unit winning a prize in a particular month vary from time to time.

ISAs and existing TOISAs

5.12 NS&I offer cash-only mini-ISAs and maintain existing TESSA-only ISAs (TOISAs). A TESSA-only ISA may contain the original capital, but not the interest, from a matured TESSA.

Exercise 6

List the NS&I products which have the following features.

(a) Tax-free returns
(b) Available for those over age 16
(c) Available to trustees
(d) Produce a guaranteed return

Charging structure

5.13 There is no charging structure for NS&I products as such. The costs of administration are taken into account before the interest rate is declared on the various accounts, bonds and certificates.

Method of purchase and sale

5.14 NS&I products can be purchased and sold via Post Offices in many cases, or by post directly from NS&I.

Risk

5.15 NS&I products are backed by the government and therefore the risk level is minimal. Many of the products offer a guaranteed rate of interest which makes them very secure. The only risk in such circumstances is a rise in interest rates. In all cases capital is secure.

5.16 Up-to-date information is available on the NS&I website at *www.nsandi.com.*

Chapter roundup

In this chapter we have studied:

- The characteristics of deposit investments

- The main types of account available from banks, building societies and NS&I

- The uses of deposit investments in portfolio construction, in particular the importance of considering inclusion of NS&I products

Quick Quiz

1   A grandparent has already recently invested £3,000 for a child in the current issue of Children's Bonus Bonds and now has a further £2,000 to invest for growth. What could be a suitable NS&I deposit product for the child?

2   A woman aged 60 wants a low risk investment with a regular guaranteed income. What NS&I investment might she select?

3   A higher rate taxpayer thinks interest rates will rise over the next two years and wants to invest £5,000 in a deposit type investment. What scheme might he choose and why? (He does not require income.)

4   James is a second year student. His father has given him £4,000 to supplement his student loan. He will not need all this money immediately. What deposit accounts might he use?

5   Eric and Ethel are both aged 65 and have £100,000 to invest in deposit based investments for three months. They are both basic rate taxpayers. What account or deposit type investment would you suggest?

The answers to the questions in the quiz can be found at the end of this Study Text. Before checking your own answers against them, you should look back at this chapter and use the information in it to correct your answers.

Answers to exercises

2   Your friend is in reality obtaining no real growth on his capital: he is simply rolling up his interest. The rate of interest is not guaranteed, it will vary over the years and there is no guarantee that the interest will exceed inflation in times of high inflation. Only an asset-backed investment such as property and shares will provide inflation-proofing for capital but this is not guaranteed. In this case the investor should obtain an increasing income from rent or dividends *plus* capital appreciation as the value of the property or shares increase. Index Linked Gilts and Index Linked Savings Certificates provide protection from inflation.

3   The risks involved in deposit type investments are as follows.

(a)   The rates are normally variable and will reduce in line with interest rate falls, so there is no guarantee of the level of income.

(b)   If a fixed rate account is chosen, interest rates may rise and the investor is stuck with a lower interest rate on his account for the balance of the term.

(c)   There is no real hedge against inflation (see answer to Exercise 2). The only investments to give real long term growth of income and capital are the asset-backed investments such as property and shares.

(d)   There is a risk that the institution with whom the money is invested may go into liquidation.

The investor can reduce risk by spreading his investment, having some in fixed rate, fixed term and some in variable rate accounts with easy access. If he is concerned about the security of the bank or building society, he can spread his capital among a number ensuring that in each case the amount in his account will be covered by the Financial Services Compensation Scheme.

6   *National Savings & Investments products*

(a)   Tax free - Savings Certificates, Children's Bonus Bonds, Premium Bonds, Cash mini ISA.

(b)   Available to those over 16 - all accounts except Children's Bonus Bonds, which may be bought by those who are 16 or over, for children under 16.

(c)   Available to trustees – Savings Certificates, Income Bonds, Pensioners Bonds, Capital Bonds, Investment Account.

(d)   Guaranteed returns – Savings Certificates, Children's Bonus Bonds, Capital Bonds and Pensioners Bonds.

PRACTICE QUESTION 2: DEPOSITS (30 Marks)

James Evans has just sold his house for a sum of £150,000 and is living in rented accommodation while he searches for a cheaper house. He has been forced to make this move because he has been made redundant and as yet he has not found alternative employment. Should he deposit the money in:

(a) His current account
(b) An onshore building society account (any type)
(c) An offshore building society account (any type)
(d) A money market deposit
(e) A unit trust cash fund?

Explain how each account works and which you think would be most suitable having regard to his current and future situation. (25 marks)

Is there further information you need in order to advise him properly? (5 marks)

The answer to the practice question can be found at the end of this Study Text

Chapter 3

FIXED INTEREST SECURITIES

Chapter topic list	Syllabus reference
1 Introduction to fixed interest securities	2.2
2 Gilts	2.2
3 Worldwide bond markets and Eurobonds	2.2
4 Local authority bonds	2.2
5 Corporate bonds	2.2
6 PIBS and PSBs	2.2

Introduction

In this chapter we examine the different types of fixed interest securities. These investments fall into the low risk category. We will look at their individual features, pricing and analysis of return, risk, tax treatment, cost and method of purchase and sale and their uses in the construction of an investment portfolio.

1 INTRODUCTION TO FIXED INTEREST SECURITIES

1.1 (a) A fixed interest security may be a loan to a government, UK or overseas, to a local authority, to a corporation or to a building society. The security pays a fixed rate of interest and has a known maturity value provided that the stock is held until its redemption date. Government securities and corporate bonds are negotiable and can therefore be traded in the market.

(b) A client can obtain the advantage of a fixed interest security by an indirect route. He can purchase a guaranteed income bond offered by an insurance company. Such a bond could pay a guaranteed income of, say, 5.0% net pa for three years with the return of the capital at the end of the period. The insurance company would have purchased fixed interest securities, possibly gilts, to enable them to offer such a guarantee. Another indirect method of investment is the purchase of a unit trust, OEIC or an insurance company investment bond which is offers a fixed interest fund. With such a fund, a professional fund manager will run a portfolio of fixed interest securities. Investors will be paying for this expertise in the management charges.

(c) Debt instruments are subject to the provisions of the FSMA 2000 and as such advisers must be authorised to advise on and arrange deals in those securities.

We will now look at the features of the various types of fixed interest security.

2 GILTS

Introduction to gilts

2.1 (a) UK government securities are known as **gilts** or **gilt-edged securities.** The government first borrowed from the City of London in the sixteenth century but the secondary market only became fully developed in the nineteenth century. Government securities are called 'gilt-edged' because they were initially indeed gold-edged documents backed by a promise from the government.

(b) The issue of these securities helps the government to fund its borrowings and to replace the capital from maturing issues. The size of the gilt market depends on the government's borrowing needs. At some times the government is in a position to repay maturing issues without the need to borrow more. At such times, the gilt market reduces.

(c) Gilts are issued by the government at various times for different terms and rates of interest. Therefore the investor has a wide choice of securities to meet individual needs. We will now look at the various types of gilt available.

Types of gilt

2.2 Gilts are classified in groups depending on their term to redemption. The Government's Debt Management Office classifications for gilts are as follows.

(a) **Shorts** are gilts with seven years or less to redemption. (Some newspapers still define shorts as gilts with five years or less to maturity.)

For example, Treasury 4 pc 2009

(b) **Mediums** have between seven and fifteen years to redemption. (Or, in some newspapers, five to fifteen years.)

For example, Treasury 8 pc 2015

(c) **Longs** have a period in excess of fifteen years to redemption.

For example, Treasury 6 pc 2028

During the life of a long dated gilt it will, of course, move through the categories, so that the Treasury 6 pc 2028 will become a medium dated gilt and eventually a short dated gilt.

(d) **Undated** gilts have no stated redemption date. The government promises to pay the interest indefinitely, but has the option of redeeming the stock at any time.

For example, War Loan 3.5 pc

War Loan is unlikely ever to be redeemed. The only time that the government would be likely to repay this stock is if interest rates fell below 3.5% and they could refinance the borrowing at a lower coupon.

(e) **Index-linked.** The first index-linked gilt was issued in 1981 and originally only pension funds could purchase it. However, from 1982 onwards index-linked gilts were available to all investors. These gilts have their income and redemption payments linked to the Retail Prices Index (RPI). It is the RPI figure eight months before each payment which is used in the calculation. The figure in brackets after the description of the stock shows the RPI base for indexing.

Example: Index-linked 2 pc Treasury 2006 (69.5).

We will now look at how the index-linking works.

Suppose that an index-linked gilt is issued at a coupon of 2½% over a five year period. Suppose that over this period the RPI rises by 20%. Then, at redemption, the investor who has held the gilt since issue will receive a capital return of £120 for every £100 invested. The interest on the investment will also have risen by 20% to 3%.

(f) **Gilts with a spread of redemption dates**. Some gilts have a spread of redemption dates.

For example, Treas 5½pc 2008 –2012.

This designation states that the government can repay the gilt at any time between the years 2008 and 2012. In practice, they will only repay it if they can replace the borrowing with a new issue with an interest rate below 5½%. If not, they will hold on until the last possible moment.

Features of gilts

2.3 (a) **The coupon**. The rate of interest on a gilt, known as the coupon, reflects the rate of interest which the government needed to offer at the time of issue in order to attract funds. Hence you will see that Treasury 2015 was issued at 8%, clearly at a time when interest rates were much higher than they are today.

(b) **Description of a gilt**. We will now look at the description of a particular stock to understand its meaning.

Example: Treasury 5 pc 2012

The description means that the government will pay the investor £5 per annum interest for every £100 of stock held.

The nominal or **par value** of the stock is the price at which the stock is issued and will be redeemed. So, in the above example each £100 of stock will be repaid in the year 2012 by £100.

However, during the term of the gilt the market value of the gilt will change according to demand. On 23 May 2005, the price of this gilt is £103.94. If you were to buy the gilt on that date you would therefore buy approximately $100 \times 100/103.94 = £96.21$ nominal of stock for £100. Therefore at redemption you would suffer a loss. You would have paid £100 but only receive back £96.21.

You could instead have purchased the long gilt Treasury 4¼% 2032, price at 23 May 2005 £98.97. You would then receive $(100 \times 100/98.97 =)$ £101.04 nominal of stock for £100 invested. At redemption you would receive £101.04 in return for an investment of £100. You would have made a gain on redemption, in 2032, although the interest received would be at the lower annual rate of 4.25%.

(c) **Identifying a stock**. The title of the stock, say, 'Treasury' or 'Exchequer' is generally of no consequence. Most gilts are registered securities. This means that the security is held in the name of the investor. If the word 'loan' appears in the title, this denotes a **bearer stock**. Such a stock is not registered in an individual's name and the only proof of ownership is the possession of the certificate.

(d) **Gilt repos**. A gilt repo (a sale-repurchase agreement) is an agreement whereby one party sells a government bond to a second party and then repurchases it from him at a later date at a given price. The given price is calculated taking into account the loss of interest on the money which has been paid for the security.

(e) **Gilt strips** were introduced in 1997. Before the introduction of gilt strips, the investor always purchased the right to a series of fixed coupon payments and a final redemption payment. With strips, it is possible for the individual coupon payments to be 'stripped' away and traded separately.

Exercise 1

Define the following expressions as they relate to gilts.

(a) Coupon
(b) Redemption
(c) Nominal value

Pricing

2.4 (a) The price of gilts is affected by supply and demand. If investors want to buy gilts, the prices will tend to rise (surplus demand). Similarly prices are likely to fall if a government is running a big deficit and issuing a large number of new gilts (surplus supply).

(b) Short dated gilts can be sensitive to changes in bank interest rates. As interest rates rise and fall, the price of gilts falls and rises. Suppose that in 2006 the government issued a Treasury 4 pc 2011 gilt. If in 2007 the government wish to increase their borrowings by the issue of a further gilt but this time they need to pay an interest rate of 5% for a gilt with a five year life, then the first issue will now be less attractive and a new investor will wish to pay less than £100 for every £100 of stock.

(c) For any **longer-term** increase in interest rates that is expected, the price change of long-dated gilts is likely to be greater than on short-dated gilts. This can be explained by considering the following example.

If interest rates increase from 5% to 6%, then the price of a gilt currently yielding 5% must fall to compensate for the loss of interest. If the gilt has five years to redemption, the price will fall to compensate for a 1% loss of interest for five years. However if the gilt has 12 years to run, then the price must fall to compensate for a much greater loss of interest. Therefore the professional investor will make a better return on long dated gilts if his assumptions about longer-term future interest rate changes is correct.

(d) The price of long-dated gilts is not so directly influenced by **short-term** interest rate changes. The holders of long-dated gilts are concerned about possible changes in government or economic policies and the effects these may have on inflation and interest rates. If investors believe there is likely to be a change in government and that a future government may not be able to control inflation, then the price of long-dated gilts may be depressed because of this.

(e) Gilt prices may be affected by changes in exchange rates. If sterling is weak against other currencies, interest rates could rise and gilt prices will be kept down.

(f) Sometimes the state of the equity market can have a direct effect on gilt prices. After the stock market 'crash' of 1987, gilts offered higher returns than equities. Many investors switched into gilts and consequently gilt prices rose.

Analysing the return on gilts

2.5 When an investor purchases a gilt, he needs to be able to quantify the return on his investment. There are a number of calculations he can make.

Interest yield

2.6 The interest yield also known as the income yield, flat yield or running yield is a calculation made to ascertain exactly how much interest an investor will obtain from the purchase of a particular gilt. Let us look at an example.

2.7 Suppose that an investor purchases Treasury 8 pc 2015 while the current price of the stock is £133.31. He will not receive an income of 8% of his investment per annum. The **interest yield** is:

$$\frac{\text{Coupon}}{\text{Market price}} \times 100 = \frac{8.00}{133.31} \times 100 = 6.0\%$$

Yield to redemption

2.8 The *Financial Times* includes calculations of the previous day's gross yield to redemption on gilts. This is a more important figure as it takes into account in the overall return to redemption both the interest earned and the capital gain or loss annualised over the remaining term. On the same date as that used in the example in paragraph 2.9 above, the published figures are as follows.

Treasury 8 pc 2015 - yield to redemption 4.47%

This figure indicates a capital loss if the stock is held to redemption because the yield to redemption is lower than the interest yield of 6.00%.

Treasury $4^{1}/_{4}$% 2032 - yield to redemption 4.67%

The price of the gilt is 93.42, and so the interest yield is $(4.25/93.42) \times 100 = 4.55\%$. The redemption yield figure indicates a capital gain if the stock is held to redemption because the yield to redemption is higher than the interest yield.

The formula for calculating the gross yield to redemption is:

Interest yield + Annualised capital gain (or loss) to redemption

2.9 The calculation requires the use of compound interest tables or a computer program. However, it is important to understand the meaning of the two expressions and their relevance in the selection of a suitable gilt.

The net redemption yield is the gross redemption yield less tax.

Exercise 2

Calculate the amount of stock you would purchase if you invested £100,000 in:

(a) Treasury $5^3/_4$% 2009, current price £109.40
(b) War Loan $3^1/_2$%, current price £75.13

Also calculate the interest yield.

Yield curve

2.10 The redemption yield is used to compare gilts. Gilts with similar periods to maturity will have similar yields to redemption. Yields to redemption vary because of the length of time a gilt has left to run.

2.11 A graph of yields for different gilts shown against the time they have left to maturity is called a **yield curve** (see below). When the normal investment rule applies, ie the longer to maturity, the higher the yield, this is known as the normal or positively sloping yield curve.

2.12 When the yield on short-term gilts is high, this may lead to an inverted or negative yield curve. This would happen if interest rates and inflation were expected to fall in the future.

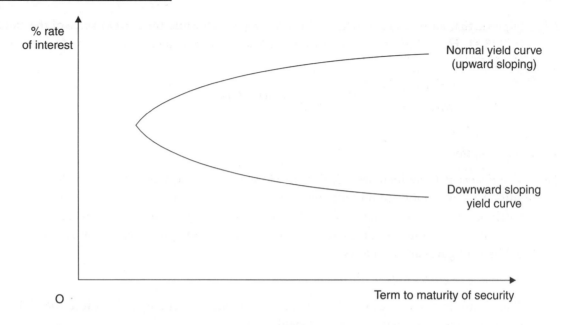

Exercise 3

What effect might the following circumstances have on the gilt market?

(a) The resignation of the Prime Minister
(b) An unexpected reduction in interest rates

Risk

2.13 (a) If an investor buys a gilt at issue and holds it until redemption, there is no risk to his capital or interest return. His original capital will be repaid at redemption and he will have received a fixed rate of interest for the term.

(b) However, an investor who buys a gilt in the market incurs a risk. He may buy today at a yield of 4% only to find that this same gilt can be bought in 12 months time for a yield of 5.5%. Timing can be very consequential in the purchase and sale of gilts.

(c) Investors who buy and sell gilts short term, ie actively trading, incur additional risk. They are predicting interest rate rises or falls and if they make a mistake they can suffer a substantial loss of capital, particularly if they have invested in the more volatile long-dated gilts. Frequent traders will need to take account also of transaction (dealing) costs.

Taxation

2.14 (a) Interest received from gilts and other fixed interest securities is taxed as **savings income,** in the tax year in which it is paid. Depending on the band in which the taxpayer's income falls, this means it will be taxed at:

- 0% for non-taxpayers
- 10% for starting rate taxpayers
- 20% for basic rate taxpayers, or
- At 40% for higher rate taxpayers

(b) Interest on gilts is paid gross, unless:

(i) The investor elects to have 20% tax deducted at source, or

(ii)   Tax has been deducted at source on a gilt purchased before 6 April 1998 and the investor has not elected for gross payments

(c)   **Lower coupon gilts** will be relatively more attractive to **higher rate taxpayers**, because income is a less significant element of the return. **Higher coupon gilts** will be relatively more attractive to **lower rate taxpayers**.

(d)   Gains made by individuals who hold gilts are not subject to capital gains tax but losses cannot be offset against other gains for tax purposes.

(e)   If the fixed interest securities are purchased via a pooled fund, such as a unit trust or investment bond, the taxation situation will be different (see Chapters 5 and 6).

Costs and methods of buying and selling

2.15   (a)   Most investors will purchase or sell gilts via a broker. The broker will be able to carry out the transaction swiftly and confirm the price to the client.

(b)   The broker will charge commission on the transaction, either buying or selling. The commissions are lower than for transactions in equities. The commission might be, for example, 1% of the first £7,000 falling to 0.125% on the balance. There is no stamp duty paid on the transaction (no PTM levy due on gilt purchases and sales also).

Example of the cost of buying a gilt
If the client wanted to invest £10,000 in Treasury 6 pc, the charges may be:

	£
1.0% on £7,000	70.00
0.125% on £3,000	3.75
Total cost	73.75

There may be a minimum commission charge of, say, £25.00.

(c)   Gilt transactions are for cash settlement which means that the cheque is required on the day following purchase.

(d)   The smaller investor can purchase gilts via the Bank of England Brokerage Service direct. This system of sale and purchase is much cheaper. The charge is 0.7% on the first £5,000 then 0.375%, with a £12.50 minimum on purchases (no minimum on sales). There is, however, a disadvantage: the deal cannot be executed immediately and the client does not know the price at which he is dealing.

(e)   When purchasing the gilt stock, the investor will be quoted a **clean price** but pay the price plus a number of days accrued interest, the **dirty price**. The reason for this is that the government pays interest twice yearly on gilts. When a gilt is purchased there is some interest to be added which is owed to the seller. The interest is accrued daily throughout the year.

Example

If an investor pays £100 for a purchase of gilts with a coupon of 10% sixty days after the last payment of interest, he will pay:

Clean price	£100.00
Interest	60/365 × £10 = £1.64
Dirty price	£101.64

(f)   If a gilt is quoted 'ex div' then it is purchased without its imminent interest payment. If it is 'cum div' then the purchaser is eligible for the interest payment. Gilts are usually quoted ex dividend approximately five weeks and two days before payment. In this instance an amount is deducted from the price paid to compensate for the loss of interest for the period of interest forgone.

Exercise 4

James Richmond invests £20,000 in Treasury 7 pc 2008 when it is at a price of 105. He uses a stockbroker for the transaction. The commission is 1% on £10,000 and 0.125% on the excess.

(a) Calculate the total cost of the transaction.
(b) Calculate the cost if he had purchased the stock via the Bank of England Brokerage Service.

New issues of Government Stock

2.16 (a) The **Debt Management Office (DMO)** (an agency of the Treasury) is responsible for the long-term funding of the government borrowing requirement and consequently is responsible for the issue of gilts.

(b) The DMO decides on gilt issues to be offered. Details are announced, together with applications to tender on a specific day. A minimum tender price is fixed. Stock that does not find a buyer on tender is then retained by the government for sale by the DMO and released to the market on 'tap'. This method gives the DMO the maximum amount of flexibility and control.

(c) Sometimes a block of gilts is issued offering the same terms as an existing gilt. This is known as a 'tranche' or 'tranchette'.

(d) In the last few years the government has favoured the method used by the US treasury bond market, the auction system. The main features of the **gilt auction** are as follows.

(i) The intention is to sell all the stock.

(ii) There is no minimum price set for the stock, although the DMO still reserves the right to refuse bids which it believes are too low.

(iii) The bidders are institutions known as **gilt edged market makers (GEMMs)**.

(iv) Individuals can submit non-competitive bids. These are then accepted at the average acceptance price. This is allowed for amounts up to £500,000 nominal value.

(e) There is such a thing as a 'reverse auction'. In this case investors can offer their stock back to the government who buy it back at the most favourable price thus reducing their net borrowings. In this case, the government is a net repurchaser of stock.

Exercise 5

What are the meanings of the following expressions?

(a) A reverse auction
(b) A tranchette

Uses

2.17 (a) Banks and building societies are purchasers of short-term gilts. They need liquid assets to pay out depositors.

(b) Insurance companies are purchasers of long dated gilts to match their liabilities on maturing policies.

(c) Pension fund managers are purchasers of index-linked gilts. The funds they manage need to provide benefits which are based on earnings. Earnings roughly keep pace with inflation. Therefore, the purchase of an index-linked gilt provides an income which keeps pace with inflation and a capital return to match their liabilities.

(d) Pension fund managers and insurance companies will be purchasers of all types of gilts to provide a balance within the funds they manage. The explanations in (b) and (c) are examples of particular uses they have for gilts.

(e) The individual investor may purchase gilts for a number of reasons.

    (i) To provide a regular and guaranteed income.

    (ii) To provide a secure investment giving a known return of capital and interest.

    (iii) A low coupon gilt could be used to fund for a known event in the future, such as school or university fees. The redemption dates could be picked to coincide with the date when funds were required.

(f) Now let us look at some of the tax reasons why individual investors buy gilts.

    (i) A higher rate taxpayer will wish to use a low coupon gilt and thus receive a good overall return, most of which relates to a non-taxed capital gain.

    (ii) A non-taxpayer may be attracted to a high gross interest even if it means a loss of capital if the stock is held to redemption. The purchase of such a stock could be a useful way of funding, say, nursing home fees.

Exercise 6

Make a list of the types of client for whom it may be advisable to hold gilts in their portfolios.

---

3 WORLDWIDE BOND MARKETS AND EUROBONDS

3.1 There is a worldwide bond market. Other governments and international companies issue bonds. The small investor is unlikely to become involved in such stock other than through a pooled investment such as a unit trust.

3.2 **Eurobonds** are fixed interest securities issued for governments and companies in several countries at once by a syndicate of banks. The stock is in bearer form. (This means that the stock is not registered in any person's name. The certificate carries the right to interest, and coupons are attached for submitting to the registrar to claim interest.) Interest is paid annually. The minimum nominal amount of stock which can be purchased is generally high, so many small investors will be precluded.

3.3 Note the following definitions.

Eurobond   A fixed interest security issued either by governments or large companies in a currency other than that of the country or market in which it is issued.

Eurosterling   Sterling deposits held by foreign institutions outside the UK.

3.4 Foreign bonds may also be denominated in the currency of the country in which they are issued by a foreign corporate body. Investment in bonds of a different currency involves **risk arising from exchange rate fluctuations** which could significantly affect returns when measured in the investor's own currency.

4 LOCAL AUTHORITY BONDS

4.1 Some local authorities have issued fixed rate bonds in the past as a means of borrowing money. Given Government restrictions on local authority finances, there are only a few such bonds available now and the market is small.

4.2 Local authority bonds available include **dated and undated bonds**.

4.3 **Yearling bonds** are local authority bonds issued for one year and six days.

4.4 Interest is paid half-yearly, net of 20% tax but, on receipt of a form R85, interest can be paid gross to a non-taxpayer.

Tax situation

4.5 Local authority bonds are **qualifying corporate bonds** and therefore interest is taxable but the bonds are exempt from capital gains tax. Interest is taxable as **savings income**.

Risks

4.6 There is a risk, as with all fixed interest investments, that interest rates will rise while the bond continues with a fixed rate of interest for the remainder of the term.

4.7 The bonds are secured by the assets of the local authority. There is potentially a very small risk, but local authority bonds will have slightly higher yields than an equivalent gilt to reflect the slightly higher risk.

5 CORPORATE BONDS

5.1 A **debenture** is a fixed interest security issued by a company for a fixed term - some are quoted on the London Stock Exchange. The term **corporate bonds** is now used widely to refer to bonds issued by corporations rather than governments. Corporate bonds often have a higher yield than government bonds because bonds issued by corporations are usually riskier than those issued by governments. Corporations have limited resources from which to pay interest on their debt. Governments can always increase taxation to meet their liabilities.

Features of corporate bonds

5.2 We will now look at some features of corporate bonds.

(a) Companies need to borrow money. Sometimes this money is borrowed from banks, sometimes from investors by the issue of debenture or loan stock.

(b) Trustees are responsible for the operation of the loan stock. In particular the trust deed protects the position of the lender in the event of the company winding up and limits the other debt the company can issue.

(c) The position of the lenders on the winding up of a company will depend upon whether the debenture is secured or unsecured. It may be secured upon a fixed asset such as a property or a floating charge of assets. The security upon a fixed asset provides the greatest security.

(d) The company issuing the loan will have to repay interest from profits and also find the capital to make repayment on redemption. There is a risk that they will not be able to do this. Credit rating agencies such as Standard and Poor's rate Government and corporate bonds, and the ratings used are summarised in the **Table** below. Government bonds will be rated as AAA or AA. Corporate bond ratings go through to D on level of risk. Bonds from issuers with a rating of Baa or above from Moody's or BBB and above from Standard & Poor's or Fitch are termed **investment grade bonds**.

Credit risk	Moody's	Standard & Poor's	Fitch
Prime	Aaa	AAA	AAA
Excellent	Aa	AA	AA
Upper medium	A	A	A
Lower medium	Baa	BBB	BBB
Speculative	Ba	BB	BB
Very speculative	B, Caa	B, CCC, CC, C	B, CCC, CC, C
Default	Ca, C	D	DDD, DD, D

Types of corporate bond

5.3   There are a number of different types of debenture or loan stock.

(a)   **Unsecured loan stock** can also be issued and this is the least protected security in the event of default. In such an event the holders only rank with other unsecured creditors such as suppliers.

(b)   A **convertible loan stock** offers the investor a fixed interest rate (usually lower than a straight fixed interest security) plus the option to convert into the company's ordinary shares at a later date on a pre-stated formula. Its other features are as follows.

(i)   It is almost always an unsecured loan stock.

(ii)   It pays a fixed rate of interest until it is converted and on conversion it becomes an ordinary share, identical to one purchased directly.

(iii)   The attraction of this stock is that it offers the security of a fixed interest security. The interest must be paid to the loan stock holders before any dividend payment is made to the shareholders. However, it also carries the option of switching into the ordinary share if the company's results are good.

(iv)   The investor can retain the original value of his capital. On repayment corporate bonds simply repay the original investment, but the conversion option gives the chance of some capital appreciation. The option can be exercised if at an advantageous price and, if necessary, the shares sold immediately. Let us look at how the conversion option works.

When the bond is issued the conversion terms will have been pitched at slightly above the share price at the time. So, if the share price was 75p, the conversion terms may have been that £1 of loan stock could be converted into one ordinary share. If three years later the price of the share is £1.50 then it makes sense to convert. However, during the period the price of the convertible stock will also have risen to reflect the attraction of the conversion option.

(v)   When purchasing a convertible loan stock the investor has to analyse the conversion premium. Those stocks offering high yields are likely to carry a high conversion premium and are in character more like an ordinary loan stock. Those stocks with a lower conversion premium are likely to have a lower yield and a more volatile price. These stocks are in most respects more like the share to which they can be converted.

(vi) *Calculating the conversion premium*

Example

A convertible loan stock has a convertible ratio of 10.2, ie for every £100 of loan stock given up 10.2 ordinary shares will be provided.

On the date of conversion the share is trading at 500p and the convertible at £80 the conversion price is £80/10.2 = 784p

$$\text{The conversion premium} = \frac{\text{Conversion price less current price of share}}{\text{Current price of share}}$$

$$= \frac{784 - 500}{500} = 56.8\%$$

(c) **Zero coupon bonds**. This type of bond pays no interest at all. The return comes entirely as a gain at redemption. Therefore, a bond issued at 50p might be guaranteed to be repaid at 100p.

Prices and methods of buying and selling debentures

5.4 (a) *Prices*. As stated above, the initial interest rate or redemption terms offered must be attractive to investors. After issue, bonds can be traded on the market and the price of the bond will vary according to interest rates in the same way as gilts.

For example, if a debenture offers a rate of 8% and interest rates rise to 10%, the price of the bond will have to fall to compensate for the loss of interest to the investor.

(b) The credit rating of the company can affect the price. If the credit rating of the company falls bond holders will fear that the company will not be able to pay the interest on the loan or repay the capital at redemption and the price will fall.

(c) Corporate bonds are negotiable stock and can be purchased and sold via a stockbroker.

Risk

5.5 (a) The investor in a corporate bond takes the risk that interest rates will rise while he is locked in to a fixed rate security. He can then sell it on the market but he will not receive a good price as the yield has become unattractive.

(b) The investor may be concerned that the profits of the company will be insufficient to pay the interest and repay the debt. There is, therefore, a higher risk than with a government security and investors will expect to receive a higher return in compensation. Large companies which are financially secure will not need to offer an interest rate much above the government's. Smaller companies will have to offer very attractive rates to persuade investors to take the risk.

(c) Another consideration is that although an investor may be happy to lend to the government over a period of, say, 25 years, he might only be happy with a short term loan to a company.

Uses

5.6 (a) A debenture could be useful for a client wanting a higher income than may be achieved from a gilt. He must be made aware of the higher risk he is taking.

(b) Convertible loan stock could be appropriate for the client who is fearful of the equity market yet feels he needs some exposure to equities. In this way he has a secure income and if the company shares perform well he has the right to equity.

(c) As convertible loan stocks could complicated investments the less sophisticated client will be best advised to enter the market via a pooled investment such as a unit trust.

(d) A zero coupon bond could be useful for a client who does not need income but requires capital in the future and does not wish to take undue risk to obtain this capital growth. The capital may be required for school or university fees.

Exercise 7

Make a list of the type of clients for whom you think an investment in the following securities would be suitable. Give reasons for your answers.

(a) Unsecured loan stock
(b) Convertible loan stock on a low conversion premium
(c) Zero coupon bond with a life of nine years

Loan notes

5.7 **Loan notes** are generally issued in connection with corporate takeovers. They are normally short-term bonds carrying a variable rate, offered to shareholders in an acquired company in exchange for shares, with the purpose of deferring or avoiding capital gains tax.

5.8 Since the exchange is paper-for-paper, it does not count as a disposal for CGT purposes. Loan notes can normally be redeemed at six-monthly intervals, allowing the investor to crystallise gains in stages to take advantage of their annual CGT exemption. However, there will be no additional taper relief for the period the loan notes are held.

5.9 The interest rate on loan notes is typically pitched slightly below money market rates, giving the investor an incentive not to hold on to them any longer than is necessary.

6 PIBS AND PSBS

6.1 **Permanent Interest Bearing Shares (PIBS)** were introduced in 1991. They are a form of share in a building society and are a means by which building societies raise capital. The features of PIBS are as follows.

(a) Interest is paid at a fixed rate, half yearly. However there is no obligation on the building society to pay the interest in any one year. If they do not pay it, they are under no obligation to roll it over to the next year (non-cumulative). It is highly unlikely that the building society would not pay the interest. This would only happen in a time of financial restraint.

(b) The interest rate is usually higher than gilts because of the higher risk.

(c) The share is irredeemable, it has no redemption date. The only time it would be repaid by the issuing building society would be on liquidation, in which case the PIBS holders would be the last creditors to be repaid.

(d) PIBS holders are members of the building society and would qualify for distributions on demutualisation.

6.2 Where a building society has subsequently demutualised, PIBS are automatically converted into **perpetual subordinated bonds (PSBs)**. The name comes from the fact that they are low down in the order for payment against other loans, often described as **deeply subordinated.** As part of the rules associated with this type of instrument, the issuer reserves the right to **withhold payments of interest** where they have insufficient income. Very few (if any) will default, but the risk premium on this type of investment makes the yield higher than other corporate bonds and gilts. The market in these investments is relatively illiquid, resulting in larger buying/selling price spreads than with other investments.

Risk

6.3　(a)　As with all fixed interest securities, if interest rates rise, the share price of a PIBS / PSB will fall and the fixed interest will look less attractive.

(b)　We have highlighted above the risks to capital and interest.

(c)　An ordinary investor in a building society is protected by the **Financial Services Compensation Scheme**, while PIBS/PSB holders are not.

Uses

6.4　(a)　PIBS/PSBs should primarily be used by institutions because of their high risk profile. They are not normally a direct investment for the small investor.

(b)　Interested small investors would be well advised to invest via a collective investment. The investor participates in a well spread portfolio of PIBS/PSBs. Income is often paid quarterly. There is a high minimum investment (perhaps £20,000) and upfront charges of entry into the fund.

(c)　A private investor with a large portfolio may use PIBS / PSB as part of his spread of assets particularly if he wishes to use them to avoid capital gains tax.

(d)　As mentioned above, PIBS give membership rights in the society that issues them. This has made PIBS attractive to so-called 'carpetbaggers' who hold a minimum investment in the hope of a windfall on demutualisation.

Tax position

6.5　(a)　Interest from PIBS/PSBs is paid gross. Income tax due will be collected through the taxpayer's tax return. As with other fixed interest securities, the income is taxed as **savings income,** meaning that basic rate (22%) taxpayers pay tax on the income at 20%.

(b)　No capital gains tax is paid on sale because the shares are classified as qualifying corporate bonds.

Method of purchase and sale

6.6　(a)　PIBS/PSBs can be purchased through a stockbroker.

(b)　The shares are bought and sold on the Stock Exchange and settlement takes about five days.

(c)　PIBS and PSBs can only be dealt in round amounts varying from 1,000 shares to 50,000 shares.

(d)　Although originally used primarily by institutional investors, the securities can be purchased by individuals.

Exercise 8

'PIBS? Aren't they some sort of building society account?' Respond to this question, listing the characteristics of PIBS and in particular its risks.

Chapter roundup

In this chapter we have studied:

- The characteristics of various types of fixed interest security including their risk profile
- The influence of changes in interest rates on fixed interest securities
- Methods of analysing the returns from different fixed interest securities
- The uses of fixed interest securities in portfolio construction

Quick Quiz

1 State an indirect method of investing in a short dated gilt.

2 Given an example of an irredeemable loan stock.

3 In what circumstances might a private investor buy an index-linked gilt?

4 What do you call a graph comparing different gilt yields with the period to redemption?

5 How is the interest from a gilt taxed?

6 What are the methods used by the Bank of England to place a new issue of gilts on the market?

7 How do you buy a local authority bond?

8 Why does a debenture carry a higher risk than a gilt?

The answers to the questions in the quiz can be found at the end of this Study Text. Before checking your own answers against them, you should look back at this chapter and use the information in it to correct your answers.

Answers to exercises

1 (a) *Coupon* - The rate of interest paid by a fixed interest bond
(b) *Redemption* - The repayment at maturity of a fixed interest security
(c) *Nominal value* - The face value of a share or security

2 Treasury $5^3/_4$% 2009 – Price: £109.40. £91,408 of nominal stock purchased. Interest yield = (5.75/109.4) x 100 = 5.26%.
War Loan $3^1/_2$ % - Price: £75.13. £133,103 of nominal stock purchased. Interest yield = (3.5/75.13) x 100 = 4.66%.

3 (a) The value of gilts may fall because of lack of confidence.
(b) The price of gilts may rise because existing issues become more attractive.

4 (a) Costs of purchase of Treasury stock value £20,000 via a stockbroker:

1.0% on £10,000 = £100.00
0.125% on £10,000 = £12.50

Total cost £112.50

    (b)   Cost of purchase of Treasury stock, value £20,000 via the Bank of England Brokerage Service.

           0.7% × £5,000 + 0.375% × £15,000 = £91.25

5   (a)   A reverse auction occurs when the government buys back gilts.

     (b)   A tranchette is the issue of a block of gilts on the same terms as an existing issue.

6   The types of person who may need gilts in a portfolio are as follows.

    (a)   A person seeking a guaranteed income (perpetual annuity)

    (b)   A non-taxpayer who wants a high gross income

    (c)   A higher rate taxpayer who purchases a low coupon gilt for tax-free capital growth (There is no capital gains tax payable on a gilt held by an individual.)

    (d)   A person requiring a secure investment (Both income and capital return are known from the outset.)

    (e)   For a low coupon gilt, someone wanting to fund for a known outlay, such as school or university fees

    (f)   A person requiring an indexed-linked income and an inflation proofed return of capital, who may purchase an index-linked gilt

7   (a)   The type of client who may purchase an unsecured loan stock is one who is seeking a higher income than he could secure from gilt. He must be prepared to take a little more risk with his capital.

    (b)   The type of client who may purchase a convertible loan stock is one who is seeking a secure income but also some exposure to the equity market.

    (c)   The type of client who may purchase a zero coupon bond is one who needs no income immediately but requires capital in the future. He will only be taking a small risk with the security of his capital.

8   PIBS are not like a building society account. It is an irredeemable loan raised by a building society. Its features are as follows.

    (a)   Interest is paid at a fixed rate.

    (b)   There is no obligation on the building society to pay the interest in any one year.

    (c)   If they do not pay the interest the building society is under no obligation to roll it over to the next year.

    (d)   The interest rate is usually higher than that available on gilts.

    (e)   The share is irredeemable. In the event of a liquidation the PIBS holders would be the last creditors to be repaid.

    (f)   When a building society demutualises, PIBS are automatically converted into Perpetual Subordinated Bonds.

PRACTICE QUESTION 3: FIXED INTEREST (30 Marks)   *27 mins*

(a) Tom Downs is single and a basic rate taxpayer. He has inherited £20,000. He needs no immediate income. He knows that in five years time he will give up his job and at that time he will wish to repay his mortgage. He is only prepared to take a minimal risk.

   (i)   List the deposit or fixed interest investments he could consider.   (5 marks)
   (ii) Describe the investment you think is most suitable and explain why.   (10 marks)

(b) Mrs Watts, aged 65, is seeking your advice. She pays higher rate tax. She has £50,000 to invest. Her investment criteria are that she wants low risk investments and a regular income.

   She would like to set aside £10,000 for investment for her grandchildren, Jane and Tim aged 8 and 12 (£5,000 each).

   (i)   Describe two investment which would be suitable to give her an income (using only fixed interest or deposit investments).   (8 marks)

   (ii) List two investments which would be suitable for the grandchildren (again using only fixed interest or deposit investments) and briefly state your reasons for the choice.
                                                                              (7 marks)

The answer to the practice question can be found at the end of this Study Text

Chapter 4

PACKAGED INVESTMENTS - REGULAR SAVINGS

Chapter topic list	Syllabus reference
1 Introduction to packaged investments for regular savings	2.3
2 Endowment policies	2.3
3 Traded endowment policies	2.3

Introduction

In this chapter we examine the different types of packaged investment primarily offered by insurance companies which can be used for regular savings. The packaged investments outlined in this chapter fall into the low risk category. There are packaged investments which carry a higher risk and these will be discussed in later chapters. We will look at their individual features, tax treatment, charging structure, risk, method of purchase and sale and use in the construction of an investment portfolio.

1   INTRODUCTION TO PACKAGED INVESTMENTS FOR REGULAR SAVINGS

1.1   The small or unsophisticated investor may find that his route to the investment of his choice is through a fund managed by professionals. He may be wary of approaching a stockbroker but be happy with the concept of an insurance company product which appears to be user friendly and to satisfy his investment needs.

1.2   Over the last 30 years or so, insurance companies have moved away from their traditional role of providing primarily protection policies to a position where they market investment products to meet various needs. In this chapter we will look at products which can be used for regular savings purposes.

2   ENDOWMENT POLICIES

2.1   The with profit **endowment policy** is a regular premium savings policy for a fixed term. The term may be between 10 and 25 years. Few new endowment policies are now being written, although many existing policies are in force, particularly as repayment vehicles for mortgages.

2.2   Premiums will be paid monthly, quarterly, half-yearly or annually. Policies taken out before 14 March 1984 only benefit from **life assurance premium relief (LAPR)** at 12.5% on the premiums paid.

2.3 The with profit endowment policy offers the investor a **guaranteed sum assured**. This is normally quite low as the main aim of the policy is to provide a savings medium.

2.4 A **bonus** is added each year to the sum assured: this is known as a reversionary bonus or annual bonus. Once added this bonus cannot be taken away. On maturity or earlier death an additional bonus, known as a vesting or terminal bonus, is added to the accrued sum assured and reversionary bonus. The terminal bonus can be a high percentage of the total return.

2.5 Before declaring the reversionary bonus, the insurance company values its life fund and declares a surplus for the year. The actuaries then recommend how much of the surplus can be allocated to the with profit policyholders with the balance going to reserves. (In the case of a proprietary office provision will need to be made for the shareholders' dividends.) Although the performance of the life fund can vary from year to year depending on investment performance, nevertheless by calling on reserves, if necessary, the insurance company should be able to declare a smooth pattern of bonus over the years. The terminal bonus reflects more directly the insurance company's returns in its life fund close to the maturity of the policy.

2.6 The Financial Services Authority (FSA) permits insurance companies to quote the returns on endowment policies assuming growth rates of 4%, 6% and 8% pa.

Types of endowment policy

2.7 There are a number of other types of endowment policy which should be mentioned in this section.

Low cost endowment

2.8 As you will remember from your previous studies, a **low cost endowment policy** is effectively a package combining two elements: a with profit endowment and a reducing term assurance. In the construction of the package, the actuary assumes that a certain level of bonus is added to the with profit endowment element each year. The term assurance reduces annually by an equal amount. If bonus levels are greater than assumed, a profit will be achieved. This policy is most likely to be used in connection with a mortgage. The aim of the policy is to provide maximum cover for a given premium. As a large part of the premium is being applied to term assurance, the investment returns will be lower than with a full endowment policy.

Flexidowment

2.9 A possible disadvantage of a fixed term endowment is just that: it has a fixed term. This is, of course, an advantage for the investor who knows when he wants the proceeds. For most clients, plans are not that precise. A parent may want to save up for his children's weddings, but who knows if they will marry or when? Hence, the flexidowment gives the flexibility needed.

The policy runs to a maturity date normally the policyholder's 65th birthday. In addition the policy is broken down into segments; for example if there is a monthly investment of £100, there may be ten segments of £10 each. From year ten onwards it is possible for the policyholder to encash segments of his policy without penalty. He will still be eligible for terminal or vesting bonus (which is normally not paid on early surrender).

Tax exempt Friendly Society policies

2.10 **Friendly societies** can offer endowment policies with an investment into a tax exempt fund.

(a) The maximum premium investment into the tax exempt fund is £270 per annum per person (including children) if paid annually or £300 if paid more frequently than annually – eg, £25 per month if paid monthly. (£25 × 12 months = £300.)

(b) As previously mentioned, the particular advantage of a friendly society is that its life fund is tax exempt, although weighed against this are the charges on the policy, which can be relatively high.

(c) Investments with friendly societies can be made into traditional with profit or unitised funds. The FSA allows friendly societies to provide quotations showing returns of 5%, 7% and 9% pa, given of the tax-free status of the funds.

(d) Friendly societies can also write ordinary business of any amount in a taxed life fund.

(e) **Baby Bond** is a registered service mark of the Tunbridge Wells Equitable Friendly Society and is the name for a savings plan with that society marketed for purchase on behalf of a child.

Unit linked endowment

2.11 A unit-linked endowment policy is a fixed term policy into which regular premiums are made.

(a) Most contracts have minimum life cover, simply 75% of the premiums paid over the term of the policy. This is done to maintain the qualifying status of the policy.

(b) Some policies are designed only to accept large premium payments, say over £100 per month with the minimum amount of life cover to keep the policy qualifying. These policies are known as **maximum investment plans**.

(c) Whatever the size of the premium, the investor has a choice of funds into which his premiums can be invested, including UK Equity, Property, European, Pacific, America, Fixed Interest and Cash.

(d) The premium is invested in the chosen fund or funds and units are then cancelled to pay for the life assurance and charges. The choice of fund will of course depend on the client's **attitude to risk**.

(e) The use of monthly premiums means that the client can make use of **pound cost averaging**, which was mentioned earlier in this Study Text. An example of the effect of pound cost averaging in the purchase of units is shown below. You will see that the unit price varies, so the number of units purchased by the same premium varies from month to month. Fewer units are purchased when the units are more expensive.

Monthly contribution of £30.00 purchasing units in a Far Eastern Fund

Month	Offer price	Units purchased
August	208.40	14.395
September	201.20	14.911
October	210.50	14.252
November	201.40	14.896
December	181.40	16.538
January	182.30	16.456

(f) Switches between funds are allowed. Normally there is one free switch each policy year and subsequent switches can be made at a small cost such as £20.

Tax treatment

2.12 **Premiums** for new endowment policies do not enjoy tax relief. **Proceeds** from endowment policies are tax-free regardless of their tax status so long as the policy is a qualifying one.

Exercise 1

Do you remember the qualifying rules for life policies? See if you can write them down. If you have forgotten them, look at the Appendix to Chapter 5.

Charging structure

2.13 There is a different charging structure depending on whether the policy is a traditional with profits arrangement or a unit linked policy.

With profits policies

2.14 It is difficult for the insurance company to clearly set out the charges of a traditional with profits policy. The advent of commission disclosure has led to many insurance companies abandoning traditional with profits policies, partly because of the problem of quantifying the costs of the policy to the policyholder in the key features document.

As a savings vehicle, the traditional endowment policy is expensive in charges and the policyholder is paying for life assurance which he may not need. A simpler method could be to split out the protection and savings needs. Protection might be provided by term assurance and the savings by a regular contribution to an ISA or a unit trust or investment trust savings plan.

Unit linked policies

2.15 The charges on a unit linked policy are explicit. There is typically a 5% - 6% bid/offer spread on the purchase of units, a monthly policy fee which may be indexed and an annual management charge, of perhaps 1%. In order to extract the setting up charges, the insurance company uses one of the following methods.

(a) Low allocation of units for the first 12 to 24 months.

(b) The use of initial and accumulation units. The first 12 or 24 months premiums are used to purchase the initial units which carry a heavier charge. Thereafter premiums are invested in the accumulation units.

Exercise 2

A client is deciding on a suitable savings medium for £100 per month. He is a basic rate taxpayer. He is not eligible to start a new ISA in the current tax year and his choices are:

(a) A building society account
(b) A unit linked endowment policy
(c) A friendly society policy

Describe to him in writing:

(a) The features of each plan including term, access and penalties
(b) The taxation of each contract
(c) The charging structure of each policy
(d) The risk associated with each policy

Risk

2.16 (a) The investment risk involved in a with profits endowment policy is low. The policyholder has a guaranteed sum assured to which a reversionary bonus is added and once added, cannot be removed however poor future performance may be. The only risks are that future bonus rates will drop and that the terminal or vesting bonus may be low or non-existent.

(b) There is, of course, a risk on early encashment. The surrender or paid-up values will include penalties which cannot be assessed in advance. In fact in many with profits policies there will be no surrender value in the first 12 months. There could also be a tax implication on early encashment of such a policy.

(c) Policyholders will be covered by the **Financial Services Compensation Scheme** which provides that, in the event of an insurance company going into liquidation, the policyholders will be protected to the extent of up to 90% of their benefits. Similar protection is available to the holders of friendly society policies.

Method of purchase and sale

2.17 (a) Endowment policies are purchased from an insurance company following a recommendation from a company direct salesman, a tied agent or an independent financial adviser.

(b) The products are designed to be held to maturity. Early encashment brings penalties which normally cannot be quantified until the time of withdrawal. The surrender values for traditional with profit policies are calculated by the actuary at the time of request.

(c) If the policyholder cannot maintain premiums either a surrender value is paid out by the insurance company or the policy becomes paid-up which means that no further premiums are paid and the life cover reduces. A reduced benefit is then paid out at maturity.

(d) There is now another alternative available to the policyholder who can no longer afford his premiums. There is a market in second-hand with profit endowment policies. In many cases the return from selling the endowment policy in the second-hand market is greater than the surrender value quoted by the insurance company. Second-hand **traded endowment policies** are discussed later in this chapter.

Uses

2.18 (a) An endowment policy might be used in a portfolio when an investor wishes to build up capital for a specific need in the future. However, new endowment policies are less tax-efficient than ISAs and in recent years there has been **regulatory pressure** for advisers to recommend alternatives. As already mentioned, there is little new business although many existing policies remain.

(b) Charges are higher than for other forms of investment. Endowments are not very flexible and early encashment can only lead to penalties and lack of the final or terminal bonus. The Key Features Document issued to investors should highlight these facts.

(c) Clients who hold older endowment policies with tax relief on premiums may wish to maintain premium payments. The tax relief adds to the overall return.

(d) An endowment policy has some advantages for a higher rate taxpayer. Whilst the investor is paying premiums he suffers no personal tax liability and on encashment the benefits are tax-free. During the term of the policy his fund is suffering tax at the rate paid by the insurance company which will be lower than his personal rate of tax.

(e) Saving via an endowment policy might be used in school fees planning. In this case there is a need for savings and protection. If the policyholder dies early, the endowment policy pays out a death benefit, which can be used for future school fees. If an ISA or other savings plan had been used, the capital available on the investor's death would only be the amount saved to date plus growth, if any. On the other hand, a savings plan can be supplemented inexpensively by a term life assurance policy to provide life cover.

(f) Friendly society policies offer tax advantages to basic and higher rate taxpayers because the life fund is tax exempt. Although there is this tax advantage, this can be outweighed by poor investment performance, so the choice of a society with a good past performance record is important (although of course this does not guarantee good future performance). Charges may also be high.

(g) Friendly society policies could be appropriate for children. Policies can be taken out in the child's own name, for example by parents, grandparents or godparents.

(h) Endowment policies have sometimes been used as savings plans for children. A parent may wish to save for a specific number of years, say, until the child reaches age 18 or 21. The policy can be written on the life of the parent in trust for the child. The policy will mature at the required age. The parents will act as the trustees and the proceeds will be paid to them tax-free on maturity. Only a very few insurance companies are able to issue policies in the name of a child with immediate cover. Other insurance companies are able to write the policy in the name of the child but the death benefit does not become effective until the child reaches age 16. In the event of death prior to this age, only the premiums paid to date are returned.

Exercise 3

Do you think that an endowment policy written on the life of one parent, with both parents acting as trustees, is a sensible way of saving money for a child?

List the advantages and disadvantages of the scheme.

(i) Investors who effected endowment policies prior to 24 February 1988 may have a valuable option written into their policy. The option states that at the end of the fixed term of the policy the capital may remain with the insurance company, continue to be invested and an 'income' can be withdrawn from the capital which is tax free. In order to achieve this facility the policyholder must pay a notional premium of £1 per annum. This facility has been withdrawn for new policies.

(j) Endowment policies have frequently been used as a means of repaying interest-only mortgages. Reliable investment performance needs to be achieved in order to secure sufficient funds to repay the loan. Poor performance of some unit linked funds and reducing with profit bonus payouts have led people to query the desirability of this method of mortgage repayment and, as already mentioned, the amount of new business is low.

3 TRADED ENDOWMENT POLICIES

Introduction

3.1 Because of changing financial circumstances, such as those following redundancy, divorce or early retirement, policyholders may wish to encash their endowment policies. They may need the cash or alternatively they may no longer be able to afford to pay the premiums.

(a) Their first course of action is to approach the insurance company for a surrender value quotation.

(b) A second option is to sell the endowment policy on the traded market. It may be possible to beat the quoted surrender value by up to around 35%.

3.2 The traded policy market has grown tremendously in recent years. The policies sold in this way are sometimes referred to as **traded endowment policies (TEPs)** or **second hand endowment policies (SHEPs)**.

Type of policies suitable for trading

3.3 The policies bought and sold are with profit endowment policies – generally those which have been in force for five years and have varying maturity dates. The policies may be either qualifying or non-qualifying.

Valuing a policy for trading

3.4 (a) A policy should only be sold in the market if a higher price can be achieved than the surrender value quoted. The market value of a traded endowment policy will depend on:

(i) The current surrender value quoted, maturity date of the policy and reversionary bonus paid to date

(ii) The long-term outlook for bonus payouts and in particular terminal bonus of the company in question and the financial strength of the company

(b) The purchaser of the endowment policy needs to calculate a possible maturity value based on current terminal and reversionary bonus rates. He then needs to see what effect there would be if the bonus rate changed. Most market makers will provide tables to assist the investor in this calculation.

(c) The yields on those policies with fewer years to run until maturity will be less affected by falls in reversionary bonus. These are the policies which are most attractive to investors.

Selling and buying a policy on the traded market

3.5 (a) *The seller.* If a policyholder wished to sell a policy, the procedure would be as follows.

(i) After the necessary research, the policyholder would agree to sell the policy through a market maker, broker or auctioneer.

(ii) Once the policy had been sold, it would be handed over to the purchaser. The sale price would be paid and a deed of assignment would be executed in favour of the purchaser.

(b) *The purchaser*

(i) The purchaser will serve a Notice of Assignment on the insurance company (Policies of Assurance Act 1867) so that, in the event of a claim, the proceeds would be paid to him rather than the life assured.

    (ii)   The purchaser would be responsible for payment of future premiums.

    (iii)   The purchaser would need some method of ensuring that he was informed should the life assured die. Upon the death of the life assured prior to maturity, the benefits would be paid to the purchaser.

    (iv)   If the policy ran its course, the proceeds would be paid to the purchaser on maturity.

Tax treatment

Tax situation for the seller

3.6   (a)   If the policy being sold is a qualifying one which has been in force for ten years or three-quarters of the term, if less, then there is no tax liability on the seller.

    (b)   If the policy being sold is non-qualifying, or has been in force for less than ten years or three-quarters of the term, then a chargeable event will occur. If the price raised exceeds the premiums paid then a charge to higher rate income tax could occur. The method of calculating the tax charge would be the same as calculating the charge to tax on the encashment of an investment bond. The gain would be subject to tax at 20% (2004/05) for a higher rate tax payer. The tax charge would also apply if, after applying top-slicing relief to the gain and adding this to the policyholder's income, it brought him into the higher rate tax bracket.

Tax situation for the purchaser

3.7   (a)   At maturity or on the death of the life assured or the owner, the proceeds of a **qualifying policy** may be subject to **capital gains tax**. The calculation will be made taking the proceeds and deducting the purchase price, expenses, premiums paid and indexation. Indexation will not apply for policies purchased after 5 April 1998. In this instance taper relief will be relevant. Polices purchased prior to 5 April 1998 will have both indexation and taper relief applied to any gain. If a gain results in excess of the annual allowance for capital gains tax purposes, then tax will be paid at the appropriate tax rate.

    (b)   The maturity or the death of the life assured (which gives rise to a benefit) or owner under a non-qualifying policy will automatically give rise to a chargeable event. The chargeable gain will be calculated by taking into account the proceeds less the premiums paid throughout the life of the policy by both the seller and buyer. Top-slicing relief will apply but if the gain once added to the purchaser's income pushes him into higher rates of tax then the whole gain will be subject to tax at 20% (2005/06).

    (c)   The proceeds from a non-qualifying policy may be subject to **capital gains tax** if the owner of the policy has already exceeded his annual exemption for capital gains tax purposes. However, the taxable capital gain is reduced by any amount which is subject to income tax, ie the chargeable gain, so double taxation should not apply.

    (d)   A higher rate taxpayer may be able to reduce the potential tax charge by investing jointly with a spouse who is a basic rate taxpayer or by assigning the policy to the spouse for no payment. As he or she had not received it for money or money's worth, there will be no liability to tax on the maturity value.

Charging structure

3.8 The cost of buying and selling endowment policies depends on the method used which is described in 'method of purchase and sale' (see below).

Risk

3.9 There is no risk for the seller of an endowment policy in the traded endowment market. He has already decided that he no longer needs the policy or he cannot afford it. The price he obtains will be better than the surrender value, so he has made a profit and should be happy. The buyer does of course run risks, as follows.

(a) The future reversionary bonus of the provider will not continue at current rates and, indeed, may fall substantially due to market conditions.

(b) The future reversionary bonus of the provider will not continue at current rates and indeed, may fall substantially due to weakness in the financial strength of the insurance company.

(c) The insurance company may be taken over and that this may have an adverse affect on long term bonus rates. (In the short term, he might receive additional bonus or 'windfall' shares.)

(d) The terminal bonus paid on maturity may be substantially less than predicted.

Exercise 4

A client approaches you and says he is interested in purchasing a traded endowment policy to mature in eight years time. He does not know which policy to choose.

Explain to him what features he should consider.

Methods of purchase and sale: the market

3.10 Endowment policies can be bought and sold *via*:

(a) Market makers
(b) Brokers
(c) Auctioneers

We will now consider the function of each member of the market.

The market maker

3.11 (a) The market maker buys policies and holds them on his books until a suitable buyer can be found.

(b) Market makers will be regulated under the **Financial Services and Markets Act 2000** by the FSA. There will be no charges for the buyer or the seller to pay. The market maker will secure his profit on the difference between the buying and selling price of a particular policy. If the client has been introduced by an independent financial adviser (IFA), commission will normally be paid to the intermediary.

Brokers

3.12 The brokers approach a number of market makers on behalf of a client who is either buying or selling a policy. The idea is to achieve the highest price for the client who is selling or the best investment for the client who is buying. The market maker's commission is then split between the broker and the IFA.

Auctioneers

3.13 (a) This is the oldest method of buying and selling policies, first introduced in 1843 by Foster and Cranfield, who still hold three auctions a month.

(b) Fees of one-third of the excess over the insurance company's surrender value are charged to the seller. Sellers can decide to impose a reserve price below which they will not sell.

Notes

Although we have dealt in this section primarily with the first time buying and selling of traded endowment policies, at least one of the market makers now offers a tertiary market. They will buy policies back again.

It is possible to buy into the traded endowment market via an investment trust. In this way the purchaser is not buying one policy for a specific period but participating in a portfolio of policies.

Exercise 5

A client says he wants to surrender his 25 year endowment policy in year 16 as he has now repaid his mortgage.

(a) Explain the disadvantages of terminating the contract.

(b) Assuming that he still wishes to proceed, explain that he could sell the policy and how this process would work.

Uses

3.14 Traded endowment policies may be used in the following circumstances.

(a) As a low to medium risk rated investment for an investor who is interested in with profit type investments but does not want to commit himself to a ten year savings scheme.

(b) As an investment for a client in poor health who may not be acceptable to the insurance company if he applied directly to them for an endowment policy.

(c) To provide a fund for a known future event such as school or university costs. Second-hand policies could be used if the client had capital available and was prepared to take a medium risk.

3.15 In making recommendations for the use of these policies within a portfolio it is important to consider the following.

(a) The **investor's likely tax situation** on encashment.

(b) The **lack of liquidity** in the scheme, ie once the policy is purchased the investor will normally hold it for the balance of the term. This objection could be overcome by the purchase of a traded endowment investment trust. In this way the investor participates in a fund of many policies with different maturity dates. He should be able to encash all or part of his shares at any time.

(c) **Compliance**. The adviser is responsible for compliance even when the relevant information is provided by a market maker. The adviser must ensure that a second hand bond is a suitable recommendation taking into account other options. He must explain the method of assignment of the policy, the claims procedure and the tax situation.

Chapter roundup

In this chapter we have studied the characteristics and uses of the packaged policies with regular premiums offered by insurance companies, with profit and unit linked endowments, friendly society policies and traded endowment policies (TEPs).

Quick Quiz

1   What do you understand by a non-qualifying policy?

2   What do you understand by the expression 'pound cost averaging'?

3   What is the maximum regular premium which can be paid into a Friendly Society tax-exempt fund?

4   If a basic rate taxpayer has purchased a TEP, what tax may he have to pay on maturity of the policy?

The answers to the questions in the quiz can be found at the end of this Study Text. Before checking your own answers against them, you should look back at this chapter and use the information in it to correct your answers.

Answers to exercises

1   See Appendix.

2   (a)   *Building society account*

Features

Term	Flexible
Access	Yes
Penalties	No
Taxation	Interest subject to tax
Charging structure	Taken into account when interest rate declared
Risk	Low

(b)   *Unit linked endowment policy*

Features

Term	Ten years
Access	None without penalties
Penalties	Yes
Taxation	Tax-free return at the end of ten years. Life fund taxed
Charging structure	Initial charges and annual management charge
Risk	Medium to high depending on the fund selected

(c)   *Friendly society tax-exempt policy*

Features

Term	Ten years
Access	None without penalty
Penalties	Yes
Taxation	Tax-free return at the end of ten years. Tax-free roll-up in fund
Charging structure	Initial charges and annual management charge
Risk	Low if with profits fund selected, medium if managed fund selected. Friendly societies are unlikely to offer very high risk funds

3   *Advantages*

   (a)   The policy is on the life of a parent so if the parent dies there is a tax-free lump sum death benefit.

   (b)   The parents are trustees of the benefits so they can decide how and when to release the money to the child.

   (c)   A term can be selected to provide a tax free lump sum at a specific age, say 18 or 21.

   Disadvantages

   (a)   The scheme is not flexible and charges may be high.

   (b)   It may be difficult to obtain benefits before the end of the term other than by surrender or policy loan. There would be penalties on a surrender.

   (c)   Tax is being paid on the life fund. Normally a child will be a non-taxpayer, so possibly another scheme could be used where tax paid on interest could be reclaimed so long as it did not exceed £100 per annum.

4   The features to consider when selecting a traded endowment policy are as follows.

   (a)   The current surrender value of the policy

   (b)   The maturity date of the policy

   (c)   Reversionary bonus paid to date

   (d)   Long-term outlook for bonus payouts of the company being considered and in particular terminal bonus

   (e)   The financial strength of the company being considered

5   (a)   The disadvantages of terminating the endowment policy are as follows.

      (i)   There will be a penalty imposed because the policy will not run its full course.

      (ii)   As the policy has been in force for 16 years, the policyholder will lose the added incentive of life assurance premium relief which applies to the premiums paid to this policy.

      (iii) He may lose a substantial amount of terminal bonus which would normally be paid at maturity.

   (b)   The client could sell his policy rather than surrendering it. In this case there is a chance that he could receive a larger return than the quoted surrender value. The client could sell his policy via:

      (i)   A market maker
      (ii)   A broker
      (iii) An auctioneer

   Whichever method is selected, if the client discovers he can obtain a better price than the surrender value quoted, he will sell. The policy will then be assigned to the new owner who must continue to pay premiums. The client will receive the sale proceeds.

The practice question at the end of Chapter 5 covers topics included in this chapter.

Chapter 5

PACKAGED INVESTMENTS – LUMP SUM SCHEMES

Chapter topic list	Syllabus reference
1 Introduction to lump sum packaged investments	2.3
2 Investment bonds	2.4
3 With profit bonds	2.3
4 Guaranteed bonds	2.3
5 Specialist bonds	2.4
6 Annuities	2.3
7 Back to back arrangements	2.3

Introduction

In this chapter, we examine the different types of packaged investment offered primarily by insurance companies for lump sum investment. The risk profile of the products is varied. We will look at their individual features, tax treatment, charging structure and use in the construction of an investment portfolio.

1   INTRODUCTION TO LUMP SUM PACKAGED INVESTMENTS

1.1   In the last chapter we looked at the use of packaged products for the regular saver. Investors may have a need for a packaged investment when they seek to invest a lump sum.

1.2   These investors purchase security and investment expertise for the management of the capital through a package. We will now look at the features of a number of these products.

2   INVESTMENT BONDS

Features

2.1   (a)   The insurance companies offer non-qualifying single premium whole of life policies as a lump sum investment vehicle. Such non-qualifying policies are variously advertised as 'investment bonds', 'property bonds', '**single premium bonds**' or 'single premium life assurance bonds'.

       (b)   A single payment is made and units are purchased in a fund or funds of the investor's choice.

       (c)   The investor has the choice of a wide range of funds. Those traditionally offered are detailed below.

(i) **Managed fund.** This fund invests in UK and overseas equities, fixed interest, cash and sometimes property. It is the manager's responsibility to balance the investments to achieve the best return. It is a fairly conservatively run fund without exposure to undue investment risk. It is the fund most often selected by the investor who has little or no experience of investing in the stockmarket.

(ii) **Cash fund.** This fund invests in the money markets and is normally used by investors as a haven between switches or when they are close to withdrawing their capital and wish to consolidate their gains.

(iii) **Gilt and fixed interest fund.** This fund invests in UK gilts, overseas bonds and corporate bonds. The return should be steady, if unexciting.

(iv) **UK equity fund.** This fund, as its name implies, invests in UK shares. The shares can range from blue-chip to smaller company shares. This is a higher risk fund. It is the manager's responsibility to pick his stocks well to achieve, hopefully, top quartile performance.

(v) **Overseas equity or international fund.** This fund invests in shares in the UK and overseas. The UK companies in the portfolio will normally be companies who secure a high percentage of their income from overseas earnings. This fund is a high risk fund and may be more volatile than the UK equity fund because of market and currency changes.

(vi) **Distribution fund.** Some insurance companies offer a distribution fund. The investment philosophy of the fund is to generate income from the portfolio. In order to achieve this the manager may invest in gilts, preference shares, or property (yielding rental income) as well as ordinary shares. The income achieved by the investments whether dividend, interest or rental income is kept in a separate fund and distributed to the bondholders monthly, quarterly or half-yearly. In this way if a client is taking a withdrawal from a bond, the value of the underlying investment is not being eroded by 'income' withdrawals. The withdrawal of income is still subject to the chargeable gains rules.

(vii) **Property fund.** This fund invests in commercial, industrial and retail units both leasehold and freehold. The distribution of the fund will depend upon the investment manager's view of which sector is likely to perform well in the existing economic situation. Because of the illiquidity of property the fund carries a special condition that encashments can be delayed for up to six months if market conditions are difficult. This rule is included to protect the remaining investors. Otherwise a property may have to be sold at an unrealistic price in the event of a run of withdrawals from the fund. A number of property funds have imposed this condition from time to time.

(viii) **Unitised with profit fund.** This type of fund is discussed in more detail later in this chapter.

(ix) **Specialised funds.** Most insurance companies offer a range of specialised unit linked funds. These funds invest in specific geographical areas such as Europe, South East Asia, Japan and North America. It is even possible to invest in specialised unit trust funds although there may be an element of double charging. All these funds carry a higher risk because of investment in one specific area and also the currency risk.

(d) The bond normally allows the investor to spread his capital between a number of funds and to switch between funds. The charges to use the switch facility are nominal. Usually the investor is allowed one free switch per annum and subsequent switches are at a flat charge of, say, £25.

(e) The investor can withdraw his money from the bond at any time, normally without penalty. As we have already seen there may be a restriction imposed on withdrawal from a property fund (see (c) above).

Exercise 1

What restriction may be imposed on an investor withdrawing money from a property fund?

(f) The investor can take an 'income' from his investment bond by making use of a withdrawal facility. This facility allows for up to 5% of the original investment to be withdrawn each policy year with no immediate tax charge. The withdrawals are taken into account when calculating the final gain when the bond is encashed (see tax treatment of investment bonds in the appendix to this chapter and below). The 'income' can be taken monthly, quarterly, half-yearly or annually.

Tax treatment

2.2 An investment bond is a **non-qualifying whole of life policy** and therefore the following rules apply.

Taxation of proceeds

2.3 A 'chargeable event' may give rise to charge to income tax being incurred on the proceeds of the bond. A chargeable event may occur in the following circumstances.

(a) The death of a life assured if this gives rise to benefits under the policy
(b) The partial surrender of benefits
(c) The total surrender of benefits
(d) The assignment of the bond for money or money's worth
(e) The maturity of the bond

There is no chargeable event in the following circumstances.

(a) The assignment of a bond between spouses
(b) An assignment which is not for money's worth
(c) An assignment as a security for a debt

A partial surrender

2.4 The policy holder has the right to a 'notional allowance' of 5% per annum of the total premium paid which can be taken as a withdrawal. If the allowance is not used, it is allowed to be carried forward to the next year. These withdrawals can be taken up to 100% of the premium paid. If the holder exceeds the cumulative allowance then a chargeable event will occur.

Example: Bond purchased for £10,000 in 2000

Year	Cumulative allowance	Surrender	Taxable gain
2001	£500	0	0
2002	£1,000	0	0
2003	£1,500	£1,000	0
2004	£1,000	£2,500	£1,500
2005	£500	£500	0

Calculating the gain

2.5　Chargeable gain = (encashment value + previous withdrawals) – (original investment + all previous chargeable excesses)

The previous chargeable excesses (withdrawals above 5%) are excluded because they have been taxed already.

Example

Client purchases an investment bond for £10,000, withdraws £600 per annum for five years and then surrenders the bond for £15,000.

The chargeable gain is: (£15,000 + £3,000) – (£10,000 + £500) = £7,500

Taxing the gain

2.6　The process of taxing the gain is as follows.

(a)　The gain is divided by the total number of years the bond has been in force, or by the number of years since the last excess over the cumulative allowance occurred.

(b)　The 'slice' obtained is added to the holder's income to ascertain the rate of tax applicable to the slice. If the slice falls in the 10% or 22% tax bands, there is no further tax to pay.

(c)　If higher rate of tax is applicable to the slice, then the whole of the gain will be subject to higher rate tax *minus* 20%, ie 40% – 20% = 20% (2005/06). The reason is that the insurance company has already paid tax in the life fund.

Example of taxation of total surrender of an investment bond where investor pays only a small amount of higher rate tax

2.7　In the tax year 2005/06 Andrew, who has a taxable income (after personal allowances) of £31,000, encashes a bond for £30,000. The bond was purchased for £10,000 in 1995. The bond has been in force for exactly 10 years. The gain is £20,000 and the top-slice is £2,000.

If the 'slice' of £2,000 is added to Andrew's income this will just put him into the higher rate tax band. The calculation of tax is as follows.

(a)　The first £1,400 (which is below the higher rate tax band) is not subject to tax, because the insurance company has already paid tax on the fund.

(b)　The balance of £600 is subject to tax at 20% = £120.

(c)　We now multiply the answer by the number of years investment (10 years). 10 × 120 = £1,200 tax to pay on the gain.

Example of the use of segmentation on surrender of investment bond

2.8　It is important for a higher rate taxpayer that the investment bond is segmented as this may be advantageous if the investor wishes to take surrenders, the taxation on total surrender being more advantageous than partial surrenders.

We will look at an example. If Jim, who is a higher rate taxpayer, purchases an investment bond for £100,000 and withdraws £22,000 in year 3 he will have exceeded his annual allowance by £7,000 (3 × £5,000 = £15,000). The chargeable gain of £7,000 will be subject to top-slicing.

If, however, Jim had taken out 100 policies of £1,000 and assuming the total fund was now worth £110,000, he could totally encash 20 policies. In this case, the chargeable gain will be £2,000, which will be subject to top-slicing. (Purchase price 20 × £1,000 = £20,000; encashment value 20 × £1,100 = £22,000.)

Example of topping up investment bonds

2.9   Bill wishes to invest a further amount in an investment bond. It is preferable for him to add it to an existing unit-linked bond rather than effecting a second bond, if the life office concerned offers a topping up facility. The reason for this is shown below.

(a)   Bill purchases one single premium bond for £20,000 in 1995 and a second bond for £20,000 in2000. The bonds are with separate insurance companies. In 2005, Bill wishes to withdraw his money. The first bond purchased is now worth £30,000 (a gain of £10,000, which will be divided by 10 for top-slicing purposes). The second bond is worth £25,000 (a gain of £5,000, which will be divided by 5 for top-slicing purposes). Therefore the top-slice will be £1,000 + £1,000 = £2,000.

(b)   If, however, Bill had added the second £20,000 to the original bond, the situation would be different. The top-slicing relief is based on the full policy term, even if some of the profit is provided by a premium paid in the middle of the term. The gain would be £15,000 which will be divided by 10 for top-slicing purposes. Therefore the top-slice will be £1,500.

If Bill is close to the higher rate tax band and he used this second method (b), this may mean he has no tax to pay as he has a smaller 'slice' to add to his income.

2.10   Persons who may be liable to pay the tax on the proceeds of a bond:

(a)   The policyholder, if he is still the owner

(b)   If a policy is held in trust, the settlor is liable to pay the tax but he can claim it back from the trustees

Note. If the bond has been assigned for money's worth, the owner may be liable to capital gains tax on the proceeds.

Exercise 2

John Jenkins effects an investment bond in July 1998 for an amount of £40,000. He takes no withdrawals until August 2001. He then takes withdrawals of 5% of the original investment for each of the next four years, up to and including August 2004. In August 2005 he takes a withdrawal of £5,000. Will a chargeable event occur at this stage and if so, what will be the amount of the chargeable gain?

Charging structure

2.11   (a)   There is typically an up-front charge which is a 5% bid/offer spread.

(b)   In addition there will be an annual management charge, typically of around 0.75% to 1.0% of the value of the fund.

Risk

2.12 (a) The client will select his own fund or funds and can therefore choose his own level of risk.

(b) The majority of funds available are investing in equities or other securities the value of which can go down as well as up.

(c) Although gilt and fixed interest funds are classified as low risk, nevertheless the capital value of the assets can fall particularly if there is an increase in interest rates.

(d) Insurance companies impose fairly high charges on an investor in an investment bond. These charges can have an effect on performance.

(e) If an investor is taking a high level of withdrawal from the bond or in times of poor fund performance, it is possible for the value of his original investment to fall. (This may not happen if capital is invested in a distribution fund.)

Method of purchase and sale

2.13 Bonds are purchased directly from the insurance company. The insurance company is responsible for making withdrawal and final encashment payments.

Uses

2.14 (a) An investment bond may be used by an unsophisticated investor as a first step into the equity market. The paperwork to set up the bond is straightforward and the client is not bothered with dividend payments, warrants and scrip offers he does not understand.

(b) Advisers should take care when recommending a bond rather than, say, an investment or unit trust. They should be aware of the compliance requirement that 'you must not advise a client to buy a packaged product if you are aware of a generally available packaged product which would **better** meet his needs and circumstances'. The charges levied on an investment bond are higher than a unit or investment trust. In addition the insurance company pays capital gains tax within the life fund whereas unit trusts and investment trusts do not. For these reasons the performance of an investment bond may be inferior to a similar unit or investment trust.

(c) An investment bond offers certain tax advantages for a higher rate taxpayer. The insurance company fund pays tax at 20% on investment income whereas the client would have a personal tax rate of 40%. The client can also take advantage of the 5% withdrawal to defer taxation until, possibly, a time when he is a basic rate taxpayer.

(d) If an investment bond is held by a higher rate taxpayer and his or her spouse is a basic rate taxpayer, consideration should be given to assigning the policy to the spouse prior to encashment. The assignment is not for money's worth so there is no CGT or IHT liability under current legislation. Under current legislation, on encashment no tax should be paid on any gain.

Exercise 3

A wary investor (a basic rate taxpayer) says she is unsure of unit trusts and investment trusts but likes the idea of an investment bond. Explain to her the advantages and disadvantages of making an investment in the bond.

---

3 WITH PROFIT BONDS

Features

3.1 (a) A **with profit bond** is simply an investment bond. A unitised with profit fund is added to the choice of unit linked funds offered by the insurance company. (It is a hybrid of a with a profit and unit linked fund.)

(b) In some with profit bond contracts there is the facility for the holder of units in the with profit fund to switch to other funds within the unit linked range. Other bonds are constructed in such a way that no such choice is available.

(c) A lump sum is invested in the product which is a non-qualifying whole of life policy. The capital is used to purchase units in the with profit fund. When the bonus is declared it is either:

(i) Added to the contract in the form of extra units, or
(ii) The price of the unitised with profits fund rises to reflect the bonus addition

(d) A terminal bonus may be added after, say, five years to reward the long-term investor.

(e) The with profit bonus system gives a smoothing effect so this is a low to medium risk investment suitable for a cautious investor.

(f) It must be stressed that there is no guarantee of the rate of future bonus which will be declared to the unitised with profit policyholders. However, the bonus once added cannot be removed except on early surrender (see below on the MVR).

(g) Most insurance companies reserve the right to make a **market value reduction (MVR)** to the proceeds of a with profit bond if it is surrendered at a time of adverse stock market conditions. The adjustment must be made, otherwise the amount being withdrawn by the investor will exceed the value of the underlying assets. Such a reduction will not be applied on death or on dates specified in the contract, eg on encashment after seven years.

(h) Income can be withdrawn from the with profits bond by use of the 5% withdrawal system. Alternatively, it is possible to take a complete withdrawal of the bonus each year. However, taking into account charges, this latter course of action could result in a reduction in the value of the original investment.

Tax treatment

3.2 The tax treatment on total encashment or withdrawals of 'income' is exactly the same as for all investment bonds. A chargeable event occurs and, as we have seen, this may give rise to a charge to tax at 20%.

Charging structure

3.3 Charges are taken from the contract in a number of ways.

(a) The allocation to units may be reduced and a bid/offer spread applied to the purchase of units.

(b) 100% allocation to units is given, the bid/offer spread remains but penalties, on a reducing scale, are imposed on withdrawal during the first five years.

(c) An annual management charge will be made of around 0.75% to 1.0%.

Exercise 4

As the adviser to a client, you are reviewing two with profit bonds. The with profit past performance and potential future performance of both companies is comparable. One company offers 100% allocation but penalties on withdrawal during the first five years and the other reduced allocations but no penalties.

State which you might select and explain why.

Risk

3.4 The risks associated with investment in a with profit bond are as follows.

(a) The rate of bonus currently being declared by the insurance company may not be continued. This is particularly relevant when an insurance company offers an initial rate in excess of the market 'norm' simply to attract monies.

(b) The promise of terminal bonus in the future may not be fulfilled.

(c) If the bonus rate of the insurance company falls it may be difficult to remove monies from the bond. If there is a large exit of monies the insurance company may impose a **Market Value Reduction**. The other problem is that the investor may still be within the penalty period and cannot exit without a loss.

(d) If the investor removes the total bonus as income, taking into account charges, this latter course of action could result in a reduction in the value of the original investment.

(e) If the investor has chosen a with profit only bond he may find future investment choice restricted. For example, he may wish to change to a higher risk fund. In a normal unit linked bond he could switch funds, but with a with profit only bond he would need to encash and repurchase. This could give rise to a tax charge.

Method of purchase and sale

3.5 The with profit bond is purchased from an insurance company who will also pay out the proceeds when it is eventually encashed or the life assured dies.

Uses

3.6 (a) A with profit bond is a suitable investment for a client prepared to take low to medium risk.

(b) A with profit bond could be viewed as the 'next step up' from the building society and deposit type investments.

(c) A with profit bond must only be recommended as a long term investment because of the up front charges and possible penalties on early encashment.

(d) A with profit bond should be part of a spread portfolio. If an MVR was applied to the fund, the client should have other funds to fall back on and could possibly delay encashing the bond until the MVR had been removed.

(e) A with profit bond is a simple investment for the unsophisticated investor. There are no dividends, scrip issues or problems with the tax return while the monies remain invested.

(f) A with profit bond could be a suitable investment for a higher rate taxpayer who is also cautious. For him the fund is suffering tax at 20% or 22% whereas he is paying tax at a

BPP
PROFESSIONAL EDUCATION

higher rate. If he uses the 5% withdrawal facility he may delay or avoid taxation. Equally he may avoid tax on encashment if he is then a basic rate taxpayer.

4   GUARANTEED BONDS

Features of guaranteed income bonds

4.1   (a)   A **guaranteed income bond** is a single premium investment scheme which gives a double guarantee. The level of income is guaranteed and so too is the return of the original investment.

(b)   The bond can be constructed in a number of ways, although the outcome for the investor is much the same. The construction methods are as follows.

(i)   A single premium investment bond.

(ii)   A series of non-qualifying endowment policies. Using this method, one bond is encashed each year to pay the income and the encashment of the final bond repays the capital.

(iii)   A combination of a temporary annuity and a deferred annuity. Using this method the temporary annuity pays the income and the deferred annuity repays the capital at maturity. This method may have advantages for non-taxpayers, basic rate and higher rate taxpayers (see *Tax treatment* below).

(c)   Whichever construction method is used, a guarantee of the return of the original investment on death must be incorporated in the bond.

(d)   Some insurance companies simply offer a tranche of guaranteed income bond money and once this is exhausted the bond is withdrawn. These promotions are often attractive and offer a rate in excess of the current interest rates.

(e)   Other insurance companies offer guaranteed income bonds on a regular basis. However, the rate of guarantee they offer varies according to changes in interest rates. It must be stressed that once a client purchases the bond the income is guaranteed for the term of the contract (whatever happens to base rates in the meantime).

(f)   The bond runs for a fixed term, say one to five years. The investor selects the term to suit his needs.

(g)   The bond guarantees a fixed rate of income for the selected period. The income is normally paid annually in arrears although some bonds offer a monthly income.

(h)   The income from the bond is paid net of basic rate tax so there is no further tax liability for an investor who is a basic rate taxpayer. A non-taxpayer cannot reclaim the tax.

(i)   The bond guarantees the return of the capital at the end of the selected period.

Exercise 5

Describe the various methods of constructing a guaranteed income bond.

Tax treatment of guaranteed income bonds

4.2   (a)   If the guaranteed income bond is constructed from non-qualifying policies and most are, then the following situation arises on encashment.

(i) The basic rate or non-taxpayer has no further tax liability because the life fund has already paid tax.

(ii) The higher rate taxpayer may suffer an additional tax charge of 20% on his income.

(b) If the bond is constructed as a temporary and deferred annuity, then the tax situation for non-taxpayers and higher rate taxpayers may be improved. The income generated by the temporary annuity will be split into a capital and an interest content and only the interest content will be taxed. The non-taxpayer can therefore obtain a tax-free income, rather than one paid net of tax. The higher rate taxpayer may also find a marginal advantage, particularly if he is not a higher rate taxpayer in every year that he receives his income.

Charging structure of guaranteed income bonds

4.3 There is no explicit charging structure. The insurance companies charges are taken into account before declaring the interest rate to be offered on the income bond.

Risk associated with investing in guaranteed income bonds

4.4 The risk the investor takes is that interest rates will rise, in which case he is locked into a contract which must run its full course. Surrender values are available but are usually poor.

Method of purchase and sale of guaranteed income bonds

4.5 The bond is purchased from the insurance company. The insurance company is responsible for repaying the capital at the end of the fixed term and also paying the regular income to the client.

Uses of guaranteed income bonds

4.6 (a) A guaranteed income bond may be used by an investor needing a regular and guaranteed level of income.

(b) A guaranteed income bond may be used if the investor needs a monthly income. The interest rate will be at a lower rate than the annual income. Sometimes it may be preferable for the client to hold back sufficient capital to use as income for the first year and then opt for an annual income version.

(c) A guaranteed income bond will be used by a cautious investor. The risk is low.

(d) The net rates available on guaranteed income bonds are normally in excess of the rates being offered by other deposit type investments such as banks and building society accounts.

(e) A guaranteed income bond could be used by clients who are retired and wish to boost their spendable income. It is more useful to taxpayers than non-taxpayers.

(f) A guaranteed income bond is issued by an insurance company so the investor is protected by the Financial Services Compensation Scheme.

(g) A guaranteed income bond is not necessarily a suitable investment for a non-taxpayer as the income is paid net and he has no way of reclaiming the tax. The only time a guaranteed income bond would be used in such circumstances is if the interest being quoted was substantially better than the gross rates which could be obtained elsewhere.

(h)   A guaranteed income bond is not necessarily suitable for a client who is a higher rate taxpayer because of the likely charge to tax on encashment. The rate on offer in the market should be compared with the guaranteed rate before committing to the investment. On maturity some insurance companies do offer the facility to roll the money over for a further period into a new bond. This may be of advantage to an investor who suddenly finds himself a higher rate taxpayer in the year of maturity.

Exercise 6

(a)   A non-taxpayer has the choice of a local authority bond paying 5.75% gross over 5 years or a guaranteed income bond paying 6.0% net. Which should he choose?

(b)   A higher rate taxpayer requiring income has the choice of a 5-year guaranteed income bond paying 6.0% or a with profit bond with a 5% withdrawal. He has no need for the capital at the end of five years. Which do you think he should choose and why?

Guaranteed growth bonds

4.7   **Guaranteed growth bonds** have similar features, tax treatment, charging structure, risk and method of purchase and sale as a guaranteed income bond except that the income is allowed to roll up and is paid out with the capital at the end of the term.

Uses of guaranteed growth bonds

4.8   (a)   A guaranteed growth bond could be used in a portfolio for a cautious investor requiring a guaranteed return over a fixed period.

(b)   The net return from a guaranteed growth bond would need to be compared with the tax free return from, say, the NS&I Five Year Certificate. The bond should generally only be used if the interest rate were better or the client already had the maximum holding in the current issue of NS&I Savings Certificates.

(c)   A guaranteed growth bond should not be used for an investor who is likely to be a higher rate taxpayer in the year of encashment (see tax situation for guaranteed income bonds).

(d)   A guaranteed growth bond could be used by an investor who needed money at a specific time in the future, say for school or university fees or to set money aside for capital gains tax liabilities.

(e)   A guaranteed growth bond is likely to be used by investors of all ages, whereas guaranteed income bonds tend to appeal to the elderly.

Features of guaranteed equity bonds

4.9   (a)   The **guaranteed equity bond** is yet another type of investment bond.

(b)   There are a number of versions of the plan.

(i)   The capital may be invested in an equity linked fund with a guarantee that at the end of a specified period, usually five years, the investor will at least get the return of his capital. The insurance company arrange the guarantee usually by use of traded options.

(ii)   The capital may be invested in a scheme which offers a return linked to the growth in an index such as the FTSE 100 Index over the given period or return of the original capital, whichever is greater. The fixed term is usually five years.

    (iii)   The capital may be invested in a scheme which offers the opportunity to lock into the growth in the FTSE 100 if the index exceeds a certain limit. These 'lock-ins' occur regularly during the term of the scheme.

  (c) The schemes detailed above are all geared to growth. Schemes can also be offered giving a guaranteed income. Such incomes are usually high when compared with current interest rates. The guaranteed return of capital at the end of the period takes into account the income already paid. For example, if such a bond offered an income of 8% net for five years, the guaranteed capital return would be 60% of the original investment.

Tax treatment of guaranteed equity bonds

4.10   As the schemes are based on investment bonds and are non-qualifying products, the return, if greater than the original investment, could be subject to tax for a higher rate taxpayer. A basic rate or non-taxpayer would have no tax to pay. (See tax treatment of single premium bonds.)

Uses of guaranteed equity bonds

4.11 (a) A guaranteed equity bond could be used by a cautious client who is interested in stock market investments but wishes to restrict his risk.

  (b) A guaranteed equity bond should only be used by a client who can hold the bond for the full term. If he encashes early he will only receive the value of the units which could be low.

  (c) A less cautious investor should receive a better return by direct investment into a FTSE 100 or equity fund. The investor is paying for the guarantee in the guaranteed equity fund which restricts the potential performance. Another disadvantage is that many schemes do not credit the investor with the income generated by the FTSE 100 shares.

  (d) As the guaranteed equity bond is a single premium investment bond for a fixed term, it is not considered suitable for a higher rate taxpayer for the reasons already cited for guaranteed income and growth bonds.

Exercise 7

A client is very cautious and requires a high guaranteed income. Would you recommend a guaranteed income bond or a guaranteed equity bond with income facility? Give reasons for your choice.

---

5   SPECIALIST BONDS

5.1   In Section 2 we looked at the features of the normal investment bond. There are a number of specialist bonds which should be considered. These are as follows.

Personal portfolio bonds

5.2   A **personal portfolio bond** allowed a client wishing to invest an amount in excess of say £50,000 to choose his own stockbroker to run his bond portfolio rather than buying units in the insurance company's various funds. If the client already had an equity portfolio the shares would have to be sold before investment in the bond took place. This could give rise to a charge to capital gains tax.

5.3   The personal bond operated in all other respects exactly like a normal bond. For example, the investor could make use of the 5% withdrawal facility.

5.4   The points made above about personal portfolio bonds have been written in the past tense because it is likely that this product has largely become 'a plan of the past' following the Inland Revenue's attack on them in the 1998 Finance Bill.

5.5   For those bonds caught by the legislation, the tax charges are draconian. They took effect from policy years ending after 6 April 2000 and impose an annual 'deemed' gain of 15% of the premiums paid plus deemed gains from previous years. There is a further deemed gain on any chargeable event in addition to the normal chargeable event gains. When the bond is surrendered, however, the amount of the termination chargeable event gain will be reduced by the amount of previous deemed gains.

5.6   Holders of these bonds would probably have encashed them before the introduction of the annual charge. Personal portfolio bonds are now only offered by offshore offices to non-UK residents.

Broker bonds

Features

5.7   (a)   In the 1980s, many intermediaries introduced broker bonds. One insurance company would be selected to carry out all administration. However, instead of the client investing in, say, the managed fund of the XYZ Insurance Company, his money would be placed in a fund run by the intermediary.

(b)   The broker fund was made up of the XYZ Insurance Company's unit linked funds but the intermediary decided the mix of the funds which made up his own managed or broker fund.

For example, the broker bond portfolio might consist of 50% UK, 20% North America, 5% Japan, 10% Far East, 10% Europe, 5% cash.

(c)   It is important to understand that the insurance company's investment managers still buy and sell the underlying assets and are responsible for the running of the funds. The intermediary simply defines the split between different geographical areas.

(d)   In recent years the regulatory authorities have become concerned about the management of broker bonds. Special authorisation is now needed to run such a fund and the intermediary must be able to prove that he is giving 'better than best' advice when he is recommending his broker fund rather than the insurance company's managed fund.

(e)   When recommending his own fund, the intermediary must give the client full information regarding the extra charges related to the fund and the fund's past performance. He must further account to the client on a half-yearly basis for the investment performance of his fund and compare this with the insurance company's managed fund performance over the same period. In addition the adviser must compare performance to a published index or sector average which is appropriate to the investment objectives and strategy of the broker bond. A report published in 1999 showed a 2% underperformance of these funds compared to non-broker funds.

(f) Many life offices have withdrawn from the broker bond market because of restrictions imposed on them by regulators. The regulations state that the life office should satisfy itself about the competence of the broker to run such a fund and must monitor his performance.

Tax treatment

5.8 The tax treatment of a broker bond is the same as for any investment bond.

Charging structure

5.9 The intermediary charges an additional annual management fee for the investment advice he gives. In many cases it has been proved that this extra charge is not warranted. Few broker funds have outperformed the insurance company's managed fund.

Risk

5.10 The investor suffers an additional risk because he is in the hands of the intermediary who may make disastrous decisions about the distribution of the fund.

Method of purchase and sale

5.11 The investor will buy his bond from the insurance company. The insurance company will be responsible for settlement on encashment, whether total or partial.

Uses

5.12 The uses of a broker bond would be the same as for an investment bond. It would be relevant for the same clients as outlined for investment bonds in Paragraph 2.14 above. The only difference is that the intermediary would have to justify his use of his own broker bond with attached extra charges.

Exercise 8

Investment bonds are criticised as being expensive. Describe the charging structure of an investment bond.

Offshore bonds

Features

5.13 (a) UK life offices who have offshore subsidiaries issue insurance bonds from their offices in the Channel Islands, Isle of Man, Dublin and Luxembourg.

(b) The bonds they issue are still non-qualifying life policies with the same facilities as onshore policies. The underlying funds suffer little or no tax, unlike UK life funds, and so income can 'roll up' gross.

(c) The costs of offshore products can be higher than onshore because the insurance company is unable to offset expenditure against income for tax purposes.

BPP
PROFESSIONAL EDUCATION

(d) An offshore bond should be maintained for as long a period as possible. Because of higher charges, it could take five years for the value of the offshore fund to start to edge ahead of the UK fund for a basic rate taxpayer, and longer for a higher rate taxpayer.

(f) Withdrawals of up to 5% of the original investment may be taken for 20 years without an immediate tax liability. If the 5% allowance is not used in one year, it can be carried forward to the next.

Tax treatment

5.14 (a) The taxation of offshore policies on encashment is more stringent than for a similar onshore product. The chargeable gain on a bond is subject to lower, basic and higher rate tax. The gain is calculated using the formula:

Chargeable gain = (Encashment value + Previous withdrawals) *less*
(Original investment + Previous chargeable excesses)

This calculation is best understood by studying an example.

Example of the calculation of taxation on encashment of an offshore bond. In 1995 Mr Stevenson purchases a bond for an amount of £100,000. He takes a withdrawal of 7% of the original investment for nine years (£63,000). In 2005 he encashes the bond for £140,000.

The tax calculation is:

Chargeable gain = (£140,000 + £63,000) – (£100,000 + £18,000)

£203,000 – £118,000 = £85,000

The gain of £85,000 would be top sliced by the number of years in force (10), and £8,500 added to the investor's income to see if higher rate tax applied. If it did, then the whole of the gain £85,000 would be subject to higher rate tax.

There is a difference on top slicing an offshore bond. The divider used is always the years since inception, not the years since the last chargeable event, as with an onshore bond.

(b) If the investor had been non-resident for tax purposes for part of the time that he had held the bond, then he would be given relief for the time he was non-resident. For example, if he was non-resident for five of the ten years that he held the bond, then the chargeable gain on encashment would be reduced by 50%.

(c) If the investor is non-UK resident when the bond is encashed, then there will be no UK tax consequences.

Charging structure

5.15 (a) The charges for an offshore bond are typically higher than for an onshore one. A typical charging structure could be 6% initial charge with 1.5% annual management charge.

An alternative might be an initial charge of 1.5% for five years with 0.5% to 1.25% annual management charge. In this case an early surrender penalty would apply of 7.5% in year one reducing to nil in year six.

(b) The costs of offshore products are more expensive than onshore because the insurance company is unable to offset expenditure against income for tax purposes.

Risk

5.16 (a) The funds offered to the investor within an offshore bond range from deposit through with profits to specialised and currency funds. The client can chose to take the level of risk he requires.

(b) Some clients may feel that there is a risk associated with investing offshore. However, most of the companies offering these bonds are subsidiaries of very large UK insurance companies and most of the countries in which they operate have an investor protection scheme similar to our own.

(c) Most offshore insurance companies offering investment bonds are FSA-regulated.

Method of purchase and sale

5.17 Most of the offshore insurance companies deal only through IFAs. Literature must be obtained directly from the offshore company with whom the IFA will deal directly.

Uses

5.18 An offshore bond could be particularly useful in the following circumstances.

(a) A client who seeks confidentiality for his investments. However, the adviser should bear in mind the money laundering prevention requirements.

(b) An expatriate may find an offshore bond useful. His money will roll up tax-free. As we have already seen in the tax calculation, an expatriate will not be liable to tax on gains for the time he is non-resident in the UK for tax purposes.

(c) A foreign national may find an offshore bond useful. As a non-UK taxpayer, a foreign national will not be subject to UK tax on encashment. However the adviser must check on the tax situation ruling in the country in which the client is resident for tax purposes.

(d) A client who may become non-resident, perhaps someone who hopes to retire abroad, could invest in an offshore bond while still a resident in the UK. However the adviser should check the tax situation in the country to which the client may retire to ensure that the tax treatment of the bond proceeds will not be draconian.

(e) A non-taxpayer could use an offshore bond. In this case money could roll up in a virtually tax-free fund and on encashment any chargeable gain will not be subject to tax. However this may not be a worthwhile exercise because the high charges imposed on the bond may wipe out the tax advantage.

(f) High net worth clients previously used offshore products within a trust to mitigate income and inheritance tax. One of the best known reasons for writing an offshore bond in trust was to take advantage of the 'dead settlor provision'. In this case a bond was effected on more than one life (insurable interest is not essential for offshore policies). On the death of the settlor the bond did not automatically cease because there was still a life assured. The remaining life or lives assured held the bond until the tax year after the settlor's death and then there was no tax to pay. The reason for this was that the gain on the bond was treated as part of the settlor's income. As the settlor had no income in the next tax year, there was no tax to pay. This loophole has now been closed.

The dead settlor loophole has been closed for all chargeable events occurring on or after 6 April 1998. The person now liable for tax following the settlor's death will depend upon whether the trustees are UK residents or non-UK residents for tax purposes. If the trustees are UK resident, the trustees will be liable to tax on the gain at the rate of 40% applicable to trusts. The gain will be taxable in the financial year in which the chargeable event occurs. If the trustees are non resident for tax purposes, the tax charge will fall upon the beneficiaries who are ordinarily resident in the UK and receive a benefit out of the trust. No tax will be paid until the beneficiary receives such a payment and then it will be payable at his or her rate of tax.

(g) A higher rate taxpayer could use an offshore bond to defer payment of tax on this gain until he was a basic rate taxpayer.

Exercise 9

(a) List the types of client for whom an offshore bond may be a suitable investment.
(b) List the types of client for whom an onshore bond may be suitable.

High income bonds

5.19 **High income bonds** can produce guaranteed income levels, at levels depending on market conditions when the bond is purchased. The total returns will be based on the movements in one or more equity indices. Derivatives (call options) are used to enhance income. If the indices rise, the options will generate profits. If the indices fall, the premium is lost, but the capital invested is protected. The **guaranteed** minimum return will typically be the value of the original investment less the income paid out over the term. The typical expectation for this type of investment is to get a **return** of the original investment at the end of the term (in addition to the income paid out), but again this is **not guaranteed**. Growth on top of this may be a possibility for some bonds, but it is unrealistic to expect much. This type of investment will appeal to those needing a high guaranteed income. The additional risks taken with this type of investment can lead to a return of the original capital as well as the income, where similar income levels with other investments would almost certainly deplete the capital.

6   ANNUITIES

Features

6.1 (a) An **annuity** is a guaranteed income paid by an insurance company in return for the deposit of a lump sum. The terms of the payment of the income will depend upon the type of annuity purchased.

(b) In all cases the capital used to purchase the annuity is lost, although the consequences of early death can be safeguarded by including guarantees or capital protection.

(c) The payment of the income can be monthly, quarterly, half-yearly or annually either in advance or in arrears.

(d) If the income is paid in arrears it can be paid **with or without proportion**. This means that upon the death of the annuitant if the payment is with proportion, a balance will be due to the estate and if without proportion, this will not be the case.

Example. Frank Baker effects an annuity with payments made quarterly in arrears with proportion. The last annuity payment was made on 25 June 2005. Frank died on 25 August 2005. As the annuity was 'with proportion', two months income will be due to Frank's estate.

(e) Annuity rates quoted by an insurance company are linked to the return on long dated gilts and vary with changes in interest rates. Most insurance companies only guarantee their quotations for a maximum of 14 days.

(f) It is sometimes possible to obtain an improved annuity rate for a client who is in very poor health (an **impaired life annuity**). Medical details will be required by the insurance company. Enhanced rates are now available for annuitants who smoke and/or are overweight.

(g) The interest rates for women requiring annuities are generally lower than for men of a similar age because their life expectancy is longer.

Types

Immediate annuity

6.2 With an **immediate annuity,** a purchase price is paid and the insurance company agrees to pay a guaranteed income to the annuitant for the rest of his life.

(a) It is possible to include a guarantee within the annuity so that payments are made for a minimum of five or ten years regardless of survival. The longer the guaranteed period selected the lower the initial income which is paid (guaranteed annuity).

(b) It is possible to completely protect the purchase price of the annuity by use of a capital protection. This means that, when the annuitant dies, the insurance company adds up the amount paid out in gross annuity payments and, if this is less than the original investment, the balance is returned to the estate (capital protected annuity).

Example of the workings of a capital protected annuity

Bernard Cook aged 73 takes out a capital protected annuity, purchase price £10,000, gross annuity £1,100 per annum. Unfortunately he dies after eight payments have been made (£8,800) so there will be a return of the balance, £1,200 to the estate.

Temporary annuity

6.3 With a **temporary annuity,** the insurance company pays a guaranteed income to the annuitant for a fixed period (for example five years) or until earlier death.

Joint life and last survivor annuities

6.4 **Joint life and last survivor annuities** are used primarily by married couples who want to ensure that the income from their annuity continues until the last death. This type of annuity can be used by any two people. The income available may be lower than a single life annuity if the second life is younger or female.

Sometimes joint life annuities reduce by one-third or one-half on the first death. If a reduction is taken, the annuity rate will be higher.

Increasing annuities

6.5 There are various types of **increasing annuity**.

(a) With the basic type, the income payable by the insurance company will increase by an agreed amount, eg 5% per annum. The introduction of such an increase can considerably reduce the initial income.

(b)   The annuity will increase in line with the RPI. The initial income is considerably lower than a conventional level annuity.

(c)   The amount of the annuity is linked to the performance of a **unit linked fund**. The amount of income received each year will therefore vary.

(d)   The amount of the annuity is linked to the performance of a **with profit fund**. In this case the income varies according to the bonus declared.

Deferred annuities

6.6   (a)   A **deferred annuity** allows for a single payment to be made or a series of regular monthly or annual payments. The annuity is paid out at a later date for the remainder of the annuitant's life with or without a guaranteed period.

(b)   Sometimes a cash option is available on the vesting date.

(c)   Should the annuitant die prior to the vesting date, the payments made will be returned with or without interest.

Annuity certain

6.7   An **annuity certain** is paid out irrespective of the survival of the annuitant. A deferred annuity certain is often used in school fees planning. Fees are not required immediately, so the annuity is deferred but then paid for a specified period irrespective of the survival of the annuitant, who could have been a grandparent.

Capital protected annuity

6.8   With a **capital protected annuity**, when death occurs, the total annuity payments made are compared with the initial purchase price. If there is a shortfall, a lump sum payment is made to the estate of the annuitant. This payment will not be subject to income tax but may be subject to inheritance tax. The cost of providing this capital protection will reduce the income available from the annuity.

With profits annuity

6.9   The fall in long-term interest rates over the 1990s and early 2000s made traditional annuities more expensive. With profits and investment linked annuities arose as an alternative to conventional annuities or, in the case of pensions, fund withdrawal (income drawdown). A **with profits annuity** is an annuity that has many of the same options as a conventional annuity, for example, on payment frequencies, spouse's annuities and guaranteed periods. The only difference is that the amount of each instalment depends on investment returns.

6.10   The funds for a with profits annuity are invested in a mixed fund, rather than just gilts or fixed interest funds. The actuary of the fund declares a reversionary bonus (or annual bonus) and funds are set aside for years when investment performance is not so good. This smoothes out the volatility of the investment returns. In good years you may not see as much growth as with unit linked annuities but in bad years you should not see dramatic falls in income. Typically the price of with profits units increases at the current bonus rate, and cannot fall. There may also be a built in guarantee that an MVR will not be applied.

6.11   Where a bonus rate has been anticipated on the annuity, there is a risk that the bonus rate may be lower than predicted and in these circumstances the guaranteed income could reduce. In order to ensure that this is not the case it is wise to use an anticipated bonus rate that is below the current rate, so that if bonuses do fall there is some in built leeway.

Unit-linked annuities

6.12 With **unit-linked pension annuities**, the amount of the annuity paid is the bid value of a pre-determined number of units each month. The purchaser of a unit-linked annuity is making an assumption about the future rate of growth in the unit price, as compared with the with profits annuity, for which an assumption is made about future bonuses. The higher unit price growth is assumed, the lower will be the initial annuity and the less likely it will be that the annuity income will grow in the future. If there is substantial exposure to equities in the unit-linked funds, there could be potentially high returns, but there is risk that returns could be disappointing. Because of the possibly resulting volatility in income, unit-linked annuities may only be suitable for those who have alternative sources of retirement income.

Pension annuities

6.13 (a) When an employee or self-employed person wishes to take his benefits from a pension policy or occupational scheme, he will have an option to take the fund available and purchase his pension from a different provider if better rates can be provided.

(b) If an employed person exercises this option from an occupational scheme, it is known as a **compulsory purchase annuity**.

(c) The option available under a personal pension or a retirement annuity is known as an **open market option**.

(d) The pension purchased can be level or increasing, on a single or joint life basis payable monthly, quarterly, half-yearly or annually, with or without guarantees and with level or reducing spouse's benefits.

Tax treatment

6.14 The taxation of an annuity depends on whether it is a **purchased life annuity (PLA)**. A PLA is an annuity bought with money already belonging to the individual and on which any tax liability has already been met. Consequently, a PLA receives favourable tax treatment.

(a) If an annuity is regarded as a PLA then part of each income payment can be treated as a return of capital, the capital content, and part as interest. Only the interest content is taxed.

(b) The capital content is fixed at outset by reference to a mortality table agreed by HMRC (formerly the Inland Revenue). All insurance companies must quote the same capital contents.

(c) The capital content is calculated by dividing the purchase price by the annuitant's expectation of life. The idea is that if the annuitant dies exactly when predicted by the tables, 100% of the purchase monies will have been returned via the capital content portion of each payment. Thus for a female aged 93, the whole of the annuity payment will be treated as a return of capital.

(d) In order for the annuity to be treated as a purchased life annuity, a form PLA1 must be completed by the annuitant.

(e) The insurance company will submit the form PLA1 to HMRC. If they agree that the annuity qualifies, HMRC will send form PLA3 to the annuitant confirming the situation and a form PLA4 to the insurance company, giving them authority to deduct tax only from the interest content of the annuity.

(f) The insurance company will then tax the interest content as follows.

  (i) If the annuitant is a basic rate taxpayer he will be paid the capital content plus the interest content net of 20% tax.

  (ii) If the annuitant is a higher rate tax payer, the insurance company will make payments as in (f) (i) above and the annuitant will account to HMRC for the higher rate tax after the submission of his annual tax return.

  (iii) If the annuitant is a UK resident and a non-taxpayer the insurance company will pay out the total annuity gross. In order for this to happen the annuitant will have competed an R87 confirming that his income is below a certain limit. This will have been submitted to HMRC for approval.

  (iv) If the annuity is held on a joint basis and one of the annuitants is a non-taxpayer then the insurance company will pay 50% of the income tax-free and tax the balance on the capital and interest basis.

  (v) If the annuitant is a non-resident and satisfies one of the following requirements, the insurance company may pay out the annuity without deduction of tax.

    (1) He is a British subject.

    (2) He is or has been employed by the British Crown.

    (3) He is a person employed by a missionary society or any state under the protection of the Queen.

    (4) He is a resident of the Channel Islands or the Isle of Man.

    (5) He is a person previously resident in the UK who is now resident abroad for reasons of the health of himself or a member of his family resident with him.

    (6) She is a widow whose husband was in the service of the Crown.

  (vi) All annuities dependant upon human life can be treated as purchased life annuities except:

    (1) Any annuity already treated as part interest and part capital, ie annuity certain

    (2) Any annuity where life assurance tax relief or retirement annuity relief has been given

    (3) Any annuity purchased by a sponsored superannuation scheme

    (4) Any annuity purchased in recognition of another's service in any office or employment

    (5) Any annuity purchased in pursuance of any direction in a will or by virtue of a will or settlement

(g) **Taxation of annuities not treated as purchased life annuities**

  (i) The income from pension annuities such as open market option and compulsory purchase annuities are taxed as earned income. Insurance companies pay the income out to the pensioners through the PAYE system. In some cases, if no pension provision has been made for a loyal employee, a pension may be purchased at the time he or she leaves. This is called a **Hancock annuity**. Such an annuity would also be taxed as earned income.

(ii)   The income from an annuity certain is not dependant on human life and so it is not a purchased life annuity. However each payment can be treated partly as a return of capital and partly as interest so long as the annuity is paid to the person who provided the purchase monies. As the annuity is for a certain period, say five years, the purchase price is simply divided by the number of years to determine the capital content. Thus, an annuity certain with a purchase price of £10,000 and a term of five years will have a capital content of £2,000.

(iii)   A deferred annuity will not automatically be treated as a purchased life annuity. Non-pension deferred annuities offer a choice of a lump sum or an annuity. If the lump sum is taken, it is a chargeable event and a tax liability could arise for a higher rate taxpayer. If the annuity is taken, it will be treated as a purchased life annuity.

(iv)   Annuities for beneficiaries under wills or trusts are not treated as purchased life annuities. The insurance company will deduct basic rate tax from the whole annuity payment.

Charging structure

6.15   There is no explicit charging structure with an annuity. The insurance company's charges are taken into account before stating the current annuity rate. However, many insurance companies deduct a policy charge from each annuity payment. The charge is higher for monthly than for annual payments of an annuity.

Risk

6.16   The risks associated with annuities are as follows.

(a)   The loss of capital to the purchaser.

(b)   In most cases an annuity provides a fixed income which will reduce in purchasing power over the years.

(c)   If an increasing annuity is selected, the annuitant has to live many years to be in a 'gain situation' because payments start at a very low level.

(d)   If an income linked to the performance of a unit linked or with profits fund is selected, the annuitant runs the risk of poor performance and an annuity which varies from payment to payment.

(e)   An annuity is a fixed income. If interest rates increase, the annuitant is tied into a fixed annuity based on a lower rate.

Uses

6.17   An annuity may be used in the following circumstances.

(a)   An immediate annuity could be used by an elderly person who needs to increase income, perhaps to meet long term care fees. A five or ten year guarantee or capital protection could be introduced to safeguard the capital used.

(b)   An immediate annuity could be used for a very elderly client, as the tax free content of the annuity will be relatively high.

(c)   An immediate annuity could be used by elderly people whether single or married who wish to increase income and who have no dependants. In this case, the loss of capital is not a problem.

(d)   In some instances an immediate annuity could be used as part of a portfolio to boost income. The fact that the amount of the annuity is fixed is not such a problem if income from other investments has an element of indexation.

(e)   An immediate annuity could be used by an elderly person who pays no tax in order to achieve a high tax-free income.

(f)   A temporary annuity may be used in a back to back arrangement (see below).

(g)   A temporary annuity may be used for a short period to make up for a loss of income if it is known that there will be an increase in income at the end of the period or capital will be forthcoming, for example to fill the gap between early retirement and state retirement age.

(h)   Annuities certain may be used for school fees packages.

7   BACK TO BACK ARRANGEMENTS

7.1   Many clients need a high level of income plus some security of capital. We have already seen in this chapter that a guaranteed income bond or a with profit bond may meet such a requirement. We will now look at other methods of achieving the same objective.

A **back to back arrangement** is an arrangement when an adviser or insurance company puts together two different types of investment. The aim normally is to create an income and at the same time preserve capital. On other occasions a scheme could be designed to create capital growth or even to provide a fund for inheritance tax purposes.

Types

7.2   We now look at the various types of investments which can be 'back to backed'.

The split capital plan

7.3   (a)   In this plan, the adviser splits the capital available and places part in an investment which will create income and part in a scheme to give capital growth. The actual split will depend upon the term of the investment and the income required.

(b)   The investments used to create the income could be as follows.

(i)   A temporary annuity which would pay regular income.

(ii)   A series of gilts which could be encashed to create income. This could be tax efficient as the proceeds would be free of capital gains tax.

(iii)   A series of investment trust zero coupon preference shares (see Chapter 6).

(iv)   A cash deposit.

(c)   The investment to create long term growth could be:

(i)   An Individual Savings Account (see Chapter 8)
(ii)   A unit trust (see Chapter 6)
(iii)   An investment trust (see Chapter 6)
(iv)   A single premium investment bond

An example of the workings of such a scheme would be as follows.

Paul is a male aged 40 attained with £20,000 to invest for five years to provide income. He invests £10,000 in a five year temporary annuity yielding an income of, say, £1,792 per annum net of tax.

The balance of £10,000 is invested in Individual Savings Accounts. (Paul is married, and he and his wife each invest £5,000). The aim of the ISA investment is that the capital will grow to £20,000 in the five year period to replace the original investment. At the end of the period the income from the annuity will cease. However, there would be no need to encash the Individual Savings Accounts and, if income was required, this could be withdrawn tax-free from ISAs.

Feeder plans

7.4 (a) With feeder plans, the adviser invests the majority of the capital available in a temporary annuity, leaving sufficient to pay the first premium to a regular savings scheme.

(b) Let us look at a number of types of scheme.

(i) A feeder plan to an endowment policy (a growth scheme)

The temporary annuity is set up for a fixed term, say 10 years and the first premium is paid to a ten year (or longer term) endowment policy. If the endowment is for a longer period so, too, is the temporary annuity.

In each successive month or year the temporary annuity produces a net income which is sufficient to pay the premium to the endowment assurance.

At the end of ten years the endowment policy matures with a tax-free sum available to the investor.

(ii) *A feeder plan to an endowment policy (a growth and income plan)*

The temporary annuity is set up for a fixed term, say 10 years and the first premium is paid to a ten year (or longer term) endowment policy. If the endowment is for a longer period so too is the temporary annuity.

In each successive month or year the temporary annuity produces a net income which is sufficient to pay the premium to the endowment assurance and also to provide an income to the investor.

At the end of ten years the endowment policy matures with a tax-free sum available to the investor. It is hoped that the return will be at least equal to the original investment.

(iii) *A feeder plan to a whole of life policy (to provide a tax-free fund to be used to pay inheritance tax)*

An immediate annuity is purchased and the first premium is paid to a whole of life policy. The whole of life policy is written in trust for named beneficiaries.

In each successive month or year the annuity produces a net income which is sufficient to pay the premium to the whole of life policy.

On the death of the life assured the immediate annuity ceases, unless it is still within the guaranteed or capital protected period, and the whole of life policy pays out a tax-free lump sum to the beneficiaries.

(iv) *A feeder plan to a whole of life policy (to provide income and a tax-free fund to be used to pay inheritance tax)*

An immediate annuity is purchased and the first premium is paid to a whole of life policy. The whole of life policy is written in trust for named beneficiaries.

In each successive month or year, the annuity produces a net income which is sufficient to pay the premium to the whole of life assurance and also to provide an income to the investor. On the death of the life assured the immediate annuity ceases, unless it is still within the guaranteed or capital protected period, and the whole of life policy pays out a tax-free lump sum to the beneficiaries.

Tax treatment

7.5 The tax treatment of these plans depends on the combination of products used and the reader should refer to the relevant section in the book to check on tax treatment. The taxation of annuities was covered earlier in this Chapter. You may find it useful to work through the following example.

7.6 **Example**

Mr Smith, a 70 year old widower, is investing £25,000 into a ten-year temporary annuity. The gross annuity rate is £3,250 for every £10,000 invested, of which £2,000 is the capital element. Mr Smith's total income from pensions is £36,000.

(a) Calculate the annual annuity paid to Mr Smith by the insurance company
(b) Calculate the net increase in Mr Smith's income

7.7 **Answer**

(a) Gross annuity income $= £25,000 \times \dfrac{£3,250}{£10,000} = £8,125$

Capital element $= £25,000 \times \dfrac{£2,000}{£10,000} = £5,000$

Taxable element is £8,125 less £5,000	=	£3,125
Tax deducted at source is 20% of £3,125	=	£625
Net income = £(8,125 – 625)	=	£7,500

(b)

	£
Current income	36,000
Taxable element of annuity	3,125
Total income	39,125
Less personal allowance (2005/06)	(4,895)
Taxable income	34,230

This means that £1,830 (£34,230 less £32,400) is subject to tax at 40%.

Note. The annuity interest element is savings income and further tax is only paid in respect of that part of the interest element exceeding the higher rate tax threshold of £32,400, ie £1,830.

Credit is given for 20% at source and so only a further 20% of £1,830 (or £366) is payable.

Net increase in annual income is £7,500 – £366 = £7,134.

Charging structure

7.8 (a) The charging structure will depend on the combination of investments used. Endowment policies are covered in Chapter 4, and annuities are covered in the current chapter.

(b) The charging on the feeder type arrangements which involve life assurance products is likely to be higher than the split investment schemes which involve, say, the purchase of gilts, zero coupon preference investment trust shares, personal equity plans or ISAs.

Risk

7.9 (a) The schemes outlined are designed to give the investor a high level of income which, if a temporary annuity is used, will be guaranteed. There is, of course, a risk that interest rates will rise and then what appeared to be a high income loses its appeal.

(b) However, because the schemes are designed to provide a high income, this may mean that insufficient capital is invested in the 'capital appreciation' portion of the scheme and therefore the capital growth is poor and the original investment cannot be returned.

(c) There is also the risk that, if the capital appreciation is being sought from the purchase of equity based investments, such as ISAs, unit trusts or investment trusts, the investment returns may be low if a poor performing fund is chosen, if there is a stock market crash or if the initial investment is made when the market is high.

(d) Many back-to-back schemes are only designed for a five year term which may be too short an investment period to obtain the returns required.

(e) If an endowment policy is the chosen investment, the returns may be eaten up by high charges.

Method of purchase and sale

7.10 The method of purchase and sale will depend on the investments chosen. Some schemes are marketed as packages and will be purchased and sold *via* one insurance company. Some advisers may choose products from different providers, so purchases and sales may be more complex.

Uses

7.11 (a) A back to back arrangement using split capital may be used for an investor needing a high level of income but also an exposure to equities. He must be informed of the risk involved with the equity investment particularly if the scheme is only for a short period. However, the equity investment need not be encashed at the end of the term and can be retained to improve investment performance.

(b) A back to back arrangement using a feeder fund may be used by a cautious investor who requires an income but wishes to use with profit funds as he perceives this to be safer than equities. This investor will need to be warned of the high charges involved and the potential that the capital will not be returned in full at the end of the investment period because of a fall in bonus rates. This situation is likely to happen if too high an income is withdrawn from the plan.

(c) A back to back arrangement using an annuity and a whole of life plan written in trust is a well established method of providing tax-free funds to pay inheritance tax. It is normally advisable to purchase the annuity and whole of life from different insurance companies to avoid HMRC treating the scheme as an 'associated operation'. If both contracts are purchased from the same insurance company, HMRC could say that correct underwriting had not been carried out because the insurance company was receiving a substantial amount of capital to purchase the annuity and therefore had a vested interest in securing the business, ie an associated operation; the purchase of one contract, the annuity, facilitating good terms for the life assurance policy.

Chapter roundup

In this chapter we have studied:

- The characteristics and uses of all types of investment bond
- The characteristics and uses of various types of annuity and the rules of taxation of annuities
- The structure and uses of various types of back to back arrangement

Quick Quiz

1   List the fund types normally offered by an investment bond.

2   Which type of guaranteed income bond would be most tax efficient for a non-taxpayer?

3   What is a Market Value Reduction?

4   Why are insurance companies reluctant to offer intermediaries the option of running broker bonds?

5   Why are the charges on offshore bonds higher than on onshore bonds?

6   What type of annuity has a capital content?

7   When would you use a form R85?

8   What does the expression 'the annuity is paid without proportion' mean?

9   How is the pension from a retirement annuity taxed?

10 Name two methods of creating a back-to-back arrangement?

11 What contracts would you use if you wanted to use a back-to-back arrangement for inheritance tax purposes?

The answers to the questions in the quiz can be found at the end of this Study Text. Before checking your own answers against them, you should look back at this chapter and use the information in it to correct your answers.

Answers to exercises

1   An investor withdrawing money from a property fund may have his encashment delayed for up to six months. This could happen if there was a run on the fund and the manager was having to sell property to pay out the claims.

2   No chargeable event will occur because the cumulative surrenders do not exceed the cumulative allowances (see below).

Policy years	Cumulative allowances	Surrenders	Cumulative surrenders
1998/99	£2,000	0	0
1999/2000	£4,000	0	0
2000/01	£6,000	0	0
2001/02	£8,000	£2,000	£2,000
2002/03	£10,000	£2,000	£4,000
2003/04	£12,000	£2,000	£6,000
2004/05	£14,000	£2,000	£8,000
2005/06	£16,000	£5,000	£13,000

3   The advantages of the investment bond are as follows.

(a)   Easy administration
(b)   Wide choice of funds including a managed fund
(c)   The ability to switch funds without a personal tax charge and at low cost
(d)   The ability to take a 5% withdrawal to provide income
(e)   The bond is open-ended and can be encashed at any time
(f)   If the client is still a basic rate taxpayer on encashment there should be no further tax to pay

The disadvantages are as follows.

(a)   The life fund pays tax on the investment

(b)   The charges are high

(c)   There could be a charge to higher rate (not basic rate) tax on partial surrender or final encashment if the client is then a higher rate taxpayer

4   If the adviser believed that the client would retain the bond for a period in excess of five years, then he would be sensible to select the 100% allocation and penalties. The reason for this is that the client has a larger amount invested upon which the bonus allocation will be added. The with profit bond should not be selected for a period of less than five years but if, for some reason it was, then the lower allocation without penalty may be a better choice.

5   A guaranteed income bond can be constructed in the following ways.

(a)   A single premium investment bond
(b)   A series of non-qualifying endowment policies
(c)   A combination of a temporary annuity and a deferred annuity

6   (a)   The non-taxpayer should select the guaranteed income bond. Although normally this type of scheme would not be a recommendation for a non-taxpayer because he could not reclaim tax, nevertheless in this case it should be selected because the net rate is better than the gross rate being offered by the local authority.

(b)   The with profit bond should be selected, because the 5% withdrawal gives rise to no immediate tax charge. There is also the potential for increased bonus declarations.

7   The guaranteed income bond because in most cases this offers a higher guarantee than the guaranteed equity bond.

8   The normal up-front charge on the bond is a 5% bid/offer spread. In addition there is an annual management charge of 0.75% or 1.0% of the value of the fund.

9   (a)   An offshore bond may be suitable for the following.
    (i)   A client who may become non-resident
    (ii)   A non-taxpayer who could invest in a fund with virtual tax-free roll up
    (iii)   A foreign national
    (iv)   An expatriate who could enjoy tax-free roll up
    (v)   A client seeking confidentiality for his investment

(b)   An onshore bond may be suitable for the following.
    (i)   An unsophisticated client wanting to put 'a toe' into the equity market
    (ii)   A higher rate taxpayer who wished to make use of the 5% withdrawal
    (iii)   A higher rate taxpayer who knows he will be a basic rate taxpayer when he takes the proceeds

PRACTICE QUESTION 4: PACKAGED INVESTMENTS (30 Marks)   *27 mins*

(a)   (i)   Describe how an endowment policy might be used as a savings policy for a child.

(8 marks)

(ii)   Outline the advantages and disadvantages in the policy.   (7 marks)

(b)   (i)   Describe the taxation of a purchased life annuity.   (6 marks)

(ii)   List the types of annuity which receive alternative tax treatment.   (3 marks)

(iii)   Describe the tax treatment of one of these annuities.   (6 marks)

The answer to the practice question can be found at the end of this Study Text

APPENDIX

TAXATION OF THE PROCEEDS OF LIFE POLICIES HELD BY INDIVIDUALS

1   There is a difference in the treatment of the proceeds of a life policy depending upon whether it is qualifying or non-qualifying. A whole of life, endowment or temporary life policy can be qualifying or non-qualifying.

    (a)   *Qualifying policy.* These are policies which satisfy certain conditions under Schedule 15 of the Income and Corporation Taxes Act 1988 (ICTA 1988), as follows.

        (i)   The policy must secure a capital sum which is either payable only on death or payable on the earlier of death or disability (and, in the case of an endowment, on survival of a specified term).

        (ii)   The premiums must be payable annually, or more frequently, for a period of ten years or more (or, in the case of an endowment, three quarters of the term if this is less than ten years).

        (iii)   The premiums paid in any one period of 12 months must not exceed twice the amount of premiums paid in any other 12 month period.

        (iv)   The premiums paid in any one period of 12 months must not exceed 1/8th of the total amount of premiums paid over the first ten years (whole of life policy) or in the term of the policy (endowment policy).

        (v)   In a whole of life policy, the sum assured must not be less than 75% of the total premiums payable should death occur at age 75.

        (vi)   In an endowment policy, the sum assured must not be less than 75% of the total premiums payable during the term of the policy.

        (vii)   The benefits may include the right to participate in profits, the right to benefit in the event of disability, the right to a return of premiums in the event of death under a specified age, say, 16, but not any other capital benefits.

        Note. Certain policies do not have to satisfy the above rules; mortgage protection policies, family income benefit policies, industrial assurances.

    (b)   *Non-qualifying policy.* This is a policy which does not satisfy the above rules, or a policy which did originally satisfy the rules but subsequently the benefits or premiums have been changed.

2   *Tax relief on premiums.* No tax relief is available for premiums paid to qualifying policies effected after 13 March 1984. Premiums paid on policies effected before 13 March 1984 still enjoy Life Assurance Premium Relief (LAPR) if the following rules are observed.

    (a)   The person paying the premium must be a UK resident.

    (b)   The policy must be written on the life of the person paying the premium or his/her spouse.

    (c)   Relief is available on premiums up to £1,500 or one-sixth of income, whichever is the greater.

The tax relief is at 12½% and is deducted from the premium. The relief is lost if the policy becomes non-qualifying or the term or if the benefits are altered.

3   *Taxation of proceeds.* A 'chargeable event' may give rise to a charge to income tax being incurred on the proceeds of a life policy. A chargeable event may occur in the following circumstances.

    (a)   The death of a life assured, if this gives rise to benefits under the policy

    (b)   The partial surrender of benefits

    (c)   The total surrender of benefits

(d)   The assignment of the policy for money or money's worth

(e)   The maturity of the policy

There is no chargeable event in the following circumstances.

(a)   The death of a life assured or the maturity of a qualifying policy where all the premiums have been paid up to date

(b)   The assignment of a policy between spouses

(c)   An assignment which is not for money's worth

(d)   An assignment for money's worth if premiums have been paid for ten years or three-quarters of the term, whichever is appropriate

(e)   A surrender if premiums have been paid for ten years or three-quarters of the term, whichever is appropriate

(f)   An assignment as a security for a debt

Where there is no chargeable event in respect of a life policy, there is no charge to income tax irrespective of the taxation position of the individual policyholder. If a chargeable event occurs, a chargeable gain calculation must be made.

4   *A partial surrender.* The policyholder has the right to a 'notional allowance' of 5% per annum of the total premiums paid which can be taken as a withdrawal. If the allowance is not used it is allowed to be carried forward to the next year. These withdrawals can be taken up to 100% of the premiums paid. If the policyholder exceeds the cumulative allowance then a chargeable event will occur.

5   *Calculating the gain*

Chargeable gain = (Encashment value + Previous withdrawals) – (Original investment + All previous chargeable excesses)

Previous chargeable excesses are excluded because they have been taxed already.

6   *Taxing the gain.* The process of taxing the gain is as follows.

(a)   The gain is divided by the total number of whole years the policy has been in force. When a chargeable event arises as a result of an excess on partial surrender, the gain is divided by the number of years since any previous excess on part surrender or by the number of years since the last excess over the cumulative allowance occurred.

(b)   The 'slice' obtained is added to the policyholder's income to ascertain the rate of tax applicable to the slice. If it is at basic rate, there is no further tax to pay.

(c)   If the rate of tax applicable to the whole slice is in excess of 40%, then the total gain will be subject to tax at 20%. The reason is that the insurance company has already paid tax in the life fund. If part of the slice falls in the basic rate tax band and part in the 40% tax band, only that proportion of the gain which falls into the 40% tax bracket will be subject to 20% tax. (See the example in this chapter, Paragraph 2.7.)

7   Persons who may be liable to pay the tax on the proceeds of a life policy:

(a)   The policyholder if he is still the owner

(b)   If a policy is held in trust, the settlor, who is liable to pay the tax but can claim it back from the trustees

Note. If the policy has been assigned for money's worth, the owner may be liable to capital gains tax on the proceeds.

Chapter 6

COLLECTIVE INVESTMENTS

Chapter topic list	Syllabus reference
1 Introduction to collective investments	2.4
2 Unit trusts	2.4
3 Unit trust cash funds	2.1
4 Investment trusts	2.4
5 OEICs	2.4
6 Exchange traded funds	2.4
7 Comparing investment funds	2.4

Introduction

In this chapter we examine the different types of collective investments. These investments fall into the medium to high risk category. We will look at their individual features, tax treatment, charging structure, pricing, methods of purchase and sale and their uses in the construction of an investment portfolio.

1   INTRODUCTION TO COLLECTIVE INVESTMENTS

1.1   A collective or pooled investment is a scheme in which the money of a large number of small investors is pooled to purchase shares or other securities. By doing this, investors can participate in a much larger spread of investments than they could individually own and in this way they reduce their exposure to risk.

1.2   **Collective investments** include unit trusts, open ended investment companies (OEICs – also called Investment Companies with Variable Capital or ICVCs) and investment trusts.

2   UNIT TRUSTS

Features

2.1   A **unit trust** is a UK vehicle for pooled investment in shares and/or securities. An investor buys units from the unit trust manager. Funds under management by unit trusts exceed £200 billion.

2.2   It is possible for the investor to purchase units in a wide range of funds. These are broken down into categories by the Investment Management Association (IMA). Official sector definitions are given below.

IMA UK Sector definitions

Funds principally targeting income - Immediate Income

UK Gilts
Funds which invest at least 90% of their assets in UK Government securities (Gilts)

UK Index Linked Gilts
Funds which invest at least 90% of their assets in UK Index Linked Government securities (Gilts)

UK Corporate Bond
Funds which invest at least 80% of their assets in Sterling-denominated (or hedged back to Sterling), Triple BBB minus or above bonds as measured by either Standard & Poor or equivalent – Moodys Baa or above. This excludes convertibles.

UK Other Bond
Funds investing at least 80% of their assets in Sterling-denominated (or hedged back to Sterling) and at least 20% of their assets in below Triple BBB minus bonds as measured by either Standard & Poor or equivalent, convertibles and preference shares.

Global Bonds
Funds which invest at least 80% of their assets in fixed interest stocks. All funds which contain more than 80% fixed interest investments are to be classified under this heading regardless of the fact that they may have more than 80% in a particular geographic sector, unless that geographic area is the UK, when the fund should be classified under the relevant UK heading.

UK Equity & Bond Income
Funds which invest at least 80% of their assets in the UK, between 20% and 80% in UK fixed interest securities and between 20% and 80% in UK equities. These funds aim to have a yield of 120% or over of the FT All Share Index.

Funds principally targeting income - Growing Income

UK Equity Income
Funds which invest at least 80% of their assets in UK equities and which aim to have a yield which is in excess of 110% of the yield of the FT All Share Index.

Funds principally targeting capital - Capital Growth/Total Return

UK All Companies
Funds which invest at least 80% of their assets in UK equities which have a primary objective of achieving capital growth. (This sector further divides into: Ethical, Index trackers, Active managed.)

UK Smaller Companies
Funds which invest at least 80% of their assets in UK equities of companies which form the bottom 10% by market capitalisation.

Japan
Funds which invest at least 80% of their assets in Japanese equities.

Japanese Smaller Companies
Funds which invest at least 80% of their assets in Japanese equities of companies which form the bottom 10% by market capitalisation.

Far East including Japan
Funds which invest at least 80% of their assets in Far Eastern equities including a Japanese content. The Japanese content must make up less than 80% of assets.

Far East excluding Japan
Funds which invest at least 80% of their assets in Far Eastern equities and exclude Japanese securities.

North America
Funds which invest at least 80% of their assets in North American equities.

North American Smaller Companies
Funds which invest a least 80% of their assets in North American equities of companies which form the bottom 10% by market capitalisation.

Europe including UK
Funds which invest at least 80% of their assets in European equities. They may include UK equities, but these must not exceed 80% of the fund's assets.

Europe excluding UK
Funds which invest at least 80% of their assets in European equities and exclude UK equities.

European Smaller Companies
Funds which invest at least 80% of their assets in European equities of companies which form the bottom 10% by market capitalisation in the European market. They may include UK equities, but these must not exceed 80% or the fund's assets. ('Europe' includes all countries in the MSCI/FTSE pan European indices.)

Cautious Managed
Funds would offer investment in a range of assets, with the maximum equity exposure restricted to 60% of the Fund. There would be no specific requirement to hold a minimum % non-UK equity. Assets must be at least 50% in Sterling/Euro and equities are deemed to include convertibles.

Balanced Managed
Funds would offer investment in a range of assets, with the maximum equity exposure restricted to 85% of the Fund. At least 10% must be held in non-UK equities. Assets must be at least 50% in Sterling/Euro and equities are deemed to include convertibles.

Active Managed
Funds would offer investment in a range of assets, with the Manager being able to invest up to 100% in equities at their discretion. At least 10% must be held in non-UK equities. There is no minimum Sterling/Euro balance and equities are deemed to include convertibles. At any one time the asset allocation of these funds may hold a high proportion of non-equity assets such that the asset allocation would by default place the fund in either the Balanced or Cautious sector. These funds would remain in this sector on these occasions since it is the Manager's stated intention to retain the right to invest up to 100% in equities.

Global Growth
Funds which invest at least 80% of their assets in equities (but not more than 80% in UK assets) and which have the prime objective of achieving growth of capital.

Global Emerging Markets
Funds which invest 80% or more of their assets directly or indirectly in emerging markets as defined by the World Bank, without geographical restriction. Indirect investment e.g. China shares listed in Hong Kong, should not exceed 50% of the portfolio.

UK zeros
Funds investing at least 80% of their assets in Sterling denominated (or hedged back to Sterling), and at least 80% of their assets in zero dividend preference shares or equivalent instruments (i.e. not income producing). This excludes preference shares which produce an income..

Note: The above sectors also require funds to be broadly diversified within the relevant country/region/asset class. Funds that concentrate solely on a specialist theme, sector or single market size (or a single country in a multi-currency region) would be incorporated in the Specialist sector (see below).

Funds principally targeting capital protection

Money Market
Funds which invest at least 95% of their assets in money market instruments (i.e. cash and near cash, such as bank deposits, certificates of deposit, very short term fixed interest securities or floating rate notes). These funds may be either "money market funds" as defined by SIB, or "securities funds" as long as they satisfy the criterion of concentrating on money market instruments.
Protected/Guaranteed Funds

Funds, other than money market funds which principally aim to provide a return of a set amount of capital back to the investor (either explicitly guaranteed or via an investment strategy highly likely to achieve this objective) plus some market upside.

Specialist Sectors

Specialist
Funds with a single country (other than the UK, Japan or the US) or a single sector theme.

Technology & Telecommunications
Funds which invest at least 80% of their assets in technology and telecommunications sectors as defined by major index providers.

Personal Pensions
Funds which are only available for use in a personal pension plan or FSAVC scheme.

Exercise 1

Which type of unit trust fund should an investor choose if he wants a safe capital investment and returns slightly better than retail interest rates?

2.3 Within the UK All Companies sector, Tracker or Index funds are funds designed to mimic the performance of a particular index such as the FTSE All Share Index or the FTSE 100 Index. These funds have lower charges because they are cheaper to run. There is less need for a highly qualified and highly remunerated fund manager.

2.4 A unit trust is an open ended fund. This means that the size of the unit trust varies with the number of units in issue. If investors wish to invest in the fund, new units are created to meet demand and the manager invests the money raised in shares or other securities (depending on the type of fund).

2.5 Investors sell back their units to the manager who must buy them back. The manager will normally be able to match the units being bought back with the demand for units. Thus, in normal trading there will be no need to raise cash from the sale of securities. However, following a market setback which undermines investor confidence, the situation may be different. In this case, many investors may wish to sell, few may wish to buy and the manager will need to sell securities in order to settle with the investors.

2.6 A unit trust, as its name implies, is a trust operated by trustees, often a bank or insurance company. The trust deed is a contract made between the trustees and the manager. The trust deed will specify how the trust is to be managed, what types of investments it can hold and the maximum charges it can make. If charges are to be raised above this ceiling, a unitholders meeting must be held. In fact, if any changes are to be made to the trust deed, these must be approved by a meeting of unitholders.

2.7 Let us look at the role of trustees of a unit trust.

   (a) The trustees must have gross capital of at least £4 million.

   (b) They must be independent from the management group.

   (c) They must ensure that the investors are protected.

   (d) They must ensure that the managers act in accordance with the trust deed.

   (e) They must hold or find a suitable custodian to hold the securities of the fund. The securities will be held in the name of the trustees.

(f) They may replace the manager if they believe he is not acting in the best interest of the investors or if he is in financial difficulties.

(g) The trustees will have to remove the manager if the majority of the unitholders vote to this effect. The manager cannot, however, be removed without the consent of the Financial Services Authority (FSA).

(h) The trustees must establish and maintain a register of unitholders. The register will list names, address, number of units held and the date on which the holding was registered.

(i) The trustees are responsible for ensuring that an annual report and accounts is prepared and also for the publication of half-yearly results (the interim report).

2.8 The role of trustee and manager must be clearly divided. We will now look at the role and duties of the manager.

(a) The manager must be authorised to carry out investment business in the UK. He will most probably be authorised by the Financial Services Authority.

(b) He must manage the fund in accordance with the trust deed.

(c) He must have adequate financial resources.

(d) He is responsible for the day to day running of the trust which includes keeping a record of units.

(e) He is responsible for investment decisions.

(f) He is responsible for administration, although sometimes a separate company may be employed to take on this role.

(g) He is responsible for promoting the fund.

(h) He is responsible for supplying the trustee with any information he requires.

(i) He is responsible for conducting the business in such manner as not to breach the rules of his regulator and should he do so, he must report such a breach.

2.9 The trust must be authorised by the Financial Services Authority and the directors of the management company approved by the FSA in order for it to market its units to the UK general public. Authorisation is also required in order to obtain CGT exemption for the fund.

2.10 There are a number of unauthorised unit trusts, namely exempt trusts, used by pension funds and charities. As the word 'exempt' implies, these funds suffer no CGT and income is paid to investors without deduction of tax.

Exercise 2

Define the role and responsibility of the trustee of a unit trust. What powers has he, should he not be satisfied with the manager of the unit trust?

FSA rules: the CIS Sourcebook

2.11 The first set of FSA regulations covering authorised unit trusts (AUTs) and OEICs/ICVCs is found in the FSA's **Collective Investment Schemes** Sourcebook coded **'CIS'** in the FSA Handbook. **'ICVC' (Investment Company with Variable Capital)** is an alternative term that can be used to refer to an OEIC.

2.12 CIS currently runs in parallel with a new set of FSA rules contained in a new Collective Investment Schemes Sourcebook named 'COLL'. Funds have until **13 February 2007** to switch to the new COLL rules. From that date, CIS will no longer apply for any scheme. In this section, we outline the **CIS** rules first, and then we look at **COLL**.

Types of authorised fund

2.13 For CIS purposes, there are the following categories of authorised fund:

- Securities schemes (funds for transferable securities, including equity funds and bond funds)
- Money market schemes
- Futures and options schemes
- Geared futures and options schemes
- Property schemes
- Warrant schemes
- Feeder funds
- Fund of funds schemes
- Umbrella schemes

2.14 Funds may be **UCITS schemes**, meaning that they conform to the European UCITS Directive and can be marketed throughout the European Economic Area (EEA).

Investment rules

2.15 Authorised fund managers of AUTs and ICVCs must ensure that, taking account of the investment objectives and policy of the authorised fund as stated in the most recently published prospectus of the authorised fund, the scheme property of the authorised fund aims to provide a **prudent spread of risk**.

2.16 The CIS Sourcebook sets out the securities in which funds may invest. These must be **freely transferable securities**. The trust deed of an AUT will state that the trust may invest in FSA-permitted securities and will identify any further narrower investment rules of the trust itself. Investment limits will be set out in the scheme particulars or fund prospectus.

2.17 At least 90% of a securities fund must be invested in **approved securities**: these are securities listed in an EEA state or in another recognised and regulated eligible market. The eligible markets used must be listed in the scheme particulars. **Unlisted (unapproved) securities**, which can make up 10% by value, may include units in other collective investment schemes constituting up to 5% of the value of the fund.

2.18 The following **concentration rules** are designed to ensure that authorised funds have a certain amount of spread or diversification.

- Not more than 10% of the total value of the fund may be held in the shares of a single company.

- The holdings exceeding 5% must not add to more than 40% of the fund in aggregate.

2.19 These rules mean that the most concentrated fund with the fewest holdings would have four holdings of 10% of the fund value each, with twelve further holdings of 5% each. Thus, a fund must have **at least 16 holdings** although in practice, funds typically have many more than this.

2.20 Funds may also **not hold more than 10% of the voting shares** of a particular company. A fund management company must not have more than 20% of the voting rights in a single company across all its funds.

2.21 A fund with more than 35% of its value in **government fixed interest securities** from a single issuer (eg, UK Government gilts) must invest in at least six different issues of stock. A single holding of a government fixed interest security must not exceed 30% of the fund value.

2.22 Equity funds and bond funds are allowed to use forward contracts or **derivatives** (futures, options or contracts for differences), to help reduce risk and costs or in the interests of efficient portfolio management that is 'economically appropriate'. A securities fund may hold a maximum of 5% of its value as **warrants** (securities giving an option to buy shares).

2.23 Funds are now available that specialise in derivatives, since legislation was introduced to permit futures and options funds, geared futures and options funds, option funds, property funds and warrant funds.

Cash and borrowings

2.24 Funds may hold cash only to provide **liquidity** and **cash flow**. **Borrowings** by AUTs and ICVCs must be temporary and not persistent. Temporary borrowing is permitted against future cash flows but must not exceed, on any business day, 10% of the value of the scheme property. These types of funds cannot use borrowing as a means of **gearing** its portfolio in the way that an investment trust can.

FSA cancellation rules

2.25 To comply with **FSA cancellation rules,** firms selling unit trusts and OEICs must allow investors who have received advice 14 days in which to cancel their investment. The cancellation period does not apply for sales made at a distance rather than face-to-face.

2.26 Written notice of the right to cancel must be given:

- Before the agreement is concluded, and
- Within eight days after the agreement being concluded

2.27 The notice must be completed and returned by the customer within 14 days for the purchase to be cancelled. If those who are eligible choose to cancel their units and the market has fallen, they will receive the **offer price** on the date of cancellation. This could be less than their original investment. If the market has risen they will not benefit from the rise and will only be refunded their original investment.

2.28 If a firm does not give to a **retail customer** information about his cancellation rights, the contract remains cancellable and the retail customer will be not liable for any shortfall.

COLL Sourcebook

2.29 As stated above, the FSA has introduced a New Collective Investment Schemes Sourcebook (**COLL**) that will replace the previous Sourcebook for Collective Investment Schemes (**CIS**). COLL applies to ICVCs (ie, OEICs) and authorised unit trusts. COLL provides a regime for product regulation, with the objective of protecting the consumer, and also implements requirements of the UCITS Directive. Until **13 February 2007** when the CIS rules ceases to apply, authorisation of collective investment schemes under COLL remains optional and so the new COLL rules currently only affect some schemes.

2.30 COLL is designed as a two-tier approach, comprising:

(a) **Retail schemes**, which are promoted to the general public, and
(b) **Qualified investor schemes** (QIS), for institutions and expert private investors

2.31 **Retail schemes** are either **UCITS retail schemes** or **non-UCITS retail schemes**. However, there have been relatively few applications to set up non-UCITS retail schemes.

2.32 With **QIS**, fewer consumer protection rules apply than for retail schemes. QIS can invest in a very wide range of assets, with no significant limitation on the spread between buying and selling prices other than whatever is stated in the scheme documentation.

2.33 With regard to **gearing**, QIS are permitted to **borrow** up to 100% of the net asset value of the fund. QIS are also permitted to hold 'short' positions profiting from falls in prices and can charge performance fees. These possibilities make QIS very similar to **hedge funds**.

2.34 A retail UCITS scheme is very similar to existing UCITS schemes, with the following limits (based on percentage of the scheme's value) applying:

- 20% limit on investment in other collective investment schemes
- 10% limit on investment in unapproved (unlisted) securities

2.35 Under COLL, there are the following new investment limits for non-UCITS retail schemes.

- 35% limit for investing in other collective investment schemes
- If a scheme does invest in a second scheme, that second scheme must not itself have more than 15% of its value invested in other collective investment schemes
- 20% limit on aggregate investment in unapproved securities and unregulated schemes

2.36 For **UCITS funds** replicating ('tracking') an index, the **concentration** limit is raised under COLL rules to permit a holding of 20% in a particular share, and up to 35%, but only for one share and only in exceptional market conditions. **Non-UCITS funds** under COLL have no concentration limits. Under the new rules, both UCITS and non-UCITS retail schemes can invest in a variety of types of instrument, including **warrants and derivatives**, within their overall investment objectives, provided that they apply a risk management procedure.

2.37 A non-UCITS retail scheme can invest in an even wider range of assets, including gold or 100% investment in immovable property. Non-UCITS schemes can also **borrow** up to 10% of the fund value on a **permanent** basis, while UCITS retail schemes are only permitted to borrow on a **temporary** basis.

2.38 Under the COLL rules, redemptions in non-UCITS retail schemes and QISs may be:

- Limited for up to six months in the case of property funds and in schemes offering a guaranteed return
- Deferred to the next valuation point if redemptions exceed 10% of the value of the fund, with proper disclosure to investors

2.39 COLL permits the **creation of units** on a **forward pricing basis** to take place up to **24 hours** after the relevant valuation point (previously, 2 hours).

2.40 In the past, the market capitalisation of some shares within an index has made it difficult for funds to track an index within the previous regulations. Under new rules, **index-tracking funds** are permitted to invest up to 20% of the fund value in particular share in order to replicate an index, or up to 35% in a single share in exceptional market conditions.

2.41 COLL also allows fund managers to charge **performance-based fees,** either at fixed fee rates or based on the value of the fund. Overall, the new COLL arrangements are designed to allow flexibility in product design by scheme providers, coupled with the retention of consumer protection based on the needs of different classes of investor.

Tax treatment

Taxation of the unit trust

2.42 (a) Dividends are received with a 10% tax credit and the unit trust has no further tax liability on such income.

(b) Income from overseas securities, cash and fixed interest securities is subject to reduced corporation tax of 20%.

(c) Any income received by the trust from currency, futures and options is exempt from corporation tax. Any gains made from similar sources are also exempt.

(d) The capital gains made within a unit trust are exempt from capital gains tax.

Taxation of the individual investor

2.43 **Taxation of income.** The taxation of income received from a unit trust varies, depending on its source. Under the '**bond fund test',** income can be received from either an equity unit trust (with at least 40% of the assets invested in equities) or a non-equity unit trust. We will look at the treatment of both types of income.

(a) **Income from equity unit trust.** The dividends from an equity unit trust are subject to income tax and are received by the investor with a tax credit of 10%. We will look at the taxation situation for different types of taxpayers.

(i) If he is a basic rate or starting rate taxpayer he has no further tax to pay.

(ii) If he is a non-taxpayer, he cannot reclaim the tax credit.

(iii) If he is a higher rate taxpayer he will have a liability to pay a further 22.5% tax on the gross dividend.

(b) **Income from a non-equity unit trust.** The payments from a non-equity unit trusts will be treated as payment of interest and will be paid net of 20% tax. The tax situation for the different taxpayers will be as follows.

(i) If he is a basic rate taxpayer he has no further tax to pay.

(ii) If he is a non-taxpayer he may reclaim the tax deducted.

(iii) If he is a higher rate taxpayer he will have a liability to pay a further 20% tax ie 40% higher rate tax less the 20% paid.

Under **proposed changes** announced in the **2005 Budget,** the '**bond fund test'** will be removed at a future date, and funds will be able to make interest and dividend distributions in the same period in proportion to the interest and other income received.

Exercise 3

Study the list of categories of unit trusts and decide which sector will pay out its dividends with a tax credit and which will treat the payment as interest.

2.44 **Taxation of capital gains**. If the investor makes a capital gain on the realisation of a unit trust, this may be subject to capital gains tax. The calculation for capital gains tax is:

Profit = Proceeds (less sale expenses) less original purchase price less indexation allowance up to April 1998 less tapering relief from April 1998

The profit thus calculated could become subject to capital gains tax if:

(a) After taking into account the capital gains tax indexation allowance, the gain is in excess of the annual capital gains allowance (£8,500 for 2005/06), or

(b) The gain is below the annual capital gains allowance but the investor has already made use of this in other transactions

2.45 **Methods of reducing the capital gains tax**

(a) The investor may have other capital losses which could be offset against this gain.

(b) The investor may consider transferring the holding of units into a spouse's name prior to the sale if he or she has not used up the annual capital gains tax allowance.

Income equalisation payments

2.46 Between distributions of income from a fund, the unit price includes the value of any income received by its underlying assets since the previous distribution. On the first distribution of income after the purchase of units, the trust will pay out to the new unit holder the income which has accrued between the date of purchase of the units and the distribution date. In addition as the unit holder has paid for income accrued before he purchased the units this amount will be refunded to him as a capital payment. The total amount received by the unit holder should therefore be the same as the full dividend received by the original unit holders. The refund of capital, known as **income equalisation**, is tax free.

2.47 The equalisation payment is treated as a **discount** on the **purchase price** of the units. This discount **reduces** the **acquisition cost** and effectively **increases** any **capital gains** that could result on disposal, potentially giving rise to a higher CGT charge.

Inheritance tax: non-UK domiciliaries

2.48 Since 16 October 2002, inheritance tax is not chargeable on holdings by non-UK domiciliaries (or trusts set up by non-UK domiciled settlors) in authorised unit trusts and Open-Ended Investment Companies (OEICs), which are covered in Section 5 of this chapter.

Charging structure

The initial charge

2.49 (a) The manager will normally impose an **initial charge**. This covers his dealing costs when purchasing the assets of the fund and commission payments.

(b) The unit trust manager offers his units for sale at an offer price and he quotes a price to buy back units, the bid price. The spread between offer and bid prices is typically between 5% and 6% but the manager is allowed to operate within a wider band up to nearer 10%. This may happen from time to time, for instance in a strongly falling market when the manager is suffering huge outflows of money. He is then dealing on a bid basis, which means that those selling will receive a relatively low price, but those buying also face a lower price, to their advantage. If a trust is dealing on an offer basis, then those buying are paying the highest possible price for their units.

(c) The spread on gilt and fixed interest trusts is usually lower than on equity funds at around 3%. This partly reflects the lower costs of purchasing these securities.

(d) Cash and money market funds normally have a 'nil' initial charge.

(e) Built into the initial charge is the intermediary's commission of say 3%. The spread or initial charge can be reduced if the intermediary is fee based or is prepared to renounce his commission for any reason. If the general public purchase the units directly from the provider, they may suffer the full bid/offer spread.

(f) From time to time, unit trust managers reduce their initial charge with a special offer. The manager may seek to promote a particular fund by offering a discount on the spread for a limited period.

(g) At launch the units trade at a fixed price for the launch period which is usually two weeks the (launch period may be up to 21 days).

(h) There is a move to trading units on a single price. This happens with Open Ended Investment Companies (OEICs) (see later in this Chapter).

Annual management charges

2.50 Unit trusts are subject to an **annual management charge** usually of between 0.5% and 1.5% which is normally deducted from the income of the fund. The management charge varies. It may be higher for overseas funds and lower for cash and money market funds.

Risk

2.51 (a) A unit trust is a pooled fund and as such the risk is lower than investing directly into equities because of the 'spread' of investments.

(b) The risk involved in investment in a unit trust depends upon the trust selected by the investor. If he selects a cash fund there is only the risk of interest rate fluctuations. If he selects, say, a specialist South East Asia fund or emerging markets fund, then the investment and currency risks can be very high.

(c) The unit trust itself is constituted under a trust and it is the responsibility of the trustees to ensure that it is properly managed. Unit trusts are authorised under the Financial Services and Markets Act 2000. Unit trust management companies are regulated in respect of the management of the trust and in respect of marketing by the FSA. The investor has access to a complaints process and to the Financial Ombudsman Service. In the event of an adviser firm or provider becoming insolvent and unable to repay the investor, the

Financial Services Compensation Scheme will pay out a maximum of £48,000 (100% of the first £30,000 and 90% of the next £20,000).

Method of purchase and sale

2.52 (a) As outlined above, units are purchased from the manager at the offer price and bought back at the bid price. The price for the units is calculated as follows:

Value of the assets in the trust

Add dealing costs such as stamp duty (0.5%) and brokerage

Add cash and accrued income

Divide by number of units issued

Add on the initial charge and round to four significant figures

(*Note*. It is proposed to abolish the current 0.5% stamp duty and replace it with a 0.2% flat charge.)

This price can be fixed at two different times and the manager must state clearly which time is employed. The two methods employed are as follows.

(i) **Historic pricing.** Using this method the fund is valued at the close of business on say Thursday, and the units are bought and sold on Friday based on Thursday's valuation. In a falling market this means that the manager is paying out too much for the units he is buying back. The price does not really reflect the value of the assets at the time of the deal. Managers must move to forward pricing on request or if the market moves by 2% or more since the last valuation.

(ii) **Forward pricing.** Using this method of valuation the investor buys or sells units at the next price to be calculated. So he is unaware of the price at which he will deal until the contract is completed. The time for valuing the fund may be mid-day or the close of business. Some funds even value twice daily. T the valuation must be at least 2 hours before the opening of any market in which the fund holds in excess of 40% of its assets. Under CIS rules, the manager must create units within 2 hours of the valuation point. Under COLL, he must do so within 24 hours of the valuation point.

(b) Since the stock market crash of 1987, when managers suffered badly from historic pricing and moved to forward pricing without warning the investor, forward pricing is more common.

(c) The minimum amount invested in a trust as a single payment is typically £500.

(d) It is possible for investors to save into a unit trust scheme ISA on a monthly basis, in which case the minimum contribution might be £25 or £50 per month.

(e) The investor may purchase income units or accumulation units. With **income units**, the investor's share of the income of the fund is distributed to him half-yearly or quarterly. With **accumulation units,** the income is reinvested at each distribution and the price of the units rises accordingly. It is possible to purchase income units and reinvest the income in which case additional units are purchased.

(f) Units could be purchased on-line, by a telephone call or by written instructions.

(g) Upon receipt of instructions, the units will be purchased at the next valuation point and a contract note issued. The client will be expected to settle on receipt of this.

(h) In some instances the unit trust company issue a certificate as proof of ownership of the units and this will be dispatched within 21 days. Many unit trust managers are now moving to non-certificated units which means that the contract note alone is proof of ownership.

(i) If an investor wishes to sell his units, the transaction can be carried out in a similar manner as a purchase. The deal can be conducted on line, either by telephone or by letter. The certificate or a form of renunciation will need to be signed indicating that the total or part of the holding is to be sold.

(j) Some managers offer a **share exchange scheme**. This allows the investor the opportunity to sell existing shares at an advantageous price. Sometimes the unit trust manager will buy the shares for one of his funds or, alternatively, the shares will be sold via a stockbroker but on better dealing terms. The investor will normally get a better deal if the manager wants to buy the shares for his own funds. (This is likely to occur with blue-chip shares.) Although it is called 'share exchange', the sale of the shares and the purchase of the units are two separate transactions, so a charge to capital gains tax may arise.

Exercise 4

See if you can define the following expressions in connection with unit trusts.

(a) Bid price of units
(b) The spread
(c) Historic pricing
(d) The contract note
(e) Share exchange

Uses

2.53 Unit trusts are a useful investment medium for both experienced and inexperienced investors.

(a) The purchase of a unit trust is a useful way for a client to obtain professional fund management skills if he does not have sufficient capital to interest a stockbroker.

(b) The purchase of unit trusts is useful for a client who wishes to enter the equity market without taking too much risk. The risk is reduced by the pooled fund.

(c) Although it is more expensive to buy gilts via a gilt and fixed interest fund than directly, nevertheless the unit trust gives the client entry into a well spread and managed fund.

(d) UK equity unit trusts can be used to create a potentially rising stream of income for a client.

(e) Unit trusts are a useful way of obtaining overseas exposure within a portfolio of any type. Clients holding a share portfolio of UK equities may use unit trusts for their overseas exposure unless they have enormous amounts to invest directly into foreign shares.

(f) Unit trusts are a method of entering specialist markets such as commodities or property in which the small investor would have neither sufficient resources nor expertise.

(g) Unit trusts are a method of entering high risk markets with a known exit route. The manager must buy back the units whereas the individual may have problems selling individual shares.

(h) Unit trusts may be a cheaper way of entering the equity market than via an investment bond.

(i) When unit trusts are used in a portfolio there will normally be a spread across geographical areas, with emphasis on growth or income as required. The mix of geographical areas will depend on the risk the client is prepared to take.

Exercise 5

In what circumstances may a unit trust manager reduce his charges?

---

3 UNIT TRUST CASH FUNDS

3.1 Unit trusts can offer **cash funds** which rival the returns offered by banks and building societies. The unit trust invests its funds in money market instruments and thus secures a high (variable) rate of interest with security of capital. The charges on such a fund are low. There is no bid/offer spread. The investor incurs no cost on buying or selling his units. There is an annual management charge. Such a fund may offer a very competitive rate of interest even for a small investment such as £500.

Tax situation

3.2 (a) Interest paid to the investor is made net of 20% tax.
   (b) Non-taxpayers must reclaim the tax deducted from HMRC.

Method of purchase and sale

3.3 Units in a cash fund are purchased directly from the manager by telephone or post. A similar method is used for the sale of the holding.

Uses

3.4 Although a unit trust cash fund could be used in any of the circumstances outlined in Paragraph 2.22, it is normally a scheme for the more sophisticated investor because of the method of access to capital. Such an investor could use the fund in the following circumstances.

(a) As an alternative to a building society, if the rate of interest currently available from the unit trust was more attractive.

(b) For instant access funds, because money can be withdrawn without notice. A unit trust cash fund cannot be used as a current account as it does not offer full banking facilities.

(c) For smaller amounts of capital, where the rate offered may be more attractive than a bank or building society would offer for the deposit of a similar sum. The reason for this is that the investor has purchased units in a pooled investment and higher money market rates are available to the total cash funds available for investment.

(d) For an active investor who may use such a fund as a home for cash while he is waiting to enter the market or between investments. If he subsequently invested in one of the 'in-house' unit trusts, advantageous charges may be applied on the switch of funds.

4 INVESTMENT TRUSTS

Features

4.1 (a) **Investment trusts** have been in existence for around 140 years. Foreign and Colonial Investment Trust was the first to be founded in 1868 with the 'aim of giving the investor of moderate means the same advantage as the large capitalist'. In mid-2003, there were 371 trusts in total, with total assets in the region of £50 billion.

(b) Investment trusts are companies quoted on the London Stock Exchange. Whereas other companies may make their profit from manufacturing or providing goods and services, an investment trust makes its profit solely from investments.

(c) Each investment trust is a separate quoted company. The number of shares issued is fixed and would normally only change if there is a rights issue or share split. Thus, an investment trust is often referred to as a **closed-end fund**.

(d) Investment trusts can issue various classes of share.

(e) Investment trusts must comply with the rules of the Companies Act and the Stock Exchange. Each investment trust company has its own board of directors and a memorandum and articles of association. The directors are responsible for making sure the company is properly run. However, they normally delegate the responsibility for investment decisions to a manager.

(f) The investment trust manager will be authorised to carry out investment business by FSA.

(g) The Stock Exchange lays down rules for a company seeking a listing as an investment trust as follows.

   (i) The investment manager must have adequate experience.

   (ii) There must be an adequate spread of investment risk.

   (iii) The company must not be actively involved in the management of the companies in which it invests.

   (iv) The trust must not to a significant extent be a dealer in investments.

(h) A few investment trusts, including Alliance and Second Alliance Trust and Scottish Investment Trust, are self managed with all the administration and investment management being done in-house. Most are run by investment management groups, such as Flemings and Hendersons who are responsible for several separate investment trust companies.

(i) To be approved as an investment trust by HMRC, a company has to meet requirements set out in s 842 Income and Corporation Taxes Act 1988, as amended. The requirements are as follows.

   (i) The investment trust is resident in the UK and is not a close company.

   (ii) Its income is derived wholly or mainly from shares or securities.

   (iii) It does not invest more than 15% of its assets in the shares or securities of any one company.

   (iv) All its ordinary share capital is listed on the London Stock Exchange.

   (v) Its articles of association prohibit the distribution of dividend surpluses arising from realisation of investment.

   (vi) It does not retain more than an amount equal to 15% of the income it receives from its investments in shares or securities.

4.2 An investment trust can issue a number of different type of shares. We will now look at these in detail.

(a) **Ordinary shares**

   If an investor buys ordinary shares in an investment trust company, he has a right to a dividend and to attend and vote at the annual general meeting of the investment trust.

If an investment trust wishes to raise more capital by the issue of more shares, it can do this by a rights issue (see Chapter 7) or the issue of C (conversion) shares. These shares bear their own cost of issue. Initially the shares are quoted separately until the money raised is fully invested. The shares are then converted to ordinary shares.

(b) **Preference shares**

   (i)   The dividend under a preference share is fixed. In the event of a trust being wound up the preference shareholders would have priority over the ordinary shareholders.

   (ii)   **Stepped preference shares**. The dividend under this share increases at a pre-set amount. There is also a pre-set capital growth.

(c) **Split capital shares**

   (i)   Whereas the ordinary shares in a traditional investment trust produce both income and growth, the idea behind the **split capital trust** was that some investors required income and others capital growth.

   (ii)   The split capital trust has one portfolio designed to produce income and growth. The trust can issue a number of different classes of share. The shares it issues are income shares or capital shares. Those who select the income obtain a higher income because their investment earns dividends from *all* the shares in the portfolio. Similarly, those who own the capital shares will be rewarded by the capital growth on the entire portfolio at redemption date once the holders of other types of share have been repaid. Some investors will buy both types of share.

   (iii) A split capital trust will operate for a fixed term, seven or ten years would be normal.

   (iv)   When the trust is wound up the assets are first distributed to the income shareholders. How much is returned to them will depend on the terms of the fund but normally they would expect to be returned their original investment, although this is not guaranteed.

   (v)   **Annuity shares** are shares issued at say £1 but on winding up the investor may receive back only 1p. Obviously in the meantime he has enjoyed a high income.

   (vi)   Some split capital funds issue **zero dividend preference shares**. These shares receive no income. They offer an almost guaranteed return on a fixed date and take priority over capital shares on winding up.

   (vii) Some investment trusts offer highly geared ordinary income/hybrid shares. These shares produce a high level of income but include a high risk on capital. The shareholders only have a right to the capital which remains after the preference shareholders have been repaid.

(d) **Debenture stock**

   The investment trust company may borrow money by the issue of debenture stock. The company pays a fixed rate of interest for a fixed term. Sometimes a company may issue stepped interest debenture stock. The interest on this stock starts lower but rises over a period.

(e) **Unsecured loan stock**

   This is another type of borrowing. The interest paid is likely to be higher than on debenture stock. It is, however, less secure and has a low priority on the winding up of the trust.

(f) **Convertible loan stock**

   This is loan stock with a fixed rate of interest but which gives the investor the right to convert to ordinary shares at a specific price at a known date in the future.

(g) **Warrants**

A **warrant** is the right to buy shares in the future at a stated date and at a set price. If the price of the shares has risen it makes sense to exercise the warrant. However, if the price has fallen the warrants may become useless. The price of a warrant is very low compared with the price of an ordinary share in the same trust. Warrants can be bought and sold on the market. Some split capital trusts issue warrants which give the right to buy capital shares but not income shares. Another type of warrant is the subscription share. This pays a dividend.

Exercise 6

Explain the following terms as they refer to Investment trusts.

(a)   Split capital trusts
(b)   Zero dividend shares
(c)   Warrants

4.3   We list below the categories and definitions of investment trusts available (Source: Association of Investment Trust companies (AITC)).

Investment trusts: AITC classifications

Country specialists: Europe. Investment trusts with at least 80% of their assets in Europe.

Country specialists: Far East. Investment trusts with at least 80% of their assets in Far East.

Country specialists: other. Investment trusts with at least 80% of their assets in one or two countries.

Europe. Investment trusts with at least 80% of their assets in Europe.

European emerging markets. Investment trusts with at least 80% of their assets in European emerging markets.

European smaller companies. Investment trusts with at least 80% of their assets invested in the shares of European Smaller Companies.

Far East - excluding Japan. Investment trusts with at least 80% of their assets in Far Eastern securities, including a Japanese content of less than 20%.

Far East - including Japan. Investment trusts that have at least 80% of their assets in Far Eastern securities, including a Japanese content of over 20%.

Global emerging markets. Investment trusts that have at least 80% of their assets in global emerging markets.

Global growth. Investment trusts whose objective is to produce a total return to shareholders from capital and some dividend income. They also have less than 80% of their assets in anyone geographical area with at least 20% in UK-registered companies.

Global growth & income. Investment trusts whose objective is to produce a total return to shareholders from capital and dividend income growth and which have a portfolio yield around 150% of its benchmark index. They also have less than 80% of their assets in any one geographical area with at least 20% in UK-registered companies.

Global high income. Investment trusts whose objective is to achieve a portfolio yield around 200% of the yield of their benchmark indices. They also have less than 80% of their assets in anyone geographical area with at least 20% in UK-registered companies.

Global smaller companies. Investment trusts whose policy is to invest at least 80% of their assets in the shares of smaller and medium sized companies. They also have less than 80% of their assets in any one geographical area with at least 20% in UK-registered companies.

Hedge funds. Investment trusts whose policy it is to invest in Hedge Funds.

Japan. Investment trusts with at least 80% of their assets in Japan.

Japanese smaller companies. Investment trusts with at least 80% of their assets invested in the shares of Japanese smaller sized companies.

Latin America. Investment trusts with at least 80% of their assets in Latin America.

North America. Investment trusts with at least 80% of their assets in North America.

North American smaller companies. Investment trusts with at least 80% of their assets invested in the shares of North American Smaller Companies.

Overseas growth. Investment trusts whose objective is to produce a total return to shareholders from capital and some dividend income. They also have less than 80% of their assets in any one geographical area with at least 80% of their assets overseas.

Overseas growth & income. Investment trusts whose objective is to produce a total return to shareholders from capital and/or dividend income growth and which have a portfolio yield around 150% of the FTSE World (Ex UK) Index. They also have less than 80% of their assets in any one geographical area with at least 80% of their assets overseas.

Private equity. Investment trusts which have a significant proportion of the company's portfolio invested in the securities of unquoted companies, which are subject to directors' valuations.

UK growth. Investment trusts whose objective is to produce a total return to shareholders from capital and some dividend income. They also have at least 80% of their assets in UK-registered companies.

UK growth & income. Investment trusts whose objective is to produce a total return to shareholders from capital and dividend income growth and which have a portfolio yield around 150% of the FTSE All-Share Index. They also have at least 80% of their assets in UK-registered companies.

UK high income. Investment trusts which have at least 80% of their assets in UK-registered companies and which aim to achieve a portfolio yield around 200% of the yield of the FTSE All-Share Index.

UK smaller companies. Investment trusts whose policy is to invest at least 80% of their assets in the shares of smaller and medium sized UK-registered companies.

Sector specialists

Alternative energy. Investment trusts whose policy is to invest in companies with significant focus on alternative energy and energy technology.

Biotechnology/life sciences. Investment trusts whose policy is to invest in companies specialising in Life Sciences or Biotechnology.

Endowment policies. Investment trusts whose policy is to invest in with-profits endowment policies or life assurance policies.

Financials. Investment trusts whose policy is to invest in companies specialising in the financial services sector.

Liquidity funds. Investment trusts whose policy is to invest in a portfolio of liquid funds.

Mining and natural resources. Investment trusts whose policy is to invest in a portfolio of mining and metal securities and natural resources.

Property. Investment trusts whose policy is to invest in the shares and securities of property companies.

Restaurants, pubs & brewing. Investment trusts whose policy is to invest in the equity of companies operating in the restaurant, brewers and pub sectors.

Smaller companies media comms & IT. Investment trusts whose policy is to invest in smaller companies specialising in media, communications and Information Technology.

Tea plantations. Investment trusts whose policy is to invest principally in the management companies controlling interests in tea plantations and related businesses.

Tech, media & telecomm. Investment trusts whose policy is to invest in technology, media and telecommunications.

Utilities. Investment trusts whose policy is to invest in the securities of utility and utility-related companies.

Zero preference shares. Investment trusts whose policy is to invest substantially in zero dividend preference shares.

4.4 Gearing

(a) We have seen that the investment trust company can borrow money by the issue of debenture and loan stock. The company may also borrow short term from the bank.

(b) The aim of borrowing money is to put the company in a position to purchase more shares and thus increase the income and net asset value of the trust. It is hoped that the earnings from the increased portfolio will outweigh the cost of the borrowing.

(c) Investment trust companies with large borrowings are referred to as being 'highly geared' and are more risky than those who have little or no borrowings. Gearing is expressed as the percentage amount by which the net asset value per share would rise if the value of the shares doubles. A gearing factor of 100 means that the company has no borrowings. If it is below 100 this means that the fund owns assets other than equities, possibly cash and gilts. If a company has a factor of 200, it is highly geared.

(d) Gearing works well when markets are rising and the value of the assets from the investment of the borrowed money is increasing. However when a market is falling the manager can lose more money than he has borrowed and he still has the interest to pay!

(e) **Example of gearing**

Gearing works as follows. If an investment trust raised £500,000 through an issue of shares to the public, it may choose to borrow a further £500,000. In total therefore there will be £1 million to invest.

If the fund gains 25% in value the fund will have grown by £250,000, which is profit to the shareholders, once the loan has been repaid. Had the fund not borrowed, there would only have been a profit of £125,000. The downside is that gearing can have a similar negative effect if a loss is made.

Tax treatment

4.5 We will now look at the taxation of the trust and the taxation of the individual holder of shares in an investment trust. (Bear in mind that the tax treatment will be different if the shares are held in an ISA.)

Taxation of the trust

4.6 Taxation of income

(a) Dividends are received with a 10% tax credit and the trust has no further tax liability on income.

(b) Income from overseas securities, cash and fixed interest securities will continue to be subject to corporation tax having taken into account expenses such as debenture interest, overseas loan interest and management expenses.

4.7 Taxation of capital gains.

Most investment trusts will be approved under s 842 Income and Corporation Taxes Act 1988 as amended by s 117 Finance Act 1988 and s 55 Finance Act 1990. If they are thus approved then the trust will have no tax to pay on capital gains it makes on its investments.

Taxation of the individual holder of an investment trust

4.8

(a) Income tax is paid on dividends received, with a 10% tax credit. There will be no further tax liability for a basic rate or starting rate tax payer. A non-taxpayer cannot reclaim the tax credit. A higher rate taxpayer will have a liability to pay a further 22.5% tax on the gross dividend.

(b) If the investor makes a capital gain on the realisation of an investment it may be subject to capital gains tax.

The calculation for capital gains tax is:

Profit = Proceeds (less sale expenses) less original purchase price less indexation allowance up to March 1998, less taper relief from April 1998. The profit thus calculated could become subject to capital gains tax if:

    (i) After taking into account the capital gains tax indexation allowance and taper relief, the gain is in excess of the annual exemption, or

    (ii) The gain is below the annual exemption but the investor had already made use of this in other transactions.

(c) There are methods of reducing the capital gain.

    (i) The investor may have other capital losses which could be offset.

    (ii) The investor may consider transferring the holding into a spouse's name prior to sale if he or she has not used up the annual exemption.

(d) Debenture or loan stock holders receive interest less 20% tax with a certificate for the tax deducted.

Charging structure

4.9

(a) **Dealing charge.** The costs of purchasing an investment trust vary depending on whether the investor buys directly from the company via the savings and investment scheme or through a stockbroker. The dealing charge through a stockbroker may be 1% commission, subject to a minimum fee of, say, £20 plus stamp duty of 0.5%. The dealing cost via the savings and investment scheme is likely to be lower.

(b) **Cost of buying shares.** There is also the cost of buying the shares. The price quoted will be the middle market price. The spread between the buying and selling price is likely to be 1.5%.

(c) **Annual management charge**. The fund will normally suffer an annual management charge between 0.3% and 1%.

(d) **Stamp duty** is chargeable at 0.5%, as for other direct share purchases.

Risk

4.10 (a) A share in an investment trust normally carries a lower risk than a share in a normal trading company. The reason for this is that the investment trust share is a share in a fund of many shares. This pooling reduces the risk.

(b) The amount of risk the investor bears relates to the type of share he selects. Examples of high risk shares are shares in specialist funds such as technology and shares in highly geared companies. At the other end of the spectrum if the investor selects a zero preference share or a debenture, his risk is lower.

(c) The operation of an investment trust is subject to the Companies Act, the Financial Services and Markets Act and Stock Exchange regulations. In the event of a liquidation, shareholders have the same rights as a shareholder in a trading company. They also have the protection of the Financial Services Compensation Scheme.

(d) A highly geared trust presents a risk as the cost of borrowing could lead to poor returns even if the stock market is performing well.

(e) The investor in a split capital trust should understand the order in which the shares are paid out at the wind-up date. This will normally be: zero dividend preference shares, stepped preference shares, income shares and then finally capital shares. The capital shares offer the highest risk: there is a chance of high capital return, but equally the shares could be worthless.

Method of purchase and sale

4.11 (a) Investment trusts can be purchased via a stockbroker or through the investment trust's own savings and investment scheme.

(b) Most small investors will purchase via the savings scheme whether they are investing lump sums or regular amounts. The minimum lump sum may be £250 and the minimum regular savings £25 per month. The manager uses the money collected in from his savings scheme to buy shares in the stock market. He then allocates the shares and a certificate is issued.

(c) Most savings and investment schemes also have arrangements for selling shares.

(d) If the investor deals via a stockbroker the deal with most probably be conducted over the telephone and the stockbroker will then issue a contract note for settlement.

(e) From time to time, a new investment trust will be launched. The issue is often advertised in the national press. The investor can complete the application form and submit this with the appropriate cheque. This is a cheap way of acquiring an investment trust because there are no fees or commissions to pay.

(f) Share exchange schemes are available via the savings and investment schemes. They work on similar lines to that described for unit trusts.

Factors to be considered when purchasing an investment trust

4.12 When buying an investment trust share, the investor should normally consider the following factors.

(a) The share price
(b) The net asset value
(c) The discount or premium
(d) The yield
(e) The hurdle rate/asset cover

We will look at these factors separately.

(a) **Share price.** To make a decision on the share price, the investor may need to monitor performance for a few months before purchase or have access to detailed research.

(b) **Net asset value (NAV)**

    (i) The net asset value of an investment company is the net worth of the company's assets expressed in pence per share.

    (ii) The value of the company's total assets is arrived at by totalling the value of all shares at mid market price (unlisted investments at directors valuations), cash and other net current assets, then deducting loans and preference capital at nominal value. The figure is then divided by the number of shares in issue.

    Example

    An investment trust company has assets worth £20 million, liabilities of £5 million and 15 million ordinary shares.

    $NAV = (£20m - £5m)/15m = 100p$

(c) **Discount or premium**

    (i) The share price is of course subject to supply and demand and it is unusual for the share price to match the NAV.

    (ii) If the share price is less than the NAV the share is said to be trading at a **discount** and if the share price is more than the NAV then the share is trading at a **premium**.

    (iii) Sometimes the investor secures a bargain if he buys at a discount, ie he is buying £110 worth of asset for £100. However there may be a good reason for the low price and the discount may widen still further.

    (iv) Some funds, particularly high income funds, trade at a premium. Sometimes investors are reluctant to purchase shares at a premium because they do not feel they are getting good value for money. If this becomes a problem a fund manager may consider having a rights issue.

    (v) Most trading companies will have a rights issue to raise funds, but investment trusts do not need to do this as they borrow primarily from the banks or through loan stock. An investment trust can use a rights issue to reduce the premium.

    (vi) The investment trust rights issue will allow existing investors to purchase more shares at a price below the market price. The shareholder has an option, if they do not wish to exercise their right to buy more shares they can sell this right in the market. The effect of the rights issue should be to reduce the premium.

    (vii) The discount or premium on a split capital trust is a 'package' - a combination of the discount or premium of its various shares classes.

(d) **Yield.** The yield of the share is arrived at by dividing the gross dividend per share paid over the last 12 months by the current market price of the shares and multiplying by 100.

(e) **Hurdle rate/asset cover.** These measurements are important when considering a zero dividend preference share. The hurdle rate denotes the percentage by which the underlying trust's assets must grow each year to meet the redemption price of each class of share in the split capital trust. The asset cover indicates the progress the fund manager has made to date to cover the redemption price. Such information can be obtained on a monthly basis from the Association of Investment Trust Companies. A negative hurdle rate would indicate that the fund could shrink and still repay each class of shareholder what is due.

Uses

4.13 (a) The use of investment trusts can be considered in all situations when the adviser would recommend a unit trust. The reasons for this are the lower charges and frequently better performance of investment trusts compared with unit trusts and OEICs.

(b) Placing investments in a well spread portfolio of investment trusts is a cheap method of exposing a client to the equity market via a pooled fund.

(c) Investing in investment trusts allows the client an exposure to overseas and other specialised markets.

(d) The income shares in a split capital trust can be used to provide a high level of income for a client with only a small amount of risk to capital.

(e) A zero dividend share may be used to provide funds at a known date in the future, for example, to provide for school fees.

(f) The investment trust is a more complex animal than a unit trust. So there are some situations when an unsophisticated client may feel happier with a unit trust despite the increased charges.

(g) The use of capital shares in a split capital trust allows a higher rate taxpayer to capture the performance of the UK stock market without the taxable income generated by direct investment into the market.

5 OEICS

The OEIC framework

5.1 **Open Ended Investment Companies (OEICs)** are managed, pooled investment vehicles in the form of companies. They invest in securities with the objective of producing a profit for investors. Unlike unit trusts, the OEIC structure is recognised throughout Europe. The possible prospect of UK participation in economic and monetary union (EMU) and the single European Market helped to drive the UK to adopt this form of pooled investment, in addition to the unit trust. Regulations made under the European Communities Act brought OEICs into existence in the UK in 1997.

5.2 These regulations provided for the incorporation in the UK of OEICs that fall within the scope of the **UCITS (Undertaking for Collective Investment in Transferable Securities)** Directive. This means they can invest only in **transferable securities** (for example, listed securities, other collective investment schemes, certificates of deposit). UCITS must be open ended. UCITS certification allows the fund to be marketed throughout the European Economic Area (EEA). If it is marketed in the UK, an OEIC must be **authorised** by the Financial Services Authority (FSA).

5.3 With the implementation of the Financial Services and Markets Act 2000 (FSMA 2000), the range of UK authorised OEICs was extended to be similar to that of unit trusts, including money market funds and property funds for example, and (as we have seen) OEICs are now alternatively termed **Investment Companies with Variable Capital (ICVCs)**. Authorisation as an ICVC defines the regulations (ie, the Treasury's ICVC Regulations, as well as further FSA regulations) with which the fund must comply.

5.4 The FSA's transitional **COLL Sourcebook** rules, as described earlier in this Chapter, apply for OEICs/ICVCs as well as unit trusts. OEICs can be set up as UCITS retail schemes or non-UCITS retail schemes, or QISs. The COLL rules, which will apply to all funds only by 13 February 2007, were summarised earlier. **CIS** rules (as for unit trusts) apply to OEICs that have not adopted the COLL regime.

5.5 Both OEICs and unit trusts are types of **open-ended collective investments**, and the term **funds** is often used to cover both types of scheme. However, with a unit trust, the units held provide beneficial ownership of the underlying trust assets. A share in an OEIC entitles the holder to a share in the profits of the OEIC, but the value of the share will be determined by the value of the underlying investments. For example, if the underlying investments are valued at £125,000,000 and there are 100,000,000 shares in issue, the net asset value of each share is £1.25.

5.6 The holder of a share in an OEIC can sell back the share to the company in any period specified in the prospectus.

5.7 The various **permitted types of OEIC** are as for unit trusts, including for example futures and options funds and geared futures and options funds, except that OEICs cannot be feeder funds. (Feeder funds can only be used for pension purposes, and exist only for holding units in other funds.)

5.8 An OEIC may take the form of an **umbrella fund** with a number of separately priced **sub-funds** adopting different investment strategies or denominated in different currencies. Each sub-fund will have a separate client register and asset pool.

5.9 Classes of shares within an OEIC may include **income shares**, which pay a dividend, and **accumulation shares**, in which income is not paid out and all income received is added to net assets.

5.10 **OEICs** are similar to investment trusts in that both have **corporate structures**. The objective of the company in each case is to make a profit for shareholders by investing in the shares of other companies. They differ in that an investment trust is a **closed-ended investment** and an OEIC is **open-ended**. The open-ended nature of an OEIC means that it cannot trade at a discount to NAV.

5.11 An OEIC may have a number of share classes in a particular fund or subfund. The fund could be an 'Umbrella Fund' and regulations state that investors must be able to switch between any of the subfunds in that umbrella.

5.12 OEICs are similar to the continental European equivalent **SICAV** and both are **UCITS (Undertaking for the Collective Investment in Transferable Securities)**. SICAV stands for **Société d'Investissement à Capital Variable** (investment company with variable capital). A SICAV is an open ended investment fund similar to an FCP (see below) except that an SICAV has a share capital (which is equal to the net assets of the fund).

5.13 **FCP** stands for **Fonds Commun de Placement**, a European standard common fund structure. An FCP is not a distinct legal entity and therefore has a management company acting on its behalf. An FCP is not liable for the obligations of the management company.

The structure of OEICs

5.14 An OEIC has an **Authorised Corporate Director (ACD)**, who **may be the only Director**. The responsibilities of the **ACD** include the following.

- Day-to-day management of the fund
- Pricing of the fund
- Management of the investments
- Dealing in the underlying securities
- Preparation of accounts
- Compliance with OEIC regulatory requirements

5.15 In order to ensure that the **ACD** acts in the interests of **investor protection**, there is a **separate, independent** depository. The responsibility of the **depository** is similar to that of a trustee for a unit trust and covers the following.

- Overseeing the management of the investment company
- Protecting the interests of the investor
- Valuation and pricing of OEIC shares
- Dealing in shares for the OEIC
- The payment of income distributions
- Generally overseeing the ACD
- Ensuring that the ACD is acting in accordance with his investment powers
- Ensuring the ACD is acting in accordance with his borrowing powers

5.16 The ACD and the depository must be regulated by the FSA, and approved as '**authorised persons**'. FSA rules cover the sales and marketing of OEICs, and there are cancellation rules.

5.17 The following requirements apply to OEICs.

- There must be an **Annual General Meeting**.

- **Unaudited interim and audited final reports** must be made to the holders of shares each year, complying the **Statement of Recommended Practice for authorised funds**.

- **Short form accounts** may be prepared but full financial statements must be provided on request.

Pricing, buying and selling

5.18 The shares in the OEIC express the entitlement of the shareholders to the underlying fund which, like a unit trust, is valued of a Net Asset Value basis. With equities, there are a limited number of shares available in each company and an individual must sell the share before another can buy. Because an OEIC is open-ended, the number of shares in issue can be **increased** or **reduced** to satisfy the demands of the investors.

5.19 OEICs are **single priced instruments**. Therefore, there is no bid/offer spread with OEICs. The buying price reflects the value of the underlying shares, with any initial charge reflecting dealing costs and management expenses being disclosed separately. **Costs of creation** of the fund may be met by the fund.

5.20   A further charge, known as a **dilution levy,** may be made at the discretion of the ACD. The **dilution levy** may be added to the single price, or deducted from the redemption price. The purpose of such a levy is to protect the interests of the shareholders in general and may be charged if the fund is in decline or is experiencing **exceptionally high levels of net sales or redemptions** relative to its size. This levy, if charged, is paid into the fund and not to the managers.

5.21   When the investor wishes to **sell** the **OEIC,** the **ACD** will **buy** it. The money value on sale will be based on the **single price** less a **deduction** for the **dealing charges**. The price may be further reduced by any **dilution levy**. The **ACD** may choose to **run a box**. Shares sold back to the ACD will be **kept** and **reissued** to investors, reducing the need for creation and cancellation of shares.

5.22   The **register of shareholders** must be **updated daily** and include all shareholdings of the ACD and those held in the box (if there is one) as well as those of the investors.

Taxation of OEICs

5.23   **OEICs** themselves face a tax regime similar to that faced by **unit trusts**. Except for fixed interest funds, interest, rent and foreign dividends not taxed at source is subject to a 20% corporation tax charge. UK dividends received will suffer no further tax. Capital gains within an OEIC are exempt from CGT.

5.24   **Distributions** (dividends) paid to investors in an OEIC are taxable in the same way as the distributions from unit trusts.

- Equity fund dividends are paid with a **tax credit** of 10% that satisfies the **tax liability** for basic and lower rate taxpayers. **Higher rate taxpayers** are liable to an additional 22.5%.

- Fixed interest funds pay interest with 20% tax deducted, which satisfies the liability for basic rate taxpayers. Higher rate taxpayers and discretionary trusts must pay 20% more and starting rate taxpayers can reclaim 10%.

5.25   **Non taxpayers** may **reclaim** tax on interest distributions, but not equity distributions. For investors' OEIC holdings outside a tax-advantaged wrapper such as an ISA, **capital gains tax** will be chargeable on disposals. There is no UK stamp duty to pay on purchases of OEICs.

5.26   Where an OEIC is based **offshore,** the distributions will **not be taxed** internally. This will provide a **benefit** to non-taxpaying investors, and a cashflow benefit to tax paying investors.

Advantages of OEICs for the investor

5.27   As for unit trusts, the general advantages of collective investment outlined at the beginning of this Chapter apply to OEICs. Like unit trusts, there is a wide range of types of fund available.

5.28   The introduction of OEICs was expected to lead to a **reduction in costs for the investor** and **transparency of charges**. At the same time, there is **no dilution** in **investor protection**.

5.29 The charges with **OEICs** may be lower than for unit trusts, particularly in respect of **cost of entry (setting up)** and **exit (encashing the investment)** due to single pricing. Annual management costs are not set out as a separate charge as with unit trusts. It is still possible to quantify the costs by looking at the **total expense ratio (TER)** of the company. Figures for this are available in the public domain, allowing investors to make valid comparisons between investment managers.

5.30 For the investment industry, an advantage of OEICs is that they are **widely recognised throughout Europe**.

6 EXCHANGE TRADED FUNDS

6.1 **Exchange traded funds (ETFs)** are a relatively new type of open ended fund which has proved very popular in the USA.

6.2 ETFs:

(a) Track share indices (eg the FTSE – 100 in the UK, or the S&P 500 in the USA)
(b) Have prices quoted in real time throughout trading hours

6.3 Low charges and the fact that no stamp duty is applied to purchases of ETFs are attractions of ETFs. However, the fact that ETFs generally only track indices is a limitation.

6.4 In theory, the price of ETFs should closely follow the underlying index, although in practice the price may diverge from the net asset value by perhaps 1%.

7 COMPARING INVESTMENT FUNDS

Feature	Unit Trusts	OEICs/ICVCs	Investment trusts
Legal structure	Trust	Company	Company
Nature of fund	Fund expands and contracts on demand (open ended)	Fund expands and contracts on demand (open ended)	Fixed number of shares in issue (closed ended)
Investors' holdings	Units	Shares	Shares
Regulation	Manager and trustee authorised by FSA. Unit trust authorised by FSA. Marketing regulated by FSA.	Company registered under a special corporate code. Manager (who is the ACD) and depository (trustee) authorised by FSA. OEIC authorised by FSA. Marketing regulated by FSA.	Registered under the Companies Act. Subject to Stock Exchange listing rules and HMRC approval. Manager authorised by FSA. Marketing of savings schemes regulated by FSA.
Independent oversight	By trustee	By depository; optional independent directors.	Stock exchange requires independent board
Investment restrictions	Clearly defined rules on what investments the manager may take.	Clearly defined rules on what investments the manager may take.	Almost unlimited investments allowed subject to Articles of Association and approval of the board
Borrowing powers	Limited ability to borrow	Limited ability to borrow	Extensive abilities to borrow (gearing/ leverage)

Feature	Unit Trusts	OEICs/ICVCs	Investment trusts
Compensation	Covered by FSCS if intermediary/ manager/trustee collapsed	Covered by FSCS if intermediary/ manager/trustee collapsed	Covered by FSCS if intermediary/ manager/trustee collapsed
Share classes	Two classes of unit based on dividend/ reinvestment of income (income/accumulation)	Multiple classes of share fund or sub fund possible with differential charges and currencies allowed	Multiple share classes possible but complex
Entry/Exit charges	Initial and annual charges but generally no exit charges	Load/no load options likely	Entry and exit transaction charges normally levied
Equalisation	Compulsory	Optional	Not applicable

Chapter roundup

In this chapter we have studied:

- The different categories of unit trust

- The functions of the trustees and manager of a unit trust

- The taxation of unit trusts and unit trust investors

- The methods of buying and selling and the charging of unit trusts

- The features of an investment trust

- Points to consider when purchasing an investment trust: price, net asset value, yield, discount and premium

- The methods of buying and selling and the charging of investment trusts

- The taxation of investment trusts and investors

- OEICs/ICVCs

- Exchange traded funds

Quick Quiz

1   What is a unit trust tracker fund?

2   Why is a unit trust called an 'open ended fund'?

3   What is the initial charge likely to be on a gilt and fixed interest unit trust?

4   What are the two methods of pricing which a unit trust manager can employ?

5   What is a unit trust 'accumulation unit'?

6   List the types of share an investment trust may issue.

7   What is the difference between an investment trust debenture stock and an unsecured loan stock?

8   What would a gearing factor of 180 indicate?

9   Does an investment trust pay tax on capital gains?

10   What do the letters 'NAV' mean?

The answers to the questions in the quiz can be found at the end of this Study Text. Before checking your own answers against them, you should look back at this chapter and use the information in it to correct your answers.

Answers to exercises

1 The investor should chose a money market fund if he wants a low risk investment with base rate returns.

2 (a) The trustees must have gross capital of at least £4 million.

   (b) The trustees must be independent from the management group.

   (c) The trustees must ensure that the investors are protected.

   (d) The trustees must ensure that the managers act in accordance with the trust deed.

   (e) The securities of the trust are held in the name of the trustees.

   (f) The trustees must hold these securities or place them in safe custody.

   (g) The trustees may replace the manager.

   (h) The trustees must establish and maintain a register of unitholders.

   (i) The trustees are responsible for making sure annual report and accounts are prepared, also the publication of half-yearly results.

   As stated above the trustee has the power to remove the manager if he feels he is not acting in the best interest of the investors. The consent of FSA must be obtained for the removal of the manager.

3 The equity sector will pay out its dividends with a tax credit and the fixed interest and cash sector will treat payments as interest.

4 (a) Bid price of units — The price at which the manager will buy back units

   (b) The spread — The difference between the bid and offer price

   (c) Historic pricing — Dealing at a known price set by a valuation of the fund on the previous day

   (d) Contract note — The contract note is confirmation that a stockbroker or intermediary has purchased or sold units or shares

   (e) Share exchange — This scheme is offered by investment houses and insurance companies to would-be-customers. It allows the investor who is about to purchase a pooled investment to pay for all or part of the deal by the sale of previously held shares. The shares are sold on preferential dealing charges

5 A fund manager may reduce his charges:

   (a) On the launch of a new fund for a limited period (2 weeks)
   (b) If units move to a bid basis
   (c) If the manager offers units at a 'discount' as a promotion

6 (a) Split capital trusts
   (b) Zero dividend shares
   (c) Warrants

PRACTICE QUESTION 5: COLLECTIVE INVESTMENTS (30 Marks)   *27 mins*

(a) Using notes in a list form, compare and contrast the features of a unit trust and an investment trust.   (8 marks)

(b) Two clients had £20,000 to invest in 1993. James purchased UK equity units in P & G Fund unit trust. Bob bought units in the same fund but through an investment bond. James has taken his dividends from the fund and Bob has taken a 5% 'withdrawal' from the bond throughout the term.

In 2005 the unit trust will generate a gain after indexation and taper relief of £42,000 and the investment bond is worth £33,600.

   (i) Calculate the amount of tax (of any kind), if any, that the investors would have to pay on the final proceeds, on the assumption that they both have a taxable income of £40,000.

   (ii) Comment on the following.

      (1) The methods James and Bob could have employed to reduce the tax they had to pay.

      (2) Why did the investors receive different amounts on encashment even though they invested in the same fund?   (22 marks)

The answer to the practice question can be found at the end of this Study Text

Chapter 7

EQUITIES

Chapter topic list	Syllabus reference
1 Introduction to equity investments	2.5
2 Types of ordinary share	2.5
3 Non-voting shares	2.5
4 Warrants	2.5
5 Preference and convertible shares	2.5
6 Tax treatment of shares	2.5
7 Factors associated with investment in shares	2.5
8 Changes to share capital	2.5
9 Method of purchase and sale of shares	2.5
10 A new offer of shares	2.5
11 Cost of investing in shares	2.5
12 Share option schemes	2.5

Introduction

In this chapter we examine the main features of shares and outline the different classes of share available. Equities (ordinary shares) fall into the medium to high risk category of investments. We will look at tax treatment, cost of investment, risk, method of purchase and sale and the use of shares in the construction of an investment portfolio.

1 INTRODUCTION TO EQUITY INVESTMENTS

1.1 (a) Ordinary shares, or equities, are by far the most important type of security issued by UK companies.

(b) Shares are bought and sold by private investors, large institutions such as life assurance companies and pension funds and foreign investors.

(c) The proportion of ordinary shares held by private investors has declined rapidly over the last three decades and at the same time the impact of the institutional investors has increased. Nevertheless there are still private investors in the market.

(d) The private investor buys ordinary shares in the hope of an increasing dividend stream and increase in the value of the capital invested.

1.2 Many smaller 'Limited' companies are private companies, which may be owner-managed and cannot offer their shares to the general public. The use of the term 'limited' indicates that shareholders have limited liability: if the company fails, shareholders can lose their entire investment in the company but the company's creditors cannot pursue the shareholders for any further money.

1.3   To offer shares for sale to the public, a company must be a 'plc' (**public limited company**).

- Such a company can seek a **full listing** (or **quotation**) on the **main market** of the London Stock Exchange (LSE), or

- It may join the less closely regulated **Alternative Investment Market (AIM)** that is also operated by the London Stock Exchange. (AIM shares cannot be held in an ISA.)

- There are also '**Ofex**' companies whose shares are traded 'off-exchange', with much less **liquidity**: that is, buying and selling at any particular time may be difficult.

Features

1.4   (a)   Public limited companies quoted on the Stock Exchange issue shares which can be ordinary, preference, convertible preference and warrants, as risk capital and loan stock.

(b)   Each ordinary share will have a nominal value, such as 25p. This will in no way reflect the market value of the share. Ordinary shares are described by the name of the company and the nominal value of the share.

(c)   The Financial Times produces daily lists indicating the share prices of most companies whose shares are traded in the London Stock Exchange. The shares are divided into various sectors.

Measuring performance

1.5   It is possible to measure the relative performance of shares by reference to a number of **share price indices,** as follows.

FT Industrial Ordinary Share Index (FT 30 Share Index)

1.6   (a)   This index commenced in 1935 and was based on 30 major industrial shares. It has been superseded by indices based on a larger sample of shares.

(b)   The original intention of this index was to measure market movements over the short term, so it ignored dividends. The object was to help predict market trends and to provide measures of market volatility. All the shares in the index were given equal weighting. The size of the company was ignored.

(c)   Despite only identifying 30 shares, the index represents around 25% of the market value of all UK equities.

(d)   Because of its make-up, this is not a very useful index to use to compare the performance of a typical investment portfolio and it is rarely used.

FTSE 100 Index

1.7   (a)   The **FTSE 100 ('Footsie') index** was introduced at the end of December 1983. The Footsie is the most widely followed 'barometer' of the UK stock market, and covers around 80% of the total stock market capitalisation. It is a weighted arithmetic index of the top 100 companies in terms of capitalisation. This means that each company in the index is weighted according to its market value. Therefore a movement in the price of a large company has more effect on the index than a movement in the price of a small company.

(b)   The shares included in this index represent both manufacturing and service industries. The index enables futures and options contracts to be linked to the performance of the UK stock market.

(c)   Like other FTSE indices, the FTSE 100 Index does not include dividend payments: in other words, it is a **price index** and not a **total return index**.

FTSE All-Share Index

1.8   The **FTSE All-Share Index** monitors the performance of around 750 shares. The index is broken down by industrial sector. The index measures price movements but also shows average yields, the PE ratios and a measure of total return, ie share price movement and dividend income.

FTSE 250 and FTSE 350 Indices

1.9   (a)   The **FTSE 250 Index** is a weighted arithmetic index of the 250 shares below the top 100 companies in terms of capitalisation.

(b)   The **FTSE 350 Index** is a weighted arithmetical index of the shares in the FTSE 100 and the FTSE 250 Index.

(c)   The idea of these indices is that they give a more accurate indication of the movement in the markets because they monitor performance between the FTSE 100 Index and the FTSE All Share Index.

FTSE techMARK Indices

1.10   FTSE '**techMARK**' covers innovative technology companies. There is a techMARK All-Share Index for all techMARK shares, and a techMARK 100 Index which *excludes* the largest techMARK companies.

FTSE Small Cap Index

1.11   **FTSE Small Cap Index** is comprised of companies with the smallest capitalisation of the capital and industry segments of the All-Share Index. This index represents approximately 2% of the total UK market capitalisation. Again, there is a variant that excludes investment trusts.

1.12   The FTSE Small Cap index is calculated in real time, and a review of constituent companies is now held quarterly.

FTSE Fledgling Index

1.13   The **FTSE Fledgling Index** is made up of around 500 to 600 companies that are smaller in size than those in the FTSE Small Cap Index. The Fledgling Index represents approximately 1% of UK market capitalisation. There is a version of the Fledgling Index that excludes investment trusts.

1.14   The Fledgling Index is calculated at the end of each trading day, and a review of constituent companied is held annually in December.

Other indices

1.15 **FTSE World Indices**. These indices indicate price movements in all the world markets expressed in terms of the local currency of US dollars, yen, deutschmarks and sterling.

1.16 **Dow Jones Industrial Average**. This widely used American index originally started in 1884 and originally included only 11 shares. It later increased to 30 shares. The index is similar to the FT 30 Share Index.

1.17 **Nikkei**. This is the most widely quoted index for the movement of share prices on the Tokyo stock market. This is not a weighted index, so the movement of the price of a small company in the index can affect the index as much as the share movement of the large capitalised company. The index is an average of the prices of 225 shares.

1.18 **DAX**. This is a weighted arithmetical index of 30 companies listed in Germany which includes dividends: therefore it is a **total return index** rather than a **price index**.

1.19 **Hang Seng Index**. This index measures share movement in the Hong Kong market. It is a weighted arithmetic index of the share prices of 33 companies.

Exercise 1

Describe the various indices which are available to monitor the performance of the UK stock market. Which index do you think is the most useful and why?

---

2 TYPES OF ORDINARY SHARE

2.1 **Ordinary shares**

(a) The purchase of an ordinary share in a company gives the investor the right to a dividend, if paid, and the right to see the annual accounts.

(b) Companies quoted on the London Stock Exchange must provide their shareholders with half-yearly results which indicates the size of the interim dividend.

(c) Each voting ordinary share carries one vote and the ordinary shareholder has a right to vote at the annual general meeting. The voting at the annual general meeting is normally to approve the accounts, agree the dividend, elect directors and appoint auditors. The shareholders should also be asked to vote on other significant matters such as a change in share structure.

2.2 **Deferred ordinary shares**. These shares are now rare. They may give the shareholder greater voting rights or rights to a higher dividend. In some cases the shares do not qualify for a dividend until the company's profits have reached a prescribed level or until a particular date.

2.3 **Golden shares**. Following privatisation the government are left with golden shares in some companies. This gives them a casting vote should they need it, for example to stop a take-over. A golden share only lasts for a limited time and most have expired.

2.4 **Partly paid shares**. Partly paid shares became a common theme of the privatisation issues. The shares are paid for in instalments. Paying the instalment is a legal liability and not an option. If the holder does not wish to pay the instalment he should sell the share in the market before the obligation falls due otherwise his entitlement to the share is lost and he is only entitled to a return of his payments to date.

3 NON-VOTING SHARES

3.1 Some companies have two types of shares: O shares and A shares. The O shares have preferential voting rights over the A shares. This type of structure has been used in family controlled companies as a means of raising more cash without losing control. The A shares have **limited or no voting rights** and their market value is usually lower because of their lack of voting rights. It is less usual now for a company to adopt this type of structure, which is frowned upon by some investors because of the restrictions to voting rights.

Exercise 2

(a) What are the rights of an ordinary shareholder?
(b) What types of share may have been issued at the time of a privatisation?

---

4 WARRANTS

4.1 (a) A **warrant** is not a share as such. It is a right for the owner to subscribe for shares in the future at a known price, the subscription or **strike price**. This price will normally be fixed above the current price of the share when the warrant is issued. Let us look at an example.

(b) If the price of the ordinary share is 125p at the time the warrant is issued, the strike price may be fixed at 150p. If the share price has risen to 200p by the time the warrant can be exercised, it obviously makes sense to do this. If the price of the ordinary share is below the warrant price then the warrant is virtually valueless. The warrants have a separate price from the ordinary share and can be dealt in separately.

(c) Warrants carry no voting rights or right to a dividend.

Exercise 3

Compare the rights of an ordinary shareholder with the rights of a warrant holder.

4.2 In Chapter 10, we also discuss **covered warrants.**

5 PREFERENCE AND CONVERTIBLE SHARES

Features

5.1 **Preference shares** form part of the share capital of a company. The share pays a fixed rather than variable amount of dividend and the investor ranks ahead of the ordinary shareholders in the event of a liquidation but after the loan and debenture holders.

Types

5.2 There are a number of types of preference share, as follows.

(a) **Participating preference shares.** The holder of this share stands a chance that if the company does well he will receive his fixed dividend plus an extra dividend.

(b) **Cumulative preference shares.** The company is under no obligation to pay a dividend to its preference shareholders in the same way that it must pay the interest to its debenture or loan stock holders. Thus, if the company does not pay a dividend for a year or more, when it resumes dividend payments those shareholders who hold cumulative preference shares will receive arrears of dividends. These arrears must be paid before the ordinary shareholders can receive their dividend.

(c) **Redeemable preference shares.** Redeemable preference shares have a set redemption date akin to a loan stock but the holder receives dividends, not interest payments.

(d) **Convertible preference shares**

   (i) These shares offer a fixed dividend plus the opportunity to convert to ordinary shares at pre-set dates on pre-set terms.

   (ii) Convertible preference shares normally have a higher market price than the ordinary share of the same company because of the guaranteed dividend and the potential gain on conversion. If the investor does not convert by the last permissible date he forfeits his right.

Exercise 4

What do you think are the advantages of holding a convertible preference share rather than an ordinary share?

---

6 TAX TREATMENT OF SHARES

6.1 The individual who owns shares which are not held within an ISA will pay tax as follows.

(a) **Income tax** will be paid on dividends received. The dividends are paid with a 10% tax credit. There is no further tax to pay for a **basic rate taxpayer** or a **starting rate taxpayer**.

A **non-taxpayer** cannot reclaim the tax credit.

A higher rate taxpayer has a liability to pay another 22.5% tax on the gross dividend.

(b) If the investor makes a **capital gain** on selling shares, it may be subject to capital gains tax.

The calculation for capital gains tax is:

Profit = Proceeds (less sale expenses), less original investment less indexation allowance up to April 1998, less taper relief from April 1998

The profit thus calculated could become subject to capital gains tax if:

   (i) After taking into account the capital gains tax indexation allowance and taper relief, the gain is in excess of the annual exemption (£8,500 for 2005/06), or

   (ii) The gain is below the annual exemption but the investor has already made use of this in other transactions

There are methods of reducing the capital gain.

   (i) The investor may have other capital losses including losses brought forward which could be offset.

   (ii) The investor may consider transferring the holding into a spouse's name prior to sale if the spouse has not used up the annual exemption.

7   FACTORS ASSOCIATED WITH INVESTMENT IN SHARES

Shares as part of a client portfolio

7.1   (a)   Ordinary shares could usually be used in a well spread portfolio for a client who has total investments in excess of, say, £100,000. This would normally give scope, along with deposit and fixed interest investments, to have a portfolio of shares in excess of £50,000. This gives sufficient opportunity to purchase a range of shares in different sectors and thus to spread the risk. Smaller portfolios should incorporate pooled investments such as unit or investment trusts.

(b)   Ordinary shares should only be considered if the client is well aware of the risks associated with individual company share ownership.

(c)   Except for the active share trader, equities should generally only be used for long term investments. Over the short term, losses are more likely and buying and selling costs will be more significant. To avoid excessive exposure to risk from a particular share, equities should normally only form part of a portfolio. A client should always have other assets which can be more easily realisable. Although equities may be sold relatively quickly, the price might be unfavourable at the time funds are required.

(d)   There are certain types of shares which could be used by any client. For example, a cumulative preference share will give a guaranteed rate of dividend and could be useful in the construction of a portfolio for income.

(e)   A well run portfolio of shares could outperform pooled investments (which involve additional charges) and also fixed interest and deposit funds, at least over the longer term.

7.2   All shares carry a risk because there is no guarantee of dividend or of return of capital. However there are degrees of risk and there are ways of defining the risk level.

Assessing the risk of investing in ordinary shares

7.3   The investor needs to take into account the potential growth and profitability of the company in which he will invest. The recent profit of the company and its balance sheet can be checked. He should also check to see if the company will be affected by interest rate or currency changes.

7.4   When considering a company's profit, the investor should be looking at the **operating profit**. A company's operating profit is:

Turnover *less* **Direct costs of production**

If the operating profit is expressed as a percentage of sales, we get the operating margin.

The investor will need to investigate whether the operating margins are improving from year to year, indicating that the company is trading efficiently. If they are not, it is an indication of falling turnover or increasing expenses.

7.5   The investor should compare the operating margins of a number of companies in a particular sector to analyse which is trading most efficiently.

7.6   The investor can take the analysis one stage further by looking at **pre-tax profit**. This takes into account indirect costs such as interest and holding company management costs and is defined as:

Pre-tax profit = Operating profit − Indirect costs

This figure does not mean a great deal on its own but may be interesting if compared with another company in the same trading sector.

7.7 The next stage is to compare profit after tax or **net profit**. The amount of tax which is deducted will vary from company to company depending upon such things as capital expenditure and overseas trading.

Exercise 5

Define:

(a) Operating profit
(b) Pre-tax profit
(c) Net profit

7.8 Once the investor knows the net profit, he can work out the earnings per share. To calculate the **earnings per share** (answer expressed in pence):

Net profit ÷ Number of shares in issue

Thus if a company had 120,000 shares and its net profit was £15,000 the earnings per share would be 125p.

The calculation could be different in a number of situations.

(a) If a company's subsidiary was partly owned by someone else. In this case the minority interests would have to be deducted from the net profit before calculating the earnings per share.

(b) If there are preference dividends to be paid. These dividends must be deducted from net profit before carrying out the calculation.

7.9 The investor may want to know the **net dividend paid per share**. This is calculated as follows.

Dividend paid/number of shares qualifying for the dividend

Thus, if Company X has 120,000 shares qualifying for a dividend and pays a dividend of £12,000, the net dividend paid per share is 10p.

7.10 Now that he knows the net dividend paid per share, the investor can take this a stage further and calculate the dividend yield.

The dividend yield is the relationship between the dividend and the current price of the share. The **dividend yield** is calculated as follows.

$$\frac{\text{Net dividend}}{\text{Share price}} \times 100\%$$

7.11 To make a judgement on the safety of his future dividend flow, an investor could make the following calculation of **dividend cover**.

$$\frac{\text{Earnings per share}}{\text{Net dividend per share}}$$

A low dividend cover implies that a company may be unable to keep up similar dividend payments in the future. If the dividend cover is relatively high, the company is better able to maintain dividends if profits fall.

7.12 The investor must decide whether he wishes to buy a large company 'blue-chip' share which may have a low risk factor and be easily marketable or a small company share which will have a higher risk and potentially higher reward but may be difficult to sell.

7.13 The investor may want to check the company's borrowings. If a company has high borrowing relative to its net assets it is said to be highly **geared**. This may be fine in a period of low interest rates when the money borrowed can be used to make profits and the interest payments on the debt are low. However, if interest rates rise the extra profitability can quickly disappear. These companies carry a higher risk.

7.14 The investor should check the gross yield on the share.

The formula to calculate the **gross yield** is:

$$\frac{\text{Gross dividend per share}}{\text{Share price}} \times 100$$

Thus, if the gross dividend per share is 8% and the price 240p the gross yield is 3.3%. This yield will obviously change with the share price and the dividend. This is not a very satisfactory method of comparing companies because the investor does not know how much the company will pay out in dividends in future years.

7.15 A better measurement for comparing companies is the **price/earnings (P/E) ratio**, sometimes known as the **earnings multiple**. Dividends are not taken into account in this equation. This formula is:

$$\frac{\text{Share price}}{\text{Earnings per share}}$$

This calculation tells the investor how highly the share is priced relative to its earning power.

If a company has a high P/E ratio, this is probably because it is anticipated that the company is likely to produce above average earnings growth. If some misfortune hits the company, the share price will inevitably fall and so too will the P/E ratio.

Exercise 6

(a) What is the formula to calculate a P/E ratio?
(b) What does a low P/E ratio indicate?

7.16 In this section we have looked at various methods of analysing the potential return from a share. We will now summarise this.

(a) If a share has a high yield it may be suitable for a client needing a high level of income but he must remember that there is no guarantee that the dividend will continue at the same level.

(b) A high P/E ratio may indicate that the market are forecasting continued growth.

(c) Companies with high gearing may be an exciting ride but the risk is high!

(d) If the dividend cover is low this may imply that the company will not be able to maintain the current level of dividend.

The Efficient Markets Hypothesis and chartism

7.17 We have looked at some basic principles of some methods of analysing how a share can be valued and forecasting whether it will continue to give good growth and dividends. From these calculations it may be possible to pick a share which is undervalued. This method of selection could be called 'picking winners' and assumes that the investor knows something the market does not and has not yet incorporated into the share price.

7.18 However, there is a theory (the **efficient markets hypothesis**) that the market is very efficient and the price of securities will reflect the market's best estimate of their expected return. So, if this hypothesis is correct, there will be no undervalued securities. In this case, all the investor must decide is the level of risk he wishes to take.

7.19 Another group of professionals who must not be overlooked are the chartists. **Chartism** involves analysing charts and graphs of share price information, spotting past trends and patterns and using them to forecast future movements.

Exercise 7

Describe the points that a potential investor may take into account before purchasing an ordinary share in a public limited company.

Risk involved in investing in special types of share

7.20 (a) **Warrants**

   (i)   If the investor has been given warrants as part of a package deal there is no risk. The investor has not paid for them so even if he never exercises them he has not made a loss.

   (ii) If the investor has paid for the warrants there is a high risk that if the agreed price is too high, it will not be sensible to buy the shares and consequently he will suffer a total loss.

(b) **Preference shares**

   (i)   These shares carry a lower risk than an ordinary share but a higher risk than a loan stock. There is a lower risk than with an ordinary share because the dividend is guaranteed. If the share is a cumulative preference share then the investor knows he will never lose out on his dividend.

   (ii) There is a higher risk than for the holder of a loan stock because, if the company goes into liquidation, the preference shareholders rank after the loan stock holders.

   (iii) The shares carry no voting rights.

(c) **Convertible preference shares.** These shares are a half way house between a fixed interest security and an equity. The share carries a fixed dividend so there is reduced risk but the opportunity of converting to an ordinary share if the price is right at the time.

Exercise 8

List the following type of share in risk order starting with the highest risk category at the top of your list.

(a) Convertible preference share
(b) Ordinary share in a blue-chip company
(c) Redeemable preference share
(d) A warrant
(e) An ordinary share in a company with a low market capitalisation

---

8 CHANGES TO SHARE CAPITAL

8.1 From time to time, companies make changes to their share capital, after agreement from their shareholders. We now discuss a number of situations that may occur.

Share splits

8.2 If the company feels that the price of its shares is too high or there are too few shares on the market, a company may seek to split its shares. To give an extreme illustration, shares in Coca-Cola were first available in 1919, at a price of $40. The same shares today would be worth around $4 million each. Investors would only be able to buy a share if had $4 million to invest. Share splits can be necessary to bring the share price to a more readily marketable figure.

Example

If the current shares of a company have a par value of £1 the company could arrange a four for one split. The investors would each receive four shares for the current one. Each new share would have a par value of 25p. Thus, there would be four times as many shares on the market. The price per share would have dropped and the company would have achieved its objective.

This scheme would have no financial implications for the company, other than the cost of administration. There would be no movement in the real asset value of the company.

8.3 A company could carry out the exact reverse operation. It could reduce the number of shares on the market thus, increasing the price per share. The reason for doing this may be to attempt to raise the status of the company and its share, which may have been treated by the market as highly speculative 'penny shares'.

Rights issues

8.4 (a) Once a company is floated on the stockmarket it can raise further equity by the issue of more shares known as a **rights issue**. The terms 'rights issue' or **'pre-emption rights'** are used because the new shares are offered first to the existing shareholders.

(b) The purpose of the issue is to raise capital, perhaps to facilitate a take-over, for expansion or to refinance debt.

(c) A prospectus will be issued setting out the terms and reasons for the issue. The prospectus will state that the rights issue will be offered to all shareholders on the register of shareholders on a particular day.

(d) The Stock Exchange will adopt a different date as the cut-off date. Shares sold prior to that date will be treated as **'cum rights'** ie with the right to the issue and after that date, **'ex rights'**. This fact will be made clear in the listings of prices in the *Financial Times* and other newspapers by an annotation of xr.

(e) Allotment letters will be issued to shareholders giving them full details. The investor has 21 days to decide whether to accept the rights or sell in nil paid form.

(f) Existing shareholders could be offered, say, two new shares for every five held at a price below the market price. This is not necessarily the bargain it may seem because once the rights issue is completed and the extra shares are on the market the price will most probably fall. The following is a very simple example of what may happen after a rights issue. There are other factors which could affect the price.

Example

Let us say that an investor is offered two new shares for every five he holds. The current market price of the ordinary share is 200p, the price for the new shares 160p.

	£
5 existing shares at 200p	10.00
2 new shares at 160p	3.20
	13.20
Value of one share = £13.20/ 7 =	189p

This means that if an investor does not take up the rights issue the value of his remaining shares will most probably fall. However, he can sell his rights and receive cash in compensation.

(g) The allotment letters are negotiable instruments and can be bought and sold in the market on a 'nil paid' basis. If no action is taken the rights are usually sold on behalf of the shareholder and a cheque would be sent to him for the settlement value.

Bonus issues

8.5 A **bonus (or scrip or capitalisation) issue** is a means by which a company turns part of its reserve into new shares. The company may offer the existing shareholders a one for one scrip offer. Thus a shareholder will receive one extra share for every one he holds at no cost. It is in fact just a book keeping exercise. The market capitalisation of the company remains unaltered. Let us look at an example.

(a) *Existing situation*

	£
Ordinary share capital (20p shares)	100m
Profit and loss account reserve	600m
Revaluation reserve	200m
Capitalisation	900m

(b) The company uses £100m of profit and loss reserve to create 500m new fully paid shares.

(c) New situation

	£
Ordinary share capital (20p shares)	200m
Profit and loss account reserve	500m
Revaluation reserve	200m
Capitalisation	900m

8.6 The effect the scrip issue will have on the price of the share is that, in the example given above, the price will reduce by 50%. The investor now holds two shares, so he has made no loss. However the increased number of shares on the market and the reduced price may make them more marketable.

Scrip dividends

8.7 Some companies give their investors the choice of receiving their dividend in the form of additional shares to the value of the net dividend. This is known as a **scrip dividend**. It is good for both investor and company. The investor receives more shares without incurring dealing costs and the company retains the funds.

8.8 As it is generally attractive to the company to retain funds, a company sometimes offer an enhanced scrip offer in excess of the cash value of the dividend.

Exercise 9

What are the reasons:

(a)   For a company to have a rights issue?
(b)   For a split in shares?
(c)   For a scrip issue?

---

9   METHOD OF PURCHASE AND SALE OF SHARES

9.1   The investor will purchase his shares from the stock market via his broker or online via internet dealing mechanisms. Brokers are linked by computer and telephone. Investors will ask their broker to buy and sell shares and the broker will use either the **Stock Exchange Electronic Trading System (SETS)** or the **Stock Exchange Automated Quotation System (SEAQ)**. In some circumstances the broker may deal **over the counter (OTC)**.

SETS

9.2   Large capitalisation shares are traded on **SETS**. This is an **order-driven** system, unlike **SEAQ** which is **quote-driven**. Investors submit orders to the SETS system via LSE member firms. The information is transmitted electronically and orders are automatically executed where possible. SETS sends out information (orders, transactions, other messages) via a broadcast public feed.

SEAQ

9.3   **SEAQ** operates for trading in smaller company shares and where investors choose not to use SETS for large capitalisation shares.

The market comprises **market makers**, who nominate the shares in which they wish to make a market, and **brokers**. Some brokers are allowed to act in **dual capacity** as market maker and broker. Many large banks operate in this dual capacity.

9.4   *Example of the purchase of shares*

Let us suppose a client, Mr Stone, wishes to buy some shares in BPP Holdings plc. He may approach his stockbroker. If the stockbroker is not a market maker, he will look on his computer screen using Stock Exchange Automated Quotation System.

The SEAQ system will tell him:

(a)   The prices quoted by the market makers
(b)   The number of trades reported above £1,000
(c)   The best bid and offer prices from market makers quoting the price

The stockbroker will then be able to tell Mr Stone the lowest quoted price for BPP shares. If it is only a small deal, the broker can use SEAQ and trade automatically by computer.

The broker will then send Mr Stone a contract note for settlement. Mr Stone will typically have to settle for his BPP shares within three or five days of the deal, although longer settlement periods are possible.

The contract note will contain the following detail.

Name of client
Reference number
Date and tax point

Timing of transaction
Number of shares purchased
Price of security
Total value of purchase
Stamp duty
Commission

Once settlement has been made the purchase will be registered with the company concerned who will issue a certificate and put Mr Stone's name on its register of shareholders.

9.5 The pattern for the sale of a security would be similar to the purchase. Once the deal has been agreed a sale contract note would be issued together with a stock transfer form. The stock transfer form would be completed and returned with the necessary share certificate.

9.6 The main settlement system used is called **CREST (Certificateless Registration of Electronic Stock and Share Transfers)**. The aim of the scheme is to achieve immediate registration of purchase or sale and immediate settlement. Members of CREST will have stock accounts within the system which will be reflected by an entry on the company's register. The fastest settlement, previously five-day settlement ('T + 5'), has now reduced to three-day settlement ('T + 3').

It is advantageous for investors who deal regularly to become members of CREST via a nominee company. Dealing through such a company should result in achieving better prices than via a paper transaction (which is still permitted), swift settlement of trades and no requirements for signed transfer forms or share certificates.

9.7 When describing the system for the purchase of the shares, we mentioned that the client approached his stockbroker to carry out the transaction. He could just as easily have dealt via his bank.

9.8 If a client does deal via a stockbroker there should be clear lines of instruction.

9.9 The stockbroker can deal for the client in one of three ways.

(a) **Execution only dealing service**. In this case the stockbroker simply carries out the client's instructions.

(b) **Advisory or non-discretionary**. In this case the stockbroker makes recommendation but the client makes the final decision.

(c) **Discretionary**. In this case the client will typically have a substantial portfolio. The stockbroker will have authority to buy and sell without reference to the client. However, a carefully worded agreement will lay down the parameters for transactions, for example, the amount of risk the client wishes to take or the types of securities he wishes to consider.

If stockbrokers offer this management service they usually operate via a nominee account. This means that all securities are held in the name of the nominee company rather than the name of the individual client. The client's dividends may also be paid into a nominee bank account, if required. The client still receives the contract notes and is the beneficial owner of the shares. The reason for the nominee account is to speed up transactions because the directors of the nominee company can sign for all transactions rather than the client having to be contacted on all occasions.

Normally the stockbroker would charge an annual management charge for this management service either instead of, or on top of, dealing charges.

Exercise 10

Outline the services offered by a stockbroker to a private client.

---

10   A NEW OFFER OF SHARES

10.1   We will look at how a new company comes to the stock market and offers its shares for sale. There are two main methods: a **placing** and an **offer for sale**.

A placing

10.2   (a)   If the company uses this method, its own stockbroker will offer a certain number of the company shares to its own clients.

(b)   For issues above £25m, shares must be offered to other institutions. With an issue in excess of £50m, 50% of the shares must be offered to other institutions.

An offer for sale

10.3   This method offers a certain number of shares to the general public at a fixed price. The programme of events for such a launch will be as follows.

(a)   Pre-launch publicity will be arranged.

(b)   Pricing and underwriting. The price will have been discussed at great length with the company's bank and broker.

(c)   Underwriting will be arranged. A merchant bank will underwrite the issue. This means that the bank will buy all the shares on offer for a commission should the general public not want them. The underwriters usually spread the underwriting risk amongst a number of fund managers (sub-underwriters).

(d)   The prospectus will be issued giving details of the company, the directors and the financial prospects for the company. The prospectus must comply with the terms of the Companies Acts. The prospectus will include the fixed price for shares. Sometimes the offer is made on a tender basis and the minimum tender is recorded in the prospectus. The prospectus will include an application form which the applicant must complete and return with a cheque.

(e)   Advertising. The offer will then be advertised in leading newspapers. The advertisement will include an application form.

(f)   Subscriptions will then be received. When all the applications have been received the offer will either be under or over subscribed.

(g)   If the offer has been made on a tender basis the company, aided by its advisers, will fix a single pricing figure and those applying with a price equal or above will receive an allotment of shares. The price will be pitched at such a level that all the shares will be sold but an active market can be maintained.

(h)   Letters of acceptance will be sent out.

(i)   First dealing in the shares will commence.

Offers for sale are expensive to arrange. Therefore this is only a suitable method for large companies raising significant funds. The placing is more suitable for small companies.

Exercise 11

What sort of companies may bring their shares to the market via an offer for sale?

Why is it expensive?

11 COST OF INVESTING IN SHARES

11.1 The costs of investing in shares are as follows.

(a) **Purchase cost**. The purchase cost or spread is the difference between the bid and offer price of the share. This is the market maker's spread and could be say 2% for a liquid share or up to 5% for a less easily traded share.

(b) **The broker's commission**. This could be say 1.5% on a deal up to £7,000 with a minimum charge of £25. Execution only services, including online brokers, are generally cheaper than this.

(c) **Stamp Duty and SDRT**. 0.5% Stamp Duty Reserve Tax (SDRT) is payable on the amount of **purchases** of UK equities settled through CREST, rounded up to the nearest 1 penny. 0.5% Stamp Duty is payable on purchases of UK equities not settled through CREST, rounded up to the nearest £5. Stamp duty on stock registered in Ireland is charged at 1%.

(d) **Panel of Takeovers and Mergers Levy**. The PTM levy is a flat £1 on either sales or purchases in excess of £10,000.

11.2 Below is an example of the cost of the purchase and sale of securities, to the value of £10,001 in each case.

Cost of purchase

	£
Shares	10,001
Brokerage commission 1.5%	150
SDRT at 0.5%	50
PTM levy	1
Total cost	10,202

Cost of sale

	£
Shares	10,001
Brokerage commission 1.5%	150
PTM levy	1
Total cost	10,152

12 SHARE OPTION SCHEMES

12.1 Share schemes are provided so that directors and senior employees can invest in the company and participate in the financial success towards which they are contributing. Such schemes are an increasingly important part of the remuneration package of key executives.

12.2 The general position is that if a director or an employee is granted an **option** to acquire **shares**, then when he exercises it there is a charge as specific **employment income** on the market value of the shares minus the sum of what he paid for the option and what he paid for the shares. If he assigns or releases the option for money, or agrees (for money) not to exercise it or to grant someone else a right to acquire the shares, he is likewise taxable on the amount he gets minus the amount he paid for the option.

12.3 In general, there is no income tax charge on the **grant** of an option. However, for options granted up to 1 September 2003, if the option could be exercised more than ten years after grant, there was a specific employment income charge at the time of grant. The charge was on the market value of the shares that could be acquired at the time of the grant minus the sum of what the director or employee paid for the option and what he would have to pay for the shares (taking the lowest price at which he could acquire the shares). Any amount taxable under this rule is deducted from the amount taxable on any later specific employment income charge in relation to the same option.

12.4 National insurance contributions are payable by both an employee and employer when gains are realised on the exercise of an **unapproved share option** and where the shares are readily convertible into cash. The employer and employee may agree that the employee should bear the employer's NICs, as well as his own. In this case the amount of employer NIC paid by the employee can be deducted from the taxable gain arising on the exercise of the option.

12.5 Successive governments have recognised the need to encourage schemes that broaden share ownership among employees or reward personnel. A number of special tax efficient **approved** schemes exist, such as those explained below.

Employee share ownership trusts (ESOTs)

12.6 ESOTs enable shares to be distributed to employees through a specially established trust. This scheme is similar to a profit sharing scheme but is wider in scope and does not have a restriction on the value of shares that may be distributed. Shares must be distributed to employees within a maximum of 20 years of their acquisition by the trust. Broadly, all employees (except part-time directors, who must be excluded) must be eligible on similar terms.

12.7 The trust established by the ESOT can receive funds to buy shares from a number of sources, principally from the company establishing the ESOT (the founding company), from subsidiaries of the founding company and by borrowing.

12.8 The shares can be transferred to employees exercising options under savings-related share option schemes (see below). The shares can also be transferred by the trustees to an all employee share plan (see below) without a chargeable event occurring.

Savings-related share option schemes

12.9 An employer can set up a scheme, under which employees can choose to make regular monthly investments in special 'Save As You Earn' bank or building society accounts called **Sharesave accounts**. Employees can save a fixed monthly amount of between £5 and £250. The investments are made for three or five years, and a tax-free bonus is then added to the account by way of interest. The employee may either withdraw the money or leave it for another two years. If he leaves it in the account, another tax-free bonus is added.

12.10 At the withdrawal date, the employee may take the money in cash. Alternatively, he may use it to buy ordinary shares in his employer company or its holding company. The price of these shares is fixed when the employee starts to save in the account, by granting the employee options to buy shares. The option price must be at least 80% of the market value at the date the options are granted.

12.11 The only tax charge is to capital gains tax, on the gain on the shares when they are finally sold. This gain is computed as if the employee bought the shares for the price he actually paid for them.

12.12 A scheme must be open to all employees and full-time directors, and on similar terms. Part-time directors may be included, but can be excluded. However, a minimum qualifying period of employment (of up to five years) may be imposed, and there may be differences based on remuneration or length of service.

12.13 Anyone who has within the preceding 12 months held over 25% of the shares of a close company which is the company whose shares may be acquired under the scheme, or which controls that company either alone or as part of a consortium, must be excluded from the scheme.

Company share option plans (CSOPs)

12.14 An employee can be granted options on shares under a CSOP. There is no income tax on the grant of an option, on the profit arising from the exercise of an option between three and ten years after the grant or on the disposal of the shares. Capital gains tax will, however, arise on the gain made when an employee eventually sells his shares.

12.15 To obtain HMRC approval, schemes must satisfy the following conditions.

(a) The shares must be fully paid ordinary shares.

(b) The price of the shares must not be less than their market value at the time of the grant of the option.

(c) Participation in the scheme must be limited to employees and full-time directors. Options must not be transferable. However, ex-employees and the personal representatives of deceased employees may exercise options; personal representatives must do so within one year after the death. The scheme need not be open to all employees and full-time directors.

(d) No options may be granted which take the total market value of shares for which an employee holds options above £30,000. Shares are valued as at the times when the options on them are granted.

(e) If the issuing company has more than one class of shares, the majority of shares in the class for which the scheme operates must be held other than by:

(i) Persons acquiring them through their positions as directors or employees (unless the company is an employee controlled company)

(ii) A holding company (unless the scheme shares are quoted)

(f) Anyone who has within the preceding 12 months held over 10% of the shares of a close company which is the company whose shares may be acquired under the scheme, or which controls that company either alone or as part of a consortium, must be excluded from the scheme.

12.16 The tax exemption is lost in respect of an option if it is exercised earlier than three years or later than ten years after grant, or within three years after the employee last exercised an option on which the tax exemption was obtained. However, neither of these three year waiting periods need be observed when personal representatives exercise the options of a deceased employee (but the ten year rule still applies).

12.17 Schemes may be altered so that in the event of the company concerned being taken over, employees may exchange their existing options for equivalent options over shares in the acquiring company.

12.18 The costs of setting up approved share option schemes (both savings related and company share option plans) are deductible in the same way as the costs of setting up profit sharing schemes, and with the same nine month rule (see above).

Share Incentive Plans (SIPs)

12.19 Employers can give up to £3,000 of 'free shares' a year to employees with no tax or NICs through a **Share Incentive Plan.** These were previously called All-Employee Share Ownership Plans (AESOPs).

12.20 Employees can buy **partnership shares** with their pre-tax salary up to:

(a) Maximum of 10% of gross earnings, subject to an upper limit of £1,500 per tax year

(b) Maximum monthly contributions of £125

(c) Any minimum monthly contributions as specified in the plan but this minimum cannot be more than £10.

Purchases do not affect pension contribution limits. Employers can give up to two free 'matching shares' for each partnership share purchased. The matching shares, up to a maximum of £3,000, are in addition to the £3,000 of free shares and must be provided on the same basis for all employees.

Chapter roundup

In this chapter we have studied:

- The main characteristics of shares
- The features of different types of share
- Methods of measuring investment returns
- New issues of shares
- Broker services, methods and charges of dealing via a stockbroker
- The main UK and overseas indices
- Share option and employee share ownership scheme hange traded funds

Quick Quiz

1   What do the letters SEAQ stand for?
2   How much is the Panel of Takeover and Mergers levy?
3   What do the letters CREST stand for?
4   Name two methods of changing the share capital of a company.
5   Does a preference share carry a higher or lower risk than an ordinary share?
6   Is a warrant a share?
7   How do you calculate the gross yield on a share?
8   What is the implication of a high dividend cover?
9   Name three types of preference share.
10 What would the letters xr mean after a share price listing?
11 What would the letter A after the name of a share indicate?
12 What is the maximum monthly saving an individual can pay into a Sharesave scheme?

The answers to the questions in the Quick Quiz can be found at the end of this Study Text. Before checking your own answers against them, you should look back at this chapter and use the information in it to correct your answers.

Answers to exercises

1   The main indices measuring the performance of the UK stock market are as follows.

(a)   *FTSE All Share Index* - This index monitors the performance of around 700 shares and is broken down in industrial sectors.

(b)   *FTSE 100 Index* - This index is a weighted arithmetic index of the top 100 companies in terms of capitalisation. Each company is weighted according to its market value.

(c)   *FTSE Mid 250 Index* - This index is a weighted arithmetic index of the 250 shares below the top 100 companies.

(d)   *FTSE 350 Index* - This index is a weighted arithmetic index of the shares in the FTSE 100 and the FTSE mid 250.

Each index provides different information and which index will be the most useful for your purposes depends on the information you require. However, if you want a good idea about the performance of the market as a whole, the FT Actuaries All Share Index is probably the most useful because it monitors the performance of more companies and the information is broken down into industrial sectors, which is useful for comparison purposes.

2   (a)   The rights of an ordinary shareholder are as follows.

(i)   The right to vote at the AGM
(ii)   The right to a dividend if one is paid
(iii) The right to vote on significant changes to the share structure of the company

(b)   Partly-paid shares were often issued at the time of a privatisation.

3   The warrant carries no voting rights or rights to dividend. See the answer to Exercise 2 on the rights of an ordinary shareholder.

4   The convertible preference share offers a fixed dividend plus the opportunity to share in the equity of the company at a later date if the price is right. The ordinary shareholder has no idea of the size of the dividend from year to year and in fact there is no guarantee that one will be paid.

5   (a)   *Operating profit* - The profit made by a company as a result of its trading activity. The profit is arrived at after deducting the direct costs of production.

(b)   *Pre-tax profit* -This is operating profit less indirect costs but before the deduction of corporation tax.

(c)   *Net profit* - Profit less taxation.

6   (a)   The formula to calculate a P/E ratio is:

$$\frac{\text{Share price}}{\text{Earnings per share}}$$

(b)   A low P/E ratio indicates poor performance and poor earnings potential.

7   A potential shareholder may take into account the following points before buying a share.

(a)   Potential growth and profitability of the chosen company
(b)   Operating profit, pre-tax profit and net profit
(c)   P/E ratio of the share
(d)   Dividend yield and dividend cover
(e)   He should check the company's borrowings to make sure it is not too highly geared

8   Listing from highest to lowest risk:

(a)   Warrant
(b)   Ordinary share in a company with low market capitalisation
(c)   Ordinary share in a blue-chip company
(d)   Convertible preference share
(e)   Redeemable preference share

9   (a)   A company will have a rights issue to raise further equity.

(b)   A company may split its shares if there are not that many on the market (to increase liquidity) and the price per individual share is high.

(c)   A company may have a scrip issue as a means of turning some of its reserve into new shares.

10   A broker offers the following services to a private individual.

(a)   A dealing service
(b)   Advisory or non-discretionary service
(c)   A full discretionary service

11   An offer for sale will only be used by a large company as a means of bringing its shares to the market. The reason is that it is very expensive because of the costs of publicity, a prospectus, advertising, etc.

PRACTICE QUESTION 6: EQUITIES (30 Marks)

27 mins

Mrs Jones holds £10,000 nominal of Treasury 9.5% 2010 and 10,000 25p J Sainsbury plc shares. The Financial Times gives the following information.

	Price	*Interest yield*	*Yield*	*Redemption yield*	*P/E*
Treasury 9.5% 2010	98	9.69		10.37	
J Sainsbury plc	381		3.9		12.7

(a) Calculate the current value of Mrs Jones's holdings. (5 marks)

(b) Explain 'interest yield', 'redemption yield' and 'yield'. (15 marks)

(c) How much income is Mrs Jones likely to obtain from these investments, is it guaranteed and how will it be taxed? (10 marks)

The answer to the practice question can be found at the end of this Study Text

Chapter 8

INDIVIDUAL SAVINGS ACCOUNTS AND PERSONAL EQUITY PLANS

Chapter topic list	Syllabus reference
1　ISAs	2.4
2　PEPs	2.4

Introduction

In this chapter we examine the different types of Individual Savings Account and Personal Equity Plan. We will look at their individual features, tax treatment, charging structure, pricing, methods of purchase and sale and their uses in the construction of an investment portfolio.

1　ISAS

Individual Savings Accounts

1.1　An ISA is an **Individual Savings Account,** a form of tax-efficient savings plan. ISAs came into existence from 6 April 1999, as a replacement for Personal Equity Plans (PEPs) and TESSAs. The Government has indicated that ISAs are to be available until April 2010, at least. An **ISA manager** must have HMRC approval.

Eligible ISA investors

1.2　An eligible ISA investor is anyone who:

- Is aged **18 or over,** or **aged 16 or over in the case of a cash ISA**

- Is resident and ordinarily resident in the UK for tax purposes, or is a Crown employee working abroad and subject to UK tax on earnings, and

- Has not subscribed to any maxi ISA, or any mini ISA of the same type as is to be applied for, in the same tax year

1.3　If the ISA holder ceases to be resident and ordinarily resident in the UK, the ISA can remain open and retain the UK tax benefits, but no new contributions can be made. There may be tax to pay in the foreign jurisdiction to which the investor emigrates. It is not possible to hold an ISA jointly or as a trustee for someone else.

Types of ISA

1.4 There are (since April 2005) **two** types of 'component' in an ISA, namely **cash** and 'stocks and shares'. An ISA may offer both components (a '**maxi ISA**') or just one of them (a '**mini ISA**'). Separate **mini ISAs** (one for each component) may be taken out during each tax year, or a maxi ISA may be taken out, but a mini ISA and a maxi ISA cannot be taken out in the same year.

1.5 From 6 April 2005, the separate **insurance component** was abolished and that component was merged with the stocks and shares component. From 6 April 2005, the stocks and shares component is able to hold eligible life insurance products and **medium-term stakeholder products** (explained further below).

1.6 A **TESSA-only ISA (TOISA)** could only accept a cash component and this had to be from the capital proceeds (not the interest) from a maturing TESSA (Tax Exempt Special Savings Account). TESSAs no longer exist, and the last possible date for transfers from maturing TESSAs into a TOISA passed in October 2004. Therefore, all existing TOISAs have already received the transfer-in of funds from the TESSA.

1.7 **CAT (Charges, Access, Terms) standards** are **withdrawn** for **new ISAs**, with effect **from 6 April 2005**. Existing CAT standard ISAs will continue to operate under the same terms. However, providers will no longer be able to market ISA products using the CAT standard. The CAT standards have been withdrawn for ISAs because of the introduction of the new range of **risk-controlled stakeholder** products available from 6 April 2005.

ISA investment limits

1.8 The annual ISA contribution limits are summarised in the Table below. The limits for the tax year **2005/06** are expected to apply unchanged until 5 April 2010.

	ISA component	2005/06 to 2009/10 annual limit
Mini ISA	Cash only	£3,000
	Stocks and shares only	£4,000
Maxi ISA	Cash component	£3,000
	Stocks and shares component	£7,000 *less* amount invested in cash component

1.9 Once funds are withdrawn from an ISA, they cannot be paid back in without counting as a new subscription. The ISA subscription limits apply to the total **payments in** to the account during the tax year.

1.10 Shares acquired from an approved profit-share scheme, share incentive plan or all-employee share option scheme may be **transferred directly** into the stocks and shares component of a maxi ISA or a stocks and shares mini ISA. The value of the shares at the date of transfer will count towards the normal stocks and shares annual limit. They must be transferred within 90 days of the exercise of the option or release from the profit-sharing scheme.

1.11 Other subscriptions to ISA managers must generally be in the form of cash rather than, for instance, by means of existing shares. (If an investor wants to continue to hold shares he or

143

she currently holds, but within the ISA wrapper, it is necessary to sell the shares, and then re-purchase within the ISA. This will normally incur dealing costs, although some providers may waive some of the costs.) Subscriptions can be either lump sum or via regular savings schemes.

Cash component

1.12   The following can be included in the **cash component** of a maxi ISA or a cash mini ISA.

(a)   Cash deposited with building societies, credit unions and UK or European banks. Such accounts will have interest credited gross.

(b)   Units in a money market fund holding cash deposits, or in a qualifying 'fund or funds' which invests solely in money market funds

(c)   Funds and (from 6 April 2005) life insurance and stakeholder products qualifying for the cash component by passing the '5% test' – see below

(d)   The National Savings & Investments cash mini ISA

Stocks and shares component

1.13   The following may be held in the stocks and shares component of an ISA.

(a)   **Shares** issued by a company (other than an investment trust or fund - see below for rules on collective investment schemes) which are listed on a recognised stock exchange. (Shares on the Alternative Investment Market (**AIM**) **cannot** be held in an ISA.)

(b)   **Corporate bonds** issued by a company incorporated anywhere in the world, with a residual term of at least five years when first held in the ISA. Either the securities themselves must be listed or the company issuing them must be listed. The bonds may be:

- Debentures/loan stocks
- Permanent Interest Bearing Shares/Perpetual Subordinated Bonds
- Convertibles
- Zero coupon/deep discount bonds
- Loan notes

(c)   **Gilts and government bonds**, including strips, from any country in the European Economic Area (EU plus Norway, Iceland and Liechtenstein) with a minimum residual term of five years when first held in the ISA.

(d)   UK authorised **unit trusts and OEICs**. Money market funds, futures and options funds, geared futures and options funds, property funds and feeder funds are specifically excluded.

(e)   Shares in UK-listed **investment trusts** that do not have any property income.

(f)   Shares acquired from an **approved profit-share scheme, share incentive plan** or **all-employee share option scheme**, if transferred within 90 days of the exercise of the option or release from the profit-sharing scheme.

(g)   From **6 April 2005**, medium-term **stakeholder products** and **life assurance products** qualifying for the stocks and shares component under the 5% test.

(h) **Cash**, but only **for the purposes of investing** in qualifying 'stocks and shares' (interest received on cash within the 'stocks and shares' component being subject to a 20% charge).

Stakeholder products and the 5% test

1.14 From 6 April 2005, expanded ranges of risk-controlled **'stakeholder' products**, which can be sold with a **simplified advice regime,** have become available. Some of these can be held in ISAs.

1.15 Medium-term stakeholder products and life assurance products are permitted in the stocks and shares component. To qualify, these products must be similar to equity investments (shares) rather than cash investments.

1.16 The **5% test** is applied to decide whether a **fund** or **stakeholder or life assurance product** is more like a cash investment (qualifying for the **cash component**) or like an equity investment (qualifying for the **stocks and shares component**).

- Investments guaranteeing a return of at least 95% of the original capital invested qualify for the cash component
- Others qualify for the stocks and shares component of an ISA or PEP

1.17 **Collective investment schemes** and **linked long-term funds** meeting stakeholder requirements must be single-priced. They must have no more than 60% of their value in listed equities, and must be appropriately diversified.

ISA tax advantages

1.18 Income received from investments in an ISA is free of income tax. (But see below regarding interest on cash.) The 10% tax credit attached to UK dividends on shares held within an ISA cannot be reclaimed.

1.19 There is a tax credit of 20% reclaimable on bond interest paid in the stocks and shares component of an ISA or an insurance ISA.

1.20 **Interest** in the **cash component** of an ISA is tax-free. Interest paid on cash held temporarily in a **stocks and shares** or **insurance** ISA component is subject to a flat rate 20% charge before being credited to the account, but higher rate taxpayers will suffer no further liability to income tax.

1.21 Disposal of ISA investments is **exempt from capital gains tax**. However, the other side of the coin is that there is no allowance for ISA losses to be offset against gains made elsewhere.

1.22 There is **no minimum holding period** to obtain the tax advantages. There is **no requirement to declare** ISA income or capital gains on a tax return to HMRC.

1.23 The tax advantages of stocks and shares ISAs are less attractive now that tax credits on dividends can no longer be reclaimed. The main tax advantages of such ISAs are for:

- Higher rate taxpayers, who are liable to additional tax on dividends received outside the tax-advantaged ISA wrapper

- Those whose capital gains exceed, or would otherwise exceed, the annual CGT allowance. (Remember that such people will include some basic rate taxpayers, as well as some higher rate taxpayers.)

Transfers between ISA managers

1.24 ISA managers are required to allow transfers, although a manager is not required to accept a transfer in. The investor may transfer an ISA to a different manager in the year of subscription, but then the entire ISA subscription for that year must be transferred. After the first year, partial (or full) transfers between ISA managers are permitted.

1.25 Securities within the ISA can be re-registered in the new manager's name. They do not have to be sold and re-purchased. If a manager returns ISA proceeds to the investor, this will be treated as a withdrawal.

1.26 Transfers between different investment components are not allowed at any time. It is not possible to transfer individual investments between a maxi ISA and a mini ISA or *vice versa*. However, an ISA from previous years' subscriptions can be transferred to a different type of ISA. For example, a maxi ISA can be transferred to a mini or maxi ISA, or *vice versa*. The component parts of the ISA must retain their identity after transfer.

1.27 No transfers are allowed between a Personal Equity Plan and an Individual Savings Account (ISA).

ISA types

1.28 The following are types of ISA.

- **Self-select ISAs.** The investor selects his own equity or bond investments, generally on an execution-only basis. There is likely to be a periodic charge made by the Plan Manager, but dealing costs are likely to be similar to those for trading securities outside an ISA.

- **Managed ISAs.** A stockbroker may use an ISA as the wrapper for part of a larger equity portfolio, principally to take advantage of the capital gains tax exemption.

- **Unit trust and OEIC/ICVC ISAs.** ISAs are a popular means of investing in unit trusts and Open Ended Investment Companies. High yield bond funds have proved particularly popular. There is now often a wide choice of funds available from which the investor might choose one or more for the ISA. Additionally, ISAs may be invested in any UCITS that has FSA recognition.

- **Investment trust ISAs.** There is a narrower choice of investment trusts than unit trusts / OEICs, but many groups offer investment trust ISAs. There may be management charges in addition to those levied within the trust itself, to pay for administration of the ISA wrapper. Of course, it is possible to invest in unit trusts, OEICs and investment trusts within the same ISA, if the Manager permits it.

- **Corporate ISAs.** Some listed companies offer ISAs for investment in their own shares. The ISA will normally be administered by external managers. Charges may be kept low by a subsidy from the company concerned, to reflect the costs that would otherwise be incurred on registration of individual shareholdings.

- **'Guaranteed' ISAs.** Some ISAs 'guarantee' a stockmarket index-linked return at the end of a specified period. These ISAs are generally based on funds holding derivatives and cash deposits.

- **Cash ISAs.** Various instant access and term accounts are available. Particularly in the case of TOISAs, some offer a stockmarket index-linked return instead of a return linked to interest rates.

Exercise 1

List the main differences between an equity and corporate bond fund.

Charges

1.29 The following charges may apply to ISAs.

(a) **Unit trust and OEIC/ICVC** funds held in ISAs may carry initial charges of up to 5%, but commonly this charge is discounted, down to zero in some cases.

(b) **Investment trust** ISAs may carry a management charge in addition to the charges internal to the trust.

(c) Charges on **direct investments** in an ISA may be paid to the manager separately from and on top of the ISA subscription. Dealing commissions and stamp duty must come out of the invested subscriptions.

(d) **Annual charges** of 0.5% to 1.5% of the fund value are typical. Some managers make a fixed charge, for example £25 plus VAT per half year, irrespective of the value of the investments.

(e) There may be a charge on **termination** or on **transfer** of the ISA.

(f) Purchase and sale of shares, including shares in investment trusts, will generally incur **broker's commission**, which may be at a percentage rate, possibly with a minimum and maximum charge per deal, or it may be at a fixed rate per deal.

(g) There are charges for **dividend collection** in some self-select ISAs.

(h) Many managers levy a charge if holders of ISAs with direct shareholdings wish to receive copies of **annual reports** via the manager or want to vote in or attend shareholders' meetings.

2 PEPS

2.1 **Personal equity plans (PEPs)** were introduced in 1986 to encourage investment in UK quoted companies. Subsequent amendments to the legislation increased the subscription levels and extended greatly the number of qualifying investment that could be held within the plan.

2.2 The Finance Act 1998 announced that from 6 April 1999, **no new investment** in PEPs would be possible. However, any PEPs in existence at 5 April 1999 generally retain their tax-free status indefinitely. In addition, transfers can continue to be made between approved PEP managers. It is possible to transfer part of a PEP (as well as the whole of a PEP) to another manager.

2.3   Any individual, aged 18 or over, who was resident and ordinarily resident in the UK, could invest up to £6,000 (by lump sum or instalments) per tax year in a general PEP. In addition, he could invest up to £3,000 per tax year in a single company PEP, which invests only in the shares of one company. Since 6 April 2001, there has been no distinction between general and single company PEPs and existing holdings can be merged.

Eligible PEP investments

2.4   Since 6 April 2001, the rules on qualifying investments have been aligned with those for ISAs. So, an existing PEP can be used to hold equities, unit trusts, OEICs/ICVCs, permitted government stocks and corporate bonds. As with ISAs, 'self-select' PEPs are available.

PEP tax reliefs

2.5   Provided that a PEP meets all the necessary conditions, the investor is entitled to the following **reliefs on gains and income** arising from a PEP. These are the same as for ISAs, except in respect of interest paid on cash (see later below).

   • All capital gains on disposals are free of tax.
   • All withdrawals of capital are free of capital gains tax.

2.6   All dividends and interest payments are exempt from further income tax. The 10% tax credit on dividends cannot be reclaimed. The tax reliefs will continue to apply if a UK-resident PEP holder becomes **non-UK resident**. Disposals of PEP assets at a loss do not give rise to allowable losses for capital gains tax purposes.

2.7   As with ISAs, PEPs can be advantageous to those who expect to have fully used their annual capital gains tax exemption, and to higher rate taxpayers, who have to pay additional tax on dividends received outside PEPs and ISAs.

2.8   The rule on **interest paid** on cash held in **PEPs** is different from the rule for **ISAs**. Interest on cash in a PEP is credited without deduction of tax. The investor may withdraw up to £180 in interest each year without a tax charge. If this limit is exceeded, all of the interest is taxable at 20%. However, this is unlikely to occur in practice as proceeds of share sales can normally be withdrawn ahead of interest income.

2.9   Cash is only allowed to be held for re-investment purposes, and the PEP manager should check that uninvested cash is not being held for excessive periods. On the **death of the investor,** the PEP ceases to be exempt from tax as from the date of death. The account must be encashed and forms part of the deceased's estate.

Exercise 2

Can PEP funds be transferred into an ISA, or will they need to be kept separate?

Chapter roundup

In this chapter we have studied:

- Tax benefits of PEPs and ISAs

- Eligibility rules for PEPs and ISAs

- Different types of PEP and ISAs

- Use of different types of PEP funds and ISAs

Quick Quiz

1   What is the maximum amount which can be invested in the stocks and shares element a maxi-ISA in 2005/2006?

2   What is the normal tax treatment of interest received on cash held in:

   (a)   A cash mini-ISA
   (b)   A stocks and shares ISA
   (c)   An existing PEP?

3   Can transfers be made between PEP managers?

4   What are the minimum ages for investing in ISAs?

The answers to the questions in the quiz can be found at the end of this Study Text. Before checking your own answers against them, you should look back at this chapter and use the information in it to correct your answers.

Answers to exercises

1   The main differences between a corporate bond and an equity fund are as follows.

    (a)   Risk - the equity fund caries a higher risk because the underlying investment of the fund is shares as opposed to the corporate bond fund, which is loans.

    (b)   Income - The corporate bond fund will be capable of producing a higher income. Some schemes have been designed using corporate bonds to create a guaranteed income, which cannot be achieved with an equity fund.

2   Funds in PEPs cannot be transferred directly into ISAs.

PRACTICE QUESTION 7: ISAS (30 Marks)   *27 mins*

(a)   (i)   Explain why an ISA could be an advantageous investment for a higher rate taxpayer.

                                                                           (6 marks)

      (ii)   Explain the maximum amount which such an investor and their spouse could invest in stocks and shares within ISAs.

                                                                                     (2 marks)

      (iii) Describe the type of ISA which may appeal to him if the investor is prepared to take a medium to high risks. (7 marks)

(b)   Outline the eligibility and subscription rules for ISAs.   (15 marks)

The answer to the practice question can be found at the end of this Study Text

Chapter 9

OFFSHORE FUNDS

Chapter topic list	Syllabus reference
1 Introduction to offshore funds	2.6
2 Offshore pooled investments	2.6
3 Offshore bonds	2.6
4 Direct investment in overseas equities and foreign bonds	2.6

Introduction

In this chapter we examine the different type of offshore funds. We will look at their individual features, tax treatment, charging structure, pricing, method of purchase and sale and their uses in the construction of an investment portfolio.

1   INTRODUCTION TO OFFSHORE FUNDS

1.1   The term 'offshore fund' refers to funds run from such places as the Channel Islands, the Isle of Man, the Cayman Islands, Hong Kong and Bermuda where the funds are not subject to the UK tax regime. Many offshore funds are run by companies associated with large UK unit trust groups and most of the countries mentioned above now have their own regulatory framework.

1.2   Many UK resident investors are attracted to offshore investments because they understand that there is an opportunity for almost gross roll up on their investments. Since 1979 when exchange controls were abolished, it has been easy for the UK resident to invest his money abroad in investments such as equities, bonds and OEICs. For UK residents, investment in offshore funds may be not be as advantageous as they may imagine, particularly from a tax point of view. Offshore funds can however be of advantage for the UK non-resident or the UK non-domiciled investor.

2   OFFSHORE POOLED INVESTMENTS

2.1   S 238(1) of the Financial Services and Markets Act 2000 (FSMA 2000) prohibits any authorised person from promoting any collective investment scheme to the general public in the UK unless it is an authorised unit trust, an authorised OIEC, or a recognised scheme. The Financial Services Authority recognises the following offshore pooled investment.

(a)   Funds categorised as **Undertakings for Collective Investments in Transferable Securities (UCITS)** are constituted in European Economic Area member states. These funds are automatically recognised by the Financial Services Authority and can be marketed freely in the UK.

(b) **Funds authorised in designated territories**, that is non-EU territories such as the Channel Islands, Bermuda and the Isle of Man. These funds may not be automatically recognised by the FSA. However, the FSA recognises that certain countries in which investments are based offer a similar regulatory authority and investor protection to that afforded to the UK investor onshore. These regulatory authorities are as follows.

Bermuda	Bermuda Monetary Authority
Guernsey	Financial Services Commission
Isle of Man	Financial Supervision Commission
Jersey	Financial Services Department

(c) **Individually recognised overseas schemes funds**. The FSA also provides for the recognition of overseas schemes on an individual basis.

2.2 **Non-regulated and non-recognised funds** are subject to severe marketing restrictions in the UK. Prospectuses and details can only be forwarded to investment professionals such as stockbrokers and Independent Financial Advisers (IFAs).

Exercise 1

List the three types of recognised collective investment.

Open Ended Investment Companies (OIECs)

2.3 (a) OEICs are the most common form of pooled investment in Europe.

(b) The attraction of the OEIC is that it can issue any number of types of shares. It is thus 'open-ended', because the total amount invested in the scheme can be increased.

(c) The ability to offer a wide number of types of shares has led to the concept of umbrella funds. In this instance there are many types of share under one management (the umbrella). Each share can invest in a different international sector.

(d) There is a wider range of funds offered to the investor through an offshore OEIC than an onshore unit or investment trust. The funds include UK Equity, International Equity, International Emerging Markets, International Managed, America, Europe, Japan, Latin America, India, Korea, Hong Kong, Australia, Commodities and Currency funds (in all the major currencies) and fixed interest funds (in all the leading currencies: eg yen, sterling, euro, US$).

UCITS

2.4 (a) **UCITS** are not a separate type of investment, but a classification of existing investments such as OEICs which can be marketed freely across EU borders.

(b) UCITS were created as a result of the UCITS Directive introduced by the Council for the European Communities on 20 December 1985 (updated by UCITS II). The idea of the directive was that it would introduce a framework under which a fund management group could market a fund domiciled within one member state to investors resident in another member state.

(c) Under the framework, a manager of a mutual fund certified as a UCITS in its country of domicile may not be refused permission to market the fund in another member state provided it complies with local marketing requirements.

The Directive covers:

(i)   Funds situated in the territory of a EU member state

(ii)   Publicly offered funds

(iii)   Funds investing in transferable securities (usually shares and bonds listed on a stock exchange or traded on a regulated market)

(iv)   Funds whose units can be redeemed at the request of the holder

The directive does not include:

(i)   Closed-ended funds
(ii)   Property funds
(iii)   Feeder funds
(iv)   Money market funds (except in France and Spain)

(d) **Operation of the Directive**. A fund is authorised by the regulatory authority of its domicile and it is granted a UCITS certificate. Application is then made to the regulatory authority of other member states in which the provider wishes to market the fund. After two months the fund may be marketed.

Exercise 2

What is the meaning of the following expressions?

(a)   OEICS
(b)   UCITS
(c)   Single pricing
(d)   Umbrella fund

Underlying funds of offshore pooled investments

2.5   As discussed above, there are a wide number of funds available to the investor in an offshore umbrella type fund. It is possible to invest in any of the major currencies. We will comment on the funds most frequently used by investors.

(a) **Equity funds**. The equity funds most commonly used are overseas funds such as North America, Japan and the Far East. Offshore funds often offer a better choice of individual country funds such as Korea or India.

(b) **Fixed interest**. Many UK investors, particularly non-taxpayers, may find offshore fixed interest funds attractive. The funds can be denominated in various currencies. The funds invest in bond markets across the world in both government and corporate stocks. Most bonds can be purchased by the fund to secure a yield free of tax eg. The investor can receive a high yield paid gross.

(c) **Currencies**. It is impossible to invest onshore in a currency fund. So offshore funds of this nature are popular. The funds give the international investor a method of investing in professionally managed currency funds at relatively low costs. In many instances an umbrella fund is used with many sub-shares being issued for all the different currencies.

Taxation

Taxation of offshore funds

2.6   In general terms there will be no tax paid by an offshore fund. However, there may be some withholding tax which may not be reclaimable by the fund. In addition a fund may be subject to a small amount of local tax. Jersey funds are subject to a flat £500 corporation tax and Luxembourg funds to a tax of 0.06% of the asset value each year. The expenses of an offshore fund cannot be offset against its income.

Taxation of the individual

2.7 The taxation of the individual will depend upon the status of the fund whether it has distributor status or non-distributor status.

(a) **Distributor status.** Distributor funds are those which are certified annually by HMRC as pursuing a policy of distribution of income. A fund will obtain this status if it distributes at least **85% of its net income after expenses (42.5% for commodity funds).** There is a concession for funds where the gross income in a year is very low and where the cost of distributing that income would be disproportionate to its value. The *de minimis* rule is set at 1% of the average value of the fund's assets. These funds are allowed to be certified as having distributor status.

The distributions paid from such funds are paid gross. A UK resident will have to declare this income and pay tax as follows.

(i) A non-taxpayer will have no liability to tax on the distribution.

(ii) A basic or lower rate taxpayer will pay 10% tax on the distribution.

(iii) A higher rate taxpayer will have to pay 32.5% on the distribution.

On encashment of the holding or transferring between classes of participating shares, should a capital gain arise, the investor may be liable to capital gains tax depending on his circumstances. The profits could become subject to capital gains tax if:

(i) After taking into account the capital gains tax indexation allowance and taper relief, the gain is in excess of the annual CGT exemption

(ii) The gain is below the annual exemption but the investor has already made use of this in other transactions whether on or offshore

There are of course methods of reducing the capital gain.

(i) The investor may have other capital losses which can be offset.

(ii) The investor may consider transferring the holding into a spouse's name prior to sale if he or she has not used up the annual CGT exemption.

(b) **Non-distributor status.** This category of fund is often referred to as a **roll-up fund.** In this instance, all income is accumulated in the fund. If a fund is not certified with distributor status, on receipt of a distribution or on total encashment a charge to income tax arises. A charge to **income tax** on a gain rather than **capital gains** tax can be a **disadvantage.** As the charge is to income tax there will be no annual CGT exemption to deduct and no indexation allowance or tapering allowance.

Those not resident in the UK will pay no UK income tax or capital gains tax on an offshore holding but of course they may be subject to tax charges in their new place of residence.

Exercise 3

Obtain a copy of the *Financial Times* and see if you can:

(a) Find the section in the listings headed FT Managed Funds Service - Offshore and Overseas

(b) Identify the UCITS

(c) Identify the funds with distributor status

Uses

2.8 (a) Offshore pooled investments may be useful for those who require a wider choice of funds than is available onshore. Offshore funds are particularly attractive to investors who wish to use currency funds.

(b) A fixed interest fund with **distributor** status may be useful for a non-taxpayer. His money will be invested in a fixed interest fund which is rolling up tax-free and he will receive a gross dividend.

(c) With a **non-distributor** fund, the taxpayer would pay no tax while his income was rolling up. If a higher rate taxpayer can take encashment when he will be a basic rate taxpayer, this might work to his advantage.

(d) The non-distributor fund may be useful for a UK resident who is anticipating retiring abroad. He can roll up his investment tax-free and encash it when he is no longer a UK resident and subject to UK tax. He will however, have to watch the tax treatment of his investment in the country in which he is then resident.

3 OFFSHORE BONDS

3.1 Offshore bonds were covered in some detail in Chapter 5. We highlight below the main features.

(a) The bonds are non-qualifying life policies with the same facilities as onshore policies. Many offshore bonds invest directly in offshore funds.

(b) Within a bond, switches between funds do not give rise to a personal tax liability. This is not the case with offshore funds, even if they are umbrella funds.

(c) Offshore bonds are subject to the income tax regime. Tax-deferred withdrawals are allowed by the '5%' rule.

(d) Costs of offshore products are generally more expensive than those marketed onshore because the insurance company is unable to offset expenses against income for tax purposes.

Exercise 4

Turn back to Chapter 5 and revise the features, tax and charging structure of offshore bonds.

---

4 DIRECT INVESTMENT IN OVERSEAS EQUITIES AND FOREIGN BONDS

4.1 The private investor can purchase overseas shares or foreign bonds directly through a broker.

4.2 Many large American and European companies' shares are quoted on the London Stock Exchange on the SETS and SEAQ International system. In this instance the investor can deal in sterling through a UK stockbroker. The shares he receives will, of course, be denominated in the appropriate foreign currency and may be bearer stock.

4.3 The stock is likely to be blue-chip. If the client wishes to buy other foreign stock he can deal directly on a foreign stock market through a local stockbroker. In this case charges could be higher, although in recent years discount brokers have developed low-cost services with deals being conducted via the internet.

4.4 If an investor does purchase foreign stock directly he must be prepared to deal with the collection of dividends and the payment of tax. He should check that there is a double taxation agreement in place with the relevant country, in order to avoid paying tax twice.

Chapter roundup

In this chapter we have studied:

- The FSA categories of offshore funds
- The features of OEICs, UCITS and offshore bonds
- The taxation of distributor and non-distributor funds

Quick Quiz

1   What do you understand by an FSA-recognised offshore fund?
2   What restrictions are place on non-recognised offshore funds?
3   What countries are recognised offshore funds most likely to operate from?
4   What types of investor may find a fixed-interest offshore fund attractive?
5   What is the difference in the taxation of a capital gain resulting from an investment in an offshore fund with a distributor status and one without this status?
6   Name two offshore funds which you think are high risk.

The answers to the questions in the quiz can be found at the end of this Study Text. Before checking your own answers against them, you should look back at this chapter and use the information in it to correct your answers.

Answers to exercises

1   The three types of recognised offshore collective investment are as follows.

   (a)   Funds authorised in EEA states (UCITS)
   (b)   Funds authorised in designated territories
   (c)   Individually recognised overseas schemes

2   (a)   OEICs   This is an open-ended investment company. It is a pooled investment which normally issues participating redeemable preference shares.

   (b)   UCITS   The initials UCITS stand for Undertakings for Collective Investments in Transferable Securities. It is a classification of investments which can be marketed freely across EU borders.

   (c)   Single pricing   This is a price quoted for the purchase or sale of a security. There is no bid/offer spread. There are charges, which are shown separately.

   (d)   Umbrella   This is the concept of many types of share under one fund management. Primarily used by offshore investment companies.

PRACTICE QUESTION 8: OFFSHORE FUNDS (30 Marks)   *27 mins*

(a)   What do the initials UCITS stand for?   (2 marks)

(b)   Explain the main features of the European Directive on UCITS.   (11 marks)

(c)   Does a unit trust fit the description of a UCITS?   (1 mark)

(d)   Does an investment trust fit the description of a UCITS?   (1 mark)

(e)   Describe an offshore investment which may suit a basic rate taxpayer who is prepared to take a risk. Also describe the personal tax position for the investor on income and any capital gain resulting from an investment in this fund.   (5 marks)

(f)   Describe an offshore investment which may suit a non taxpayer who wishes to secure income and take a low risk. Also describe the personal tax position for the investor on income and any capital gain.   (5 marks)

(g)   Describe an offshore investment which may suit a wealthy higher rate taxpayer who wants to take risk. Also describe the personal tax position for the investor on income and any capital gain.   (5 marks)

The answer to the practice question can be found at the end of this Study Text

Chapter 10

DERIVATIVES

Chapter topic list	Syllabus reference
1 Introduction to derivatives	2.7
2 Definition of derivatives	2.7
3 Financial futures	2.7
4 Options	2.7
5 Warrants	2.7
6 Swaps	2.7
7 Terminology	2.7
8 Uses of derivatives	2.7

Introduction

You need to have a detailed knowledge of all the types of investment we have discussed so far in this Study Text. We now consider less 'mainstream' types of investments. You are only required to have an outline knowledge of derivatives, which can be a speculative and risky investment, or alternatively may be used to reduce (hedge) risks.

1   INTRODUCTION TO DERIVATIVES

1.1   **Derivatives** are instruments based on the underlying securities of bonds and ordinary shares which enable investors to reduce risk or enhance returns on these investments. Derivatives are often only thought of in terms of increasing risk. However they can be used to reduce ('**hedge**') risk as well as to enhance returns.

1.2   Because of the volatility of the stock market, there has arisen a need for the market to develop products for the investor which will protect them against this volatility. Derivatives have been used heavily in these products.

1.3   Derivatives are mainly the domain of the professional fund manager as considerable expertise is needed to deal in this area.

2   DEFINITION OF DERIVATIVES

2.1   A **derivative** can be defined as 'a financial instrument valued according to the anticipated price movement of an underlying asset which may be a commodity, a currency or a security'.

2.2   Derivatives can be used either to hedge a position or to establish a synthetic open position. Examples of derivatives are futures, options, warrants and swaps.

We will now look at each type of derivative.

3 FINANCIAL FUTURES

3.1 The first futures market was established in the mid-1880s, in Chicago.

3.2 To understand a futures contract, we need first to understand the concept of a **forward contract**. A forward contract is an agreement reached at one point in time calling for the delivery of some commodity at a specified later date, at a price established at the time of contracting.

Example of a forward contract. A and B agree that in six months time A will deliver two tons of corn to B. B will pay £5.00 a ton. This is the cash or **spot price**.

The problem with the forward contract is that the price of £5 may be very uncompetitive in six months time. Futures allow those who must buy commodities to hedge against price changes.

3.3 A **futures contract** is a forward contract traded on an organised exchange with the contract terms clearly specified by the rules of the exchange.

3.4 A futures contract can be a contract to buy or sell commodities, currencies or securities. Commodity futures are traded in London in various markets. The Baltic Exchange deals with shipping and agricultural products, LIFFE deals with coffee, cocoa and other foodstuffs, the London Metal Exchange with metals and the International Petroleum Exchange with oil.

Financial futures are traded on the London International Financial Futures and Options Exchange (**LIFFE**).

3.5 Futures are traded on **margin** which means that the trader only has to spend a small amount of money, far below the value of the underlying security, to be exposed to the price rise or fall of that security.

3.6 A **financial future** is an agreement to buy or sell an investment at a future date at a given price. The investment can be an interest rate, a currency, shares, a commodity or an index.

3.7 Financial futures are futures contracts based on financial instruments such as currencies, debt instruments, interest rates, bonds and equities.

3.8 **Currency futures** are futures contracts calling for the delivery of a specific amount of a foreign currency at a specified future date in return for a given payment.

3.9 **Stock index futures** are futures contracts based on the value of an index. For these futures the gains or losses are determined by movements in the index. Managers can use futures to protect portfolios. For example, if the manager thinks the market will fall he can sell index futures. If the market does fall, the value of his portfolio will have fallen but he can offset this by the profit from the contract.

Let us look at an example of how this would work. Index futures are quoted in index points which are multiplied by the index multiplier (in the case of the FT-SE 100, £10 per index point). The value of a futures position is:

Number of contracts × Index multiplier × Index level

Suppose that a manager runs a portfolio of £15m. He believes the market will fall from its current index level of 6,000. He wishes to protect his portfolio, so he sells 250 contracts. That is:

250 × £10 × 6,000 = £15m

If the market falls by 250 points the fund will receive:

250 × £10 × 250 = £625,000.

So long as the underlying portfolio is invested mainly in FT-SE stock, this profit should roughly mirror the loss in the value of the portfolio and so the situation has been hedged. It is important to note that stock index futures are settled in cash not the physical delivery of the stock.

Index futures can also be used by the fund manager who wishes to move part of his fund from one geographical area to another. He can do this quickly and more efficiently by initially selling and buying futures. The physical purchase and sale of stock may be a time consuming business, particularly allowing for timing differences in settlement practices.

3.10 **Operation of the market.** The buyer of the contract has the obligation to buy the asset in the future at a price agreed today (a long position). The seller has the obligation to deliver at the agreed price (a short position). Each futures exchange has a clearing house. The clearing house stands between the buyer and the seller. The clearing house guarantees that the goods or securities will be delivered to the buyer and that the settlement of cash will be paid to the seller. Thus, the clearing house takes the risk of one party defaulting. This is sometimes known as a counterparty risk. The clearing house covers this risk by collecting margins from its members.

The London Clearing House (LCH) acts as the clearing house for LIFFE, the London Metal Exchange and the International Petroleum Exchange. LCH is owned by six major UK commercial banks. It provides an enormous guarantee of £200 million from its shareholders and the insurance market.

Exercise 1

(a) Describe a future.
(b) Give three examples of financial futures.

---

4 OPTIONS

4.1 An **option** is the right to sell or buy a commodity, currency or security at a set price (the exercise price) at any time within three months of the contract date.

4.2 Unlike the future, this is not a contract to buy and sell which must be completed. This is merely an option and the buyer will only exercise his option if it is profitable to do so. If he does not exercise the option he will lose the option money or premium.

4.3 Options in commodity futures, options in share indices, currencies, bonds and equities are traded on LIFFE.

4.4 There are two main types of option.

(a) **Call option.** In this case the owner has the option to buy a particular commodity or security at a certain price in the future. Such an option would be purchased if the buyer thought prices were going to rise. Below is an example of call option prices.

Call options

November 2000 - XYZ plc (current share price 254)

	January	April	July
240	25	35	42
260	14	24	31
280	7	15	23

This chart indicates that an investor could purchase the April 260 call option for a cost of 24p per share. One option contract would then give him the right to purchase 1,000 shares at 260p at any time between the date of purchase and April.

If the price rises to (say) 300p, the investor may exercise his option and then sell the shares into the market at a profit.

His profit will be 300p – 260p – option premium of 24p = 16p per share.

Alternatively, he could sell his option. The option will be worth the difference between the market price and the option price = 40p per share. From this he must deduct his premium, so the net result is the same whichever course of action he takes.

(b) **Put option**. In this case the owner has the option to sell a particular commodity or security at a specified price in the future. Such an option would be purchased if the buyer thought prices were going to fall or to protect a profit on an investment. Below is an example of put option prices using the example of the same share as in (a) above.

Put options

November 2000 - XYZ plc (current share price 254)

	January	April	July
240	6	10	12
260	14	18	20
280	27	29	30

In this example, if the investor thought the share price was likely to fall below 240 then he can purchase the put option April 240 for a premium of 10p per share. If the price does fall to say 200p then the investor can exercise the option and sell the shares to the writer of the option at 240p. If, on the other hand, the price of the share in April is 250p then the investor will not exercise the put option. He has lost his premium but has still protected his holding against further large price falls.

4.5 Every option involves a payment of a premium even if the option is not exercised.

4.6 **Writing a call or put**. Sometimes it can be advantageous for an investor to be the writer of the option. **Writing a call** could be useful in a scenario when a stock should be held but it is unlikely that the share price will move much in the coming months.

Example

Suppose the ABC share is currently (in April) trading at 1000p, and that the investor could sell July 1050p call options at a premium of 35p per share. This has generated an immediate return of 3.5% for three months. If the price remains static as predicted, the investor retains the premium. If the share price rises above 1050p, the investor must sell but he has his sale price of 1050p per share plus the 35p premium = 1085p per share.

In this case, the call is covered, ie the investor holds this stock. If he does not and the call is exercised, he may have to buy in stock at a high market price and could suffer a considerable loss.

Writing a put. In this instance the writer does not expect the price to fall significantly. If it does, he must supply stock which will be at a loss. However, he will retain the premium.

4.7 **Traded options.** There is a trade in the options themselves and these can be bought and sold on an exchange at any time. On the other hand, an 'over-the-counter (OTC) option' or 'negotiated option' is tailor made by a financial institution for a particular client and will not be readily tradable.

Exercise 2

(a) What is the difference between an option and a future?
(b) Give two types of financial options.

---

5 WARRANTS

What is a warrant?

5.1 A **warrant** offers the owner the right to subscribe for the ordinary shares of company at a fixed price at a fixed date in the future. Warrants are bought and sold on the market in a similar fashion to options. (Warrants have already been discussed in Chapter 7.)

Exercise 3

(a) What is a warrant?
(b) Is the price of the warrant likely to be higher or lower than the price of the ordinary share?
(c) What circumstances must apply for an investor to exercise a warrant?

Covered warrants

5.2 **Covered warrants** are a relatively recent innovation. These are warrants based on an underlying share or index which are issued by a financial institution rather than by the company itself. The warrant is called 'covered' because the issuing institution will hold the underlying asset, to cover its exposure.

5.3 **Call** warrants give a right to buy at a specified price within a specified time period, while **put** warrants give a right to sell at a specified price within a specified time period.

5.4 A call warrant may be purchased as a bet on the price of the underlying asset rising, while a put warrant may be bought as a bet on the price falling.

5.5 For example, suppose that the share of X plc trade at 120p currently (at 15 June). An investor who believes the price will rise may be able to buy a call warrant to buy at 150p by, say, 30 September. This warrant might be priced at, say 5p for each share. If the X plc share price rises to 160p, the warrant can be excised for a profit in since 160p – 150p = 10p proceeds, compared with the cost of 5p. If the share price does not reach 150p by 30 September, the warrant will be worthless on expiry. Therefore, warrants are risky investments although, if the 'bet' is correct, significant profits can be earned due to the 'gearing' effect of warrants.

5.6 A put warrant to sell X plc at 100p by 30 September could be exercised if the share price of X plc falls below 100p. The profit on exercise will depend on how far below 100p the price falls, less the initial warrant cost.

5.7 Covered warrants can be sold on in the market before being exercised, in which case part of their value will be the **time value** attributable to the hope that the warrant can eventually be exercised at a profit.

5.8 Covered warrants are even available for house price indices, as well as share prices and indices.

6 SWAPS

6.1 A **swap** involves the exchange of obligations in a transaction.

(a) **Product swap.** An example of a product swap would be a situation where Tom owns hay but requires corn. Gary owns corn but requires hay, so they swap. 'Countertrade' is a name given to barter arrangements in international trading.

(b) **Interest rate swap.** An example of an interest rate swap would be a situation where Andrew agrees to pay a fixed amount of interest on £100,000 each year for five years to Graham. In return Graham offers to pay a variable rate of interest to Andrew on the same amount of money for the same period. This swap indicates that Andrew believes interest rates will rise and Graham believes they will fall.

(c) **Currency swaps.** Currency swaps are used by international trading companies to minimise the risk of losses arising from exchange rate changes. An example of a currency swap would be a situation where company A wants to borrow US dollars but it has good credit rating in France and can borrow the required amount of money in euros. Company B, which is an American company, can borrow money in the USA in US dollars but it wants euros. The companies simply swap their loan facilities. They then have the loan in the currency they require and they pay interest in that currency.

7 TERMINOLOGY

7.1 Terms used in relation to derivatives include the following.

Arbitrage. The buying or selling of commodities, securities or currencies between two or more markets to take advantage of differences in the prices quoted in these markets.

American-style option/warrant. These are options/warrants which can be exercised before as well as on the expiry date.

At the money At the expiration of an option the option is 'at the money' if the value of the stock equals the striking price.

Bear spread. This is a combination of put options. The aim is to achieve a profit if the price of the underlying security or commodity falls.

Bull spread. This is a combination of call options. The aim is to achieve a profit if the price of the underlying security or commodity rises.

Cost of carry. The cost of financing the purchase or sale of a derivative.

Covered call. If the writer of the option owns the stock this is known as a covered call. If he does not own the stock it is a naked call.

European-style option/warrant. These options/warrants can only be exercised on the expiry date.

Exercise. If the owner uses the option, this is known as exercising the option.

Expiry. This is the date when an option, warrant or future lapses.

Hedging. Hedging is the act of reducing uncertainty about future prices of a commodity, security or currency. This can be done by undertaking forward sales or purchases on the futures market or by taking out an option which limits exposure to price fluctuation.

In the money. At the expiry of a call option or warrant, the instrument is 'in the money' if the value of the underlying stock is greater than the strike price. A put is 'in the money' if the underlying price is below the strike price.

Intrinsic value. The difference between the value of the stock and the striking price is known as the intrinsic value.

Margin. To protect the clearing house and the exchange, dealers in the market must deposit funds or securities (a margin) with their brokers before they are allowed to trade.

Out of the money. At the expiry of a call option or warrant, the instrument is 'out of the money' if the value of the underlying stock is less than the strike price. A put is out of the money if the underlying price is above the strike price.

Spot market. A spot market is a market for the sale and purchase of commodities and securities for immediate delivery as opposed to the futures market which provides for delivery at some future date.

Strike price. This is the price at which the option is exercised.

Time value. The time value is the value of an option over and above its intrinsic value. This represents the value of the possibility that the option will become worth exercising before it expires. The option's value reduces with time. The nearer to the expiry date, the closer the value is to the intrinsic value.

8   USES OF DERIVATIVES

8.1   (a)   **Futures.** Futures are used by fund managers who wish to move markets or change market allocations. The use of futures is quicker and there is saving on dealing costs.

(b)   **Options.** Options are used by fund managers to hedge against wide variations in interest rates or currencies. Options can also be used if a manager knows he will shortly receive a large input of money but fears that the market will rise sharply in the meantime.

The use of futures and options in products with a protected element

8.2   Many investors are not willing to take risks with their investments and hence the guaranteed income and growth bond market is active and competitive. The demand for risk free investments has lead to the introduction of bonds with underlying guarantees in the form of derivatives.

8.3   The principle of this type of investment is that the investor will get his money back, as an absolute minimum, when the bond matures, typically in five years time. In addition, he may also get further growth, based on the movements of predetermined stock market indices. Pre-set levels of movements in the indices will give rise to set levels of return equivalent to stock market returns. However, care must be taken in the description of this type of investment, as it will only provide the guaranteed minimum return at the end of the term. Any attempt to access the money in the meantime will result in penalties and possibly loss of capital.

8.4   The concept of an investment that guarantees to return the original investment and yet has the potential to lock into stockmarket returns is a good one to market, even if there is considerable complexity underlying it.

8.5   For potential investors, it is important for them to understand that although they will get their money back as an **absolute minimum** they will have **lost money** in real terms if this minimum is all they receive. Although inflation is currently at moderately low levels, inflation of 3% per year would mount up over five years reducing purchasing power by almost 14%.

Guarantees and stock market links

8.6   In order to achieve the combined effect of a guaranteed return and a return linked to stock markets, life companies combine various investments within the framework of the life assurance bond. Typically, a proportion of the invested money goes into low risk guaranteed growth investments such as zero coupon bond, or indeed a fixed interest deposit account. The rest goes into a derivative based on the stockmarket indices of one or more different countries.

8.7   The low risk portion of the investment ensures that under all circumstances the investors will get their money back. The role of this part of the investment is to take the money that remains invested after the bid offer spread (5% or so) and the cost of the derivative (5-15%) – some 80-90% of the original investment – and grow this back to the full value over the five year term.

8.8   There will also be a high-risk portion of the investment to buy in to one or more stock indices. These derivatives are quite unlike exchange-traded derivatives which are liquid. They are tailor made over-the-counter (OTC) derivatives, especially set up to meet the needs of buyers and sellers. The investments themselves cannot generally be traded. Each purchase of the derivative will be quite specific and will cover a set amount of investment, eg £10 million.

8.9   The fact that the underlying derivative is only available in set tranches means that bonds that use them are also only available on a limited basis. Each issue of bond will have a set size of issue and once this is gone, the company will not be in a position to sell more unless it renegotiates for a new derivative to underlie the issue. The prices of the derivative will also change rapidly, so often life companies will set an investment up with a time limit and invite investments from IFAs as intermediaries, and directly to the public. Changes in the cost of the derivative during this period will be met by the life company. When the money is in, they buy the high and low-risk investments and the term of the bond begins. If the take-up of the bond issue is not high, they can reserve the right to cancel it before they buy the deriviatives. In this case the investment money will be returned to the investors.

> ### Chapter roundup
>
> In this chapter we have studied:
>
> * The main types of derivatives
> * The main uses of derivatives

Quick Quiz

1 What is the full name of LIFFE?

2 What do the letters OTC stand for?

3 What is the role of the London Clearing House?

4 Why is a clearing house necessary in the trading of derivatives?

5 Can derivatives be used to increase or reduce risk, or both?

6 What is a warrant?

The answers to the questions in the quiz can be found at the end of this Study Text. Before checking your own answers against them, you should look back at this chapter and use the information in it to correct your answers.

Answers to exercises

1 (a) A future is an agreement to buy or sell a fixed quantity of a particular commodity, currency, or security for delivery at a fixed date in the future at a fixed price.

   (b) Three examples of financial futures are as follows.

     (i) A contract to buy or sell an investment at a future date at a given price.

     (ii) A foreign currency future. In this case it is a contract to buy or sell a specific amount of a foreign currency at a given price at a future date.

     (iii) A stock index future. This is a contract based on the value of an index in the future.

2 (a) The difference between an option and a future is that an option is the right to sell or buy a commodity, currency or security at a fixed price at any time within three months of the contract date. The future is a contract to buy or sell which must be completed.

   (b) Two types of financial options are:

     (i) A call option
     (ii) A put option

3 (a) A warrant offers the owner the right to buy the ordinary shares of the company at a fixed price at a fixed time in the future.

   (b) The price will be lower than the price of the ordinary share.

   (c) The owner of the warrant will only exercise the option if the fixed price of the warrant is less than the quoted price of the ordinary share on the date when the option can be exercised.

PRACTICE QUESTION 9: DERIVATIVES (20 Marks)   *18 mins*

(a) What is the difference between a forward contact and a futures contract?   (4 marks)

(b) Is there any obligation on the owner of an option?   (3 marks)

(c) What are the advantages of trading on a derivatives exchange rather than 'over the counter'?
                                                                          (4 marks)

(d) Describe one type of swap which can be arranged and its advantage.   (5 marks)

(e) What is the purpose of 'hedging'?   (4 marks)

The answer to the practice question can be found at the end of the Study Text

Chapter 11

OTHER INVESTMENTS

Chapter topic list	Syllabus reference
1 Introduction to other investments	2.5, 2.8-2.12
2 Property	2.12
3 Unquoted shares	2.5, 2.11
4 Commodities	2.10
5 Collectibles	2.8
6 Membership of Lloyd's	2.9
7 Film partnerships	2.11
8 Child Trust Funds	2.11

Introduction

In this chapter we examine a wide range of 'other investments'. We will look at their features, advantages and disadvantages, tax treatment, risk profile and use in the construction of an investment portfolio.

1 INTRODUCTION TO OTHER INVESTMENTS

1.1 Financial advisers tend to think only in terms of financial investments but there are a wide variety of other investments which the client can incorporate into a portfolio. The most obvious is the other asset-backed investment: property. Many clients will own a residential property and some will include commercial property in their portfolio to produce capital appreciation and a rental income. Some clients may own a holiday home. This too can be viewed as an investment. It has an intrinsic value and the ability to create income if it is leased to visitors.

1.2 Some clients may own shares in private unquoted companies and, more recently, investments in pooled schemes such as the **Enterprise Investment Scheme (EIS)** and **Venture Capital Trusts (VCTs)**. Those who are least averse to risk might wish to use commodities and collectibles as a means of accumulating capital.

1.3 In the past, the rich have seen membership of Lloyd's as another method of increasing wealth in a tax efficient manner. In this chapter we will consider whether membership is still viable and the advantages, if any.

2 PROPERTY

2.1 In the past, long term growth has been achieved from asset-backed investments such as shares and property. However, property values can fall. Up to 1989, the residential market was steaming ahead and many rushed to join in, with unfortunate results. Interest rates rose and property prices slumped. Many later had a negative amount of equity in their property, because their mortgages exceeded the value of the property.

2.2 We will now look at the various methods of investing in property.

Residential property

Advantages of residential property as an investment

2.3 (a) Many investors participate in property ownership through owning the house in which they live. One of the advantages of owner-occupation is psychological: most owner-occupiers like the security of a permanent home they own, even if it is subject to a mortgage.

(b) In the past property values have kept pace with average earnings, although the property market is susceptible to cyclical fluctuations.

(c) It is possible to use a property as part of an investor's retirement fund. She could decide to sell a large house, move down market and use the surplus funds to invest and create income.

(d) If for some reason the owner cannot live in his property for a period, say, because she is working abroad, the property can be let and used to create an income.

(e) Similarly, if a client owns a holiday home, this can be let for part of the year. The rental income will, hopefully, offset general running expenses.

(f) Residential property can, of course, be used as collateral security for a loan.

Disadvantages of residential property as an investment

2.4 (a) One of the main disadvantages of any property is illiquidity. The property can only be sold if a buyer can be found.

(b) Often the sale of a property can be protracted and the vendor may be incurring expenses during this period.

(c) If a property is leased out there may be times when a suitable tenant cannot be found. In addition there are charges involved in letting property. A letting agent may be needed to vet suitable tenants, collect rents and oversee the upkeep of the property.

Tax points on property investments

2.5 Profits from renting out property are treated as **earned income**, under **Schedule A**, for tax purposes.

- This will be taxed at the taxpayer's marginal rate of 10%, 22% or 40%.

- Each tax year's profit is taxed in that tax year.

- Mortgage interest on the property being let counts as a deductible expense to set against the letting income.

2.6 **Deductions against tax** on rents received may be claimed for the interest on loans (mortgages) to buy or improve the property, and costs of maintenance, such as insurance, cleaning, gardening, agent's commission and other reasonable management expenses (but not improvements). A wear and teal allowance of 10% of rents received can be claimed to cover the cost of furniture, fittings and fixtures for property let **furnished**, or alternatively the actual cost of replacements can be claimed.

2.7 Landlords qualify for an income tax **deduction of up to £1,500** when they install **loft or cavity wall insulation** in a dwelling which they let.

2.8 If the landlord is **non-UK resident**, the tenant or letting agent is required to deduct basic rate tax from the property income before remitting rent to the landlord. A landlord may however apply to HMRC to come within the self assessment regime, in order to be permitted to receive gross payments of rent.

2.9 If the investor owns **furnished holiday accommodation** which is let out on a frequent basis (at least 70 days in a 12 month period) he may, if he satisfies the following criteria, be able to treat the letting **as a trade**. In this case be may obtain other reliefs and allowances.

- The property must be situated in the UK.

- The property must be run on a commercial basis.

- The property must be furnished.

- The property must be available to let for not less than 140 days per fiscal year.

- The property must not normally be occupied by the same person/people for more than 31 days for at least seven months within a twelve-month period.

2.10 A holiday home (in the UK or overseas) could be a suitable asset to transfer to the client's children as a **potentially exempt transfer (PET)** if the client is considering ways of mitigating inheritance tax.

2.11 If a house is the investor's **principal private residence**, the sale of the property will be exempt from capital gains tax. If not, gains will be subject to capital gains tax.

2.12 **Stamp duty land tax (SDLT)** is a tax payable on buying property, and is charged on the purchase consideration (price) at the rates set out below. No SDLT is payable for transfers on divorce or for transfers to charities if the land is to be used for charitable purposes. The tax is rounded up to the next multiple of £5.

Consideration (residential property)	*Rate of SDLT*
Up to £120,000*	Nil
£120,001 – £250,000	1%
£250,001 – £500,000	3%
£500,001 +	4%

* The nil rate band is **up to £150,000** for (1) non-residential property, and (2) residential property in disadvantaged areas.

2.13 If an individual lets a room or rooms in his or her **main residence** as **furnished living accommodation**, then a special tax exemption called the **rent a room scheme** may apply. The limit on the exemption is gross rents (before any expenses or capital allowances) of £4,250 per year (2005/06). This limit is halved if any other person (including the first person's spouse) also received income from renting accommodation in the property while the property was the first person's main residence.

Buy to let

2.14 **Buy to let** refers to the purchase of property - usually residential property purchased by individuals - with the purpose of letting it.

(a) Various lenders are prepared to grant mortgages to 'buy to let' purchasers, typically requiring the purchaser to provide, say, 20 per cent of the capital required for the purchase. The lender may base the size of the loan on expected rents.

(b) The letting may be managed by estate agents, who will take a percentage of the rent as their fees.

(c) Gross returns - the rent received before taking account of the cost of letting such as management fees, maintenance, service charges ground rents and insurance - vary between approximately 4% and 9%.

(d) Deductions against tax on rents received may be claimed for the costs of maintenance, such as insurance, cleaning, gardening, agent's commission and other reasonable management expenses (but not improvements).

(e) For furnished lettings, the initial cost of furniture, fittings and fixtures is not allowable, but the actual cost of subsequent replacement may be claimed; or, alternatively, a wear and tear allowance of 10% of the rents received may be deductible.

2.15 'Buy to let' schemes became very popular in the late 1990s and early 2000s because of:

- Rising property values
- Readily available funds from lenders

2.16 **Advantages of buy to let**

(a) For a relatively small capital outlay, the investor can gain exposure to housing market gains

(b) As well as any capital gain, rents are earned to produce a yield and will offset interest costs

2.17 **Disadvantages of buy to let**

(a) In areas of weak housing demand or over-supply, properties may be vacant for long periods

(b) If house prices fall, losses may be suffered

(c) It may take some time to sell property in order to realise gains

(d) Capital gains will be taxed

2.18 Many clients' long-term financial plan is to sell their house at retirement, buy a property at a lower value and use the balance of the proceeds of the sale to produce increased retirement income.

Commercial property

2.19 (a) Much of the non-residential **commercial property** in the UK is the property of large institutions such as insurance companies and pension funds. These institutions may be the property developer and, once the property is built, the landlord.

(b) Such properties will be let on long leases. In the past this could be as long as 99 years. Now it is likely to be a maximum of 25, with three or five year rent reviews.

(c) The owner of the property obviously hopes that the rental income from his property will increase. The value of commercial property is normally calculated as a multiple of the rental income, for example a property could be purchased at 18 years purchase of the rent.

(d) A number of the leading estate agents in the UK produce indices of the movement in rental and capital values of commercial property. There is also an index produced by Investment Property Databank (IPD). This organisation monitors the performance of commercial properties owned by the large institutions.

(e) **Factories and warehouses** tend to produce the highest yields in the property sector and **retail** shops and stores the lowest. **Office buildings** are a third type of commercial property.

(f) Commercial property tends to follow a cyclical pattern, often in the opposite direction to the performance of the stock market.

Advantages of commercial property as an investment

2.20 (a) The price of commercial property may keep pace with inflation although this is by no means guaranteed.

(b) Property can produce an increasing rental income if good tenants can be found and maintained.

(c) Property can provide a balance in the investment portfolio reducing overall risk, as the performance of property may be opposite to the performance of the stock market. Thus, if the stock market is doing well, property may performing relatively poorly and *vice versa*.

Disadvantages of commercial property as an investment

2.21 (a) From time to time there will be slumps in the property market and these may be protracted.

(b) Commercial property may remain untenanted for many months or even years during which time there is no rental income and the underlying value of the property may also have fallen.

(c) Commercial property is very illiquid. It may take many months or even years to sell a property.

(d) Property can be expensive to manage. The buildings have to be kept up to a high standard if suitable tenants are to be found and retained. The owner will have the expense of an agent who will be in charge of the day-to-day running of the property and finding and vetting suitable tenants. Other professional advisers will need to be employed from time to time such as surveyors and lawyers to draw up suitable leases and contracts.

Exercise 1

(a) List the disadvantages of residential property as an investment.
(b) List the advantages of commercial property as an investment.

Indirect investment in property

2.22   Investors may purchase property indirectly through property shares, enterprise zone property and via pooled arrangements: property bonds and property unit trusts.

(a)   **Property shares.** If a client wants an exposure to property but does not have sufficient capital to purchase a property, he may buy property shares. To obtain an indication of the performance of property shares, the investor can make reference to the property company sub-index of the FT-SE Actuaries indices. The investor should be aware of the fact that the prices of property shares tend to be more volatile than the actual property values.

(b)   **Enterprise Zone (EZ) property.** Expenditure on industrial and commercial buildings in an enterprise zone qualifies as 100% deduction against the investor's income. The investor can make a direct investment or via a unit trust. The advantage of the unit trust is a lower initial investment and a spread of properties. Nevertheless there is a high risk within the fund. An individual who invests in such a unit trust is treated as if he has incurred a proportion of the trust's expenditure on enterprise zone property and he will qualify for industrial buildings allowances. These allowances can be set against other income for tax purposes.

(c)   **Property bonds.** For the smaller investor who obviously cannot afford to purchase a commercial property to place in his portfolio, an investment in a pooled scheme may be attractive. This can be done via a property bond or a unit trust. A property bond is an insurance company investment bond. The underlying investment of the fund is commercial and retail property which is professionally managed for the investor. (See Chapter 5 for a full explanation.)

Exercise 2

Re-read the section in Chapter 6 about property bonds and unit trusts and answer the following questions.

(a)   Why may it be difficult to exit from a property bond quickly?

(b)   What is the taxation on the individual investor of the income and capital gain resulting from an investment in a unit trust?

(d)   **Property unit trusts and OEICs.** Originally unit trusts were prohibited from directly investing in property and could only invest indirectly via property shares. This has now changed and unit trust and OEIC managers can invest directly into commercial property. At the launch of such a fund the manager must feel confident that he will attract sufficient funds to make adequate property purchases to establish a well spread portfolio. There are however restrictions on the proportion of the fund that can be invested in leases with less than 60 years to run, or in unoccupied property. There are also restrictions on holding mortgaged property, which limit gearing. No more than 15% in value of the fund assets can be invested in a single property. Additionally, there are unit trusts and OEICs that invest in property company shares. As with unit trusts and OEICs generally, the investment will be redeemed at net asset value. However, if many investors choose to sell at one time, the unit trust or OEIC may need to invoke its right to postpone encashment of units/shares until property can be sold. This makes property funds potentially illiquid.

(e)   **Property investment trusts** are pooled investments but are only permitted to invest in shares and securities of property companies, not in property directly. They are permitted to borrow, which increases the risk for the investor as well as the possible return. The share price of the trust will fluctuate with supply and demand for the share of the trust, and may be at a discount or a premium of the net asset value. A new form of tax-exempt structure similar to the **Real Estate Investment Trusts (REITs)** of the USA is expected to be introduced in the UK in the future (see below).

Real Estate Investment Trusts (REITs)

2.23 **Real Estate Investment Trusts (REITs)** are '**tax-transparent**' **property investment vehicles** which were first formed in the USA, where the name 'REITs' originated. Other countries, including Japan, the Netherlands and France, now have their own versions of **REITs**. The UK is expected to follow, with **UK-REITs** being proposed. The exact form of UK-REITs is not yet known, and there will not be legislation until **2006** at the earliest.

2.24 **Tax-transparent property investment vehicles**, such as REITs, distribute nearly all of their taxable income to investors. Provided they do this, the vehicles are granted exemption from capital gains tax and from corporate taxes. Investors pay tax on the dividends and capital growth at their own marginal tax rates, thus avoiding the double taxation that affects investors in UK property companies currently.

2.25 It is anticipated that existing UK **property companies** may choose to **convert** to become REITs. When France introduced similar funds in 2003, converting companies had to pay an 'exit tax' amounting to half of their capital gains tax liability over four years. It is expected that the UK Treasury is likely to put a similar provision in place, when REITs are introduced.

2.26 The UK Treasury hopes that introducing a UK version of REITs might bring **offshore property investment vehicles** back onshore, thus allowing them to be better regulated. However, since offshore vehicles do not pay UK tax, they might not be attracted back onshore, particularly if they have to pay a tax to convert to the new type of company.

Advantages of investing in property in a pooled investment fund

2.27 (a) The investor is 'buying' expert property management.

(b) The investor is buying into a large well spread fund. It will be spread according to type, ie office, warehousing, retail and geographically and therefore reduces risk.

(c) Although there is some illiquidity in the pooled finds, particularly in the property fund and the Enterprise Zone schemes: nevertheless liquidity is greater than with direct investment.

(d) A small amount of money can be invested in an investment bond or a property unit trust. A substantial sum would need to be committed to the purchase of even a modest commercial property.

Disadvantages of investing in property in a pooled investment fund

2.28 (a) The investor does not have direct control over the properties.

(b) It may be difficult to realise capital quickly particularly from a property bond or Enterprise Zone scheme.

(c) Enterprise Zone schemes are illiquid and high risk.

3   UNQUOTED SHARES

3.1   An investor may be invited to invest in a private unquoted company. Before making a decision he should consider the following points.

(a)   Will he have a management role and therefore any control over the activities of the company?

(b)   Will he hold sufficient shares to control the company? If not, he may have very little control over his investment.

(c)   What is the possible time scale of his investment: for example, is the company aiming to be floated on the stock market?

(d)   What are the income and capital growth possibilities?

(e)   What is the risk to his capital?

(f)   What are the tax incentives/implications?

3.2   In some instances, the investor may be better advised to make a loan to the company rather than purchase shares. A reason for this is that the payment and amount of dividends received may be erratic. Also, it may be very difficult, or impossible, to sell private company shares and therefore there is often little chance of being able to recover the capital invested. The advantage of the loan is that there is a fixed rate of interest paid and return of the capital is promised at a known date. There is also greater security on the winding up of a company.

Exercise 3

(a)   What may be the advantages of a private investor purchasing shares in an unquoted trading company?

(b)   What may be the disadvantages?

3.3   In the previous paragraphs, we have been discussing the problems that may arise if a private individual puts capital into an unquoted company. It is now worth mentioning the role of the venture capitalist in this area. The venture capital funds have been providing finance for unquoted companies in the UK for many years. The organisation with the longest track record is Investors in Industry, also known as the 3i Group. This organisation has financed thousands of businesses.

3.4   A venture capitalist will put up money for a management buy-out or to finance a growing business in return for a share of the capital. The venture capitalist will only want a limited involvement of, say, five years. At the end of this period he will want to dispose of his shares, a take-out, hopefully for a profit, either through a stock market flotation or the company being bought out.

3.5   The private investor who is interested in an investment in an unquoted company, without the total risk, may wish to consider a pooled investment such as an **Enterprise Investment Scheme (EIS)** fund or a **Venture Capital Trust (VCT)**, both of which schemes offer tax incentives. We will now look at the features of both schemes.

Enterprise Investment Scheme (EIS)

3.6   (a)   The Enterprise Investment Scheme was introduced in 1993 and has been modified a number of times since then.

(b) The purpose of the scheme was to encourage investment in unquoted shares of trading companies and to replace the old Business Expansion Scheme (BES).

(c) An **Enterprise Investment Scheme** is a fund established to invest in a range of qualifying companies. The investor has the advantage of professional management and a spread of investments.

(d) It must be stressed that there is a high degree of risk associated with this type of investment.

(e) The rules governing the scheme are as follows.

    (i)   An investor may subscribe up to £200,000 per fiscal year (2005/06) in qualifying shares and obtain tax relief of 20% on the amount subscribed. The relief cannot be obtained until the shares have been issued and the company has carried on a qualifying trade for four months. It is possible to invest prior to 6 October in a year of assessment and qualify for tax relief in the previous year. The amount which can be invested in these circumstances is £25,000, or 50% of the amount invested if this is lower than £25,000.

    (ii)   The shares must be retained for three years to keep the relief.

    (iii)   If the investor makes a profit he will not pay capital gains tax on the gain.

    (iv)   Losses on EIS shares are calculated as for capital gains tax (but reducing the cost by the 20% income tax relief) and can be offset against other taxable income or chargeable gains.

    (v)   An investor with large capital gains from the disposal of another asset can invest unlimited gains in the EIS and defer the payment of the capital gains tax.

    (vi)   Relief is not available if the investor was previously involved with the company but there are arrangements for 'business angels'. These are people who wish to invest in a qualifying company but also bring management skills, they may invest and become directors.

    (vii)   The company must carry out a qualifying activity (which excludes financial services and property based activities).

    (viii)   Investors must subscribe for new shares if they are to obtain the relief.

    (ix)   The investor must not acquire more than 30% of the issued ordinary share capital in a particular company, if income tax relief is to be claimed.

    (x)   Participation in these schemes is limited to companies with gross assets of less than £15 million before an investment and no more than £16 million after it.

    (xi)   Investors will not qualify for EIS relief if certain arrangements exist before or at the time of issue. The arrangements concerned are those for:

        (1)   The disposal of shares in the company
        (2)   The disposal of the company's assets
        (3)   The ending of the company's trade, or
        (4)   A guarantee of the shareholders' investment

    (xii)   The following property-backed activities are excluded from the EIS.

        (1)   Farming and market gardening
        (2)   Forestry and timber production
        (3)   Property development
        (4)   Operating or managing hotels or guest houses
        (5)   Operating or managing nursing homes or residential care homes

(xiii) The company must be unquoted but it need not be resident in or incorporated in the UK.

(xiv) The investor need not be a UK resident but must be liable to UK tax.

(xv) If the investor is making use of the capital gains tax relief (see (v) above), he must invest in the EIS in the period beginning one year before and ending three years after the disposal giving rise to the chargeable gain.

Example of EIS CGT deferral relief

Situation. Adam sells shares in November 2005 for £18,000. He purchased them for £5,000, before 1998. In July 2005, Adam invested £10,000 in ordinary shares in an EIS scheme or company.

CGT position

	£	£
Proceeds		18,000
Less cost	5,000	
Indexation allowance, say	3,000	8,000
Net gain		10,000
Reinvestment relief		10,000
Net chargeable gain		nil

(f) **Compliance.** An adviser recommending such a scheme must issue a **risk warning** notice drawing the investor's attention to the fact that he may have trouble selling the investment at a reasonable price and, indeed, at any price. The investor is asked to consider whether the scheme is suitable for him in the light of his financial circumstances. He must confirm that he has read the prospectus and understands the risk involved.

Exercise 4

(a) State four of the rules governing an EIS scheme.
(b) What are the tax reliefs available to a private investor in an EIS?
(c) Which particular type of investor will gain most from an EIS?

Venture capital trusts (VCT)

3.7 (a) The 1994 Finance Act established a new investment vehicle, the **Venture Capital Trust**.

(b) The venture capital trust is similar to an investment trust but it must not be a close company.

(c) The company need not be resident in the UK but it must be quoted on the London Stock Exchange.

(d) The VCT must hold at least 70% of its investments in unquoted trading companies (this includes AIM shares) but not more than 15% in any one company. At least 30% of the qualifying holdings must consist of ordinary share capital. The 70% of assets must be invested within three years of the fund's launch. The three year period of grace starts each time new funds are raised.

(e) For accounting periods ending on or after 2 July 1997 (but not in respect of funds raised by the issue of shares before that date), guaranteed loans and securities may not form part of the fixed proportion of qualifying investments which a VCT can hold to qualify for the reliefs. VCTs will also be required to ensure that at least 10% of their total investment in any company is held in ordinary non-preferential shares.

(f) For shares issued on or after 17 March 1998, the same property-backed activities are excluded from VCTs as are excluded for EIS purposes. This will not have an effect on money raised before that date.

(g) The income of a VCT must be derived wholly from shares or securities and it must not retain more than 15% of its income derived from shares or securities.

(h) VCTs may invest up to £1 million in any one qualifying unquoted trading company but the gross assets of the unquoted company must not exceed £15 million prior to the VCT investment.

(i) If the companies in which the trust invests are subsequently floated on the stock market, the trust can hold the shares within the portfolio for a further five years.

(j) The investor aged over 18 will receive a tax reduction of 40% on a new investment of up to £200,000 per year in the fiscal years 2004/05 or 2005/06 provided the investment is in a new issue of shares and the shares are held for three years. (The annual investment limit was £100,000 and the relief was at 20%, before 2004/05.) It is not necessary to be a higher rate taxpayer to claim the 40% rebate, but the rebate is restricted to the amount of income tax the investor is liable to pay.

(k) The VCT investor aged 18 or more pays no tax on dividends received or capital gains. He cannot however, offset losses on disposals against other income or chargeable gains.

(l) CGT deferral relief was withdrawn for VCT shares issued on or after 6 April 2004.

Exercise 5

(a) List the main differences between an EIS and a VCT.
(b) Do you think an EIS or a VCT carries the higher risk and why?

---

4 COMMODITIES

4.1 Trading in commodities can be a high-risk investment. Commodities such as coffee, tea, rubber, metals, grain and oil are traded on markets across the world. The main exchanges are in London and New York. In London, the Baltic Exchange deals with shipping and agricultural products, LIFFE with coffee, tea and foodstuffs, London Metal Exchange with metal and the International Petroleum Exchange with oil.

4.2 Trading in commodities can carry high risks for a number of reasons.

(a) The price of a commodity can fluctuate and may show high volatility.

(b) Weather conditions, such as drought or flood, can ruin a crop, for agricultural commodities.

(c) Economic conditions such as a recession may mean that there is less demand for commodities.

(d) The sale or purchase of a commodity usually involves dealing in a different currency, so exchange rate changes can be an issue.

(e) Wars or political uncertainty may prevent the sale or movement of a commodity.

(f) Change in attitudes or public 'scares' can reduce demand and prices quite quickly.

4.3 An investor in commodities will deal either:

(a) **For immediate delivery**. In this instance the buyer wishes to take delivery of the commodity. The trade is for immediate delivery and is known as a physical or actual. The price paid is known as the spot price, or

(b) **For delivery at a future date**. In this instance the delivery is not necessary for three months. As there is no physical delivery the investor is dealing in futures. The basics of futures were described in Chapter 10.

4.4 An investor in commodities can deal directly through a broker if he has large amounts to invest or indirectly through an offshore pooled fund investing in commodities. This type of fund still presents a high risk but it is modified by a spread, professional management and a lower minimum investment.

Exercise 6

An investor wished to invest in commodities.

(a) List the risks.
(b) How could he limit the risk?

---

5 COLLECTIBLES

5.1 The following could be considered as **collectibles**.

- Works of art
- Antiques
- Coins
- Stamps
- Veteran cars

- Wine
- Limited editions of books
- Diamonds
- Gold

5.2 Collectibles have the following features.

(a) They produce no income.

(b) They are difficult to value. Their value is usually directly related to the price another collector is prepared to pay.

(c) There are changes in fashion of collectible items, so the value can vary.

(d) They are expensive to keep because they are vulnerable to atmospheric change, burglary and so on. There is therefore the additional cost of custodianship, maybe in a bank and heavy insurance premiums.

(e) The cost of buying and selling can be high, with dealers' margins or commissions being substantial.

(f) The item may be difficult to sell in a hurry and the price raised may be a great disappointment. The valuation for insurance purposes may be far in excess of the price obtained on a sale!

(g) Specialist knowledge is required in the selection of the item.

(h) The investor is vulnerable to the unscrupulous expert.

The use of collectibles in a portfolio

5.3 (a) Most investment advisers will not be called upon to recommend an alternative investment. The client will normally already have an interest in whatever the collectible item may be.

(b) The adviser must remember that typically the client is genuinely interested in this collectible item and the possession of it will give genuine pleasure. Looking at an original Gauguin on the dining room wall will give pleasure never experienced from holding a share certificate in the hand! Therefore a small number of collectible items can be included in a well balanced portfolio without causing too many problems.

(c) Collectibles may be of particular use to a higher rate taxpayer who has no intention of disposing of the items during his lifetime. As the artefacts generate no income, he will suffer no tax whilst he holds them, there will be no CGT on death and inheritance tax can be avoided if the item is given for national purposes or the public good.

Tax position of collectibles

5.4 (a) Normally no income is generated for the individual investor, and so consequently there will be no income tax.

(b) A charge to capital gains tax is likely to arise on the disposal of most collectible items if the gain is in excess of the annual exemption.

(c) The investor must be careful that he is not treated by HMRC as trading. If he is treated in this way any gains will be subject to income tax.

(d) If the collectible item is a motor car suitable for private use, the gain on the sale will be exempt from capital gains tax.

(e) Antiques and paintings, being chattels, are exempt from capital gains tax if the sale proceeds do not exceed £6,000. If the proceeds do exceed £6,000 marginal relief is allowed: the maximum capital gain is 5/3 of the excess over £6,000.

6 MEMBERSHIP OF LLOYD'S

6.1 Lloyd's originated in a coffee shop in the City of London in 1689. In 1774 it was established in the Royal Exchange and in 1871 was incorporated by Act of Parliament.

6.2 To understand **Lloyd's membership**, we must first understand the workings of the Lloyd's market. Lloyd's is a corporation of underwriters of mainly general insurance risks (Lloyd's underwriters) and insurance brokers (Lloyd's Brokers) who place the business in the market.

6.3 Lloyd's brokers negotiate and place their clients' business with the underwriters via the working underwriter.

6.4 The underwriters have formed themselves into a number of syndicates, approximately 200. Many of the underwriters (or **names**) do not themselves work in the market. They provide the risk capital and in return they will share in the profit or loss of their syndicate. They do in fact pledge the whole of their wealth to meet claims, ie they have unlimited liability.

6.5 The syndicate's business is run by an managing agent and the underwriters' interests are looked after by a members' agent. The accounts for each syndicate are drawn up each year but remain open for a further two years because of the time required for claims to be processed. Thus, the results for the 1991 underwriting year would have been announced in 1994.

6.6 In recent years there have been a number of scandals involving Lloyd's. These scandals involved both bad professional practice and, in some cases, fraud. For the years 1988 to 1992 syndicates recorded losses of over £8 billion. As a result of such problems, Lloyd's has introduced corporate capital to the market. Corporate capital made up 87.5% of Lloyd's premium capacity in 2004. Corporate bodies are allowed to become syndicate members and a number of Lloyd's investment trusts have been established. These trusts allow the investor to spread his capital amongst a number of syndicates.

6.7 A large majority of the remaining individual members of Lloyd's are no longer underwriting, but they must remain as members until all of their liabilities have been calculated and reinsured.

6.8 Individuals wishing to become a Lloyd's name will be introduced to a syndicate by the syndicate's members' agent. The prospective member would then decide the level of risk he wishes to take. This is known as the premium income level. The member would normally deposit with Lloyd's assets to the value of 40% of the premium income level.

6.9 In addition, the member must demonstrate a minimum amount of wealth (**net eligible means**) of £300,000, excluding his principal residence, private company shares, partnership assets and chattels. No more than 40% of the assets can be in the form of freehold or leasehold property (with at least 50 years unexpired).

Tax position of Lloyd's members

6.10 (a) An individual who is a name at Lloyd's is treated as someone carrying on a trade and is taxed under Schedule D Case I. Names can set aside up to 50% of their profit free of tax as a special reserve against future liabilities.

(b) The individual's income will be made up of: insurance underwriting profit, investment income on syndicate funds, interest and dividends on investments in his Lloyd's deposit.

(c) Names are allowed to treat underwriting profits as net relevant earnings for the purposes of investing in a personal or stakeholder pension.

Risks

6.11 (a) A significant risk is the **unlimited liability** borne by individual names If the syndicate of which the individual is a member suffers large losses then the member can lose his entire wealth.

(b) The member might be able to reduce his risk by the following means.

(i) Careful selection of a syndicate (Some syndicates are known to insure higher risks with a view to higher profit.)

(ii) Becoming a member of a number of syndicates in order to spread the risk

(iii) Limiting the amount of premium income he is prepared to underwrite

(iv) Ensuring that he is satisfied with the reputation of the syndicate underwriter

(c) **Corporate membership with limited liability** is now popular, and many names have established their own companies.

7 FILM PARTNERSHIPS

7.1 **Film tax reliefs** were introduced in 1997 to encourage investment in British film-making. These reliefs were set to apply up to 1 July 2005 but have been extended to 31 March 2006.

After that, the current scheme could be replaced by a new relief for film production expenditure.

7.2 Under the existing scheme, there is a full write-off for tax purposes on production and acquisition costs on films with a budget of up to £15 million, if they have been certified as 'British qualifying' by the Department for Culture, Media and Sport. The qualification criteria include that 70% of the cost of the film should be spent on film activity in the UK.

7.3 Partnerships have typically developed because the level of capital involved is high. The individual can benefit from opening year rules for taxation of new business and losses may be relieved against general income under section 380 of the Income and Corporation Taxes Act 1988.

7.4 **Film partnerships** are a specialised form of investment and the level of risk may be high. Most film partnerships are established as general partnerships, which can be registered in the UK or abroad. Because UK partnerships limit the number of partners to twenty, investment schemes expecting a large number of investors will normally register abroad.

7.5 Where investors have borrowed money to make their investment into a partnership, they are only entitled to an income tax deduction on the interest paid on their loan if the partnership carries unlimited liability. Typically the financing of a film partnership is a vital component of the investment returns it generates and without the income tax deduction on interest paid on partners' borrowings, the investment would not be attractive.

7.6 Sometimes, a film partnership will be involved in a sale and leaseback arrangements, leasing distribution rights in the films back to the vendors in return for pre-determined streams of lease rental payments.

CHILD TRUST FUNDS

8.1 The Government aims to promote positive attitudes to saving and to improve financial capability by funding a **Child Trust Fund (CTF)** account for each child born after 31 August 2002.

8.2 CTF accounts first became available in April 2005. The CTF is initially be funded by a **Government contribution**, with a further Government contribution, probably at the same level, when the child is seven years old. The Government is consulting on making further contributions at the secondary school stage.

8.3 The Government's initial contribution is **£250,** sent out to parents as a voucher which they can present to a CTF provider. An **enhancement** (for example, £27 for a child born between 1 September 2002 and 5 April 2003) is added to reflect the time between the child's date of birth and April 2006. An **additional £250** will be paid into the CTF accounts of children in families eligible for full Child Tax Credit (CTC) with household income at or below the CTC income threshold (£13,910 for tax year 2005/2006).

8.4 A range of institutions, including banks, insurance companies and Friendly Societies provide CTF accounts. **Friends and family** (including parents) may contribute up to £1,200 a year to the account. For many, this additional contribution option will be the most significant part of the CTF scheme.

8.5 The CTF will be held for the child until he reaches 18. Types of accounts available include **cash accounts, unit trusts** and **life products**. Equity-based CTFs may be either stakeholder or non-stakeholder products. **Stakeholder products** are risk-controlled by making sure that there is a mix of investments and that risks are reduced by switching to lower-risk investments (the process of 'lifestyling') as the child nears the age of 18.

8.6 There are the following statutory **minimum standards for stakeholder CTFs**:

- Penalty-free transfers between accounts and between CTF providers (except for stamp duty and dealing expenses)

- Minimum subscriptions of no more than £10

- Asset diversification and 'lifestyling'

- Annual management charge capped at 1.5% of fund value

8.7 There is **no income tax or capital gains tax payable** on the CTF. This applies even if parental contributions have been made.

8.8 When a child reaches the age of 18, the account loses its tax benefits and there will be no restriction on how the accountholder uses the money in their CTF account.

Chapter roundup

In this chapter we have studied:

- The features of various types of property investment

- The features and tax implications of investing directly in unquoted shares and via EIS and VCTs

- The outline details of investment in commodities, alternative investments such as works of art and antiques

- The outline details and background to becoming a member of Lloyd's

- Film tax relief

- Child Trust Funds (new in 2005)

Quick Quiz

1   What are the indirect methods of investing in property?

2   What is the tax position for an investor in an Enterprise Zone property?

3   If you let out a room in your house, how much rent can you receive each year tax free?

4   What is a spot price?

5   What might be the tax position on the sale of an antique which had been held as an investment?

6   What is the role of a managing agent at Lloyd's?

7   Name four traded commodities.

The answers to the questions in the quiz can be found at the end of this Study Text. Before checking your own answers against them, you should look back at this chapter and use the information in it to correct your answers.

Answers to exercises

1   (a)   Disadvantages of residential property as an investment are as follows.

    (i)   The investment is illiquid. The house can only be sold if a buyer can be found.

    (ii)   The sale of a residential property can be protracted and costly.

    (iii)   There is no guarantee that the value of the property will increase. Many purchasers experienced negative equity in the period 1989 - 1996. Their houses came to be worth less than their mortgages.

    (b)   Advantages of commercial property as an investment are as follows.

    (i)   The value may keep pace with inflation.

    (ii)   Property can produce an increasing rental income if good tenants are found and maintained.

    (iii)   It is a good balance to a portfolio of equities. The performance of property is frequently directly opposed to the performance of the stock market.

2   (a)   It may be difficult to exit from a property bond quickly if there is a run on the fund. The manager will need time to sell property and raise cash to pay out the investors. Therefore, there is a clause written into the contract giving the manager six months to pay out the value of the units in these circumstances.

    (b)   The income from an equity unit trust is paid to the investor net of 10% tax. Any capital gain on the trust could be subject to capital gains tax subject to the individual's circumstances, for example, if he has already used up his annual CGT exemption.

3   (a)   The advantage for a private investor in buying shares in an unquoted company is that if the investor chooses wisely, he may find himself with a large shareholding in a company which is successfully launched on the market and he may then make a substantial profit.

    (b)   Disadvantages for a private investor in buying shares in an unquoted company are as follows.

    (i)   Risk to capital
    (ii)   Illiquidity of shares

4   (a)   Four of the rules of an EIS scheme:

    (i)   The company must be unquoted but it need not be resident or incorporated in the UK.

    (ii)   The investor must not acquire more than 30% of the ordinary share capital of a particular company.

    (iii)   The company must carry out a qualifying activity.

    (iv)   The investors must subscribe for new shares.

    (b)   Tax reliefs available to a private investor in an EIS:

    (i)   The private investor can subscribe up to £200,000 per fiscal year into qualifying shares and obtain tax relief of 20% (2005/06).

    (ii)   The shares must be retained for three years to gain full tax relief. If a profit is made, the investor will pay no capital gains tax.

    (iii)   Losses can be used to offset other taxable income or chargeable gains.

    (iv)   The investor with large capital gains from the disposal of another asset can invest the gains in the EIS and defer payment of the capital gains tax.

    (c)   The investor who will gain most from the EIS is one who is investing gains from another disposal and deferring payment of the capital gains tax.

5   (a)   The main differences between an EIS and a VCT are as follows.

    (i)   The composition of a VCT is different. It potentially offers a more diverse portfolio than an EIS.

    (ii)   Losses incurred on a VCT cannot be offset against other income or chargeable gains.

    (iii)   CGT deferral relief is available for EIS but not for VCT, for shares issued on or after 6 April 2004.

    (b)   The EIS carries higher risk because there is total exposure to unquoted equities, whereas the rules for the VCT allow for loan stock (although not guaranteed loan stock) within the portfolio.

6   (a)   Risks associated with investments in commodities are as follows.

    (i)   The price of the commodity can change.
    (ii)   Weather conditions can ruin crops.

(iii) Economic conditions can have an effect.
(iv) Wars or civil unrest can prevent the movement of commodities.
(v) Changes in attitudes can reduce demand.
(vi) Changes in currency rates can have an effect.

(b) The investor can limit the risk by buying units in an offshore commodities trust.

PRACTICE QUESTION 10: OTHER INVESTMENTS (30 Marks)   *27 mins*

(a) (i) Compare the permitted investment of an Enterprise Investment Scheme (EIS) and a Venture Capital Trust (VCT).   (5 marks)

(ii) What is the maximum amount which could be invested in a Venture Capital Trust (VCT) in any one fiscal year?   (2 marks)

(iii) What is the situation if an EIS share is sold at a loss?   (3 marks)

(iv) How can an investor take advantage of reinvestment relief by investing in an EIS or VCT?   (5 marks)

(b) (i) Briefly describe the workings of the Lloyd's market.   (9 marks)
(ii) What are the risks involved in being a Lloyd's name?   (3 marks)
(iii) What are the risks associated with investing in antiques?   (3 marks)

The answer to the practice question can be found at the end of this Study Text

Chapter 12

TAX PLANNING

Chapter topic list	Syllabus reference
1 Introduction to tax planning	4.1
2 Income tax - making use of allowances	4.1
3 Capital gains tax - making use of allowances	4.1
4 Tax-advantaged investments	4.1
5 Inheritance tax mitigation	4.1

Introduction

In this chapter we pull together the information we have learnt so far in this course and begin to consider tax planning for the client. We will explain the importance of understanding a client's tax position before making investment recommendations. We will study the place for tax-free investments in a portfolio, the importance of providing pensions in investment planning and finally methods of mitigating inheritance tax.

1 INTRODUCTION TO TAX PLANNING

1.1 Having a thorough knowledge of a client's tax position is essential in any tax planning exercise. Having to pay tax on an investment can considerably reduce the return, so every attempt must be made to mitigate the effects of taxation. This may be done by making full use of the personal allowances, including the capital gains tax annual exemption, the age allowance and the lower rate tax band. Tax-free investments should be employed for an investor who is a taxpayer. Use may be made of the tax reliefs available on pension contributions, EIS and VCTs, if applicable. Finally, if the client has considerable assets which he wishes to pass to the next generation, methods may be employed to mitigate the effects of inheritance tax.

Civil partnerships – from 5 December 2005

1.2 The Civil Partnership Act 2004 – coming into force on 5 December 2005 – will put same-sex couples who have formed a civil partnership on the same footing as married couples for tax purposes. For example, such couples will enjoy the inheritance tax 'spousal' exemption, but will also suffer the disadvantages, such as anti-avoidance provisions. For capital gains tax purposes, there will be only one principal private residence exemption per couple. There will be no gain / no loss treatment on intra-couple disposals.

2   INCOME TAX - MAKING USE OF ALLOWANCES

2.1   Before looking at ways of improving a client's tax and investment position, review the tax rates and main allowances for the tax year 2005/06. These are shown in the Tax Tables after the main chapters in this Study Text.

2.2   We will now consider a number of methods of making full use of the allowances.

The non-taxpayer

2.3   (a)   If the client is a non-taxpayer, the most suitable type of interest-paying investment will pay gross interest up to the maximum of the personal allowance. Investments such as the National Savings & Investments Income Bond or a gilt may be suitable.

(b)   If applicable, such clients may make personal or stakeholder pension contributions net of 22% tax relief (which they can still get the benefit of).

(c)   If a non-taxpayer is married to a taxpayer, so long as the couple are not averse to the idea, the taxpayer can transfer assets into the name of the non-taxpayer to make use of the personal allowance. However, the adviser must remember that some clients are averse to this idea and tax advantages are not the only considerations in financial planning.

(d)   *Example of scheme to make full use of the personal allowances for husband and wife*

Ted Stokes is aged 55. In 2005/06, he has an earned income of £15,500 and gross interest received of £1,000 per annum. His wife, Anne has net earned income of £1,500.

Current situation - Ted Stokes

	£	£
Total income	16,500.00	16,500.00
Less personal allowance	4,895.00	
Taxable income	11,605.00	
First £2,090 @ 10%	209.00	
£8,515 @ 22%	1,873.30	
£1,000 @ 20%	200.00	
	2,282.30	
		2,282.30
Net spendable income		14,217.70
Plus Anne's net earned income		1,500.00
Total family net income		15,717.70

Situation after investment transferred into Anne's name

Ted Stokes

	£	£
Total income	15,500.00	15,500.00
Less personal allowance	4,895.00	
Taxable income	10,605.00	
First £2,090 @ 10%	209.00	
£8,515 @ 22%	1,873.30	
	2,082.30	
		2,082.30
		13,417.70
Plus Anne's net earned income		1,500.00
Plus income from investment (within personal allowance)		1,000.00
Total family income		15,917.70
Increase in family income		£200.00

The starting rate taxpayer

2.4 (a) If the client is a **starting rate (10%) taxpayer**, the adviser should ensure that the client is paid gross interest up to the level of the personal allowance or that he can claim back tax to this amount.

(b) Dividends are paid with a 10% tax credit and interest is paid net of 20% tax, and there is no scope to claim back any tax on income above the personal allowance.

(c) Clients in this tax bracket aged under 75 may make personal or stakeholder pension contributions, and will pay premiums net of 22% tax.

(d) If the client who is a starting rate tax payer is married to a higher rate taxpayer, there is an advantage in more investments being placed in his or her name. The first £4,895 of income will be tax free. Any income above this limit will be taxed according to whether it is dividend income or investment income. Dividend income receives a tax credit of 10% and for a basic rate taxpayer no further tax is due. For a higher rate taxpayer 22.5% extra tax would be due. Interest income is taxed at 20% and no further tax is due for a basic rate taxpayer. Higher rate taxpayers have to pay an extra 20% tax.

Children

2.5 (a) If children are given money by grandparents, then advisers should recommend investing it in such a way as to make maximum use of the personal allowance. Each child has a personal allowance of £4,745.

(b) If a child is given money by their parent, the income generated is treated as the income of the parent if it exceeds £100 per parent per tax year.

Married couple and civil partnerships

2.6 The married couples/civil partnerships age allowance applies only where one spouse is born before 6 April 1935. The amount of the allowance depends on whether at least one of the couple is aged 75 or over. A tax reduction of 10% of the allowance is given. Any allowance that is wasted can be transferred to the other partner or spouse. (As already mentioned, civil partnerships formed under the Civil Partnership Act 2004 are treated in the same way as married couples for tax purposes, with effect from 5 December 2005, when the Act comes into force.)

Age allowance

2.7 (a) Higher personal allowances are given to those over 65 who have limited income. The allowance reduces by £1 for every £2 that the income exceeds the £19,500 limit (2005/06) until it reaches the normal personal allowance. If a client's income is close to the age allowance, it is important to make sure that the portfolio is invested in such a way as to maintain the higher allowance.

(b) Taking the 5% withdrawal from an investment bond can be a useful way of maintaining the allowance, as the withdrawal does not count as income. However, there is a trap. On final encashment the whole gain, without top-slicing, is treated as income in the year of encashment and could lead to the age allowance being reduced.

Calculation of income tax: non-savings and savings income

2.8 It is necessary to separate out the types of income for taxation purposes. This is illustrated in the following example.

Elizabeth is a 50-year old widow with earned income of £29,000. In addition she receives building society interest of £6,000 and gross income from a NS&I Income Bond of £1,500.

Calculation of Elizabeth's income tax liability for 2005/06

	Non-savings income £	Savings income £	Total £
Earned income	29,000.00		
Building society income (£6,000 × 100/80)		7,500.00	
Gross income from NS&I Income Bond		1,500.00	
	29,000.00	9,000.00	38,000.00
Less personal allowance	(4,895.00)		
	24,105.00		
First £2,090 @ 10%	209.00		
Next £22,015 @ 22%	4,843.30		
First £8,295* of savings income @ 20%	1,659.00		
Balance of savings income of £705 @ 40%	282.00		
Tax liability	6,993.30		
Less tax on building society income taxed at source	(1,000.00)		
Tax due	5,993.30		

*£2,090 + £22,015 + £8,295 = £32,400

This underlines the fact that savings income can suffer tax at either or both of 20% and 40%.

Exercise 1

John, who is not married, has earned income of £45,000. He receives £2,000 gross per annum from an investment in gilts, £500 per annum from a personal equity plan and £1,000 in withdrawals from a bond (original investment £20,000). Calculate John's net income after tax.

---

3 CAPITAL GAINS TAX - MAKING USE OF ALLOWANCES

3.1 Every UK taxpayer has an annual exemption for capital gains tax (CGT), currently £8,500 (2005/06).

3.2 Holders of substantial amounts of individual company shares, unit trusts or investment trusts outside ISAs and PEPs who have achieved unrealised gains may wish to make use of the capital gains tax exemption by selling securities each year to cover the tax-free gain. Following the 1998 Finance Act, it is not possible to 'bed and breakfast' securities to crystallise a capital gains tax charge by selling and immediately repurchasing the same shares, but alternative similar investments can be purchased.

3.3 Alternatively, a husband could sell certain shares and at the same time his wife could purchase a similar number of shares in the same company. Or, shares sold by individuals can be repurchased in their ISA in order to crystallise the gain for CGT purposes – a tactic called 'bed and ISA' which is not affected by the 'bed and breakfast' rules. The dealing costs and the spreads between selling and buying prices need to be taken into account when evaluating such transactions.

3.4 Clients with large portfolios can be encouraged to invest in ISAs and other investments where gains are tax-free. This leaves more scope to make use of the CGT exemption elsewhere.

3.5 Clients should make use of allowable losses to offset against capital gains, but losses on assets held in ISAs cannot be used.

3.6 If appropriate, clients may own assets jointly. In this case, they can both make use of their annual capital gains tax exemptions. If this is not possible, then one partner who has made use of his annual exemption for capital gains tax may consider transferring the asset to his spouse. She can sell it, thus using up her annual exemption.

3.7 The introduction of taper relief for capital gains tax purposes could lead to tax planning ideas for retirement or school fees. If clients are able to tie up money for a period in excess of ten years, it may be possible to produce tax free returns.

Example. Suppose that £15,000 is invested now for ten years in a unit trust. If we assume a rate of 6% growth after charges, the return will be £26,863. The gain is £11,863, but because of taper relief only 60% is chargeable. This leaves a chargeable gain of £7,118 which may be covered by the annual allowance for CGT purposes in ten years' time and will thus give a tax-free return.

Exercise 2

List five investments which are exempt from capital gains tax.

---

4 TAX-ADVANTAGED INVESTMENTS

4.1 Taxpayers should be encouraged to consider making maximum use of tax-advantaged investments.

4.2 Non-taxpayers however, can most probably achieve a similar gross return without the restriction of tying money up for, say, five years.

4.3 Tax-advantaged investments can be of key importance for a higher rate taxpayer because the savings on both income and capital gains tax (if there are capital gains above the annual allowance) can be significant.

4.4 Some tax-free investments fall in the low risk area. These are cash ISAs and NS&I Savings Certificates. Cash can be held for immediate access in the cash component of an ISA, but once cash is withdrawn, the tax relief is lost. NS&I Savings Certificates tie up the investment for a full five years for capital growth.

Exercise 3

(a) In what circumstances would an adviser use NS&I Savings Certificates in a portfolio?

(b) What is the maximum amount which can be invested in the current issue of five year index-linked NS&I Savings Certificates?

4.5 **Existing PEPs** should be retained for their tax benefits. Where affordable, investors should look to utilise their **annual ISA allowance** (£7,000 maximum in 2005/06).

4.6 Advisers may recommend tax-exempt **friendly society savings schemes**. However, the tax incentive is only useful if the performance of the funds is good and charges are not too high. Otherwise the expenses can outweigh the tax advantage.

4.7 **Pension funds** enjoy tax reliefs and we will explore their role in tax planning in Chapter 13.

5 INHERITANCE TAX MITIGATION

5.1 Before looking at **estate planning** in this section we will look at the current **inheritance tax rates and exemptions**.

IHT rates and exemptions

Inheritance tax rates 2005/06

Nil band	£275,000
Full rate	40%
Reduced rate for transfers to and charges on certain discretionary settlements	20%

Reduced tax charge on death within seven years of Potentially Exempt Transfer (PET)

Death in years	0 - 3	4	5	6	7
% of tax paid	100%	80%	60%	40%	20%

Main exemptions for IHT

Annual exemption		£3,000
Small gifts		£250
Gifts in consideration of marriage:	parents	£5,000
	grandparents	£2,500
	other	£1,000

Business property relief

Unincorporated business, shareholding in qualifying unquoted companies	100%

The above table demonstrates that for many people the fear of their family having to meet high bills for inheritance tax on their death has been removed. There is full relief from inheritance tax for most businesses.

5.2 Nevertheless we will consider methods of mitigating inheritance tax. The very wealthy still have a problem and there is always the possibility that future legislation could reduce reliefs.

Mitigating inheritance tax

5.3 Some methods of mitigating inheritance tax, particularly for wealthier clients, are as follows.

(a) Make sure that the client has made a **will** and that all planning fits around the terms of this will.

(b) Make use of the **annual IHT exemption** of £3,000. This is available for husband and wife. Thus £6,000 per annum can be transferred to children or grandchildren. In addition, if the previous year's exemption has not been used, a total of £6,000 per person can be used.

(c) Make use of the **normal expenditure exemption**. This can be employed by someone who lives well within his income. This exemption allows an individual to give away amounts in excess of £3,000 per annum. He must make the gifts regularly, say, annually and after making the gift the donor must be left with sufficient income to maintain his normal standard of living without having to resort to capital.

(d) Consider using the **marriage exemptions**, with each parent and grandparent giving the married couple the maximum amounts.

(e) Consider making **potentially exempt transfers (PETs)**. As you will remember, a potentially exempt transfer is a lifetime transfer of value which is not exempt but does not give rise to an immediate liability to IHT because it is potentially exempt if the donor survives for at least seven years.

A potentially exempt transfer may be made by an individual to:

(i) Another individual
(ii) An accumulation and maintenance trust
(iii) A trust for the disabled, or
(iv) An interest in possession trust

Gifts to a discretionary trust are chargeable to IHT.

If the donor of a potentially exempt transfer survives for seven years, the capital will be outside his estate. On death prior to this, tapering relief is applicable, see table above. The gift has some effect even if the donor does not survive the seven years. It is only the amount of the original gift which is added back into the estate and the donee has had the benefit of the growth on the gift free of inheritance tax. The potential inheritance tax charge on PETs may be protected by the use of a gift inter vivos policy.

If PETs are being used, it must be remembered that when the assets are given away there is a potential liability to capital gains tax. Therefore it is prudent to select assets which have little or no liability to this tax.

(f) Make use of **equalisation of estates** between husband and wife. This gives scope for both parties to make use of all the gift exemptions and potentially exempt transfers.

(g) Make use of **gifts between spouses**, which are exempt from IHT, and pass over capital on death which falls within the nil band.

For example, if Bill Sims leaves his entire estate of £405,000 to his wife Beryl, there is no IHT to pay until her death. If we assume that Beryl dies one year later (in 2005/06) and there has been no increase in the size of the estate, IHT of (£405,000 – £275,000) × 40% = £52,000 will become payable on the second death.

If, instead, the wills had been drawn up leaving £275,000 to the children or grandchildren on Bill's death and the balance to Beryl, the surviving spouse, then on her death in the circumstances described above, her estate would only be worth £130,000. This would fall within the nil band and no IHT would be payable. Thus, £405,000 would have been passed to the family free of IHT.

There are a number of points to be made on the above planning idea.

(i) Although the scheme saves inheritance tax, it is important that the surviving spouse is left with sufficient capital to generate the level of income required. The scheme could work well if, say, the husband has a large pension from an occupational scheme which will continue to his wife. If the couple are too heavily reliant on investment income, it may not be appropriate.

(ii) Some insurance companies have marketed a **bond and will trust scheme** intended to answer to the problem of wanting to make use of the nil band but still have a source of potential income if things go wrong.

191

The bond and will trust scheme works as follows.

Husband and wife write their wills leaving the first £275,000 to the children in a power of appointment trust and the balance of the estate to the surviving spouse.

The husband and wife take out an investment bond for £275,000 which they treat as their own investment during their lifetime taking a 5% withdrawal if necessary.

On the first death, the bond becomes the subject of the will trust. The terms of the trust give the children an interest in possession but the surviving spouse is also named as a beneficiary. The trustees have power to make loans to the beneficiaries including the spouse. Thus, in an emergency the spouse has access to some capital.

The trust finally pays out on the death of the surviving spouse.

(iii) In some instances, if the next generation have already accumulated assets which bring them into the IHT bracket, it may be more sensible to 'miss a generation' and pass capital to the grandchildren.

(iv) A deed of variation may be employed after the death of an individual if it is executed within two years of the death. Thus, if Bill had written his will leaving his entire estate to Beryl, then with agreement from the family, the estate could be rearranged to pass capital to the children. Beryl, who has given up her benefit, is not treated as making a transfer of value for IHT purposes.

Exercise 4

List the types of exemption available for inheritance tax purposes.

Life assurance and investment plans in inheritance tax planning

5.4 We will now look at various life assurance and investment plans employed to mitigate inheritance tax.

Pension plans

5.5 It is important that the death benefits under a retirement annuity or personal pension plan are written in trust so that they pass to beneficiaries on the death of the investor free of IHT. In this context, advisers should check the terms of any retirement annuities which their clients hold. Years ago it was not common for the whole of the fund to be available on death prior to retirement. Many policies only returned the premiums paid with or without interest. It is often possible for the return on death to be altered. The client suffers a small reduction in pension, but depending on circumstances, this may be worthwhile in order to secure the higher death benefit.

If the client is a member of an occupational scheme, it is important that he has completed a nomination request. This will enable the trustees of the scheme to pass the benefits to the beneficiary of his choice free of inheritance tax.

Whole of life policies

5.6 (a) Although many clients wish to pass money to their children and to save inheritance tax, they may not like the idea of passing over large sums of money to their children during their lifetime.

(b) The solution to this problem may be to use a whole of life policy. The scheme works as follows.

(i) The client effects a whole of life policy written in trust for named beneficiaries such as the children or grandchildren or under a flexible trust to allow the settlor to amend the beneficiaries if necessary.

(ii) The client pays monthly or annual premiums to the policy. The premiums are treated as potentially exempt transfers for inheritance tax purposes. However, the premiums should fall within the annual exemption of £3,000 or make use of the normal expenditure exemption.

(iii) On death the benefits pass to the beneficiaries free of all tax.

(iv) The policy may be written on a single life or joint lives. If husband and wife have written wills leaving their entire estate to the surviving spouse, a joint life last survivor whole of life policy may be effected. In this event the benefits are paid out on the death of the survivor and can be used to pay the inheritance tax if required, or alternatively, to boost the beneficiaries' inheritance. If a joint life policy is being used, premiums of up to £6,000 per annum can be paid thus using both lives assured's annual exemptions.

(c) The advantage of using a whole of life policy are as follows.

(i) Instant insurance cover is available. The settlor could pay one premium and then die. The full sum assured would still be paid to the beneficiaries.

(ii) The beneficiaries do not need to know of the existence of the policy.

(iii) The beneficiaries do not even have to be named at outset. If the settlor uses a flexible trust, he has power to appoint beneficiaries at a later date.

(iv) The policy is funded from income so the settlor still keeps control of his capital.

Exercise 5

(a) If a whole of life policy is written on a joint life second death basis under an absolute trust, what are the inheritance tax implications?

(b) What are the attractions of using a whole of life policy as a means of mitigating inheritance tax?

Funding plans

5.7 We have seen in the section above the merits of using a whole of life policy as a means of passing capital to beneficiaries free of inheritance tax. Sometimes clients do not have sufficient income to fund such a policy, or they may be wary that even if they can afford the premium today, they may not be able to in five or ten years time. The answer may be some form of funding plan. We will now consider a number of these.

(a) **Back to back arrangements**. We considered back to back arrangements in Chapter 5. If a back to back is employed for inheritance tax mitigation the contracts used are an immediate annuity and a whole of life policy on a single or joint lives last survivor basis. The following process takes place.

(i) A lump sum is paid, most of which is used to purchase the immediate annuity, with a small balance being paid as the first premium to the whole of life policy.

(ii) The whole of life policy is written in trust.

(iii) In each subsequent year the net income from the annuity is used to pay the premium to the whole of life policy.

193

(iv) On death the annuity ceases and the whole of life policy pays out the tax-free amount to the beneficiaries.

There are the following inheritance tax implications of the scheme.

(i) The purchase of the annuity has the effect of reducing the value of the estate.

(ii) The payment of the premiums into the whole of life policy will be treated as a potentially exempt transfer for inheritance tax purposes but hopefully should fall within the annual exemption or the normal expenditure rule. Care must be taken if the client is resorting to the normal expenditure rule, because only part of each annuity payment can be treated as income for tax purposes (the interest content).

(b) In some cases a client says he cannot afford to proceed with a back to back arrangement because he cannot afford to relinquish the income currently received from the capital to be employed in the plan.

If this is a problem and the original capital has been invested in, say, shares yielding 4% then it may be possible to put into effect the back to back arrangement and also replace the income in whole or part.

The method of doing this is to fund a slightly smaller whole of life policy and to use the excess income from the annuity to replace the income.

Care must be taken to ensure that HMRC (formerly the Inland Revenue) do not treat a back to back arrangement as an associated operation. If both contracts are purchased from the same insurance company, HMRC could say that correct underwriting had not been carried out. The argument would be that, because the company is receiving a substantial amount of capital to purchase the annuity, it has a vested interest in securing the business by applying lenient underwriting terms, ie an associated operation, the purchase of one contract – the annuity – facilitating good terms on the whole of life policy.

Conversion plans

5.8 (a) Some clients do not like the idea of the immediate annuity and whole of life plan because of the loss of the capital. One way around this is the use of a conversion plan.

(b) In this case, an investment bond and a unit linked whole of life policy are used on a single or joint lives last survivor basis.

(c) The majority of the lump sum is used to purchase the bond and the balance is used as the first premium for the unit linked whole of life policy. The contracts can be written on a single life or joint lives last survivor basis and written in trust for named beneficiaries or under a flexible trust.

(d) A withdrawal is taken from the investment bond of up to 5% of the original investment. This withdrawal is used to pay the premium to the whole of life policy. If there is an excess, this can be passed to the client to use as income.

(e) On death, the whole of life policy pays out a tax-free sum to the beneficiaries.

(f) However, the remaining value of the bond forms part of the donor's estate. The value may be subject to inheritance tax and higher rate income tax on any gain.

Single premium whole of life policy

5.9 (a) In some cases, a single premium unit linked whole of life policy can be used for inheritance tax mitigation.

(b) The single premium whole of life policy is often used by younger people.

(c) A capital payment is made to the policy, units are purchased in the selected fund and each month units are cancelled to pay for the life assurance.

(d) It is assumed that if the units grow at, say, 7.5% per annum, there should be sufficient in the policy to fund the life assurance premium for the client's life. If investment returns fall, the amount of cover may have to be reviewed.

(e) The policy is written in trust and on death the guaranteed death cover is paid out to the beneficiaries. The IHT situation will depend on the time the trust had been in force. The original purchase of the policy would be treated as a PET and therefore the settlor would need to survive for seven years for the capital sum to fall outside his estate.

(f) There may also be a charge to higher rate tax on the settlor's estate as a result of the chargeable event which occurs on his death. A chargeable event will occur if the surrender value is greater than the original purchase price.

Other schemes for inheritance tax mitigation

5.10 (a) Some clients like the idea of being able to make a gift but retain an interest in the gift or retain an income. The schemes outlined above allow this.

(b) Before 18 March 1986, it was possible to set up such a scheme where a **gift with reservation** was made to a trust. The Finance Act 1986 stopped these schemes. If a client was fortunate to have one in place, this can continue, but no new schemes of this type can be written and no further money placed in existing schemes.

(c) Insurance companies issued modified schemes called gift and loan arrangements.

Gift and loan plan

5.11 The gift and loan scheme works in the following way.

(a) The settlor creates a trust to which he gives £3,000 as a PET.

(b) The settlor subsequently lends the trustees a much larger amount of money, say £100,000. This is an interest-free loan repayable on demand.

(c) The original gift and the loan are invested in an investment bond. The trustees take advantage of the 5% withdrawal facility to repay the loan to the donor over a 20 year period.

(d) The inheritance tax implications are as follows.

 (i) The original gift is not chargeable to IHT as it makes use of the annual IHT exemption.

 (ii) On the settlor's death any outstanding loan is repaid to his estate from the proceeds of the bond and may be subject to IHT. The estate is also responsible for any charge to higher rate tax which may have occurred on the encashment of the bond. Whether this is payable will depend on the settlor's income in the year of death.

 (iii) The balance of the bond is paid to the beneficiaries free of IHT.

PETA plan

5.12 A PETA plan is a discounted gift scheme which works as follows.

(a) Assuming an investment of £110,000 the capital is split into two parts: £100,000 purchases a pure endowment policy which runs to age 105. £100 pays a premium to a term assurance policy. The policy has a sum assured of £100,000 to be paid on death before age 110 and is written in trust for named beneficiaries (or a flexible trust can be used).

(b) The pure endowment produces an annual bonus which is paid to the donor as income.

(c) On death which is assumed to be before age 105, the pure endowment policy only has a death value of 0.1% of the original investment plus any non-distributed bonus. This is returned to the estate. The term assurance pays out £100,000 to the trustees to distribute to beneficiaries free of IHT.

(d) The inheritance tax implications are that if the donor survives for seven years there is no IHT to pay other than on the small value from the pure endowment which falls into the estate (see (c) above). There is an added advantage. If the donor dies within the seven years, his estate does not have to pay IHT on the full value given but on a discounted value. The discounted value is calculated on the loss to the estate. For example, if a male of 65 effected such a plan for £100,000 and died within the seven year period the discounted value of the gift could be £45,000.

Series of endowment policies

5.13 (a) With this scheme, a series of single premium endowments is established with maturity dates from year 3 to age 100 of the life assured. The proceeds of each policy are written in trust for the benefit of the investor on maturity or for named beneficiaries on earlier death. At maturity the investor could take the proceeds or alternatively the trustees could extend the term by a further 10 years (not beyond age 100).

(b) Initially the scheme is a PET for inheritance tax purposes but once it has been in force for seven years it should be tax-free. No chargeable gain occurs on death because on death the endowment has no surrender value.

Offshore bonds

5.14 (a) There are a number of IHT packages produced by offshore companies. One scheme involves the purchase of a capital redemption bond which is placed in trust. The trust is a flexible power of appointment trust allowing the settlor to name his spouse amongst the potential beneficiaries. A capital redemption bond has no life assurance or lives assured and is written for a maximum of 99 years. As death does not trigger a chargeable event, the bond can be transferred through the generations.

(b) Another offshore scheme involves a series of single premium endowment policies with different terms. The endowment policies are put into an interest in possession trust as a PET. All growth thereafter is free of IHT. The settlor has a reversionary interest in the trust and the trustees can pay to him the proceeds of the endowment policies as they mature. The maturity of the policies creates a chargeable event.

(c) Another offshore plan involves a retained interest trust which splits the beneficial ownership of the plan into donor and given sections. The given section is a PET for IHT purposes and the donor section can be used to produce income.

Pre-owned asset tax

5.15 An income tax charge known as the **pre-owned asset tax** was introduced from 6 April 2005. This may tax the notional benefit received, eg from use of the home, where individuals have entered into tax planning to reduce their inheritance tax liability without completely divesting themselves of the asset. This may affect certain tax planning schemes involving the family home.

Chapter roundup

In this chapter we have studied:

- The importance of the client's tax position in investment planning

- The use of various products in inheritance tax planning

Quick Quiz

1　What rate of tax is deducted from a building society deposit account net interest payment?

2　If a father invests £5,000 in a building society account for his daughter, what are the tax implications?

3　What is the current nil rate band for inheritance tax purposes?

4　When may you use a deed of variation?

5　Why would you use an immediate annuity rather than a temporary annuity in a back to back arrangement for inheritance tax purposes?

6　How may you justify a gift out of normal expenditure for IHT purposes?

7　Name three types of insurance scheme designed to mitigate IHT.

8　What is the amount of the small gifts exemption for IHT?

The answers to the questions in the quiz can be found at the end of this Study Text. Before checking your own answers against them, you should look back at this chapter and use the information in it to correct your answers.

Answers to exercises

1

	£	£
Earned income	45,000.00	45,000.00
Gross income from gilts	2,000.00	2,000.00
Total gross income	47,000.00	47,000.00
Less personal allowance	4,745.00	
Taxable income	42,255.00	
Tax		
£2,020 @ 10%	202.00	
£29,380 @ 22%	6,463.60	
£10,855 @ 40%	4,342.00	
		11,007.60
		35,992.40
Plus tax free income from PEP		500.00
Plus 5% withdrawal from bond		1,000.00
Net spendable income		37,492.40

2　Five investments which are exempt from capital gains tax, within applicable limits:

(a)　Personal Equity Plans/ Individual Savings Accounts
(b)　EIS
(c)　VCTs
(d)　Gilts
(e)　NS&I Savings Certificates

3   (a)   An adviser might recommend NS&I Savings Certificates for a portfolio if the client wanted guaranteed capital appreciation. The return would be tax-free.

     (b)   £15,000

4   Exemptions for IHT purposes:

     (a)   Gifts between spouses
     (b)   Annual exemption
     (c)   Gifts in consideration of marriage
     (d)   Small gifts
     (e)   Gifts out of normal expenditure
     (f)   Gifts to charities
     (g)   Gifts for public benefit
     (h)   Gifts to political parties

5   (a)   The premiums paid to the joint life second death policy are gifts for IHT purposes. However, normally the amount should fall within the annual exemption (2 × £3,000 as it is a joint life policy) or, alternatively use can be made of the normal expenditure exemption. On the second death, the proceeds will be paid to the trustees who will pass the money on to the beneficiaries free of all tax, including IHT.

     (b)   The attractions of using a whole of life policy to mitigate IHT are as follows.

        (i)   It is a tried and tested method which the Inland Revenue (now HMRC) have accepted for many years.

       (ii)   The beneficiaries do not need to know that they will benefit from the policy until the settlor/s are dead.

      (iii)   The policy can be funded from income which leaves all the client's other assets free for his own use.

      (iv)   If a flexible trust is used the settlor can appoint the beneficiaries at any time.

The practice question at the end of Chapter 13 covers topics included in this Chapter.

Chapter 13

PENSIONS IN INVESTMENT PLANNING

Chapter topic list	Syllabus reference
1 Introduction to pensions in investment planning	4.2
2 Making use of pension tax reliefs	4.2
3 Making provision for income in retirement	4.2
4 Investment planning at retirement	4.2
5 Pensions simplification proposals	4.2

Introduction

Planning for retirement is one of the most important aspects of investment planning and should include the use of pension products. In this chapter we will look at the part such products play in this planning, at the different situations for the self-employed and the employed, those in pension schemes and those making provision for themselves.

In giving advice relating to the tax year 2005/06, advisers need to take account of the major changes to be made to the UK pensions regimes with effect from 6 April 2006. These changes have been referred to as 'pensions simplification' and are covered in the final section of this chapter.

1   INTRODUCTION TO PENSIONS IN INVESTMENT PLANNING

1.1 Generally the greatest advantage of membership of any pension arrangement is the tax relief which the investor receives on the contributions paid. Although some investments allow tax-free roll up, PEPs and ISAs and some low rates of tax relief, EIS and VCT, it is only pension contributions which are currently eligible for full tax relief, at 40% if applicable. But although HMRC gives tax relief on payments, the main benefit – the pension – is taxed as earned income during retirement.

2   MAKING USE OF PENSION TAX RELIEFS

2.1 In order to encourage prudent savings for retirement, successive governments have provided tax incentives to those who make such provision. These tax incentives for pension schemes are as follows.

(a) The employee and the employer receive tax relief on any contributions made (within HMRC limits).

(b) If the employer contributes to a scheme on behalf of his employee, his contribution will not be treated as a benefit in kind of the employee.

(c) An approved pension fund is normally exempt, and so it pays no tax on interest received by the fund or gains made on the realisation of assets within the fund. Pension funds cannot however reclaim tax credits on UK dividends.

(d) Certain benefits are allowed to be taken from a pension scheme free of tax, eg a tax-free lump sum at retirement.

3 MAKING PROVISION FOR INCOME IN RETIREMENT

3.1 We will now look at a number of circumstances in which a client may need to make additional provision for retirement. The different circumstances are as follows.

(a) The client who has to date made no contributions to a pension scheme. This may be because he or she had heavy expenses, such as large monthly mortgage payments or school fees, which have taken first call on his income.

(b) The client who has, to date, thought that he or she will rely totally upon the state pension benefits.

(c) The client who has been building up a business, has taken only low drawings and has made no provision for a pension.

(d) The client who has a business and has, to date, thought he would rely on the proceeds of the sale of his business to fund his retirement income. The recession may have opened his eyes to the fact that his business may not be worth as much as he originally thought. Equally he should not rely too heavily on a business asset to provide for his retirement income, particularly now that the phasing out of retirement relief from CGT has been completed (in April 2003).

(e) A client who had a career break to bring up children or to care for elderly parents.

(f) A woman client who has been recently divorced or widowed.

(g) The client who has led a peripatetic life style, not staying long enough with any employer to build up an adequate pension.

(h) The client who has a series of frozen pensions from previous employers. If he left employment prior to 1985, some of these benefits will not have kept pace with inflation.

(i) The client who has been badly advised in the past. He has pension contracts but, for reasons of high charging or poor performance, the benefits are not adequate.

(j) The client who is a member of an occupational pension scheme. He may have considered that he was in an excellent scheme. However examination of the scheme may reveal that the benefits are not as good as anticipated. The reasons could be as follows.

　(i) If the eventual pension is a percentage of the client's final salary, the definition of this final salary may be based on basic salary rather than total remuneration. This can have a significant effect on the expected level of income, particularly for a salesman or other employee who relies heavily on bonus or commission to make up the majority of the pay packet.

　(ii) Some schemes have a built-in reduction in pension. For example the eventual pension may have a deduction equal to the basic state pension.

　(iii) The employee will not be a member of the scheme for a sufficient length of time to build up a decent level of retirement income.

3.2 We have now established that many clients have made inadequate provision for their old age. The next stage in the process is to decide how much income or capital they will need in retirement.

Assessing the need for income

3.3 The assessment of how much income is needed is a complicated one. The client should consider and take into account the following points.

(a) If he were to retire today, how much income would he need? To make this judgement the client needs to list the income he is likely to receive in retirement.

Sources of pensions in retirement

(i) State pension and any additional state pension (now the State Second Pension or S2P)

(ii) Pension from previous employers' pension scheme/s

(iii) Pension from existing employer's pension scheme, retirement annuity or personal pensions

(b) Whether the pensions in his list are likely to increase in retirement and if so, by how much?

(c) Whether there are spouse's pensions provided and is so, at what level, are they 100% of the full pension or 2/3rd or 1/2?

(d) **Income from investments**. In calculating this item, the client must consider other assets which may create income.

(e) **Income from a part-time job or consultancies** which may be undertaken in retirement. However, this source of income should probably not be relied upon too heavily. In retirement the client may enjoy his leisure so much that he may not want to work, the work may not be forthcoming or illness may prevent it.

(f) We list the possible sources of income.

Assets which could be used to create income

(i) Maturing life assurance policies

(ii) Other maturing investments

(iii) Inheritances

(iv) Capital from the sale of a business

(v) Capital from the sale of, say, a holiday home

(vi) Capital from the sale of the principal residence (relevant if the client decides to retire to a smaller house)

(g) In calculating the value of the assets, the client and his adviser must take into account any tax which may need to be paid on realising these assets.

(h) The client must then repeat the exercise for his spouse, making a calculation of her possible income and assets at retirement date.

(i) The client should then turn to expenditure. How much money will he need to live on in retirement?

(i) Some of his expenditure will remain the same, subject to inflation.

(1) Council tax
(2) Insurances
(3) Household bills (although these may rise from extra consumption)

(ii) Some of his expenditure may **reduce**.

(1) The mortgage may be paid off.

(2) The children may have finished full-time education and be self supporting, but are not always!

(3) Contributions to pension scheme, permanent health insurance and possibly savings schemes will have ceased.

(4) The cost of going to work will be removed, for example the cost of a season ticket, work clothes and lunches

(iii) Some expenditures are likely to be added or **increased**.

(1) The client will be at home more, so heating and other household bills may rise.

(2) The client will want to enjoy retirement, so the cost of leisure activities such as holidays, trips to the theatre and sporting activities will increase.

(3) Premiums for health care will increase and the client may be paying premiums for long-term care.

(4) Petrol and travelling costs are likely to increase.

(j) The client must also consider that his retirement is likely to fall into three definite stages and his requirement for income will change.

Stage 1 This is hopefully the active stage when the client and spouse take holidays and enjoy their sporting and cultural activities.

Stage 2 As the client becomes older he may slow down and spend more time at home. His spending may then reduce.

Stage 3 The client may be in need of outside help to deal with the day-to-day living requirements and eventually full time care. This is an expensive stage.

(k) Consideration must also be given to the needs of the spouse, should the client die at any of the stages listed in (j) above. He will need to decide how much income his spouse will need. Will the need for income be the same, bearing in mind that the costs of running the home, for example, are much the same for one or two people?

(l) Having made these calculations, the client should have a fair idea, in today's terms, of the amount he needs to live on in retirement and the shortfall he has revealed. This, of course, is only a shortfall in today's terms. The client should be advised:

(i)   Of the effect of inflation on the value of his assets and income
(ii) Of possible changes in legislation which may affect pension provision
(iii) Of possible changes to state pension benefits

(m) How will he fill the pension gap? He must save either in a pension arrangement or some other form of investment. As stated at the beginning of this section, saving via a pension policy has some very distinct tax advantages.

Exercise 1

List the tax advantages of:

(a) Contributing to a pension scheme
(b) Contributing to an Individual Savings Account
(c) Contributing to a Venture Capital Trust

3.4 We will now look at the type of pension scheme arrangement which could be recommended.

The pension recommendation will depend upon the status of the client. We will need to find out some information.

(a) Is he self employed and, if so, does he have existing retirement annuity policies (RAPs) or personal pension plans (PPPs)?

(b) Is he employed but not eligible to join a company pension scheme? If so, does he have existing company pensions from previous employers, retirement annuities and/or personal pensions?

(c) Is he employed and eligible to join a company scheme, or already a member of a scheme?

(d) If he is a member of an occupational pension scheme, is it a final salary scheme or a money purchase scheme?

(e) If he is a member of an occupational pension scheme, is he already paying additional voluntary contributions (AVCs) or free standing additional voluntary contributions (FSAVCs)?

(f) If he is employed, is he a member of a group personal pension arrangement?

(g) If he is employed, is he contracted in or out of the State Second Pension (S2P)?

(h) If in an occupational scheme, is he or has he been a controlling director, and have his earnings been under £30,000?

Status of the client

3.5 We will now look at different possible client situations.

Self-employed

3.6 (a) In this case, the client will only receive the basic state pension if he has been self-employed all his working life. If he has not, then he may be entitled to a small amount of S2P/SERPS or the old graduated pension scheme.

(b) In this case the client can make contributions to an existing retirement annuity contract or personal or stakeholder pension plan.

(c) Under HMRC contribution limits, £3,600 gross pa can be paid into a personal or stakeholder pension plan by an eligible individual **without reference to income**.

Retirement annuity contract - maximum contributions as % of net relevant earnings (not subject to earnings cap)

Age on 6 April	%
50 or less	17.5
51 – 55	20.0
56 – 60	22.5
61 – 74	27.5

Personal pension - maximum contributions as % of net relevant earnings (subject to the **earnings cap**, which is £105,600 for 2005/06), applying where contributions exceed £3,600. The **net relevant earnings** to apply are the highest of the earnings in the current and the preceding five tax years, any of which can be selected as the **basis year**.

Age on 6 April	%
35 or less	17.5
36 – 45	20.0
46 – 50	25.0
51 - 55	30.0
56 - 60	35.0
61 - 74	40.0

(d) If the client has a large capital sum available to invest and he has made little or no pension provision in the past, he may be able to contribute this to a retirement annuity or personal pension, and may be able to make use of the one-year carry back provisions.

Exercise 2

Check your existing knowledge of personal pensions.

(a) How many years can you carry forward relief? How are past years' earnings taken into account in calculating maximum contributions?

(b) In what circumstances can you carry back a personal pension contribution?

(e) **Personal pensions** were introduced in July 1988, and if the client is taking out a new pension contract or has only been contributing to an existing policy for a few years, his contract will either be a personal or stakeholder pension policy. **Stakeholder pensions,** introduced from 6 April 2001, are effectively a type of personal pension plan conforming to standards on **charges, access** and **terms (CAT standards).** CAT standards mean that stakeholder pensions issued after 5 April 2005 have **charges** capped at 1.5% for the first ten years, and 1% thereafter. Contributions as low as £20 must be accepted, and there must be no requirement for regular contributions. Transfers in and out must be possible without penalty.

(f) The client will need to decide on the level of contribution he will have to pay to achieve his target pension income. It may well be that he cannot afford to do this at the present time. In that case he should be encouraged to make a contribution at a level he can afford with an annual review to compare actual results with the target pension. Above £3,600 pa gross, contributions are limited to an age-related percentage of **net relevant earnings** subject to the **earnings cap** (given in the **Tax Tables**). As noted earlier, instead of the current year, any of the previous five years may alternatively be taken as the **basis year** for the calculation.

(g) The client will need to decide whether he will pay regular premiums or single payments. The advantages and disadvantages of both methods are as follows.

Regular premiums

   (i) A regular contribution is an excellent method if the client is not disciplined about saving money.

   (ii) A regular premium can take advantage of pound cost averaging.

   (iii) **Waiver of premium** is possible so that contributions can continue during a period of ill health. For plans set up after 5 April 2001, this must be in a separate contract.

   (iv) The main disadvantage of the regular premium contribution is that it usually suffers heavier charges than the single payment.

Single payment

   (i) The self employed client can review his financial situation at the end of each accounting period and make the appropriate single payment depending upon his profit.

   (ii) The single payments paid in different years can be invested with different insurance companies to achieve a spread of investment.

   (iii) The single premium contract does not suffer such heavy charges as the regular premium policy.

(iv) The main disadvantage is that, in some years, the client may think he has insufficient funds to make his pension payment, thus considerably reducing the potential retirement income.

(h) It is no longer possible to take out a new retirement annuity policy. These contracts were superseded by personal pensions in 1988. However, if the client has existing retirement annuities and personal pensions, his adviser will have to recommend which type of contract will be the most suitable. Different contracts may be used in different years depending upon circumstances. The points which the adviser will take into account are as follows.

(i) It may not be possible to add to an existing retirement annuity. If the original contract was a monthly premium one, some insurance companies do not allow any increments or additional single payments.

(ii) If it is possible to add to the retirement annuity the client must be aware of the following.

(1) The minimum retirement age will normally be 60 rather than 50 under a PPP.

(2) The investment choice may be restricted. The contributions to many old retirement annuities can only be invested in the traditional with profits fund.

(3) A client with high net relevant earnings may invest in the retirement annuity. The reason is that the **earnings cap**, £105,600 in 2005/06, does not apply to retirement annuities. He may, therefore, be able to contribute a higher amount to the retirement annuity than to a personal pension. It does not always work because the higher percentage contribution to a personal pension may give a better result. (Do Exercise 3 below to see the effect of this.)

(4) It may be possible to take a larger tax free lump sum from a retirement annuity at retirement. However, if annuity rates are low, this is not necessarily so.

(iii) Even if a self-employed client uses a retirement annuity to maximise contributions, he can, at any time after age 50, transfer the benefits to a personal pension and take early retirement.

Exercise 3

(a) John is aged 48 has net relevant earnings for 2005/06 of £100,000. In previous years, his earnings were lower. He wishes to make the maximum pension contribution in 2005/06. He could make this to a retirement annuity or a personal pension plan. Which should he choose?

(b) Jeff is aged 44 and also has net relevant earnings for 2005/06 of £150,000. In previous years, his earnings were lower. He wishes to make the maximum pension contribution in 2005/06. He could make this to a retirement annuity or a personal pension. Which should he choose?

Client is employed but not eligible to join a company pension scheme

3.7 (a) In this case, the client has the same choices as we have looked at. He may contribute to a personal pension or retirement annuity or both, depending on circumstances.

(b) However, the employed person has other options.

(i) He may be able to persuade his employer to contribute to the personal pension. The combined contribution of employee and employer must be within the maximum percentage limits.

(ii) He may wish to contract out of S2P. If the client is a man under age 45 or a woman under age 40, it may be sensible to contract out using a personal pension. The contracting out decision should be reviewed on an annual basis. If the charges under the policy are low, the pivotal age may be higher. Some commentators have suggested that all people should stay contracted-in, if possible.

(iii) The client may have preserved pension arrangements from a previous employer and he may be keen to consolidate all his pension provision into one contact. The adviser will need to give very detailed advice in this area which we now look at below.

Employed person with pension arrangements from previous employments

3.8 (a) The adviser will need to gather detailed information of the previous scheme or schemes so that a full transfer analysis may be carried out. If he discovers that one of the schemes is a final salary arrangement, unless the client left the employment before 1985, it is unlikely that it will be in the client's interest to transfer because of:

   (i) Guarantees offered by final salary schemes
   (ii) Potential increases to pensions in payment and other benefits
   (iii) The initial costs of a new scheme

(b) If he discovers that the scheme was a money purchase arrangement or another personal pension, the decision to transfer must be founded on:

   (i) The initial and ongoing charges of the new scheme

   (ii) The investment performance of the funds within the existing arrangement and the choice of funds and whether this is better or worse than the proposed scheme

(c) If a transfer is made, the adviser can suggest using a personal pension plan or a **s 32 'buy out' policy**.

(d) The personal pension offers the following advantages.

   (i) It may give a higher tax-free sum at retirement, but not always.

   (ii) It may provide greater flexibility. For example the client can select a different retirement age to that stated in the previous scheme.

(e) The s 32 policy offers the following advantages.

   (i) It ensures that the **guaranteed minimum pension (GMP)** is secured. This, of course, only applies if the previous scheme was a contracted out final salary scheme. A transfer to a personal pension on the other hand gives no such guarantees. The GMP becomes 'protected rights'. The value of protected rights at retirement is totally dependent on investment performance.

   (ii) It may be possible to take all the benefits early whereas, under a personal pension plan, the protected rights portion cannot be withdrawn until age 60.

Employed person who is eligible to join a company pension scheme

3.9 (a) The adviser should find out whether the client has been a **controlling director** of any company at any time since 6 April 2000, and whether he has earned more than £30,000 pa in each tax year since that date. If both of these do not apply, the client may contribute to a personal or stakeholder pension plan as well as being a member of an occupational scheme.

(b) The adviser needs to establish what type of scheme is the client eligible to join. Is it final salary or money purchase? Then he needs to know the likely waiting period before the client can join the scheme and whether life assurance will be provided during this period.

(c) If there is a waiting period, the adviser will have to consider what advice, if any, he should be giving about immediate pension payments, bearing in mind that a short period of investment into say a personal pension will be heavily charged.

(d) The adviser will need full details of the scheme benefits.

(e) The maximum benefits which can be provided under an occupational pension scheme, whether final salary or money purchase, where a member is subject to the Finance Act 1989 regime, are as follows.

Maximum pension - 1/30 of final remuneration for each year of service up to 20 years plus spouse's 2/3rds pension.

Maximum tax free cash - the greater of 3/80 of final remuneration for each year of service or 2.25 × initial pension.

Maximum death benefit - up to 4 × final remuneration lump sum, plus spouse's 2/3rds members prospective pension. Plus a return of contributions and reasonable interest.

Note. The salary used to calculate final remuneration is restricted to the earnings cap.

(f) The adviser will need to know if the scheme is contributory or non-contributory and if it is contributory, the amount the employee will be asked to pay.

(g) The adviser will need to know the retirement age under the rules of the scheme and whether there are provisions for early retirement.

(h) The client does have a choice not to join the scheme and to opt out. In almost all cases, to opt out would not be best advice for the following reasons.

  (i) The employer will normally contribute to the pension scheme, whether it is money purchase or final salary. It is unlikely that the employer will contribute to the client's personal pension policy.

  (ii) The company scheme will most probably include death in service benefits which the employee will forfeit if he does not join.

  (iii) If the employee changes his mind at a later date, the trustees can refuse him entry to the scheme and, if he is allowed re-entry, he may have to submit medical evidence in order to obtain the life assurance benefits.

  (iv) The client will be paying the expenses of setting up his own scheme.

  (v) The amount of the client's private pension will be totally dependent upon his ability to contribute to the scheme and the performance of his pension fund. If he joins an occupational scheme and in particular a final salary scheme, it is the employer's responsibility to ensure that there are sufficient assets in the fund to provide the guaranteed pension.

(i) If the client joins the company scheme or is already a member, he may wish to transfer benefits from an existing pension scheme. The decision in this case will be different from the process explained above for transferring to a personal pension arrangement.

(j) If a transfer is proposed to a company scheme, it will be necessary for the previous scheme to quote a transfer value. The trustees of the client's existing scheme are then asked if they will accept this. If they will, then the client will wish to know the amount of additional benefit they will give him for the transfer. A comparison of benefits will then need to be carried out. The likely results are as follows.

(i) If the client is transferring from a final salary scheme to another final salary scheme or from a money purchase to a final salary scheme, the trustees of the new scheme will normally say that the transfer value will buy the member a number of additional years of service in the scheme.

Example of the purchase of additional years of service

Bob is aged 55 and the retirement age under his occupational pension scheme is 65. It is a final salary scheme with an accrual rate of 1/60ths. He transfers in benefits from a previous scheme which purchase him a further three years service. When his final pension is calculated it will be based on 13/60ths of final remuneration rather than 10/60ths.

(ii) The adviser will need to calculate whether the added years quoted will give the client a better pension than leaving it with the original scheme. In making the calculation he will need to compare other benefits such as spouse's pensions, and potential increases to pensions in payment.

(iii) The added years formula should work to the client's advantage if he is likely to receive an increasing remuneration from the date of transfer until retirement.

(iv) If the proposed transfer is from a final salary scheme to a money purchase scheme then the decision to move will be based on a comparison of benefits. In most cases it will be best advice to leave the benefits with the final salary scheme because of the underlying guarantees. There are no such guarantees in a money purchase arrangement.

(v) If the transfer is from one money purchase scheme to another then the decision to transfer is based on charges and investment performance. The adviser needs to decide if the potential investment performance under the new scheme will be better than the old and what effect the charges may have on reducing the potential yield.

Employed person in a company pension scheme but with insufficient retirement income

3.10 (a) If a client is a member of an occupational scheme and he carries out the calculation studied earlier in this chapter, it is likely that he will find that there is a shortfall of retirement income, especially if he wants to retire early.

(b) The client may use an additional voluntary contribution (AVC) to make up this shortfall in whole or part or, if eligible under the **concurrency rules** (see (e) below), he may contribute up to £3,600 pa gross to a personal pension plan.

(c) For AVCs, the client has a choice of an in-house scheme which must now be offered by all schemes or going to an outside provider, a free standing additional voluntary contribution scheme (FSAVC). Remember that a controlling director will not have the choice of an FSAVC.

(d) When making a choice of which type of AVC scheme, the client should consider the following points.

(i) If he stays with the in-house AVC scheme he may be offered a money purchase scheme. In this case he must look at the charges and the funds available for investment. Normally the charges will be low but the choice of funds may be restricted to, say, a building society or with profits fund.

(ii) The in-house AVC scheme may give him the opportunity of purchasing additional years of service. This system works in the same way as we have described for transfers. This method is attractive for the client who foresees considerable increases in his salary prior to retirement. It is, however, not a good idea if the client considers moving jobs shortly. The added years will be cut back on leaving service and then it may not seem such a good buy.

(iii) Advantages of the FSAVC are as follows.

    (1) Choice of provider

    (2) Choice of funds

    (3) Choice of retirement age: the retirement age under a FSAVC does not have to be the same as the main scheme so long as the main scheme can provide for early retirement. This gives scope for saving for early retirement even when the main scheme would appear to be giving maximum benefits.

(iv) The main disadvantage of the FSAVC is the charges.

(e) With the new regime for stakeholder pensions and other personal pension plans introduced in April 2001, personal pensions contributions of up to £3,600 pa gross should also be considered for clients in occupational pension schemes. Under the **concurrency rules**, anyone in an occupational scheme who is a controlling director in the tax year in which contribution is made or was a controlling director at any time during the previous five tax years, and anyone who earned £30,000 or more in each of the previous five tax years, is ineligible. For the purposes of both of these rules, years before 2000/01 are ignored. However, other individuals may contribute up to £3,600 pa gross to a stakeholder or personal pension plan. An advantage of personal pension contributions over AVC schemes is that 25% of the fund can be taken as a tax-free lump sum when the pension is taken.

(f) The client does have a further choice, should he wish to use some other form of investment to build up funds for retirement. That choice is an **Individual Savings Account (ISA)**.

(g) In making a choice from AVCs, a personal pension plan and an ISA (choices which are not mutually exclusive) the client should take into consideration the following points.

(i) The drawbacks of saving to provide for additional retirement benefits by means of AVCs or personal pensions.

    (1) The benefits which have to be taken as pension are taxed as earned income.

    (2) There is no facility to take a tax-free lump sum for post 8 April 1987 schemes, but this is possible with a personal pension.

    (3) Should the client select an excellent fund which performs very well, this could result in an over-funded situation. In this case, the surplus is returned to the client less tax at 32% (basic rate liability). Higher rate tax payers would suffer a rate of about 48%.

(ii) The advantages of saving to provide for additional retirement benefits by means of an ISA are as follows.

    (1) A tax-free capital sum can be taken.

    (2) The tax-free sum can be withdrawn at any time.

    (3) The investment rolls up in a tax exempt fund.

(4)   A tax-free income can be withdrawn.

An employed person who is a member of a group personal pension scheme

3.11   (a)   If a client is a member of a group personal pension arrangement or has the opportunity to become a member, it will normally be to his advantage. The points to check are as follows.

(i)   Does the employer make a contribution and if so, how much?

(ii)   Are the contributions invested with a reputable insurance company with a wide choice of funds and switching facilities?

(iii)   Is the past performance of these funds competitive: for example, are they in the top quartile in their sector?

(iv)   Are the charges on the individual policy less because the client is joining a group arrangement?

(b)   If the scheme is invested with an insurance company with poor performance or there is no reduction in charges for joining the group arrangement, the client may be better advised to effect his own personal pension with a provider of his choice with potentially better investment performance. He could then ask his employer to make a contribution. The employer may well refuse, having gone to the bother of setting up the group arrangement.

A director of his own company

3.12   (a)   If the client is a director of his own company then he has more control over his pension provision. He can choose a personal pension (retirement annuity) or an individual occupational scheme known as an **Executive Pension Plan (EPP)**.

(b)   If the director only wishes to pay modest contributions, well below the maximum allowed for personal pensions (PPP) or retirement annuities, then the PPP may be a good option. The contract is flexible allowing for retirement from age 50 (PPP) and there is very little administration.

(c)   The advantage of the executive pension plan is that a larger contribution can be made. The scheme can also provide higher tax-free lump sum benefits.

Exercise 4

(a)   An employee leaves a company pension scheme with a final salary of £150,000. He joined in 1988. What is the maximum tax-free lump sum he can take, based on eight years service?

(b)   If the same employee had a personal pension with a fund value of £200,000, what is the maximum tax-free cash sum he could take in 2005/06?

(d)   The director may wish to take advantage of a **Small Self Administered Scheme (SSAS)**. This type of scheme would give him the following opportunities.

(i)   The advantage of appointing his own investment manager who could run a portfolio of shares, gilts, property, unit trusts, investment trusts, other fixed interest securities and cash.

(ii)   To take a loan back from the fund for use by his own company.

(iii)   To use the pension fund to purchase property which may subsequently be used by his own company.

(iv) The ability to withdraw (or 'draw down') income from his pension fund at retirement rather than buying an annuity. (Although this facility is now available under all personal pensions, it is only available under those occupational schemes that allow the option, and few do in practice).

Investment choices

3.13 If a client has control over his pension scheme, he will also be able to select the fund or funds into which his contributions are placed. We will now consider the choices available to him.

Investment choice for those using retirement annuities and personal pensions

3.14 (a) If a client is still using a retirement annuity it is likely that his investment choice will be restricted to with profits.

(b) The choice under a personal pension will usually be much wider ranging from with profits and unitised with profits, through managed funds to the specialised higher risk areas such as the Far East, USA, Europe and emerging markets.

(c) The selection of funds will depend upon the client's attitude to risk.

(d) If the client is young and is prepared to take a medium to high risk he could be recommended to select an equity fund with the prospect of long term growth in excess of inflation.

(e) As a client draws nearer to retirement age he should switch the emphasis of his investment, say, first to a managed fund and gradually towards fixed interest. By the time he reaches retirement age, he should have consolidated all his gains into a totally safe fund.

(f) If the client is a sophisticated investor with large funds to commit to a personal pension plan, he may wish to consider a **Self-Invested Personal Pension plan (SIPP)**. In this instance the contract will have all the features of a normal personal pension but the client can select his own fund manager. The manager can purchase and then manage a portfolio of shares, gilts, unit trusts, investment trusts and even property. SIPPs are also available on an execution-only basis, for the individual who wishes to make his or her own investment decisions without receiving advice.

Investment choice for the member of an occupational scheme

3.15 (a) If the client is a member of a final salary scheme, he has no investment decisions to make. The decisions are made by the trustees who are guaranteeing him a certain level of pension.

(b) If the client is a member of a money purchase scheme, he may or may not have an investment decision to make. Some employers/trustees make their own decision as to the investment of the pension scheme and the members have no say. Others allow the members a small choice of funds. These are usually cautiously managed funds, for example a choice between with profits or managed fund. In these circumstances it may be wise for the younger client to select the managed fund and the older the with profits, although some would say that with profits investments should generally be avoided.

Investment choice for those investing in an AVC or FSAVC

3.16 (a) If the client chooses the company AVC scheme, he may not have much investment choice. The selected funds will usually be conservative, possibly a choice between with profits and a building society.

(b) If the client selects a FSAVC scheme, he will have a choice of with profits and a full unit-linked range. His selection will depend upon his attitude to risk.

(c) If the client is young and is prepared to take a medium to high risk, he could be recommended to select an equity fund for long term growth in excess of inflation.

(d) As a client draws nearer to retirement age he should consider switching the emphasis of his funds from more risky investments, say first to a managed fund and gradually towards fixed interest. By the time he reaches retirement, he should have consolidated all his gains in a totally safe fund.

Exercise 5

(a) What are the investment choices under a SIPP?
(b) What are the investment choices available to a member of an occupational pension scheme?

Selecting a pension provider for a personal pension, FSAVC or executive pension

3.17 The adviser will need to take into account features, charges, investment performance and company strength.

(a) **Features.** The features he should consider are as follows.

   (i) Does the contract allow for premium holidays without penalty? This feature is of particular importance to women who may need to take months or years off work to bring up children or care for elderly parents.

   (ii) Is there a facility for varying contracts, eg moving from personal pension to executive pension scheme without penalty?

   (iii) Is it possible to take the benefits early without penalty?

(b) **Charges.** The adviser will need to take note of the initial and annual management charges in the contract and the reduction in yield which may arise.

(c) **Investment performance.** The adviser will take into consideration the choice of fund and the performance of these funds. It is normally preferable to choose a company with a number of funds with consistent performance, rather than a company which has one top flight fund. If the manager of the top flight fund leaves, the investor has little choice if the other funds are poor performers. A company which has funds which have shown consistent performance over long periods should be highly regarded as a pension provider.

(d) **Financial stability.** The provider's financial stability is very important in the selection of any investment. However, with a pension contract it has even greater significance. The client will wish to invest with a company which will still be operational when he wishes to draw his pension.

4 INVESTMENT PLANNING AT RETIREMENT

4.1 In this chapter we have discussed at some length the type of advice which should be given to those planning for pension provision. As the client nears retirement age, he requires further advice. We will now look at the various types of client and the advice they may need.

Member of a final salary occupational scheme

4.2 (a) The client will want advice on whether to take the tax-free lump sum and, if so, whether he should take the maximum sum or less. The choice will depend on the following.

    (i) The client's need for the cash. Does he want to buy a new car, buy a retirement home or pay off a mortgage, for example?

    (ii) How important it is to achieve an increasing income in retirement. If the pension scheme payments increase in payment, there may be an argument for retaining as large a pension as possible so that there is a larger income to be increased each year.

    (iii) The client's state of health. If he is not in good health, the best advice may be to take the lump sum and invest it. Taking the tax-free lump sum does not affect the level of spouse's pension. This remains the same as if no cash had been taken.

  (b) The client may also want advice on a compulsory purchase annuity. The trustees can be asked to quote a transfer value and the adviser can check annuity rates to see if it is possible to purchase enhanced benefits from an alternative insurance company.

Member of a money purchase occupational scheme/group personal pension/personal pension arrangement

4.3 (a) Once again the client may want to know if they should take the tax-free lump sum. In this case the answer is almost always yes, even if he requires the total pension.

  (b) The reason for taking the maximum lump sum is that he can use this to buy a purchased life annuity. Whereas the pension from the scheme is taxed as earnings through the PAYE system, the income from a purchased life annuity, is treated partly as a return of capital and partly as income and the net result should be an enhanced income.

  (c) As the money purchase occupational arrangement is a 'piggy bank' scheme, the client has a fund and must select his benefits.

    These may be as follows.

    (i) A level pension for his life

    (ii) A level pension for his life but guaranteed to be paid for five or ten years irrespective of survival

    (iii) A pension which increases in payment whether by a set amount or linked to the RPI. He can even choose a with profit or unit linked annuity

    (iv) A pension payable to a spouse on his death (This can remain level or reduce by one-half or one-third.)

  (d) The client also has the choice of taking an **open market option** annuity. This means that the client can transfer the fund to an alternative provider if an improved rate can be achieved on the annuity of his choice.

(e) Since 1995, it has been possible to defer the purchase of an annuity from a personal pension scheme by making use of a **drawdown of income facility**. (Similar rules were introduced in 1999 for money purchase occupational schemes and buyout contracts.)

(f) The main conditions of the drawdown facility are as follows.

    (i) The income withdrawn must be within a range agreed by the government actuary and reviewed every three years.

    (ii) The income withdrawal may be taken between age 50 and 75.

    (iii) An annuity must be purchased at or before age 75.

    (iv) On the member's death a number of options are available.

        (1) The spouse or dependants can continue to take income withdrawals until she or the member would have reached aged 75, whichever is the sooner.

        (2) The spouse may purchase an annuity.

        (3) The fund can be taken as cash subject to a 35% tax charge.

(g) Selecting the drawdown facility does not affect the client's option to take part of the benefit at retirement as a tax-free lump sum.

(h) If the client does not want to take the lump sum, he may exercise another option and that is to take **phased retirement**. In this case his personal pension is broken down into, say, 1,000 policies. Benefits are taken gradually using mainly the tax-free lump sum to create tax efficient income in the early years of retirement. Using this method the annuity is purchased over a number of years thus obtaining a possible improvement in rates provided by an increase in general interest rates and the client's advancing age.

(i) If a client is a member of a money purchase or final salary occupational scheme, it would be possible for him to transfer his benefits before normal retirement age to a personal pension. He would then be in a position to use the drawdown or phased retirement methods. It is however likely that this option will shortly be introduced for occupational schemes.

Client retiring with a retirement annuity

4.4   (a) If a client has a retirement annuity, he will have the same problems as outlined above.

    Should he take the tax free lump sum? And: What type of annuity does he need?

    The answers will be the same as previously discussed.

    (b) If the client wants to make use of the phased or drawdown facility, he will have to transfer his contract to a personal pension.

    (c) He will also need to transfer his contract to a personal pension if he wishes to retire before age 60.

    (d) An open market option normally exists on a retirement annuity but, in order to exercise it, the fund must be transferred to another retirement annuity. As it is impossible to establish a new one, this means that exercising the option is virtually impossible. However, there is a way around this: the client transfers the retirement annuity to a personal pension and then exercises the open market option. He hopefully secures a better annuity rate although the tax-free cash sum may be slightly less.

Exercise 6

(a) What is an open market option?
(b) What is a compulsory purchase annuity?
(c) What is a drawdown facility?
(d) What is a phased retirement facility?

5 PENSIONS SIMPLIFICATION

Overview

5.1 In recent years, the Inland Revenue and the Department for Work and Pensions have put forward proposals for reform of pension arrangements. These proposals have led to legislation for **pensions simplification** which is contained in the Finance Act 2004. The pensions simplification proposals are expected to be brought into force on 6 April 2006. However, because the decisions people make now will sometimes be affected by the impending changes, it is important for advisers to know about the expected changes. It is also important to appreciate that not all of the changes have been finalised yet.

5.2 There is also a new **Pensions Act 2004**. The changes arising from the Pensions Act concern such matters as the funding of schemes, the security of benefits, and contracting-out requirements.

5.3 The pensions simplification proposals and pension reforms will lead to various changes from 6 April 2006, as described in the following paragraphs.

5.4 There will be a **single tax regime** for all pension schemes, to replace the currently different arrangements for different types of scheme.

Lifetime allowance and enhanced and primary protection

5.5 Under the new unified scheme, there will be a single structure of limits. There will be a **lifetime allowance** limit on the total value of funds or benefits at retirement, covering benefits from all pension sources. The lifetime allowance will be on a rising scale, starting at £1.5 million per person in 2006/07 and increasing as follows over a five year period.

Tax year	Lifetime allowance
	£m
2006/07	1.5
2007/08	1.6
2008/09	1.65
2009/10	1.75
2010/11	1.8

5.6 For the purpose of checking whether this limit is breached, the value of a pension benefit in a **final salary (defined benefit) scheme** will be converted to an equivalent fund value at a factor of 20:1, with annual pension increases being converted at a rate of 10:1. Thus, a pension benefit of £30,000 per year will be valued at £600,000.

5.7 If the value of a person's accumulated funds and benefits exceeds the lifetime allowance, a tax charge called the **recovery charge** will apply at the time that benefits are taken. The recovery charge will be at a rate of 25% of the excess fund, where benefits are taken in the form of income. The individual is permitted to take excess funds as a lump sum, in which case the recovery charge will be 55% of the excess.

5.8 If a person already has pension funds exceeding the lifetime allowance at 6 April 2006 ('**A-Day**'), he may register the value of the funds and then the registered fund will become that person's **personalised lifetime allowance**.

5.9 The personalised lifetime allowance limit will be increased annually in line with the increases in the normal lifetime allowance. This type of arrangement is called **primary protection**.

5.10 Through **enhanced protection** arrangements, it is possible to avoid any recovery charge on benefits accrued by 'A-Day' (6 April 2006), but only if the individual makes no further contributions and accrues no further benefit under registered pension arrangements.

5.11 From an investment point of view, someone who opts for **primary protection** may decide to adopt a relatively low risk approach to investment. If growth exceeds the rate of increase in the lifetime allowance, the recovery charge will be applied. This means that he would run the full risk of loss if he adopted a higher risk, higher potential return strategy, but the upside would be reduced by the potential tax charge. A lower risk approach with the pension fund might however be balanced by a more aggressive stance with other assets.

5.12 **Enhanced protection** allows the individual to benefit fully from gains. This therefore should not hamper investment strategy, and indeed this basis is likely to appeal only to those intending to adopt a more aggressive approach. Whereas primary protection can only be applied to those with a fund in excess of the lifetime allowance on 6 April 2006 (it would be of no benefit otherwise), enhanced protection can be selected by anyone – though probably only those with a fund close to the allowance are likely to be attracted by it.

Annual allowance – contributions

5.13 From 6 April 2006, there will be a new basis for the annual limit of contributions to pension schemes. Contributions will generally be limited to the greater of £3,600 (gross) per year and 100% of annual earnings, with an overriding limit called the **annual allowance**. The annual allowance will be set at £215,000 for 2005/06, rising on a pre-set five-year scale as follows.

Tax year	*Annual allowance*
	£
2006/07	215,000
2007/08	225,000
2008/09	235,000
2009/10	245,000
2010/11	255,000

5.14 For all schemes, it will be possible to take a **tax-free lump sum of 25%** of the funds, when benefits are taken and a pension is obtained. This follows the current rules for personal and stakeholder pension schemes. This is a major change for occupational pension schemes. The new rule will also apply to Additional Voluntary Contribution schemes, for which there is not currently the possibility of taking a 25% tax-free lump sum.

Retirement benefits

5.15 Retirement income will be provided by purchase of an **annuity,** or by **secured income** provided by an occupational scheme, or by **unsecured income** – this last option probably applying only to a money purchase scheme. The unsecured income is similar to the income withdrawals that are currently possible. However, with the new arrangements there will be no minimum withdrawal as at present, so an individual could take the 25% tax-free lump sum but defer taking any income benefit until later. The maximum unsecured income will be 120% of the annuity that would otherwise be available. The limits must be reviewed only every five years (as compared with every three years as is currently required).

5.16 There will be a lifting of restrictions on drawing benefits from occupational schemes while employed by the same employer, and the concept of normal retirement age will be abolished. The minimum age for drawing benefits will be raised from **50 to 55**, although this change will not be introduced until **6 April 2010.**

5.17 The general rule that an annuity must be taken by age 75 at the latest will remain under the new regime. However, there will be an additional basis available only at age 75 for money purchase schemes known as **Alternatively Secured Income (ASI)** or Alternatively Secured Pension. The ASI arrangement is designed for members of certain religious groups for whom the mortality basis of annuities is unacceptable. Under ASI, the need to purchase an income is removed. The ASI basis does however carry restrictions on the death benefits that can be made available.

5.18 There will be the possibility of **commutation of trivial pension rights** for cash where the total value of such rights does not exceed 1% of the lifetime allowance. Commutation will only be available between ages 60 and 75. If benefits have not yet been taken, a 25% lump sum will be tax-free and the remainder will be taxable. If benefits have already been taken, the lump sum will be fully taxable.

5.19 A full tax-free commutation of pension rights is possible before age 75 if medical evidence of **serious ill health** is provided.

Other provisions

5.20 A funding test specific to the scheme will replace the **Minimum Finding Requirement** for occupational schemes.

5.21 A new pensions regulator will be established to replace the current **Occupational Pensions Regulatory Authority (OPRA).**

5.22 A number of features of current pensions legislation will disappear, including the earnings cap, restrictions on concurrent membership of different schemes and restrictions on transfers between different types of pensions.

SSAS and SIPP

5.23 The investment rules for **SSASs and SIPPs** will be brought into line, which should simplify advice considerably. There will be some advantages, including the ability to invest in residential property, but it is planned that the ability to borrow to invest will be restricted to 50% of the value of the fund.

Death

5.24 Pre-retirement, the only limit on lump sum benefits will be the lifetime allowance, initially £1.5m. There will be no limitation based on earnings. The tax free nature of the benefit will continue as at present.

5.25 After retirement, if income is unsecured, the residual fund will be capable of being paid as a lump sum on death, but there will be a tax charge of 35%, in the same way as currently applies to income withdrawal arrangements. Alternatively, income benefits can be provided for a spouse or for dependants.

5.26 If an annuity has been purchased, there will generally be no lump sum benefit, unless value protection has been included (see below), but the income can continue under a guarantee provision. The annuity can also include provision for it to continue, wholly or partly, to a spouse or to dependants.

5.27 It will not be possible to pay a lump sum benefit on death after 75 however.

Effects on investment strategy

5.28 There are various aspects of the proposals which will impact on investment strategy, including the impact of the transitional arrangements already discussed.

5.29 The lifetime allowance will affect investment strategy more generally for those with substantial defined contribution funds. An individual whose fund approaches the allowance is likely to want to adopt a lower risk strategy for exactly the same reasons that apply to someone using the primary protection transitional provisions.

5.30 Alternatively, he may choose to draw benefits early, and invest elsewhere. He could draw cash and crystallise the calculation of the value of benefits relative to the lifetime allowance, but defer income. This would allow a more aggressive investment approach without any recovery charge, but death benefits would be subject to the less favourable 'death after retirement' treatment where any lump sum is subject to a 35% tax charge.

5.31 The proposal to allow income withdrawals with no minimum will mean that different considerations will apply in designing a portfolio in some cases. For example, if market conditions are weak, this will allow those who can afford to do so to delay income and this may allow a more aggressive investment strategy. This however is dependent on the individual having sufficient other resources to provide for his needs.

5.32 There are also proposals to allow greater choice for **annuity purchase**, by allowing the following two new types of annuity, not currently available under pension legislation.

(a) **Value protected annuities** where, on death, if the total of the annuity instalments is less than the purchase price paid, a lump sum will be payable. This is the same concept as for capital protected annuities which have been available for many years under non-pensions legislation. (Guarantees will still be available, but will provide for continuation of income rather than any lump sum payments as can currently occur under occupational schemes.)

(b) **Short term annuities** (previously called limited period annuities), where part of the fund is used to buy an annuity for a short term, with a maximum of five years, and a maximum age of 75 at expiry. The rest of the fund remains invested. At the end of the term, a further portion of the fund can be used to provide a further short term annuity, or the whole fund could be used to provide a lifetime annuity. Alternatively, up to age 75, income withdrawals can be used after the temporary annuity ceases.

5.33 These changes will place still more emphasis on investment choices, with more situations arising where some or all of the fund will be invested beyond the point where retirement benefits start. For example, the ability to purchase a short term annuity may widen the appeal of continued investment, because it allows the individual to avoid risk in relation to immediate income needs, whilst maintaining a longer term equity investment. Care would be needed here as the end of the short term annuity approaches. There is perhaps a case for some investments to be moved slowly towards gilts over a period to facilitate the next annuity purchase.

5.34 Generally, the broader investment issues to be considered will be as at present, although increased flexibility will always mean wider choice and greater variations in the strategy adopted.

Chapter roundup

In this chapter we have studied:

- The tax reliefs applicable to pension products

- The pension products available to the employed and self employed

- The options available under the various policies and schemes at retirement age

---

BPP
PROFESSIONAL EDUCATION

Quick Quiz

1   What state pension benefits will a self-employed person receive?

2   How much more in percentage of net relevant earnings can a 63 year old earning £75,000 contribute to a personal pension compared to a retirement annuity?

3   How much is the earnings cap for 2005/06?

4   What do the letters GMP stand for?

5   What is the effect of buying 'added years'?

6   If a FSAVC was overfunded, how much tax would have to be paid by a basic rate policy holder?

7   What do the letters SIPP stand for?

8   If you use a drawdown facility, by what age must the annuity be purchased?

9   What happens if you wish to take an open market option from a retirement annuity?

The answers to the questions in the quiz can be found at the end of this Study Text. Before checking your own answers against them, you should look back at this chapter and use the information in it to correct your answers.

Answers to exercises

1   (a)   The tax advantages of contributing to a pension scheme are:

        (i)   Tax relief on the contributions
        (ii)   Part of the benefit at retirement is tax free
        (iii)   The investment rolls up in a tax free fund

    (b)   The tax advantages of contributing to a Individual Savings Account are:

        (i)   The investment rolls up in a tax free fund

        (ii)   There is no additional tax to pay on dividends for higher rate taxpayers (although tax credits cannot be reclaimed)

        (iii)   Any gain is tax free: it is not subject to CGT

    (c)   The tax advantages of contributing to a Venture Capital Trust are:

        (i)   Tax relief at 40% (2005/06) on the contribution up to £200,000.
        (ii)   No capital gains tax to pay on any profit if the trust is held for three years

2   (a)   It is not possible to carry forward relief. However, net relevant earnings can be taken as the highest of the earnings in the current and preceding five years. (Note also the new contributions rules being introduced from 6 April 2006.)

    (b)   A personal pension contribution can be carried back for one year only, if elected by 31 January in the tax year.

3   (a)   John can pay 17.5% of £100,000 to the retirement annuity, ie £17,500, or 25% of capped earnings of £105,600, to his personal pension. The amount he could pay to his personal pension is, therefore, £26,400.

    (b)   Jeff is slightly younger. He can pay 17.5% of £150,000 to the retirement annuity ie £26,250 or 20% of capped earnings of £105,600 to his personal pension. The amount he could pay to his personal pension is therefore less, at £21,120.

4   (a)   The maximum tax-free lump sum he can receive is 3n/80ths × earnings of £100,000 = 24/80 × £100,000 = £30,000. This is because he joined the scheme in 1988.

    (b)   The maximum tax-free lump sum which can be taken from the personal pension is 25% of the fund, ie 25% of £200,000 = £50,000.

5   (a)   The investment choices under a SIPP encompass listed shares (including overseas), gilts, unit trusts, shares in OEICs, investment trusts, loan stock, futures, options, insurance policies, traded endowment policies, cash and property (with some limitations).

    (b)   The investment choices available to the member of an occupational scheme depend upon the type of scheme. If it is a final salary scheme, the employee will play no part in the investment decisions.

If the scheme is a money purchase scheme, the employer may make the investment choice, or the employee could be given a choice, say between with profits or a unit-linked managed fund.

6 (a) An open market option is the option available at retirement to the person with a personal pension or retirement annuity. They can choose to transfer the fund from the original provider if they can obtain better terms elsewhere.

   (b) A compulsory purchase annuity is the same as an open market annuity option, but it is the option which applies to the member of an occupational scheme. He can transfer his fund if he can obtain better terms elsewhere.

   (c) A drawdown facility is a method of deferring the purchase of an annuity from the proceeds of a personal pension. The purchase can be deferred until age 75 and in the meantime income can be withdrawn from the fund.

   (d) A phased retirement facility is a flexible and tax efficient method of withdrawing benefits from a personal pension. The personal pension is converted into 1,000 policies and benefits are taken gradually making maximum use of the tax-free cash in the early years. The tax-free cash needs to be used as income if the scheme is to work properly.

PRACTICE QUESTION 11: TAX AND PENSIONS PLANNING (30 Marks) *27 mins*

(a) Harry sells securities worth £100,000 and invests in a gift and loan scheme writing the scheme in trust for his three children, Sarah, Harriet and James, absolutely.

   (i) Explain how the scheme would work.   (7 marks)
   (ii) Explain all the tax implications of this action.   (8 marks)

(b) You are the pensions manager for a final salary scheme. Jim comes to see you. He says that he is thinking of joining the scheme, but he has a personal pension and he has heard that he cannot belong to two schemes. He also has a frozen pension from a previous employer and he needs advice on how to deal with this.

   (i) Explain to Jim the current situation (under 2005/06 rules) concerning his personal pension and what actions are open to him.   (7 marks)

   (ii) Explain to Jim what information you would need from his previous employer in order to give him advice about his frozen pension.   (8 marks)

The answer to the practice question can be found at the end of this Study Text

Chapter 14

COLLECTING AND ANALYSING CLIENT INFORMATION

Chapter topic list	Syllabus reference
1 Introduction to collecting client information	3.1
2 Personal information	3.1
3 Financial information	3.1
4 The client's plans and objectives	3.1
5 Establishing investment needs and attitudes	3.1
6 Analysing client information	3.2
7 The role of the professional adviser	3.2

Introduction

In this chapter we will investigate how to collect and interpret relevant client data and establish the client's attitude to risk, inflation, taxation, liquidity, term of investment and investment objectives. We will analyse a client's financial situation including the preparation of a statement of current assets and income and expenditure. From these statements we will identify planning opportunities to mitigate income tax, capital gains tax and inheritance tax.

1 INTRODUCTION TO COLLECTING CLIENT INFORMATION

1.1 Collecting accurate information about the client is essential in the preparation of correct recommendations to meet the client's aims and objectives. It is also essential to comply with the rules in the Financial Services Authority Handbook.

1.2 Frequently a client will be ill-prepared to provide the information, so data collection may be a lengthy process. Detailed information must not be overlooked. If the client does not have the information immediately to hand, for example, a booklet concerning his employer's pension scheme, he should be asked to provide this as soon as possible.

1.3 If an adviser is giving advice to a client who is in a permanent relationship, the adviser must ensure that he has full information of the partner's financial affairs and his or her aims, ambitions and attitude to risk. They may be completely different to their partner's.

1.4 Most advisers use a fact find to collect the information. A formal fact find document is not essential but it does serve as an *aide memoire* for the basic information which is required. A simple fact find is reproduced at the end of this chapter.

2   PERSONAL INFORMATION

2.1   The personal information which is required is as follows.

- Name and address
- Date and place of birth
- Residence and domicile
- Marital status
- Health, hobbies and pastimes
- Children and other dependants

We will now look at each of these in more detail.

2.2   Name and address

(a)   This is simple but essential information. An adviser needs accurate information to write to the client and one way of annoying a client is the incorrect spelling of his name!

(b)   The full and accurate address is necessary for correspondence, and if you are checking on the client for money laundering purposes by access to the electoral roll.

2.3   Date and place of birth

(a)   The date of birth is important if the adviser is to recommend life assurance or annuity products. It is always a good idea to verify this by asking to see, and keeping a certified copy of, the birth and marriage certificate (if the client is a married woman).

(b)   The place of birth may be relevant in establishing a client's domicile.

2.4   Residence and domicile

A client's residence and domicile is important for tax purposes and may affect the type of investments the adviser will recommend.

2.5   Marital status

(a)   It is important to elicit the exact marital status of the client. If he is married or in a permanent relationship, it may be a good idea to have a meeting with both partners or at least to ascertain information about the partner's investments, financial aims, objectives and attitude to risk.

(b)   If a client is separated or divorced, this may have considerable implications on any tax planning. It will be useful to ascertain details of the settlement and any maintenance arrangements.

(c)   A client may have dependent children from a previous marriage. They will need to be considered in the proposed planning.

2.6   Health, hobbies and pastimes

(a)   It is important to ascertain the state of health of the client. This is relevant if the adviser is likely to recommend life assurance or permanent health cover. Sometimes this information is difficult to elicit because clients do not like to admit to illness. The adviser needs to emphasise the importance of knowing this information before he approaches underwriters rather than after he has received adverse acceptance terms.

(b)   A client's state of health may have long term implications on financial planning. If he is in poor health it may mean that he will wish to retire early or to move to a country with a more temperate climate than the UK.

(c) Knowledge of a client's smoking habits will be needed if life assurance is to be arranged.

(d) Hobbies and pastimes have an importance for life assurance or permanent health insurance as they could lead to the need for special questionnaires and ratings. It is important to ascertain as much detail as possible at the outset so that an accurate picture of the risk can be relayed to the insurance company.

(e) Interesting hobbies may also mean that the client will wish to create sufficient income to satisfy the requirements of his hobbies, perhaps for expensive equipment or travel and in the long term early retirement, so that he can pursue them full-time.

2.7 Children and other dependants

(a) It is important to establish how many children the client has, their ages, state of health and education plans. It is useful to know if they are being privately educated and if so, the current level of fees, possible increases and who is currently paying them, whether the client or perhaps grandparents. If there are plans for the children to go to university this, too, can be a cost for the future which will need funding.

(b) If the client has been divorced he may have dependent children from a previous marriage. The adviser will need to collect exactly the same information about these children as shown in (a) above.

(c) Not all dependants are children. A client could have a handicapped son or daughter or elderly parents who are financially dependant upon him. They, too, must be taken into consideration in the financial planning exercise.

Exercise 1

Why is it essential to have full personal details of the client? List the ones you think are most important.

---

3 FINANCIAL INFORMATION

3.1 The financial information required is the following.

Employment information

Employment status
Current employment
Previous employment
Retirement benefits
Other benefits such as permanent health insurance, private medical insurance
Other fringe benefits

Income

Earned income
Investment income/unearned income
Pension income
State benefits

Expenditure

Monthly, quarterly and annual expenditure
Tax and national insurance

Assets

Property
Business assets
Investments and savings
Protection policies
Pensions
Inheritances
Trusts

Liabilities

Mortgage
Business loans
Short-term loans

We will now look at these sections of information in more detail.

3.2 **Employment information.** The adviser will need to know if the client is employed or self-employed.

(a) **Employed**

(i) If the client is employed, the adviser will want to know something of the client's ambitions. Does he seek promotion? Is he likely to obtain promotion? If he is promoted, will this lead to an increase in remuneration or perhaps a house move to another part of the country or even abroad? Exploration may discover that the client is unhappy with his job or thinks that the company who employs him may shortly be going into receivership. All such information is relevant to the financial plan which will be developed for the client.

(ii) If the client is a company director of his own business, the adviser should ask to see a copy of the latest accounts which will show the company's year end and the current financial state of the business. He will need to ask the client about the shareholding of the company. Is he a controlling director? Does his wife and family own any shares?

(iii) He should then ask about the other directors and what arrangements are in place for share transference on death or long term sickness. Is a share agreement in place?

(iv) He might then enquire about the aims of the business. What are the plans for the business? Is it expanding? What are its sources of finance? Do the directors have a long term aim of a flotation on the stock market?

(v) He will need to know about pension arrangements for directors. Is there a pension scheme? When was it established? What are the benefits? If it is a SSAS he will need to ascertain who is the pensioneer trustee and whether there are any loans to the company or property purchase.

(vi) The adviser should then turn his attention to the employees. Has the company covered any key employees in the event that they cannot work through sickness or death? Is there a company pension scheme, accident and sickness scheme, private medical insurance or permanent health insurance arrangement?

(b) **Self-employed**

(i) If the client is self-employed the adviser will need to know if he is a sole trader or in partnership.

(ii) If the client is in a partnership, the adviser will need to know if there is a partnership agreement in place.

(iii) Many of the additional questions he needs to ask, particularly about employees, will be similar to those listed for the company director.

3.3 **Current employment**. The adviser will need to know the name and address of the current employer and the client's exact occupation. It will be useful to know when the client joined service as this may be relevant for pension purposes.

3.4 **Previous employer**. If the employee has only recently moved jobs, it is useful to know the name and address of his previous employer and whether he was a member of their pension scheme. The discussion of employers may lead to the client revealing that he tends to move jobs frequently and this may be relevant in any long term commitments that the adviser may suggest.

3.5 **Retirement benefits**

(a) If the client is employed, the adviser will want to obtain full details of the employer's pension scheme and of whether or not the client is a member.

(b) The best method of obtaining the information is from an up-to-date booklet and benefit statement. An **up-to-date booklet** is stressed because very often clients produce very dog-eared and old booklets which have obviously been superseded!

(c) If the scheme is a final salary occupational scheme, the adviser will need to know when the employee was first eligible to join, was there a waiting period and if so, did his pensionable service start from the date of joining the scheme or joining the company? What is the accrual rate of the scheme: 1/60, 1/80 or even 1/40?

(d) Do pensions increase in payment? If the increases are discretionary, what is the level of recent increases?

(e) What are other pension benefits? Is there a spouse's and dependants' pension and if so, at what level?

(f) Is the scheme contracted out of S2P?

(g) He will also need to know the definition of pensionable salary. Is it total earnings, including bonus and commission or restricted to basic pay?

(h) What is the definition of final pensionable salary?

(i) What is the normal retirement age?

(j) Is there a bridging pension between 60 and 65?

(k) What are the provisions for death in service benefits? Is there a lump sum benefit and if so, how much? Are spouse's and dependants' pensions provided and if so at what level?

(l) It is important to ascertain whether the client has completed a nomination form stating the names of the beneficiaries he would wish the trustees to consider for his death benefit.

(m) It would be useful to know if there provision within the scheme for early retirement and, if so, what is the penalty, if any?

(n) Is there a provision for incapacity pensions and how are they calculated?

(o) Is the scheme contributory and if so, how much do the members pay?

(p) What are the terms of the in-house AVC scheme and does the client belong?

(q) Is the employer likely to make any changes to the scheme shortly?

(r) Has the client made a transfer in to the scheme and if so what are the additional benefits purchased.

(s) Is the scheme money purchase scheme or group personal pension?

(t) If the client is a member of the in-house AVC scheme, the adviser will need to know the following.

    (i) The level of his contributions

    (ii) The fund into which the contributions are paid

    (iii) An up-to-date fund value

    (iv) Whether all or part of the contributions are being used to provide extra death in service benefits

(u) **Retirement annuities and personal pensions**

If the client is self-employed or not a member of an occupational pension scheme, the adviser will need details of any existing retirement annuities or personal pensions.

The information he will need is the following.

    (i) Name of insurance companies

    (ii) Policy numbers

    (iii) Retirement dates

    (iv) Amount of contributions and frequency

    (v) Funds being used and up-to-date fund values

    (vi) Whether there is waiver of premium

    (vii) Details of the benefit on death, whether return of fund or return of contributions with or without interest

    (viii) Whether the death benefits are written in trust

    (ix) Whether the policies are being used to contract out of S2P (for personal pensions only)

    (x) Whether the employer is making a contribution

    (xi) Whether the client has unused reliefs from previous years which could be carried forward

---

Exercise 2

Make a list of the questions you would ask a client who is a member of a company pension scheme.

3.6   **Other benefits**. If the client is employed the adviser will need to know whether he has other benefits provided for him under a group arrangement, such as the following.

Permanent health insurance
Private medical insurance
Accident cover
Critical illness

We will now look at the detail required for each type of cover.

3.7 **Income protection insurance (IPI)**. The adviser will need to ascertain the following information.

(a) The period of deferment

(b) The level of cover

(c) Whether the cover continues to retirement age or is it only short term cover?

(d) Whether the pension contributions are continued in the event of a claim

(e) Whether the cover escalates

(f) What is the definition of disability? (Any or own occupation)

(g) Whether the client has the ability to continue the cover when he ceases employment

(h) Whether there are any exclusions attached to the cover on grounds of health or because of a hazardous pursuit

(i) Whether the client has ever claimed under the policy

3.8 **Private medical insurance**. The adviser will need to ascertain the following information.

(a) The level of cover - is it full cover or restricted in some way, for example, it only comes into effect if treatment is not forthcoming on the NHS after a six week waiting period?

(b) Who is covered under the policy? Some employers only cover the employee. He must pay if he wants his partner and children covered.

(c) Is worldwide cover provided?

(d) Has the client claimed under the policy?

(e) Is there provision for the client to continue the cover if he leaves the company?

3.9 **Accident insurance cover**. Some companies cover their employees for additional death or injury by accident insurance. If this is the case the adviser will need to know the following.

(a) The amount of the cover provided
(b) Is the cover 24-hour cover or only effective while the employee is at work?
(c) Does the scheme provide worldwide cover?

3.10 **Critical illness cover**. If there is a group critical illness policy, the adviser will need to know the following.

(a) The amount of the cover.
(b) The full terms and conditions.

3.11 **Other fringe benefits**. The adviser will need to know if there is a share option scheme. If so, the terms of the scheme and whether the client participates.

3.12 **Benefits in kind**. The adviser will need to know the value of the client's benefits in kind if he is to calculate his total remuneration, for example for the purposes of calculating maximum pension contributions.

3.13 **Income**

(a) **Earned income**

(i) The adviser will need full details of the client's income whether he is employed or self employed. He will need details of basic pay, bonuses and commissions from all sources. The client may have a hobby which may bring in extra income. However small this is it must be taken into account.

(ii) Some clients do not have two occupations but they do have two sources of income from the same occupation, for example doctors and dentists who work for the NHS and for themselves.

(iii) If the client is self-employed the adviser should look at three years' accounts or contact the client's accountant for full details.

(b) **Investment income, unearned income**. The adviser will need to have details of the following.

(i) Interest from bank and building society accounts

(ii) Interest from gilts or loan stock

(iii) Dividends from shares, unit trusts or investment trusts

(iv) Rental income

(v) Untaxed income such as withdrawals from investment bonds or income from ISAs or PEPs

(c) **Pension income**. If the client already has a pension, details must be recorded. Remember the client does not need to be of retirement age in order to have a pension. Ex-employees of the fire service or police force can be in their early fifties and be in receipt of a pension. The adviser will need to know the following.

(i) The amount of the pension

(ii) The frequency of payment

(iii) How the pension is taxed

(iv) Whether it is guaranteed for a specific period and if so, for how long

(v) Whether it will continue to the client's spouse if he predeceases her and if so, at what level

(d) **State benefits**. The adviser will need to know if the client is in receipt of any state benefits and how they are taxed. These benefits may include the following.

Child benefit
State widow's pension
Income support
Jobseeker's allowance
Special allowances in the case of disabilities

Exercise 3

(a) Is child benefit taxed?
(b) Is income support means tested?
(c) Is long term incapacity benefit now tax free?

3.14 **Expenditure**

(a) The client should be asked to list his expenditure on a monthly, quarterly and annual basis. Within the list he must remember to include tax and national insurance.

(b) The purpose of this list is to establish the level of income required to sustain the family. This is the level of income that needs to be protected by life assurance and permanent health insurance.

(c) The income and expenditure statement will also reveal if there is any surplus income over expenditure which can be used to meet savings or protection needs.

3.15 **Assets**. The adviser will need details of the following.

(a) **Personal property**. The current value of the principal residence is required together with the value of any holiday home and contents, value of cars, boats etc.

(b) **Business assets**

   (i) It is difficult to value shares but the adviser should try and ascertain the value of any shares.

   (ii) It may be easier to ascertain the value of any capital loaned to the business by the director.

   (iii) Similarly, if the client is a member of a partnership, the adviser will need to know the amount of his capital account and arrangements to pay this out on death or resignation from the partnership.

(c) **Investments**. The adviser will need full details of the following.

   (i) Bank and building society accounts
   (ii) NS&I Savings Certificates
   (iii) Shares, unit trusts and investment trusts (iv)   Gilts and any loan stock
   (iv) ISAs, PEPs
   (v) Investment bonds
   (vi) Any assets held in trust with the full details of the trust

   For each investment, the adviser will want to know the following.

   (i) The type of account
   (ii) The number of shares/units
   (iii) The funds used
   (iv) The current value
   (v) Any notice for withdrawals
   (vi) Term of the investment if relevant

(d) **Savings**. If the client has any savings schemes, such as building society accounts, ISAs, PEPs, endowments, friendly society schemes, unit trusts or investment trusts, the adviser will want to know the following.

   (i) The provider
   (ii) The amount invested
   (iii) The frequency of investment
   (iv) The funds used, if applicable
   (v) The term of the savings scheme
   (vi) Any exit penalties which may apply
   (vii) The current value

(e) **Protection policies**. The adviser would need details of all life assurance policies, IPI policies, private medical insurance, critical illness, accident and sickness insurance, long term care insurance.

   (i) **Life assurance**. The adviser will need full details of the following.

      (1) The provider

      (2) The sum assured

      (3) The term

(4)   Any ratings for poor health

(5)   Whether the policy is taken out on single or joint life basis (first or second death)

(6)   Whether the policies are written in trust

(7)   Whether the policies are assigned to, say, a building society

(8)   Whether the policies are being used to cover a loan

(9)   The amount of the premium and the frequency of payment

(10) Whether the premiums are guaranteed

(11) If the policy has an investment element, the funds to which it is linked, the number of units and current value

(12) Whether there are any policy options, such as a conversion or increasable option

(ii)   **Income protection insurance**. The details required have been covered in the section on group benefits. However, if the cover is private rather than part of a company package, the adviser should check the following.

(1)   Details of the provider

(2)   Level of cover

(3)   The deferred period, to make sure it fits with the client's conditions of employment

(4)   The situation on changing jobs. Does the provider need to be told?

(5)   The situation should the client becomes redundant. Does cover continue?

(iii) **Critical illness cover** The adviser will need to know the following.

(1)   Details of the provider

(2)   The extent of the cover

(3)   Details of whether it is stand alone critical illness or added to whole of life, endowment or term assurance

(iv)   **Accident cover** Details of the extent of the cover are require

(v)   **Long-term care insurance**. Relatively few clients are likely to already hold this cover but, if they do, the adviser will need to check the following.

(1)   The provider
(2)   Level of cover provided
(3)   Method of payment, single contribution or regular premiums
(4)   Are premiums guaranteed and if so, for how long?

(vi)   **Pensions**. The details required for most pensions has been covered under the section of financial details earlier in this chapter. However, the adviser may need certain additional information as follows. If the client has an FSAVC, the adviser will need to have the following.

(1)   Details of the provider
(2)   Details of single or regular contributions paid
(3)   Details of the funds used and an up to date valuation

Previous pensions. Many clients, both employed and self-employed, may have been members of previous occupational pension schemes. The adviser will need to have as much information as possible. This will be obtained by writing to the previous company for an up to date transfer value and full details of the scheme. The adviser will need this information to take into account when calculating the client's total pension benefits. It may also be needed if a transfer is being considered so that a full transfer analysis can be carried out.

(f) **Inheritances.** A client must be asked if he or his partner are likely to inherit capital in the future. It is useful if some idea of the amount can be supplied. Although it would not be diplomatic to ask when the inheritance is expected, nevertheless the information can most probably be obtained by asking the age of the person from whom the client is likely to inherit.

(g) **Trusts.** If the client is a beneficiary, trustee or settlor of a trust, the following information is required.

    (i)   What is the type of trust, for example is it discretionary or an accumulation and maintenance settlement?

    (ii)   The name of the trustees, the settlor and the beneficiaries

    (iii)   The assets and income of the trust

    (iv)   Whether the trustees have limited powers of investment

    (v)   The tax position of the trust

    (vi)   The terms of the trust (a copy of the trust deed would be useful)

Exercise 4

Re-read the section on trusts and make sure you can make a list of the information which is needed if a client is a beneficiary under a trust.

3.16 **Liabilities**

(a) **Mortgage.** Details of any mortgage on the client's principal residence will be needed as follows.

    (i)   Amount of loan outstanding

    (ii)   Term of loan

    (iii)   Method of repayment, ie capital and interest or interest only

    (iv)   If it is an interest only mortgage, what provision has been made to repay the loan?

    (v)   What is the rate of interest? Is it variable or fixed? Is it capped or collared?

    (vi)   Are there any early redemption penalties on the mortgage?

    (vii)   Is this a first or second mortgage?

(b) **Business loans.** It is important to know the amount and term of the loan and whether the client has given a personal guarantee for the loan.

(c) **Short-term loans.** It is important to know if the client has any credit card debts or overdrafts. This may be an indication of a client who is a poor manager of money or whose expenditure exceeds his income.

4 THE CLIENT'S PLANS AND OBJECTIVES

4.1 In the previous section we have studied fact finding. It should be reasonably easy for the client to ascertain and communicate the information. It may be more difficult to ascertain the client's plans and objectives. He may not be fully sure of them himself. Certainly he may never have consciously sat down and worked them out. The adviser will have to lead the client gently through this section of information collection. Rather than asking direct questions, the adviser may ask a series of 'What is more likely to happen?' questions or 'Do you think this may happen, or that?' or 'What would you like to happen?'

4.2 Each client will have his or her unique plans and objectives. The adviser must never 'assume'. An adviser may meet a client in his early sixties and think he is planning retirement and savings plans for his grandchildren, only to discover that the client has recently remarried a 30 year old and has a new son aged one year.

4.3 We will now look at the information which is useful to ascertain with regard to plans and objectives.

Personal plans

Short-term personal plans and objectives

4.4 (a) The adviser will need to ascertain if there is likely to be an imminent change in the marital status of the client. He may be getting divorced or be about to re-marry. Any changes of this nature could have a bearing on financial planning.

(b) The adviser will need to ascertain information about the client's family. Is it likely that he or she will have any more children? What is happening to the existing children? Are they being privately educated or are any of them about to go on to university or some further education course? If the children are in their twenties or thirties, are there imminent plans for weddings, or the birth of grandchildren? To bring the questions full circle, has the older client got grandchildren about to be privately educated?

(c) At the other end of the age span, the adviser should enquire as to whether the client's or the client's spouse's parents are still alive and if so, are they likely to become more financially or physically dependent in the next few years?

(d) The adviser will need to focus attention on the client's short term plans for his job and earnings. Is his salary likely to increase, or even decrease? Is he likely to receive any commission, bonus or dividends and if so of what amount? Is his job secure or could he be made redundant? Is his company carrying out any reorganisation? If things are going well, is the client likely to be promoted? If so, will his salary and benefits package improve?

(e) If the client mentions that his job is insecure, the adviser should enquire how easy it would be for the client to find another job and whether he has sufficient redundancy cover to meet his immediate outgoings. He may ask the client if he has considered self-employment.

(f) If a client is running his own business, the adviser will need to ascertain how profitable the business is at present and whether the client feels positive or negative about the short term results from his business.

(g) If a client is close to retirement age the adviser must ascertain his plans for retirement. When will he retire? What is the level of his pension likely to be? Will he take a part-time job? How much state pension will he obtain? Will he be moving house?

(h) The adviser will need to ascertain whether the client has any plans to move house in the near future and if so, is the move to a larger or smaller house? How will the costs of moving be met? Has the client considered the amount of the deposit, type of mortgage etc?

(i) The adviser will need to know whether the client has recently taken on any new personal liabilities, for example, bought a new car, a second homes, a boat or even paid for an expensive holiday. The client may have taken on business liabilities like a large commercial loan to build a new factory.

(j) It may well be that the client is already contemplating expenditure on additional life assurance, permanent health, private medical insurance or long term care. The adviser will need details of the proposed premiums and cover in order that he can ascertain if the client can afford it and whether the policies provides the cover required.

(k) The client may be contemplating additional expenditure on a regular savings plan or pension arrangement. Details will be required.

(l) The adviser should ascertain whether there are any immediate needs from the emergency fund, for example, the client is in desperate need of a new car. It is no good putting forward recommendations for the investment of capital if it has already been earmarked for a car purchase!

Long-term personal plans and objectives

4.5 (a) Many of the short-term plans are also long-term ones. If the client's children are very young, then his long term, rather than immediate plans, may be to fund for school and university fees and, eventually, to have a sum to pay for weddings.

(b) The adviser will need to ascertain the client's long-term plans and attitude to work. Is he hoping for promotion? Will this mean moving employer or will this mean moving house in the UK or even abroad? On the other hand has the client always had a dream to become self-employed, or to be an author or a potter? Is the client planning early retirement so he can pursue a hobby?

(c) The long-term plans concerning the main residence is important. Does the client intend to sell his house on retirement? To move to a different part of the UK or even abroad? Does he intend to live in a smaller house? Does he see his house as a means of raising capital to provide retirement income? May he need to build a granny annexe to the house to provide accommodation for aged parents?

(d) If the client runs his own business the adviser will need to know his long term plans. Does he hope to sell out the business, or to float it on the stock market? What are the provisions for him to raise capital from the business on retirement or earlier death?

(e) The adviser will need to know the client's attitude to his children. This is particularly important if the client wants advice on passing on assets to the next generation either by making use of potentially exempt transfers or by the terms of his will. Is the client concerned to pass on assets or does he take the view that he worked for his capital and so too should his children?

Exercise 5

(a) List the possible long-term personal plans of a married man aged 35 with two children aged 5 and 7.

(b) List the possible short-term personal plans of a couple aged 65 and 63 who will retire in two months time.

Financial plans

Short-term financial plans and objectives

4.6 (a) A client's short-term financial plans may be to pay off credit cards or to pay for a holiday, or Christmas presents.

(b) He may have more expensive short term financial plans such as buying a new car or investing money in a new business.

(c) If the client is considering short-term savings plans, the adviser will need to know how much he is likely to be saving and the amount of access which is required.

Long-term financial plans and objectives

4.7 (a) A client's long-term financial plan may be to secure a reasonable level of income for retirement by means for saving either in an occupational or personal pension plan.

(b) His plans may include building up capital sums by saving in, say ISAs and National Savings & Investments (NS&I).

(c) He may plan to build up capital sums to pay school fees, university or wedding expenses.

5 ESTABLISHING INVESTMENT NEEDS AND ATTITUDES

5.1 If a client has capital to invest the adviser must ascertain a number of fact before he can proceed to make a recommendation. The facts are the following: the client's tax position, the client's attitude to risk, the term of the investment, the access required and whether the client wishes to produce income or capital growth from the investment.

Tax position

5.2 As we saw earlier, a client's tax position is a very important consideration in any recommendation. The adviser should take into account the client's current tax position and also his likely tax position when the investment matures.

Attitude to risk

5.3 (a) If an adviser asks a client the question 'What is your attitude to risk?' he or she is quite likely to obtain the reply 'I am happy to take some risk.' However, the real problem is that the client may not really understand the meaning of the word 'risk'. It is the adviser's role to try and explain it to the client. Higher risk investment offer the prospect of a higher possible gain or return than lower risk investments but with a possibility that, instead of a positive return, there may be a **loss of capital**.

(b) The adviser should first categorise investments into risk sectors as follows.

> *Low risk* - Deposits such as bank or building society accounts, NS&I accounts and certificates, gilts, guaranteed income bonds and local authority bonds.
>
> *Low/medium risk* - Corporate bonds convertible loan stock, convertible preference shares.
>
> *Medium risk* - Pooled investments; investment bonds, unit trusts, investment trusts, blue-chip equities.
>
> *High risk* - Most equities, particularly smaller company shares, unquoted company shares, EIS schemes, Enterprise Zone schemes, VCTs, commercial/retail property, commodities, collectibles.

(c) The adviser should explain that even the high risk taker should have same money available on easy access or deposit.

(d) The adviser should explain that there is no real growth in deposit types investments such as bank and building society accounts.

(e) The adviser should explain that if a client needs a guaranteed return for some reason, then he must chose, say, NS&I Savings Certificates or guaranteed income bonds.

(f) The adviser should explain that normally if money is only invested for a short term it should be placed on deposit. It is unwise to take risk with short term money

(g) The adviser should explain that if a client wants to achieve long term growth, this is only likely to happen if he uses asset-backed investments such as shares or property.

(h) The adviser should explain that most clients should have a well spread portfolio of deposit, fixed interest and some asset backed investments. This allows for a spread of type and risk of investments and also of access. The percentage split will depend on the client's attitude to risk. A high risk portfolio may have a much as 75% of the fund in equities or pooled investments, a low risk only 5%.

(i) The adviser should explain that if the capital available for investment is only a small amount, then this should always, unless there are exceptional circumstances, be invested in low risk investments.

(j) The adviser should tell the client about the effect of inflation on deposit accounts.

(k) The adviser should emphasise the value of employing experts to manage money.

(l) The adviser will be aware that clients may wish to take different levels of risk depending on the reason for the investment, for example the following.

   (i) If a client needs a specific amount of money at a given time, say money for school fees, he will not wish to take too high a risk. Similarly he will not wish to take a high risk with an investment which will be built up to repay his mortgage. He may not wish to take a risk with his pension fund.

   (ii) Others who have made insufficient pension provision, may be prepared to take a risk with a percentage of the funds in order to achieve a higher return. However once the enhanced return has been achieved the client would be well advised to consolidate the gain in a fixed interest fund.

Term of the investment

5.4 The adviser needs to know for how long the client plans to invest. It is often a good idea to spread the terms of investment in fixed interest schemes. This means that the client has a flow of capital available for reinvestment which allows him to take advantage of changing interest rates and opportunities.

Access to capital

5.5 The adviser must know when the investor will need the money. It is not good advice to tie money up in a five year contract only to learn 12 months later that the client is in desperate need of the capital and exit is only available with a heavy penalty. An adviser should always recommend that the first tranche of a client's money should be held in some form of deposit fund for easy access.

Income or capital growth

5.6 The adviser should ascertain if the client needs income and if so, what sort of income as follows.

(a) Does he need income now or in the future?

(b) Does he need a level income or an increasing one?

(c) Does he need a guaranteed income?

(d) Is he prepared to take a lower income now in the hope of an increasing income in the future?

(e) Does he want some income and some capital growth?

(f) What is the frequency of payment of income required? Many clients want a monthly income and this can restrict the choice of product.

If the client wants capital appreciation, then the adviser will need to know the reason for the investment, possible term of investment and whether there may be a requirement at a later date to receive income from the capital.

Exercise 6

(a) List the investments available to a client who wants income but a low risk.

(b) List the investments which may be suitable for a client who is prepared to take a medium risk but wants to pay as little tax as possible on his investments.

Financial objectives

5.7 Having recorded the client's personal and financial plans, the adviser should then be able to summarise the client's financial objectives. The objectives could be some or all of the following.

(a) To provide protection for his family in the event of his death, sickness or redundancy
(b) To provide for early retirement
(c) To build up funds for the future
(d) To build up funds to pay for secondary or tertiary education
(e) To mitigate inheritance tax
(f) To buy or extend a house, build a granny annex, buy a second home
(g) To take out or rearrange a mortgage
(h) To invest for income
(i) To invest for capital appreciation

6 ANALYSING CLIENT INFORMATION

6.1 Once the adviser has collected all the necessary data, the next step is for him to sort this and then report to the client. The adviser may summarise the information as follows.

Statement of Assets and Liabilities
Statement of Income and Expenditure
Statement of Mortgage/Loans Summary of Investments
Summary of Protection and Savings Policies
Summary of current and previous pensions

The information can be summarised for the client using headings as shown below.

1   *Statement of assets*

Statement of assets as at ....

Asset	*Ownership*		
	Client	*Partner*	*Joint*
Personal	£	£	£
Main home			
Second home			
Contents			
Valuables			
Business assets			
Shares			
Partnership capital			
Business property			
Investment assets			
Bank account			
Building society accounts			
National Savings & Investments			
Gilts and fixed interest			
Shares			
ISAs			
PEPs			
Unit trusts			
Investment bonds			
EIS			
VCTs			
Interest in a trust			

Total assets

This statement give the totals for the investments. A breakdown should be presented on a separate statement.

The total shown in this summary may be used to calculate any IHT liabilities.

2 *Statement of liabilities*

Statement of liabilities as at ....

Liability	Home loan	Business loan	Short-term loans	Lender
Term				
Security				
Amount outstanding				
Interest rate				
Fixed/variable				
Payment per annum				
Redemption penalties				
Method of repayment				
Life cover				
Redundancy cover				
Critical illness cover				
Sickness cover				

3 *Statement of income*

Statement of income as at ....

	Client £	Partner £
Income		
Salary		
Bonus		
Commission		
Benefits in kind		
Taxable state benefits		
Pensions		
Dividends		
Interest		
Rental income		
Gross income		
Deduct		
Personal allowance		
Pension contributions		
Taxable income		
Tax		
National insurance		
Net spendable income		

The income and expenditure statements should be prepared on a monthly, quarterly and annual basis.

4   *Statement of expenditure*

Statement of expenditure as at ....

	Client £	Partner £
Expenditure		
Utility bills		
Mortgage		
Council tax		
Road tax		
TV licence		
Insurance		
Telephone		
Petrol		
Travel		
Holidays		
Clothes		
Savings		
Life assurance		
Food		
Subscriptions		
Newspapers		
Spending money (other)		
Total expenditure		

Net Income - expenditure = £.................

This statement should be used to demonstrate if there is any surplus income available for investment.

5   *Summary of protection policies as at* ....

Company	*Type of cover*	*Term*	*Sum assured/income*	*Comment*

The comment column should contain information such as the period of deferment applicable to a permanent health policy or the fact that a life policy is written in trust and details of the beneficiaries.

6   *Summary of lump sum investments as at...................*

   Company   Date of purchase   Fund   No of units   Value

7   *Statement of pension benefits as at ....*

	Company	Current fund/TV	NRD	Estimated pension	Estimated cash + pension
Personal stakeholder pensions					
Retirement annuities					
S32 buy-outs					
Occupational pension scheme					
AVC					
FSAVC					
State benefits					
Basic state pension					
S2P/SERPS					
Total					

Notes would be added stating the investment assumptions and whether pension policies were written in trust.

7   THE ROLE OF THE PROFESSIONAL ADVISER

7.1   The job of the financial adviser is the following.

   (a)   To analyse a client's financial and personal information

   (b)   To ascertain the client's plans and objectives

   (c)   To analyse the data collected

   (d)   To put forward recommendations

   (e)   To keep the client's financial affairs under review

   (f)   To provide day to day management or pass on all or part of this role to another professional adviser such as a stockbroker

   (g)   To ensure that the advice complies with the regulator's rules

7.2   *Working with other advisers*

   (a)   Many clients will already have a solicitor or accountant and if at all possible the financial adviser should attempt to work in co-operation with these advisers.

(b) Sometimes a client will need expert advice which is outside the adviser's scope of expertise, for example the following.

    (i) The client may require a discretionary managed portfolio of shares.

    (ii) The client may wish to set up a self-administered pension scheme. In this case he will need the services of a pensioneer trustee and an actuary.

    (iii) The client may wish to set up an accumulation and maintenance trust or a will trust. In this case the services of a solicitor will be required.

    (iv) The client may wish to sell his business in which case he may require the services of an accountant and a solicitor.

    (v) The client may require mortgage advice and the adviser may not have in-house expertise in the mortgage area.

(c) In some instances an adviser will not be authorised to advise on certain products, for example, if he is a tied agent, he will not be able to advise on the products across the whole market as an independent adviser would.

(d) The Financial Services Authority requires advisers to have special qualifications for specialised activities, such as pensions transfer business. If an adviser does not have authorisation, he must not give the advice and must refer the client on to someone who is authorised to give the advice.

Chapter roundup

In this chapter we have studied:

- Collecting personal and financial data from a client

- Establishing the clients investment objectives

- Analysing the client situation

- Preparation of statements summarising the client situation

Quick quiz

1 Name the items of personal information in a fact find.

2 Why does an adviser need to know about the client's state of health?

3 Why does an adviser need to know about the client's benefits in kind?

4 Name three types of investment income a client may receive.

5 Name three state benefits a client may receive.

6 Why is it important to know if a life policy is written in trust?

7 Name two short-term financial aims.

8 Name two long-term financial aims.

9 Name three facts which a financial adviser should take into account before making a recommendation.

10 Name three statements that an adviser may use in a report to a client.

The answers to the questions in the quiz can be found at the end of this Study Text. Before checking your own answers against them, you should look back at this chapter and use the information in it to correct your answers.

Answers to exercises

1   It is important to have full personal details of the client to obtain an insight into his age, marital status, his dependants, his state of health, his hobbies and so on. The most important details are the following.

Age
State of health
Dependants

2   The questions you should ask a member of a company pension scheme are the following.

(a)   Do you belong to the scheme?
(b)   Do you have a booklet?
(c)   Do you have a benefit statement?
(d)   When did you join the scheme?
(e)   How much do you pay?
(f)   Do you make any additional contributions?
(g)   Do you know what the benefits are?
(h)   What is the retirement age?
(i)   Do you know if you are contracted out of the state scheme?

These are most probably the only questions the client can easily answer. All other questions may be too technical and the advise would have to obtain the answers from the booklet or the pensions department of the employer.

3   (a)   No
(b)   Yes
(c)   Yes

5   (a)   The long-term personal plans of a married man aged 35 with two young children may be the following.

(i)   Provision of school fees for the children
(ii)   The provision of a lump sum for the children at 18 or 21
(iii)   He may want to consider early retirement
(iv)   He may want to consider a change of career when the children have grown up

(b)   The short-term personal plans of a couple aged 65 and 63 may be the following.

(i)   Providing sufficient income for retirement.
(ii)   Using their savings to advantage to provide this income
(iii)   Perhaps moving house to another location or simply to raise cash

6   (a)   NS&I Income Bond
NS&I Pensioners Bond (if aged over 60)
Building Society account paying monthly income
Guaranteed income bond
Gilts

(b)   ISAs (Stocks and shares component)
Unit trusts / OEICs   )
Investment trusts   ) Making maximum use of bed and breakfast (after 30 days) to use
Shares   ) to use up annual CGT allowance.

PRACTICE QUESTION 12: CLIENT INFORMATION (30 Marks)   *27 mins*

(a)   (i)   A new client is seeking your advice. He has investments in shares, gilts and unit trusts. List the information you would need on these investments.   (8 marks)

(ii)   Explain why you need this information.   (7 marks)

(b)   (i)   A new client says he thinks he is paying too much for his mortgage. Explain the information you would need to find out from him in order to be able to advise him.   (8 marks)

(ii)   If you find that the interest rate is too high, how may you be able to help him?   (7 marks)

The answer to the practice question can be found at the end of this Study Text

Chapter 15

CONSTRUCTING A SUITABLE PORTFOLIO

Chapter topic list	Syllabus reference
1 Introduction to portfolio construction	4.1
2 Identifying needs	4.1
3 Setting priorities	4.1
4 Constructing a portfolio	4.1
5 Taking over an existing portfolio	4.1

Introduction

In this chapter we will identify needs and priorities and then study how to construct a portfolio to meet the client's objectives. The portfolio will take into consideration the client's residency status, family finances, existing trusts, tax position, attitude to risk and need for liquidity.

1   INTRODUCTION TO PORTFOLIO CONSTRUCTION

1.1 The adviser must base his advice on the foundation of the data collected in the fact find. The facts reveal gaps in the client's financial armour. From these gaps and the client's own financial aims and ambitions, the adviser can build up a list of the client's needs and then proceed to satisfy them taking particular notice of the client's tax position, the client's attitude to risk and the client's existing investments and assets.

1.2 We will look first at how an adviser can identify needs and then explore some examples of the needs he may establish.

2   IDENTIFYING NEEDS

2.1 The adviser will identify the needs by the apparent gaps in the client's protection or investment portfolio. For example, if the client has three young children but only £5,000 of life cover, there is an obvious need for additional protection.

2.2 The adviser will study the answers the client has given regarding his own financial aims and ambitions. These needs will have to be satisfied.

2.3 The adviser may have to prioritise the needs. There may be a number of criteria for the prioritising of the needs.

2.4   It is unlikely that the client will be able to afford to satisfy all his financial needs immediately, so a list needs to be constructed. In most cases this list will give greatest priority to protection, then pension planning and finally satisfying investment needs.

2.5   The needs should be prioritised on a time basis. The client may have an immediate need to resolve a mortgage problem if he is about to move house. He may be able to give lower priority to saving for his children's weddings or a rainy day.

2.6   The needs may be prioritised on the basis of those the client must fulfil and those that it would be nice to fulfil if he could afford it, possibly in the future. For example, it is important that a married person with children has sufficient protection cover. It might be very nice if he could save £250 per month in an ISA so that he could afford to go on a cruise with his partner in ten years time, but a cruise is not an essential.

Identifying and satisfying protection needs

2.7   We will now look at some of the normal needs that an adviser will identify and how he may satisfy them.

Mortgage requirements

2.8   (a) *Identifying the need*

      (i)   It may be very easy to identify the need: the client may be about to purchase his first home.

      (ii)   The client may wish to buy a more expensive house, build a granny annex or borrow more money to build a new kitchen.

      (iii)   Other needs may not be so clear cut. A client may be finding it hard to meet his mortgage repayments or examination of the client's affairs may indicate that he is paying too much for his mortgage.

      (iv)   A client may be confused about the method he is using to repay his mortgage. Newspaper articles may have scared him particularly if he is using a low cost endowment policy to repay the loan.

  (b) *Satisfying the need*

      (i)   **The client buying a first house**. The adviser will need to discuss with him the methods of repaying a loan, capital and interest or interest only, and decide which is most appropriate. He may well inform the client that it makes sense to keep mortgage and savings requirements separate. Therefore, it may be best to chose the cheapest and most flexible route to repay the mortgage (which could be capital and interest) and invest any spare income in, say, a ISA, investment trust or unit trust savings plan.

              The adviser will also need to outline the advantages of a fixed rate mortgage particularly if interest rates seem set to rise. A fixed rate mortgage can be a particular advantage for the first time buyer because he then has a known monthly cost.

              If the client is attracted by 'glossy' deals offering cash sums and discounted rates, the adviser must make the client aware that there may be redemption penalties written into these deals.

The adviser will need to explain to the client the costs of buying a house, the stamp duty, survey fees, solicitors' fees and possibly a procurement fee paid to a mortgage broker.

The client will also need to consider the amount of capital he has available as a deposit and how much he should keep back to pay for his moving costs etc.

(ii)   **Client wanting to 'move up'.** This client will already understand the workings of a mortgage. The advice he will need is where to obtain a competitive deal for his new mortgage.

He will need to consider seriously whether he can afford the new mortgage. Some people take on large mortgages on the premise that their salaries will increase and that soon they will find the level of their mortgage payments to be more comfortably within their budget. This may be unwise. The client must be able to satisfy himself that he can meet the costs, even if interest rates rise significantly.

This client may need to consider how he will repay his increased mortgage. If he has an existing endowment policy, should he top this up, or would it be preferable to repay part of the mortgage with the endowment and the balance by means of a capital and interest mortgage?

(iii)   **The client wanting to borrow extra money.** A client may want to borrow extra money for many reasons, building an extension, replacing a kitchen, paying off credit card debts. Taking a **second mortgage** can be an expensive business. The client usually has to pay a higher rate of interest. Therefore, if possible, the adviser should try to consolidate the extra borrowing in a remortgage.

(iv)   **The client who is finding it hard to meet his mortgage repayments.** There are a number of ways that the adviser can seek to meet this need. He may advise seeking a new lender, particularly if offers from new lenders are more attractive than those from existing ones. However, there may be problems trying to obtain a remortgage if the client is already behind with mortgage payments.

The adviser may recommend that the client approaches his existing lender and asks for some sympathetic help. It may be that if the mortgage is a capital and interest one, the term of the loan can be extended, thus reducing the payments.

(v)   **The confused client.** In this case the adviser will need to explain clearly to the client the different methods of repaying a mortgage. If the client is using a low cost endowment the adviser will need to see how long the policy has been in force. He will need to ascertain certain other information; what is its current value and what is the past performance of the company? Does he consider the performance is going to be sufficient in the future to meet the mortgage requirement? The answers may lead the adviser to suggest that the premiums paid to the policy should be increased or that the client runs a second policy alongside (taking into account setting up charges) to give a spread of performance. Alternatively, he may suggest a switch to a capital and interest mortgage and advise making the policy paid-up.

Life assurance

2.9   (a)   *Identifying the need*

(i)   The need for protection should be easy to identify from the fact find.

(ii)   If the client has one or more people financially dependent upon him, then they need financial protection in the event of his death.

(iii) As we have mentioned earlier in the Study Text, it is important for the adviser to identify everyone who may be dependent upon the client. The dependants may not always be obvious: they may include children from a former marriage or elderly parents.

(iv) It is as important for the client to be protected as it is for him to protect. Thus, the fact find should identify whether the client's partner has sufficient life cover. If he or she has not, then the client may be financially vulnerable.

(v) A need may arise if the client has borrowings which are not properly covered by life assurance in the event of his death.

(vi) A need may arise if the client has insufficient life cover through his company pension scheme.

(b) *Satisfying the need*

(i) **The client with inadequate family protection.** The need for protection in the event of death is normally met by some form of term or whole of life assurance. These policies pay out a tax-free lump sum on death. We will look at some important considerations.

(1) **The term of the cover.** If the policy is designed to provide cover whilst children are being educated, then it makes sense to gear the term of the policy to the date when the youngest child may finish full time education, say age 21.

(2) **The amount of cover which is required.** In order to work this out the adviser should refer the client to the income and expenditure analysis which he completed in the fact find. The expenditure analysis will be a good guide as to how much income the family would need if the main breadwinner has died. Certain items of expenditure can be removed. It is likely that the mortgage will have been repaid. Another consideration is whether his or her partner will continue to work. If they do, then some income will be coming into the household and there will only be a need to pick up the shortfall.

(3) When the client has decided how much income is required per annum, he must then convert this into a lump sum. How this is done will depend on whether the client expects that his dependants will live off the interest and preserve the capital or use the capital towards living expenses. For example, if the client decided that the family needed an income of £10,000 per annum, assuming an interest rate of, say, 5%, this would mean that he would need to take out cover of £200,000. If, however, he felt that the capital should be used then maybe an amount of £100,000 would suffice.

(4) As the client wants to provide his family with sufficient income to meet their expenditure, the adviser may recommend that some form of family income benefit cover may be more appropriate than a lump sum benefit. A family income benefit policy pays out a tax-free income from the date of death until the end of the term. Such a policy could continue until, say, the youngest child has reached age 21.

(5) When advising on any type of protection cover the adviser should make the client aware of the effect of inflation on a fixed benefit policy. He may suggest to the client that there should be some escalation or inflation proofing built into the sum assured, for example by using **increasing term assurance** or an increasing **family income benefit** policy

BPP
PROFESSIONAL EDUCATION

(6) The adviser should meet the protection need as cheaply as possible. This can often be achieved by the use of personal pension or AVC term assurance. There is tax relief on the premiums paid for this type of cover.

(7) Protecting a client means getting tax free benefits into the right hands at the right time. Getting the benefits into the right hands means that it is important to write the policy in trust. If a term assurance is made the subject of a Married Women's Property Act (MWPA) trust, probate is not required in order for the claim to be settled.

(ii) **Providing cover for a partner/wife or husband.** Although it is natural to provide the largest amount of cover on the life of the main breadwinner, the adviser must not overlook the need to provide cover on the partner's life. If, for example, a wife dies when her children are still young, her husband may need to hire a housekeeper or nanny. This will be costly. However, the tax-free income from a family income benefit policy, taken out on the life of the partner, could provide the necessary funds.

(iii) **Providing cover for a mortgage.** If a client has an endowment linked mortgage, he automatically has a death benefit equivalent to the outstanding loan. However, if the method of repayment is capital and interest, a pension policy, ISAs or PEPs, there is still normally the need to provide a capital sum in the event of the mortgagee's death. A cheap mortgage protection policy will cover the capital and interest type loan. Level term assurance, possibly with tax relief, should meet the need of the client with a pension or PEP/ISA mortgage.

(iv) **Client with inadequate life cover through a company pension scheme.** HMRC allows an approved occupational pension scheme to offer a maximum lump sum death benefit of four times remuneration. Some occupational pension schemes only offer cover of once or twice times salary. A member of such a scheme is probably inadequately covered, particularly if he is married with a family. He may be able to increase the cover by use of an in-house or external AVC scheme.

Exercise 1

(a) In what circumstances may life assurance protection be needed?
(b) What points must an adviser take into account when recommending protection life assurance?

Income protection insurance (IPI)

2.10 (a) **Identifying the need.** Most people need to protect their income in the event that they cannot work because of illness. The need has been particularly highlighted since the government cut back on the state disability benefits.

(i) Whereas life assurance protection is primarily required by people with dependants, IPI is needed by everyone who has an earned income.

(ii) Although there is a universal need for IPI, the adviser may from time to time identify a client with a particular need for this cover. This may occur when the client has an exceptional physical skill, such as a footballer, a concert pianist or ballet dancer. Such people will be especially vulnerable to an accident or illness making them unfit to continue in their chosen profession. If they cannot play or dance, they cannot work.

(iii) IPI can be very important for the self-employed. If, say, a self-employed plumber cannot work through illness he has no income. When we were studying life assurance we considered the situation of the client's spouse or partner. In the same way it is important to consider the income needs of the family if the partner who normally looks after the home and the children is ill.

(b) **Satisfying the need.** The most important factor for the adviser to consider is how much cover the client needs. Again, he should refer the client to the income and expenditure analysis carried out in the fact find. This indicates the outgoings that the client must meet whether he is in good or poor health. In the past, insurance companies have offered a maximum IPI cover of 75% of earnings less a single person's state sickness benefit. However, now that the benefit will no longer be taxable, insurance companies have cut back the maximum benefit to 66.66% or 50%. If the client can afford it, he should aim to insure for the maximum amount.

It is also important that IPI cover is escalating. A policy is taken out today, but a claim may not occur for ten years. The purchasing power of the income in ten years' time will have reduced considerably unless there is some increase or inflation proofing included. The term of the contract is important. Many policies will run through to retirement age, 60 or 65. It may be more sensible to terminate the policy at age 60 because it makes the premium less expensive than continuing to age 65. If a client becomes ill after this age, hopefully he can draw his pension. The adviser must consider what particular deferred period will fit the client's needs. The contract of employment should be checked to confirm the length of time the employee will be paid in the event of long term sickness. A houseperson's IPI policy may meet the needs of the partner who is the prime family carer. Some companies offer limited cover, say, £10,000 per annum. If the client has a very specific skill the adviser must meet the need with a policy with a favourable definition of disability.

Waiver of premium

2.11 (a) **Identifying a need.** If a client is dependent upon his earning capacity in order to make pension contributions, then if he cannot make these payments because of long term illness his eventual pension will be reduced.

(b) **Satisfying the need.** A self-employed or employed person paying regular premiums to a new personal pension can provide for waiver of premium in a separate contract. Thus, in the event of long term illness affecting earning capacity, the benefit of the policy will not reduce.

Critical illness cover

2.12 (a) **Identifying a need.** Critical illness cover is not confined to the married person with children. It is cover needed by all types of people. A single person may have a greater need for financial help if he is diagnosed with a critical illness. He may need to pay for help and additional equipment to cope with daily living.

An IPI policy provides an income to meet living expenses. There are situations when the payment of a lump sum could be more useful. For example, such a sum could be used to pay off a mortgage and thus permanently reduce outgoings.

There may be a need for a critical illness policy if a client has a large commitment to a loan, perhaps a business loan. This may be difficult to service if he had suffered a heart attack which, in turn, prevents him from running his business profitably.

(b) **Satisfying the need.** Critical illness cover can be used as a stand-alone policy or added to term assurance, endowments or whole of life.

Private medical insurance

2.13 (a) **Identifying the need.** Many clients will list private medical insurance as one of their priorities. They may feel that they do not want their family waiting for vital treatment through the National Health Service.

Clients running their own businesses, whether self-employed or employed need private medical insurance. It is important for such a person to have access to medical attention quickly and at a time which is convenient to the smooth operation of the business.

(b) **Satisfying the need.** The need for private medical insurance can be met by a number of policies offering cover of different types. Some offer the full cover, others simply in-patient care. The client may have his own idea of the amount of cover which fits his requirements.

Long-term care insurance

2.14 (a) **Identifying the need.** The recent publicity in newspapers and on television, highlighting the plight of the elderly and the cost of long term care, has to some extent done the work for the adviser. Clients are aware that their retirement may fit into three stages; very active, slowing down and 'in need of care'. The last stage is very expensive and may involve all the client's assets being sold to pay the nursing home fees.

Single people, whether unmarried or widowed, feel particularly vulnerable as they have no one to care for them in their old age. They may be very interested in the concept of long term care cover to provide the professional care they seek.

(b) **Satisfying the need.** At the present time there is not a great deal of choice of product available on the market and the costs are high. It is expected that many more providers will enter the market and more choice and competitive pricing will then follow.

Exercise 2

List the people who especially need:

(a) Income protection insurance
(b) Private medical insurance
(c) Critical illness insurance

Identifying and satisfying investment needs

2.15 With the help of the information in the fact find the adviser will be able to establish investment needs and then prioritise these. Let us look first at the needs.

- The need for income now
- The need for income in the future
- The need for growth
- The need for income and growth

Before proceeding to satisfy these needs the adviser will need to take into consideration certain matters.

(a) The **age of the client.** If a client is young, there will be many years for his investment to grow. He may, therefore, feel able to take a higher level of risk with, say, an equity based investment. If a client is aged 65 he may be unwilling to take any risk at all. For this client the security of his capital and income is of paramount importance.

The age of the client can be important in the selection of the investment. Some investments are exclusive to certain age ranges, for example, the children's bonus bond is only available to children up to the age of 16 at entry, the pensioners' income bond is only available to those over 60. VCTs and ISAs are for individuals who are over 18, except that a cash mini-ISA can be opened from age 16.

(b) The **residence or domicile of the client** is important. If the client is non-resident or non-domiciled for UK tax purposes, it may be appropriate to use offshore investments. Other investments, such as personal pensions or ISAs will be excluded.

(c) The **client's tax position** is always important. A non-taxpayer will have different needs to a higher rate taxpayer. The question of capital gains tax and inheritance tax should also be considered.

(d) **Liquidity and access to funds**. In most cases a client should have a spread portfolio with some money on deposit in easily accessible funds.

(e) The adviser will be influenced by the **timescale of investments**. For example, a client aged 55 who wishes to retire at age 60 will not wish to tie up his capital in long term growth investments.

(f) The adviser must always be aware of the **effect of inflation** on investments. Even if he feels he can best satisfy a client's needs with fixed interest and deposit investments, the adviser must point out to the client the potential loss of purchasing power which will result from such a strategy.

(g) The adviser must be aware of the level of risk the client is prepared to take. He should normally advise against taking risk with capital which is needed for short term requirements. The use of a well balanced portfolio and of pooled funds can help to reduce risk in a portfolio.

(h) The adviser should also suggest that a client should have **diversified assets**. Many clients cling to their building society accounts, often keeping a balance of £100,000 or more. The adviser will need to persuade such a client that it is possible to move some of the capital without exposing the funds to unnecessary risk.

(i) The adviser should suggest **international diversification**. If a client has a portfolio of shares it will normally be almost exclusively UK holdings. Within the portfolio there may be companies with overseas earnings but no direct overseas investment. This can be remedied by the use of pooled specialist overseas funds using investment trusts or unit trusts.

3 SETTING PRIORITIES

3.1 It is impossible for a client's every need to be satisfied. The adviser's job is to highlight the most important need.

For the retired person, this may be to secure a high level of income. The adviser may satisfy this with the use of gilts, guaranteed income bonds and the NS&I Pensioners' Income Bond. The client may say that he would like some capital appreciation but this may be impossible to achieve other than at the risk of reducing the income.

A younger client, who is a higher rate taxpayer may wish to invest for growth and incur little or no tax liability. In this case, the adviser may suggest NS&I Savings Certificates, investment bonds or low coupon gilts.

3.2   **Satisfying the need.** We will consider this in greater detail when we discuss the construction of a portfolio. However, there are a number of important points which we will now consider.

(a)   The adviser must not overlook the fact that clients have changing needs. It is pointless for an adviser to set up a portfolio and then not manage or review it.

(b)   The client's personal circumstance may change. He may divorce, have another child, decide to buy a second home or even emigrate.

(c)   The client's investment aims may change. Originally he may have needed income. A promotion at work may mean that he is now a higher rate taxpayer and needs to invest for growth.

(d)   Legislation may change. Future governments may change the tax regime making investment easier or more difficult. Types of investments may be withdrawn, others will replace them. It is the role of the adviser to keep abreast of all these changes and advise his client of any changes which may affect his situation.

(e)   The prosperity of the world economies will change. Some economies will flourish, others may be in recession. Interest rates will rise and fall, so too will the values of shares. The adviser must be aware of these potential changes and, if necessary, switch the client's investments to advantage.

4   CONSTRUCTING A PORTFOLIO

4.1   When constructing a portfolio an adviser should be aware of the following points.

(a)   Amount of capital available for investment
(b)   The client's tax position
(c)   Access to capital requirements
(d)   The client's attitude to risk
(e)   The suitability of recommendations for compliance purposes

4.2   He will then split the portfolio into short term investments and long-term investments.

Short-term monies should always be invested in risk free areas. It is the long-term investment which can be exposed to greater risk if the client so desires.

Exercise 3

Why does a client's portfolio need to be reviewed on a regular basis?

4.3   We list below a number of portfolios, together with a risk and tax profile for each client. It must be emphasised that each client is unique and will have his own investment need. These portfolios are only examples. The investments shown are the type which could be used. The client would not necessarily have all of them in his portfolio. ISA wrappers can be used where appropriate – for example, for some cash. However, ISA investments for immediate access have the disadvantage that, once funds are withdrawn, the tax advantage is lost.

(a)   Investments in a portfolio for a client who is risk averse, a non-taxpayer needing income

Immediate Access	*Medium Term*	*Long Term*
Current account	Short-dated gilt (high coupon)	Long-dated gilt (high coupon)
Building society postal/ Internet/passbook account	NS&I Income Bond	Pensioners Income Bond (if age allows)
NS&I Easy Access Account	Local authority bond	Local authority bond
Offshore building society account		

Comments

The NS&I Easy Access Account may or may not give a better rate of interest than a building society for small investments.

An R85 will need to be completed for the building society and local authority bond in order for interest to be paid gross.

A building society postal or internet account may pay a higher interest rate than a branch-based passbook account.

The gilt will pay gross interest.

The offshore building society account will pay interest gross.

(b)   *Investments in a portfolio for a client who is risk averse, a basic rate taxpayer needing income*

Immediate Access	*Medium Term*	*Long Term*
Current account	Short-dated gilt (high coupon)	Long-dated gilt (high coupon)
Building society postal/ Internet/passbook account	NS&I Income Bond	Pensioners Income Bond (if age allows)
NS&I Easy Access Account	Guaranteed income bond	
Cash unit trust		

Comments

The client will need to declare the income received from the NS&I Income Bond and the Easy Access Account and it will be subject to tax.

A guaranteed income bond will provide an income with no further liability to tax. The rates are usually competitive.

The cash unit trust may give a higher rate of interest on a small investment because the unit trust manager can take advantage of money market rates.

(c) *Investments in a portfolio for a client who is risk averse, a higher rate tax payer seeking growth*

Immediate Access	Medium Term	Long Term
Current account	Short-dated gilt (low coupon)	Long-dated gilt (low coupon)
Building society Postal/Internet/passbook account		Onshore or offshore bond (building society fund)
Offshore cash roll-up fund		NS&I Savings Certificates
Cash unit trust		Zero preference shares

Comments

The offshore cash roll-up fund is a secure fund and defers tax until encashment and so, too, does the offshore investment bond.

The gilts have been selected with a low coupon. The client can expect a capital gain which will not be subject to CGT.

The NS&I Savings Certificates allow the client to secure a tax free return on his capital without risk.

The onshore investment bond allows the capital to roll up without personal tax liability. The life fund will pay 20% tax as opposed to the client's personal rate of 40%. There will be a tax charge on encashment.

Zero preference shares need to be selected with care.

(d) *Investments in a portfolio for a client who is a basic rate taxpayer prepared to take low/medium risk - 60% deposit and fixed interest, 40% equities - and requiring a balance of income and growth*

Immediate Access	Medium Term	Long Term
Current account	Short-dated gilt (medium coupon)	Long-dated gilt (medium coupon)
Building society postal/Internet/passbook account	Guaranteed income/ growth bond	Corporate bond ISA
Cash unit trust		Investment bond (with profits/managed)
		Unit trusts (tracker or funds of funds)
		NS&I Savings Certificates

Comments

The investments shown above could be applied to produce a well balanced portfolio of income and growth.

The NS&I Savings Certificates give a tax free return.

The corporate bond ISA allows the client a tax free return without undue risk: the interest is high but neither the income nor the capital is totally guaranteed.

The with profits investment bond or the investment bond using the managed fund allows the client to have an exposure to the equity market without undue risk. The client is paying for expert management. The charges will be higher and the taxation deduction greater than for a unit trust.

The choice of a tracker unit trust or a fund of funds unit trust, gives the client an exposure to equities but with diversification.

(e) *Investments in a portfolio for a client who is a basic rate taxpayer prepared to take medium risk - 40% deposit and fixed interest, 60% equity. The portfolio is designed for capital growth.*

Immediate Access	Medium Term	Long Term
Current account	Short-dated gilt (low coupon)	Long-dated gilt (low coupon)
Building society postal/Internet/passbook account		Investment bond (UK equity/overseas)
Cash unit trust		Convertible preference shares
		NS&I Savings Certificates
		Unit trust/investment trusts (overseas/ recovery/ special situations)
		Maxi-ISA (equity income fund)

Comments

An equity income fund is used for the ISA as this can give an increasing tax free income if required.

The investment bonds give an exposure to the UK and overseas equity markets but allow the client to take a 5% withdrawal to use as income and defer taxation, if required. Encashment can be deferred until, hopefully, the client is a basic rate taxpayer.

The unit trusts and investment trusts are selected for growth. The use of funds investing in different economies will give a spread of risk and diversification to the portfolio. The convertible preference shares give a guaranteed income with the chance of equity exposure from the conversion of the share.

(f) *Investments in a portfolio for a higher rate taxpayer prepared to take high risk - 20% deposit and fixed interest, 80% equity. The portfolio is designed for capital growth.*

Immediate Access	Medium Term	Long Term
Current account	Short-dated gilt (low coupon)	Share portfolio
Building society postal/Internet/passbook account		Offshore investment bond (specialist funds)
Cash unit trust		Maxi-ISA, stocks and shares
Offshore cash roll-up fund		Unit trust/investment trusts for overseas exposure
		NS&I Savings Certificates
		EIS and VCTs

Comments

The mix of this portfolio would depend on the funds available. The client would probably need £50,000+ for a stockbroker to be prepared to run a share portfolio.

A higher risk investor should make use of his maximum ISA allowance (£7,000 in 2004/05).

As the equity portfolio would be predominately invested in UK based companies, unit trusts and investment trusts should be used to invest in overseas funds to give the balance to the portfolio.

The investor would use up the 20% deposit and fixed interest section with cash deposits for emergencies, NS&I Savings Certificates and low coupon gilts because of the tax effectiveness of these schemes.

(g) *Investments in a portfolio for a client who is a higher rate taxpayer prepared to take a high risk - all equity except for small cash deposit. The portfolio is designed for capital growth.*

This client may hold any of the securities listed in (f) above plus:

- Commodities
- Futures
- Options
- Currencies
- Property
- Collectibles

Exercise 4

Rate the following investments as high, medium or low risk.

(a) Offshore bond
(b) PIBS
(c) EIS
(d) Maxi-stocks and shares ISA
(e) Mini-cash ISA
(f) Gilt
(g) Special situations unit trust
(h) TOISA (TESSA-only ISA)

Portfolio choices

4.4 When constructing a portfolio, an adviser has choices to make. We will discuss a number of the more common decisions he must make.

4.5 *Should investments be in equities or fixed interest securities?*

Unless the client is very risk-averse, there should probably be some exposure to equities, for long term funds. This may be through pooled fund such as unit or investment trusts. The reason for this advice is that statistics have shown in the past, that it is asset-backed investments such as equities that can generally provide a real return over inflation over most long term periods.

4.6 *If a client has a mortgage and access to some capital, should he use the capital to pay off a mortgage?*

(a) In making this decision, the client should first calculated the amount of monthly mortgage payments. Then he needs to ascertain the amount of interest he could earn on the available capital if he invested it. He can then compare the two figures. He will no doubt discover that it is impossible to obtain a return on the capital greater than the mortgage payment. Therefore, he should consider paying off the mortgage or at least reducing it to a modest level.

(b)   The only method of producing a return in excess of the building society lending rate is to invest in equities. If the client is prepared to do this and appreciates the risk, the mortgage should not be paid off.

(c)   A client who may need capital in the future should not be encouraged to pay off a mortgage. Paying off a mortgage and then having to borrow again in the near future is a futile and expensive exercise.

(d)   If the client has an endowment, ISA or pension mortgage, he would also need to take into consideration the future of the investment contract once he had paid back the mortgage in full or part.

4.7   *Should a client invest in the UK markets or overseas?*

(a)   Most clients are happy to have the majority of their money invested in the home market. They know something about the companies in which they are invested and they can watch the performance of their shares or unit trusts in the newspaper or on teletext.

(b)   The investor in the UK is not affected directly by currency fluctuations. Currency changes may, however, have an effect on the share price of individual UK companies with significant overseas earnings.

(c)   To create a well spread portfolio, a client should have holdings in other economies. In this way there is diversification. Some countries will be in recession, some in growth phases. With expert management the client may be able to take advantage of changing world economic patterns. Although exposure to currencies gives an extra exposure to risk, this too can be an advantage for the more adventurous investor.

(d)   Unless a client has a very large portfolio, it can be both difficult and expensive for him to invest in individual overseas shares. Therefore, overseas markets are often best covered by the use of investment or unit trusts.

4.8   *Property as an investment compared with equities*

(a)   The British are traditionally enthusiastic investors in property. This confidence is based on experience of what has happened in the past, which might not be repeated.

(b)   If a client wants to invest directly in commercial or residential properties, there are high management costs and risks, particularly if tenants are difficult to find and retain.

Exercise 5

(a)   In what circumstances may it make sense for a client to repay a mortgage?
(b)   If he had a pension linked mortgage what would be the effect of the repayment of the mortgage?

4.9   *Direct equity investment or pooled investment?*

The question of whether a client should invest directly in equities or via pooled investments depends very largely on how much capital is available to invest. If there is say £100,000+, then a portfolio of equities makes sense because there can be a spread of type of shares and sectors. If it is less, then unit trusts or investment trusts make sense. They allow participation in a pool of shares and access to expert management at a reasonable cost.

4.10 *Offshore or onshore investment bonds?*

There is very little advantage for a basic rate taxpayer to invest in an offshore bond. There may be an advantage for a higher rate taxpayer.

Exercise 6

State the tax situation for a higher rate taxpayer who effects an offshore investment bond.

4.11 *Tracker funds or actively managed funds?*

(a) *Arguments for tracker funds*

   (i) There are lower management charges than for actively managed funds, as little fund management expertise is needed.

   (ii) Very few managers of non-tracker funds actually outperform the index.

   (iii) Outperformance in actively managed funds is only achieved by managers taking on higher risks.

(b) *Arguments for non-tracker funds*

   (i) A good fund manager should have a goal of being able to outperform the market. He should be able to achieve this by good stock selection. This does, however, suggest a higher risk.

   (ii) Tracker funds will always slightly underperform the market because of charges.

   (iii) At times when the markets as a whole are doing badly, specialist unit trust may perform well because of the mix of shares in the portfolio.

4.12 *Investment trust or unit trust/OEIC?*

The criteria for selecting a unit trust or investment trust are as follows.

(a) *Advantages of an investment trust*

   (i) It is a share. The price and performance is less likely to be affected by a fall in the stockmarket than a unit trust. One reason for this is that as investors sell when the share market falls, the unit trust will be forced to sell assets while the investment trust will not, since the investment trust's shares will simply have been sold on to another investor.

   (ii) Charges are normally lower.

   (iii) Investment trusts have different types of shares. It is possible to achieve a higher income than with a unit trust, through the purchase of a split capital income share.

(b) *Advantages of a unit trust/OEIC*

   (i) Unit trusts/OEICs generally are not such a high risk investment. The investment trust can be highly geared which leads to volatility in the price and higher risk. The investment trust can be trading at a discount which can widen if the investors do not much like the trust.

   (ii) The price of a unit trust/OEIC reflects the price of the underlying assets.

   (iii) The unit trust/OEIC is more accessible. The fund manager has to buy back his units.

(iv) The unit trust is more easily understood by the less sophisticated investor. Such an investor may be alarmed by dividends, scrips, warrants and so on which will arise from the purchase of an investment trust.

4.13 *Investment bonds or unit trusts?*

The general belief is that in most cases the purchase of a unit trust is better advice than a bond for the following reasons.

(a) The investment bond has higher charges than the unit trust.

(b) The investment return from an investment bond has suffered tax on the life fund. A unit trust pays no CGT on its funds and therefore the performance should be better in the unit trust.

The investment bond does have a tax advantage for the higher rate taxpayer because it allows him to defer taxation.

Drawing income from a portfolio

4.14 The adviser can enable the investor to draw income from a portfolio in a number of ways.

(a) He can use deposit investments such as monthly income accounts in the building society or the NS&I Income Bond.

(b) He can use fixed interest securities such as gilts, local authority bonds, corporate bonds, convertible loan stock, convertible preference shares or corporate bond ISAs.

(c) He can use equities. Using good UK equity funds could produce an increasing income over the years.

(d) He can use withdrawals from investment bonds This method of income creation is highly suited to higher rate taxpayers.

(e) He can use a back-to-back arrangement such as a temporary annuity and ISA/unit trust/endowment policy.

In practice an adviser will use a mix of these securities to achieve the level of income required at the level of risk the investor is prepared to accept. It should be mentioned that recently packaged products have been produced paying high levels of income but relying on derivatives to secure the return of capital. The clients should be made aware of the possibility that capital could be lost in investment of this kind.

Exercise 7

List the types of securities you could use to provide an income. Against each one indicate the tax situation for a basic rate taxpayer.

---

5 TAKING OVER AN EXISTING PORTFOLIO

5.1 From time to time an adviser will be asked to take over an existing portfolio. There may be a temptation to put his own mark on the portfolio but he must follow a logical system of review.

(a) The portfolio should be structured to take maximum advantage of the client's tax situation. For example, both partners should make use of their full personal allowance.

(b) If necessary, it may be prudent to equalise assets so that both partners pay basic rate tax (instead of one paying higher rate tax and the other no tax at all).

(c)   Clients should make a will and carry out planning to minimise IHT liabilities, such as by the use of gifts and potentially exempt transfers.

(d)   The portfolio should achieve the client's requirements for either income or growth? If the requirement is income, it should be at the right level and frequency. If not, some rearrangement of assets may be necessary. Care must be taken to see if this can be done without incurring unnecessary capital gains tax. It may be necessary for assets to be passed to a spouse before disposal.

(e)   The portfolio should be constructed in line with the client's attitude to risk. Again, this may require rearrangement of assets. The client may be prepared to accept more risk than reflected in his or her current portfolio.

(f)   The past performance of the portfolio needs to be compared with the client's risk profile. Poor returns do not necessarily mean that the portfolio has been badly managed; they may simply be in line with the client's desire for a low-risk portfolio.

(g)   The percentage of investments in deposit, fixed interest and equities needs to be checked to see if it is in line with the client's requirements.

(h)   Full use should be made of any investments with tax benefits, such as existing PEPs, ISAs and possibly VCTs, where they meet the client's requirements.

(i)   The adviser will need to have a signed agreement with the client so that both parties know the agreed investment parameters.

Chapter roundup

In this chapter we have studied:

- Identifying client needs
- Satisfying client needs
- Constructing a portfolio

Quick Quiz

1   What action can you take to inflation-proof a protection life policy?

2   How must a life policy be arranged to obtain tax relief?

3   What is the effect of writing a life policy under a MWPA trust?

4   What type of life cover would you need if you have chosen to repay your mortgage by means of a PEP/ISA?

5   What is the maximum IPI cover you are likely to be able to obtain?

6   How is the benefit from an individual IPI policy taxed?

7   How much IPI cover may a houseperson obtain?

8   What is the advantage of a cash unit trust?

9   What are the main advantages of tracker funds?

10   How may an investment trust give a higher income than a unit trust?

11   What form needs to be completed to obtain gross interest from a building society account?

12   What is 'waiver of premium'?

The answers to the questions in the quiz can be found at the end of this Study Text. Before checking your own answers against them, you should look back at this chapter and use the information in it to correct your answers.

Answers to exercises

1   (a)   Life assurance protection will be needed if:

    (i)   The client has dependants
    (ii)   The client has a loan or mortgage
    (iii) The client has insufficient cover under his company pension scheme

    (b)   When recommending protection life assurance, the adviser must be aware of the following.

    (i)   *Cost.* He needs to obtain a competitive premium.

    (ii)   *Tax relief.* If at all possible the premiums should be eligible for tax relief. This can be achieved by use of pension life cover.

    (iii) *The amount of cover required.* He must take into account the effects of inflation and build in some inflation proofing to the cover.

    (iv)   *Getting the benefits in the right hands at the right time.* It is important to write policies in trust so that the money gets to the right beneficiaries as quickly as possible.

    (v)   *The term of the cover.* For example, this should fit in with the length of time the children will be dependent.

2   (a)   People who especially need income protection insurance:

    (i)   Self-employed people
    (ii)   Company directors
    (iii) Housepersons
    (iv)   Single people

    (b)   People who especially need medical insurance:

    (i)   Self-employed people
    (ii)   Company directors

    (c)   People who especially need critical illness insurance:

    (i)   Single people
    (ii)   Self-employed people
    (iii) Company directors

3   A client's portfolio needs to be reviewed on a regular basis because of changing circumstances such as the following.

    (a)   A member of the client's family may have died.
    (b)   A child may have been born.
    (c)   The client may be about to get married or divorced.
    (d)   The client may be about to be made redundant, or retire early.
    (e)   The client may be about to move house.
    (f)   The client may have been promoted.
    (g)   There may be changes in taxation which will affect the client.
    (h)   There may be changes in legislation which may affect the client.
    (i)   His investment needs may have changed.

4

Investment	Risk
Offshore bond	Medium/High
PIBS	Medium
EIS	High
Maxi-stocks ISA	Medium/High
Mini-cash ISA	Low
Gilt	Low
Special situations unit trust	High
TOISA	Low (as for cash ISA) – no new investment possible

5   (a)   It may make sense for a client to repay a mortgage:

    (i)   If he is paying more in mortgage interest than he can safely obtain by investing the capital

      (ii)   If he has no other immediate needs for the capital

(b)   If the client had a pension linked mortgage, the whole of the capital would be outstanding. The client would pay this off. The pension policy would continue until retirement age. At this stage the client could use the whole fund to provide a pension as he would no longer need the lump sum to pay off the mortgage. Or he could use the lump sum for another purpose.

6   As the offshore fund pays no tax, when a chargeable event occurs, the gain is liable to lower, basic and higher rate tax. The calculation, and top-slicing is carried out in the same way as for an onshore bond except the divider for the top-slicing is the years since inception, not the years since the last chargeable event.

7	*Security*	*Tax situation for basic rate taxpayer*
	Guaranteed income bond	Income paid net, no further liability
	NS&I Income Bond	Income paid gross but liable to tax
	Building society account, monthly income	Income paid net of 20% tax, no further liability
	Gilts	Income paid gross
	Individual Savings Account	Uninvested cash in a stocks and shares ISA has 20% tax deducted. There is no additional tax on dividends for higher rate taxpayers, but tax credits on dividends no longer reclaimable.
	Local authority bond	Income paid net of 20% tax, no further liability
	High income unit trust	Dividend paid net of 10% tax, no further liability

PRACTICE QUESTION 13: CONSTRUCTION (30 Marks)　　　*27 mins*

Bill and Sally are 65 and 63 respectively. Bill has just retired and has a pension of £8,000 per annum. If he dies before Sally she will receive a pension of £4,000 per annum. Bill and Sally receive a basic state pension (but no State Second Pension, because Bill was self-employed).

Bill and Sally own their own house, current value £75,000. They have paid off their mortgage.

Sally has recently inherited £100,000 from an aunt.

She wants to invest the money to create additional income. She is prepared to take a small amount of risk but she says she would like to be able to leave the capital to her two children when she dies.

(a)   State Bill and Sally's financial aims.   (2 marks)

(b)   Design a portfolio which meets the financial aims. Against each investment type state whether it is to be held in Bill's name or Sally's.   (18 marks)

(c)   Bearing (b) in mind, indicate against each investment the tax situation.   (10 marks)

The answer to the practice question can be found at the end of this Study Text

Chapter 16

PRESENTING REASONED RECOMMENDATIONS

Chapter topic list	Syllabus reference
1 Presenting reasoned recommendations - the report	4.3
2 Putting the recommendations into effect	4.3
3 Maintaining records	4.3
4 Monitoring the client's needs	4.4
5 Case study and draft report	4.4

Introduction

In this chapter we discuss how a reasoned report should be constructed, how the recommendations are put into effect and the importance of good liaison with the client's other professional advisers.

We look at how the recommendations are implemented and recorded and finally the process of monitoring changes in the client's circumstances.

1   PRESENTING REASONED RECOMMENDATIONS - THE REPORT

1.1   Setting out recommendations for the client in the form of a letter or a **report** is important not just for compliance purposes but also to make sure that there is good communication between the adviser and the client. In the following paragraphs we will refer to a report. The adviser can, of course, lay out his recommendations in letter form. However, if the case is complex, a report is a more structured method of setting out the recommendations.

The function of the report

1.2   (a)   The function of a report is to communicate. In this instance, a report is a more effective form of communication than the spoken word for the following reasons.

(i)   The report is a permanent record.

(ii)   The adviser can use the report as a means of confirming that he has all the correct client information.

(iii)   The client has an opportunity of reading the report in his own time and then coming to a reasoned conclusion as to whether he wishes to proceed with the advice.

(iv)   The report enables both parties to check information. The adviser checks that he has identified all the client's financial needs and the client should be able to see clearly the features and costs of the proposed scheme and how it meets his financial aims.

(v)   The report is a record for the client to keep. Therefore, in a few weeks or months time when the client has a query he can refer back to the document to see why he took a particular course of action, or the advantages of a particular contract he effected.

(vi)   The report can be used by the client if he wishes to discuss the proposals with his other professional advisers, say, his solicitor or accountant.

(b)   Another function of the report is as a discussion document. The adviser is setting out facts about the client and his objectives as he understands them. He may be wrong. Equally when the client has read the report and understood the ramifications of the proposed action he may wish to change his objectives.

(c)   The report allows the adviser to demonstrate the adviser's professionalism and technical expertise. The adviser is demonstrating that he is worthy of being properly remunerated for his knowledge, the time spent on analysing the situation and putting forward recommendations.

Exercise 1

List the functions of a report putting forward financial recommendations.

Structure of report

1.3   (a)   The report should be as simple as possible and easily understood by the reader. It will help to break down the information into logical sections. An example of such sections is shown below.

(i)   A section setting out the client's current situation (This will be information based upon the fact find.)

(ii)   A section summarising the client's income and expenditure, assets and liabilities

(iii)   A section setting out the client's financial aims and objectives, short and long term

(iv)   A section assessing the information

(v)   A section setting out the recommendations

(b)   The recommendations should be set out as clearly as possible. It is suggested that this is achieved by the use of further sections on each subject as appropriate, for example, pensions, investment and protection.

The technical information can then be contained in appendices at the back of the report.

To summarise, the headings of the report could follow the layout below.

Report for Simon and Hannah Hill

Date: 15 June 2005

1   Current situation including analysis of income and expenditure and assets and liabilities

2   Financial aims and objectives

3   Assessment of financial situation

4   Recommendations

Pensions

Protection

Investment

5   Appendix: Summary of income and expenditure

6   Appendix: Summary of assets and liabilities

7   Appendix: Schedule of existing investments

8   Appendix: Schedule of existing pension policies

9   Appendix: Schedule of proposed investments, listing funds, amounts, duration of investment etc.

10   Appendix: Schedule of recommended policies showing comparison of policies, premiums, charges and features.

An example of a case study and report is given at the end of this chapter.

Layout and language of the report

1.4   The report is an means of communication between the adviser and the client. Therefore the adviser should:

(a)   Keep jargon to a minimum. If it is essential to use technical terms they should be fully explained.

(b)   Write in short sentences and short paragraphs so that the report is easy to understand.

(c)   Use headings and subheadings to breakdown the information into sections for the purposes of clarity.

Exercise 2

What must the adviser remember about language when writing a report for a client?

Using the report to aid discussion with the client's other advisers

1.5   The client may wish to consult other advisers about the recommendation which have been proposed. The adviser should not be frightened by this prospect. He must be confident that he has the necessary expertise to be able to stand alongside the client's accountant or solicitor in giving advice. The adviser should strive to build up a good working relationship with the client's solicitor and accountant.

2   PUTTING THE RECOMMENDATIONS INTO EFFECT

2.1   When the client decides to proceed, the adviser will have to make the various investments on behalf of the client. This may involve the following.

(a)   Dealing with an insurance company and arranging medicals for life assurance and other forms of protection. The adviser may have to discuss acceptance terms with the underwriter.

(b)   The premiums will need to be collected, the policy put on risk, the policy document checked and dispatched to the client.

(c) Dealing with a unit trust, OEIC or investment trust company to buy units or shares in a particular trust, receiving and dispatching contract notes and certificates, if applicable.

(d) Dealing with building societies, banks or NS&I to arrange deposit accounts.

(e) Dealing with a client's stockbroker who may be arranging the purchase of shares or gilts on behalf of the client.

3 MAINTAINING RECORDS

3.1 Records of all transactions will have to be made for the following reasons.

(a) For the normal efficiency and organisation of the adviser's business

(b) In order to comply with FSA rules, which generally require the adviser to keep the following records for six years

    (i) Client's name and address

    (ii) Details of the terms of business letter or client agreement which was in force and the date when it was issued

    (iii) A note of any oral or written request for the adviser to purchase an investment

    (iv) A copy of each written communication sent to the client including contract notes, reports or valuations

    (v) A copy of each transaction arranged for the client: the detail of the transaction must include the following

        (1) The date the instructions were received

        (2) The date when the instructions were carried out

        (3) The time the deal was carried out must also be recorded for the purchase of unit trusts, investment trusts or shares

        (4) A record to demonstrate that the advice was suitable for the client's circumstances

        (5) A record of commission received

4 MONITORING THE CLIENT'S NEEDS

4.1 (a) Some advisers will state in their terms of business letter or client agreement that they will review the client's investments or overall situation, say, once every 12 months. It may be a more regular review if the client has an investment portfolio. A half-yearly review would be normal in that case.

(b) Other advisers contact clients on an irregular basis or wait for the client to contact them.

(c) There is a need to review the client's affairs regularly. His personal circumstances may have changed. Any of the following could have happened.

    (i) The death of a close family member
    (ii) The birth of another child
    (iii) The client may be marrying or getting divorced
    (iv) The client may be changing his job
    (v) The client may have been promoted
    (vi) The client may be about to be made redundant or take early retirement
    (vii) The investment client may feel he now needs income rather than growth

(viii) The client may be moving house

(d) There may be non-personal reasons for reviewing the client's financial affairs.

(i) Changes in taxation

(ii) Changes in legislation

(iii) New products on the market which may fit the client's financial objectives

5 CASE STUDY AND DRAFT REPORT

5.1 In the Appendix to this chapter you will find a case study and draft report.

Chapter roundup

In this chapter we have studied:

- The reasons for report writing

- The construction of a report

- The maintenance of the appropriate records of the advice given and actions taken

- The preparation of a draft report

Answers to exercises

1 Functions of a report: see Paragraph 1.2.

2 Language must be easy to understand and jargon should be avoided.

PRACTICE QUESTION 14: RECOMMENDATIONS (30 Marks)   *27 mins*

Anne Horsey is aged 42. She is a widow. She receives a pension of £4,500 per annum from her husband's previous employer. She works full-time as a 'temp'. This gives her the opportunity to take long holidays to pursue her hobby of mountain walking. Her earnings are approximately £12,500 per annum. She has made no provision for pension.

Her house is valued at £410,000 and there is no mortgage. Anne has two stepchildren, Timothy and Ben, aged 20 and 22. Both are still in full-time education. Anne's husband died two years ago. His entire estate passed to Anne, including investments valued at £146,000. Currently the money is invested in two building society accounts.

Anne now seeks advice on how best to invest the capital.

Her main concerns are the following.

(a) To be able to provide sufficient income in the future should she not want to or not be able to work

(b) To ensure that as much capital as possible passes to her stepchildren

Required

(a) Draft the 'general strategy' and 'long term investment approach' of a report.   (10 marks)

(b) In note form, draft the recommendation section of the report, specifying particular products and the reason for the selection.   (20 marks)

The answer to the practice question can be found at the end of this Study Text

APPENDIX

CASE STUDY AND DRAFT REPORT

Simon and Hannah Hill are aged 42 and 38 respectively. They have three children, Mark aged 14, Sarah aged 10 and Charlotte aged 10. Simon runs his own business: he is a self-employed optician. His wife is in partnership with him. She is also a qualified optician and works three days a week.

The children are all at independent schools, with fees of £1,500 per term each (ie, payable three times per year) for Mark and Sarah, and £1,200 per term for Charlotte. Charlotte has musical talent and her family hope that she may win a music scholarship to a private school close by. The scholarship would reduce the fees by £1,500 per annum. The school fees are met from income. Simon's mother has used up her annual exemption for inheritance tax for the last two years by giving her son £3,000 per annum. This money has been used for school fees purposes. Simon does not know whether his mother can afford to, or is inclined to, continue to make these gifts.

Simon and Hannah jointly own their home, which is a converted barn. It is valued at £210,000 and there is a repayment mortgage with an outstanding balance of £75,000. Hannah's parents were killed in a road accident a few years ago. Both of Simon's parents are alive. However, Simon's mother has arthritis and the couple know that, should Simon's father die, it is likely that his mother may need to move closer to them. They have considered converting part of the house so that she could have her own accommodation.

Simon has been paying £150 per month into a personal pension plan. His wife has no pension arrangement although she says she has a small pension scheme from her first job. Upon investigation it is discovered that this is a retirement annuity contract. They say that they would like to retire when Simon is age 55. At retirement Simon will sell his business. He says he would hope to receive, say, £100,000.

In the most recent trading year, Simon and Hannah's income from the partnership is £110,000 each. This is because they have recently received a substantial refund of VAT. Their share of the profits has been £40,000 each for the previous six trading years. Simon has no further income but Hannah has investment income from an equity portfolio inherited from her parents. This income amounts to £4,000 gross per annum.

Simon's expenditure has been listed and it appears that the couple live well within their means.

Simon and Hannah have the following assets.

Building Society instant access account	£140,000	Joint
TESSA-only ISA	£3,000	Hannah
Share portfolio	£104,000	Hannah

Simon is an only child. When his parents die, he is likely to inherit £300,000.

Simon and Hannah have made wills leaving all their assets to each other.

Simon now wants advice regarding the investment of £140,000 in the building society. He says his objectives are to increase his retirement income, to make provision for school fees and possibly to set aside, say, £500 each for the children. He is prepared to take some risk with his investments in order to gain long-term growth.

The report which follows is a draft and gives a broad outline of the points which should be covered. The appendices are not shown in full. Look particularly at the layout of the report.

REPORT FOR SIMON AND HANNAH HILL

15 June 2005

Current position

1   Simon and Hannah are aged 42 and 38 respectively.

2   They have three children Mark aged 14 and twin daughters, Sarah and Charlotte aged 10. The children are all being privately educated.

3   The current school fees are £1,500 per term for Mark and Sarah and £1,200 per term for Charlotte. It is hoped that Charlotte may win a music scholarship which will reduce her fees by £1,500 per annum. At present Simon Hill pays for the school fees out of income although for the last two years his mother has given him £3,000 as a gift. He has used this money to help with the school fees bills.

4   Simon is a self-employed optician. His wife, Hannah is also a qualified optician. She works three days a week and is in partnership with her husband.

5   *Income*

Simon's earnings from partnership	£110,000
Hannah's earnings from partnership	£110,000
Hannah's investment income	£4,000

Note. Partnership income for each of the previous six years was £40,000 each.

Expenditure

Simon and Hannah's main items of expenditure are the mortgage, £586.00 per month, the school fees £1,050 per month and Simon's pension premium £150 per month.

Appendix 1 Statement of Income and Expenditure lists Simon and Hannah's total monthly expenditure and indicates that they have net surplus monthly income of £500.00. (This is in a normal year when the joint income is £80,000.)

6   *Simon and Hannah's assets and liabilities*

Asset	Amount	Ownership
Residential property	£210,000	Joint
Building Society account	£140,000	Joint
TOISA	£3,000	Hannah
Share portfolio★★	£104,000	Hannah
Personal pension (fund value)	£11,200	Simon
Retirement annuity	★ £2,100	Hannah
Value of business, say	£100,000	
Total assets	£570,300	

★ Current transfer value.

★★For full breakdown of portfolio, see Appendix 2 Investment schedule.

Liabilities

Simon and Hannah have no credit card or short term loans. Their only liability is the repayment mortgage of £75,000.

7   Simon and Hannah have written wills leaving all assets to the surviving spouse. It is likely that their potential estates will increase in value. Simon expects to inherit £300,000. When he sells his business, this should raise an amount in excess of £100,000.

Summary of objectives

Simon and Hannah wish to invest the £140,000 currently available in the building society:

(a)   To increase their retirement income
(b)   To make provision for school fees
(c)   To provide a small investment for each child

General strategy

1   *Pension provision*

One of Simon and Hannah's top priorities must be to build up substantial funds for retirement. They should be wary of relying too heavily on the proceeds of the sale of their business upon retirement. Trading patterns can change and the business might be worth relatively little by the time the clients reach retirement age.

It makes sense to take advantage of the tax reliefs available on contributions to pension funds. To date, they have made very little provision. Simon's fund is £11,200 and Hannah's £2,100. They have indicated that they wish to retire when Simon is aged 55, only 13 years away.

To provide a pension of say 50% of their current earnings, Simon and Hannah would need a combined fund of perhaps £450,000. Simon and Hannah must make use of the maximum reliefs for tax purposes and can use some of the capital currently available to make single premium pension contributions. Tax relief will be available on these contributions up to a maximum of 40%.

Simon and Hannah should aim to make regular pension contributions of a reasonable size and to top these up with single payments, dependent upon the profitability of their business and cashflow.

Simon and Hannah should aim to build up a portfolio of pension policies, spreading the risk between a number of insurance companies and between different investment funds. They can use a mix of with profits and unitised funds to provide a balanced investment approach.

Simon and Hannah's existing pension policies should be reviewed. The choice of funds and past performance of the funds offered by the current provider needs to be examined. It is also important to check that in the event of death prior to retirement the value of the fund is returned, rather than there simply being a return of premiums with or without interest. The death benefits should be written in trust or under a nomination so that the funds pass to the beneficiaries free of inheritance tax.

2   *School fees provision*

The cost of the school fees is likely to increase, and Simon cannot rely upon continued financial help from his mother. To date he has managed the fees from income but this may become a problem if his business is less successful.

As there is now capital available, Simon can set aside some to provide for school fees in the future. It would be very costly to attempt to fund the entire school fees bill. If, say, one-third of the fees can be guaranteed, this will help to provide a feeling of security and enable the family to fulfil their ambition of privately educating the children.

There are a number of methods of funding for school fees. If a family starts planning when the child is aged two or three, then a long-term savings plan can be used. This type of scheme is impossible for the Hill family. In this case, a lump sum school fees investment plan is more appropriate. Such schemes guarantee fees for a set period of time.

3   *Investment for the children*

Simon and Hannah wish to invest small amounts of money for their children. If capital invested by a parent for a child creates income in excess of £100 per annum, it is treated as the parent's income. It is, therefore, important that an investment is selected which provides a tax-free growth. Small amounts of money invested for children should be made in secure investments without undue risk.

4   *Providing protection for the family*

In the information provided to us, Simon has not indicated the levels of life assurance or income protection cover which he and his wife hold. As they have a young family it is important that both Simon and Hannah have adequate cover. In calculating the amount of cover needed, Simon and Hannah must estimate the amount of capital which would be needed if one of them were to die while the children were still young.

In addition, Simon and Hannah should be making provision for some protection against the inheritance tax liability. At present the assets after debts and business property relief are, say, £395,300 (see assets above, £570,300 − £100,000 − £75,000). Allowing for a nil rate band of £275,000 for inheritance tax purposes, this means that £120,300 would be taxed at 40% (a liability of £48,120) should Simon and Hannah both die, say, in a road accident.

5   *Making use of tax incentives*

Simon and Hannah are both higher rate taxpayers, so if they have any capital to invest they should be making use of tax-free investments such as ISAs and NS&I Certificates (fixed interest and index-linked).

6   *Making use of existing investments*

Hannah's share portfolio should be reviewed to make sure that the investment strategy meets her investment aims. As Hannah is a higher rate taxpayer and has sufficient income, the aim of the portfolio should be to achieve capital appreciation rather than income.

The manager of Hannah's share portfolio should ensure that the maximum is invested in ISAs each year and that she is making full use of her annual CGT exemption (£8,500 in 2005/06).

7   *Making sure there is an emergency fund*

Simon and Hannah must have an easily accessible emergency fund. This may be needed to pay school fees if there is a cash flow crisis, or perhaps to provide for unexpected work on the house or car.

Long-term investment approach

1   *Building up capital*

As well as making maximum pension contributions, Simon and Hannah should aim to build up capital. This capital will be used to provide additional income in retirement. Their funds will consist of Hannah's share portfolio, any tax-free investments such as ISAs and possibly the capital which Simon will inherit from his parents.

In order to secure these funds, Simon and Hannah should be aware of the following.

(a) *Inflation.* Although inflation is currently fairly low, inflation will still reduce the purchasing power of capital significantly over a long period. Capital retained in fixed-interest or deposit accounts suffers most from the effects of inflation. Past experience has shown that a hedge against inflation is provided by asset-backed investments such as property and particularly equities (shares). Over long periods, these investments have given a real rate of return over inflation.

(b) *Diversification.* It is important that an investment and pension portfolio is well spread between types of investment and geographical areas. For example, investments can be made into gilts, deposits, property and shares (either directly or through pooled investments such as unit or investment trusts) and across global economic regions such as the UK, Europe, Japan, North America and South East Asia.

(c) *Expert investment management.* Simon and Hannah are experts in their own profession. They should look to professional fund managers to invest and manage their investments. It is important that all investments are reviewed in light of family circumstances, tax legislation and economic changes.

2   *Changing circumstances*

It is likely that the Hill family's personal circumstances will change. If Simon's father dies before his mother, there may be a need to extend the house to provide a granny annex. Such a move will require an injection of capital. This could be raised from a loan, from capital or Simon's mother may contribute. In such circumstances a substantial contribution by Simon's mother would make sense from a long term planning point of view. The gift of the capital to Simon would be treated as a potentially exempt transfer (PET) for inheritance tax purposes. If his mother then survived for seven years, the gift would be exempt from inheritance tax.

3   *Inheritance tax planning*

As we have already seen in the general strategy section of this report, there is already a substantial liability to inheritance tax should both Simon and Hannah die, say in a car accident.

The estate will increase as Simon and Hannah save more money, increase their investments, inherit capital and eventually sell their business.

Once the mortgage has been paid off, the eventual estate could be in the region of £850,000. Using today's rates, the inheritance tax liability at 40% would be £230,000 (allowing for the use of only one nil rate band).

For the long term, Simon and Hannah should consider methods to mitigate this liability. Although it is sensible to make use of the spouse exemption by leaving all assets to the surviving spouse no use is made of the £275,000 nil band for IHT purposes by the first spouse to die. If Simon and Hannah can create sufficient pension income, they should consider changing their wills. It would be more tax efficient to pass capital, up to the nil band, to the children on the first death with the remaining assets passing to the surviving spouse. In this way £275,000 × 2 = £550,000 (at current IHT rates) could be passed to the family free of inheritance tax.

In years to come, Simon and Hannah could consider passing capital to their children at the time of their marriages within the then current limits for inheritance tax-free gifts.

Simon mentions that he expects to inherit about £300,000 from his parents. As Simon and Hannah already have a fairly substantial estate, consideration might be given to passing on some of this capital directly to Simon's children, possibly by use of a deed of family arrangement (deed of variation).

Recommendations

1   Simon should invest £35,000 as a single premium personal pension contribution.

2   Hannah should also invest £35,000 as a single premium pension contribution. In her case the investment should be made to the retirement annuity contract.

3   Simon and Hannah should invest £30,000 in a School Fees Capital Plan.

4   Simon should invest £7,000 in ISAs.

5   £500 for each child should be invested in NS&I Children's Bonus Bonds.

6   A unit linked whole of life policy should be taken out for cover of £100,000 index-linked.

7   Simon should effect a further personal pension with a regular premium of £100 per month together with a waiver of premium contract.

8   Hannah should effect a personal pension with a regular premium of £250 per month including a waiver of premium contract.

9   Hannah's portfolio should be reviewed to ensure that she has made the maximum ISA contribution for the current fiscal year.

10   £26,500 should be invested in building society accounts, with £6,500 on instant access and £20,000 on 90 day access.

Points arising out of the recommendation

1   *Simon's pension contribution*

The maximum Simon can contribute to a personal or stakeholder pension plan for the current tax year is 20% of capped earnings £105,600 = £21,120 less other contributions, £1,800 (possibly increasing). If he elects to do so by 31 January 2006 and makes the contribution by then, Simon can 'carry back' further contributions to have them treated as having been made in 2004/05. Next year, under the pension simplification proposals, Simon will be able to contribute up to 100% of his income, subject to a limit of £215,000.

It is suggested that the contribution is made to a new provider in order to spread risk. We show in Appendix 3 details of the scheme recommended. The Appendix gives details of fund choice, past performance, charges and the financial strength of the insurance company selected.

We also suggest that Simon should increase his monthly contributions to the existing personal pension to £250. A further insurance company has been selected, with details in Appendix 4. Simon will then have four personal pension contracts with a selection of investment funds both with profits and unit linked. All contracts could be written to a retirement age of 55.

A waiver of premium contract should be added to the new policy to ensure that, in the event of Simon being unable to work through long-term sickness, his premium contributions continue to be paid. It should be possible to insure for a waiver of premium contribution of £250 per month even if waiver of premium does not apply to the existing policy. For policies opened after 5 April 2001, the premium waiver must be a separate contract. Each contract should be written in trust or under a nomination of beneficiary, so that the value of the fund passes to Simon's beneficiaries free of inheritance tax.

2 *Hannah's pension contribution*

As Hannah has an existing Retirement Annuity Policy (RAP), it may be possible for her to make a single premium contribution to this policy. If this is so, she can pay 17.5% of her earnings without suffering an earnings cap. By relating back (carrying back) premiums to 2004/05 – making an election to do so by 31 January 2006 – she can make use of the facility available for RAPs which allows unused reliefs to be carried forward from 1998/99 and later years.

Appendix 5 reviews the funds offered by the RAP and the past performance statistics. The choice is restricted and Hannah may have to select a 50/50 split between with profits and the managed fund.

Hannah should commence a new personal pension using a monthly contribution of £250. Details of the recommended insurance company, choice of funds, charges and financial strength are shown in Appendix 6. As Hannah is four years younger than her husband, the quotation assumes a retirement age of 51 to coincide with her husband reaching age 55. If she wishes to pay a maximum contribution to the RAP, Hannah should wait for a new tax year to start the regular personal pension contribution. The total of RPA and personal pension contributions must be within personal pension contribution limits.

Hannah should take out waiver of premium cover and ensure that the death benefit under both her policies is correctly written to ensure that the proceeds pass to her beneficiaries free of inheritance tax should she die before the retirement date.

3 *School fees capital plan*

Simon and Hannah should invest £10,000 in a school fees plan to provide fees for Mark for the next four years. The amounts will be guaranteed and increase each year by 5%. The quotation and full details are given in Appendix 7.

A further £20,000 should be invested in a similar scheme for the twins. In this case, the fee payments do not start until age 13 and they continue for five years. A deferred period has been selected to allow for some capital appreciation on the investment. The fees are guaranteed and escalate at 5% pa. See quotations in Appendix 7.

The plan selected allows for certain flexibility, fees can be redistributed between children and this may be useful if Charlotte wins the music scholarship.

4 *ISA investment for Simon*

Simon should invest the maximum £7,000 in an ISA during the current tax year. Details of the recommended scheme are attached. An income fund has been selected. The tax-free income should be allowed to roll up within the scheme. The scheme is open-ended but should be viewed as a long-term investment building up a tax-free fund for retirement.

£5,000 could be withdrawn from the building society in the next fiscal year and a further ISA purchased. A recommendation for the selection of a suitable scheme will be made in twelve months time.

5 *NS&I Children's Bonus Bonds*

The proposed investment of £500 per child could be invested in Children's Bonus Bonds for each child. A fixed rate of tax-free interest is guaranteed for five years. At the end of the period, NS&I declares a further rate and the investor can decide whether to remain or withdraw. Mark will have to withdraw in five years time but the twins can have their investment rolled over for a further five year period. The investment must mature by age 21.

The investment has been selected because it is secure and tax-free.

6 *Unit linked whole of life policy*

As we have seen from the general strategy and the long-term investment approach, the family do have a potential inheritance tax problem. This can be resolved to some extent by use of a life assurance policy. A whole of life policy can be taken out and written under a trust for the benefit of the children. Premiums to the policy will be treated as gifts for inheritance tax purposes but will normally be covered by the donor's annual exemption, currently £3,000 per annum.

A whole of life policy with a death cover of £100,000 should be written on the joint lives of Simon and Hannah. A tax-free lump sum would then pass to the children on the second death. The amount could be used in part to pay the inheritance tax liability. The recommended policy allows for some growth in the death cover through indexation. A quotation, key features document and other details are attached.

7 *Building society accounts*

The building society accounts should be taken out in joint names. Full details are attached.

Review service

It is essential that the proposed investment plan is regularly reviewed. The review will take place on an annual basis, when a full valuation of all assets will be prepared.

Remuneration

The cost of this report, implementing the recommendations and carrying out a regular review can be met by fees or commissions. Appendix 8 sets out the comparative costs and the client is asked to indicate which method is acceptable.

A copy of the company's terms and conditions of business is also reproduced in Appendix 8.

Tax position

The tax position of the schemes recommended in this report is based upon current legislation and HMRC practice. This may be subject to alteration in the future.

Appendices (not reproduced here)

Attached to this report are quotations, booklets, key features and tables as follows.

Appendix 1   Statement of Income and Expenditure

Appendix 2   Schedule of Hannah Hill's investments

Appendix 3   Recommendations for investment of a single premium pension contribution for Simon Hill

Appendix 4   Recommendation for investment of a regular premium pension contribution for Simon Hill

Appendix 5   Details of Hannah Hill's retirement annuity contract

Appendix 6   Recommendation for investment of a regular premium pension contribution for Hannah Hill

Appendix 7   Details of school fees plans for Mark, Sarah and Charlotte Hill

Appendix 8   Methods of remuneration and terms and conditions of business

Details of: XYZ ISA
PQR insurance company whole of life scheme
Sturdy Building Society accounts

Tax tables

TAX TABLES

Income tax rates

2005/06		2004/05	
Rate	Band	Rate	Band
%	£	%	£
10	1 – 2,090	10	0 -2,020
22	2,091 – 32,400	22	2,021-31,400
40	Over 32,400	40	Over 31,400

National Insurance contributions: 2005/06 rates

	Weekly	Monthly	Yearly
Class I (employee)			
Lower Earnings Limit (LEL)	£82.00	£356.00	£4,264.00
Upper Earnings Limit (UEL)	£630.00	£2,730.00	£32,760.00
Earnings Threshold (ET)★	£94.00	£408.00	£4,895.00

Employees' contributions – Class 1

Total earnings £ per week	Contracted in rate	Contracted out rate
Below £94.00★	Nil	Nil
£94.01 - £630.00	11%	9.4%
Excess over £630.00	1%	1%
		1.6% rebate on earnings between LEL and ET

Employers' contributions – Class 1

Total earnings £ per week	Contracted-in rate	Contracted-out rate	
		Final salary	Money purchase
Below £94.00★	Nil	Nil	Nil
£94.01 - £630.00	12.8%	9.3%	11.8%
Excess over £630.00	12.8%	12.8%	12.8%
		3.5% rebate on earnings between LEL and ET	1% rebate on earnings between LEL and ET

★ Earnings threshold below which no NICs payable. There is a zero band between the lower earnings limit (£82 pw) and the earnings threshold (£94 pw) to protect lower earners' rights to contributory state benefits such as basic state pension.

Class 1A (employer's contributions on most benefits) 12.8% on all relevant benefits

Class II (self-employed)   Flat rate per week £2.10 where earnings are over £4,345 pa

Class III (voluntary)   Flat rate per week £7.35

Class IV (self-employed)   8% on profits £4,895 – £32,760; 1% on profits above £32,760

BPP
PROFESSIONAL EDUCATION

Income tax reliefs

		2005/06 £	2004/05 £
Personal allowance	– under 65	4,895	4,745
	– 65 – 74	7,090	6,830
	– 75 and over	7,220	6,950
Married couple's allowance	– 65 – 74 (see note 1)	5,905	5,725
	– 75 and over (see note 1)	5,975	5,795
	minimum for 65+	2,280	2,210
Age allowance income limit		19,500	18,900
Blind person's allowance		1,610	1,560
Enterprise investment scheme relief limit (see note 2)		200,000	200,000
Venture capital trust relief limit (see note 3)		200,000	200,000

Notes

1   Either spouse must be born before 6 April 1935. Relief is restricted to 10%.

2   EIS qualifies for 20% relief.

3   VCT qualifies for 40% tax relief.

Working and child tax credits

Working tax credit	2005/06 £	2004/05 £
Basic element	1,620	1,570
Couple and lone parent element	1,595	1,545
30 hour element	660	640
Childcare element of WTC		
Maximum eligible cost for 1 child	175 per week	135 per week
Maximum eligible cost for 2 children	300 per week	200 per week
Percent of eligible child costs covered	70	70
Child tax credit		
Family element	545	545
Baby addition	545	545
Child element	1,690	1,625
Tax credits income thresholds and withdrawal rates		
First income threshold	5,220	5,060
First withdrawal rate	37%	37%
Second income threshold	50,000	50,000
Second withdrawal rate	6.67%	6.67%
First threshold for those entitled to CTC	13,910	13,480
Income disregard	2,500	2,500

Personal Pension Contributions (PPCs) and Retirement Annuity Premiums (RAPs)

	% of Net Relevant Earnings	
Age at beginning of tax year	PPCs %	RAPs %
35 or less	17.5	17.5
36 – 45	20	17.5
46 – 50	25	17.5
51 – 55	30	20
56 – 60	35	22.5
61 or more	40	27.5

Earnings limit (PPCs only)		
2005/06	£105,600
2004/05	£102,000
2003/04	£99,000
2002/03	£97,200
2001/02	£95,400
2000/01	£91,800
1999/00	£90,600
1998/99	£87,600

Maximum contribution without evidence of earnings (2005/06) £3,600 gross (£2,808 net)

Car and fuel benefits

Company cars Lower threshold CO_2 – 140g/km: 15% of list price (max £80,000 including VAT)

2005/06   Increase by 1% for each 5g/km (round down to nearest multiple of 5g)
3% supplement for diesel cars (maximum 35% of list price)
To maximum: 35% of list price (max £80,000 including VAT)

Car fuel   £14,400 × % used for car benefit

Further information:

(a) **In most cases, accessories** are included in the list price on which the benefit is calculated.

(b) **List price** is reduced by employee's capital contributions (maximum £5,000).

(c) **Car benefit** is reduced by the amount of employee's contributions towards running costs, but **fuel** benefit is reduced only if the employee makes good **all** the fuel used for private journeys.

Fixed profit car scheme (authorised mileage rates)

2005/06 rates

Car or Van		**Motorcycle**	24p
Up to 10,000 miles	40p	**Cycle**	20p
Over 10,000 miles	25p	**Passenger payments**	5p

Inheritance tax

Death rate %	Lifetime rate %	Chargeable 2005/06 £'000	Chargeable 2004/05 £'000	Chargeable 2003/04 £'000
Nil	Nil	0 – 275	0 – 263	0 – 255
40	20	Over 275	Over 263	Over 255

Inheritance tax reliefs

Annual exemption	£3,000	Marriage	– parent	£5,000
Small gifts	£250		– grandparent	£2,500
			– bride/groom	£2,500
			– other	£1,000

Reduced charge on gifts within 7 years of death

Years before death	0 – 3	3 – 4	4 – 5	5 – 6	6 – 7
% of death charge	100%	80%	60%	40%	20%

Main Social Security benefits

		From 11.4.05	From 12.4.04
		£	£
Child benefit	– first child	17.00	16.50
	– subsequent child	11.40	11.05
Incapacity benefit	– short term lower rate	57.65	55.90
	– short term higher rate	68.20	66.15
	– long term rate	76.45	74.15
Attendance allowance	– lower rate	40.55	39.35
	– higher rate	60.60	58.80
Retirement pension	– single	82.05	79.60
	– married	131.20	127.25
Widowed parent's allowance		82.05	79.60
Bereavement payment (lump sum)		2,000.00	2,000.00
Jobseekers allowance		56.20	55.65

Value added tax

Standard Rate	17½%
Annual Registration Limit – from 1 April 2005	£60,000
Deregistration Limit – from 1 April 2005	£58,000

Corporation tax

Financial Year	2005 to 31.3.06	2004 to 31.3.05
Full rate	30%	30%
Small companies rate	19%	19%
Starting rate	0%	0%
Profit limit for starting rate	£10,000	£10,000
Effective marginal rate for starting rate	23.75%	23.75%
Profit limit for starting rate	£50,000	£50,000
Small companies limit	£300,000	£300,000
Effective marginal rate for small companies	32.75%	32.75%
Upper marginal limit	£1,500,000	£1,500,000

There is a minimum 19% corporation tax charge on distributed profits.

Capital allowances

	First year allowance	Writing down allowance pa
Plant and machinery	40% ★ 50% ★★	25% (reducing balance)
Motor cars	–	25% (reducing balance) (max £3,000)
Motor cars – low emission (not more than 120gm/km)	100%	not usually applicable
Industrial buildings	–	4% (straight line)
Agricultural buildings	–	4% (straight line)
Hotels	–	4% (straight line)
Enterprise Zones	100%	–
Scientific research	100%	–
Patents, know-how	–	25% (reducing balance)

★ For small and medium sized enterprises from 2 July 1998

★★ For small enterprises in the one year period commencing 1.4.04/6.4.04 (companies/unincorporated businesses)

Small/medium sized enterprises

	Turnover (not more than)	Balance sheet total (not more than)	No of employees (not more than)
Small enterprise	£5.6 million	£2.8 million	50
Medium sized enterprise	£22.8 million	£11.4 million	250

Capital gains tax

	2005/06	2004/05
Rate	Gains taxed at 10%, 20% or 40%, subject to level of income	Gains taxed at 10%, 20% or 40%, subject to level of income
Individuals-exemption	£8,500	£8,200
Trusts-exemption	£4,250	£4,100

Taper relief (for disposals on or after 6 April 2002)

Gains on business assets		Gains on non-business assets *	
Complete years after 5 April 1998	% of gain chargeable	Complete years after 5 April 1998	% of gain chargeable
0	100.0	0	100
1	50	1	100
2 or more	25	2	100
		3	95
		4	90
		5	85
		6	80
		7	75
		8	70
		9	65
		10 or more	60

* Non-business assets held on 17 March 1998 given additional year of relief.

Retail prices index

	Jan	Feb	Mar	Apr	May	Jun	Jul	Aug	Sep	Oct	Nov	Dec
1982			79.4	81.0	81.6	81.9	81.9	81.9	81.9	82.3	82.7	82.5
1983	82.6	83.0	83.1	84.3	84.6	84.8	85.3	85.7	86.1	86.4	86.7	86.9
1984	86.8	87.2	87.5	88.6	89.0	89.2	89.1	89.9	90.1	90.7	91.0	90.9
1985	91.2	91.9	92.8	94.8	95.2	95.4	95.2	95.5	95.4	95.6	95.9	96.0
1986	96.2	96.6	96.7	97.7	97.8	97.8	97.5	97.8	98.3	98.5	99.3	99.6
1987	100.0	100.4	100.6	101.8	101.9	101.9	101.8	102.1	102.4	102.9	103.4	103.3
1988	103.3	103.7	104.1	105.8	106.2	106.6	106.7	107.9	108.4	109.5	110.0	110.3
1989	110.0	111.8	112.3	114.3	115.0	115.4	115.5	115.8	116.6	117.5	118.5	118.8
1990	119.5	120.2	121.4	125.1	126.2	126.7	126.8	128.1	129.3	130.3	130.0	129.9
1991	130.2	130.9	131.4	133.1	133.5	134.1	133.8	134.1	134.6	135.1	135.6	135.7
1992	135.6	136.3	136.7	138.8	139.3	139.3	138.8	138.9	139.4	139.9	139.7	139.2
1993	137.9	138.8	139.3	140.6	141.0	141.0	140.7	141.3	141.9	141.8	141.6	141.9
1994	141.3	142.1	142.5	144.2	144.7	144.7	144.0	144.7	145.0	145.2	145.3	146.0
1995	146.0	146.9	147.5	149.0	149.6	149.8	149.1	149.9	150.6	149.8	149.8	150.7
1996	150.2	150.9	151.5	152.6	152.9	153.0	152.4	153.1	153.8	153.8	153.9	154.4
1997	154.4	155.0	155.4	156.3	156.9	157.5	157.5	158.5	159.3	159.5	159.6	160.0
1998	159.5	160.3	160.8	162.6	163.5	163.4	163.0	163.7	164.4	164.5	164.4	164.4
1999	163.4	163.7	164.1	165.2	165.6	165.6	165.1	165.5	166.2	166.5	166.7	167.3
2000	166.6	167.5	168.4	170.1	170.7	171.1	170.5	170.5	171.7	171.6	172.1	172.2
2001	171.1	172.0	172.2	173.1	174.2	174.4	173.3	174.0	174.6	174.3	173.6	173.4
2002	173.3	173.8	174.5	175.7	176.2	176.2	175.9	176.4	177.6	177.9	178.2	178.5
2003	178.4	179.3	179.9	181.2	181.5	181.3	181.3	181.6	182.5	182.6	182.7	183.5
2004	183.1	183.8	184.6	185.7	186.5	186.8	186.8	187.4	188.1	188.6	189.0	189.9
2005	188.9	189.6	190.5	191.6								

Indexation relief was frozen at 5 April 1998 and replaced by taper relief for individuals and trustees.

Answers to Quick Quizzes

Chapter 1

1   A 'short-term' investment is one for up to three months.

2   Negative equity arises when the current value of a property is less than amount borrowed.

3   Systematic risk is the risk of a failure in a whole market, such as a fall in a stock market.

4   A real rate of return is a return in excess of the current rate of inflation.

5   A retired person is more likely to be affected by inflation because he or she is likely to be living on a fixed income.

6   Share prices are generally likely to rise if interest rates fall.

    Because the cost to companies and individuals of borrowing money reduces. Companies have to pay less interest on debt and consumers have more money to spend. Companies should be able to trade more profitably.

    Additionally, expected rates of return will have fallen. If expected yield falls, share prices will tend to rise.

7   Overseas equities broadly speaking add risk to an investment portfolio because there is both a stock market risk and a currency risk.

8   The price at which a share is quoted in the financial pages is normally the 'mid price'.

Chapter 2

1   NS&I Savings Certificates or Capital Bonds are possibilities, depending on the rate offered and the tax status of the child.

2   A Pensioners Bond (one, two or five year term) is a possibility.

3   Index-linked NS&I Savings Certificates could be suitable because, if interest rates increase, so too may inflation. He does not want a fixed rate certificate. The return is tax-free which is attractive to a higher rate taxpayer.

4   An NS&I Investment Account is a possibility, or a bank or building society account if a better rate can be found. With the NS&I account, interest is paid gross. James is unlikely to be paying tax. He can therefore elect to receive interest gross from a bank or building society account.

5   The clients could put the capital on the money market. They should compare the rates with Pensioners Bonds, Guaranteed Income or Guaranteed Growth Bonds offered by insurance companies.

Chapter 3

1   An indirect method of investing in a short-dated gilt may be via a guaranteed income bond.

2   War Loan.

3   A private investor may buy an index-linked gilt if he thinks inflation is going to rise.

4   A yield curve.

5   Interest will be paid gross but subject to tax.

6   The methods used by the Bank of England's Debt Management Office to place a new issue of gilts on the market are:

    (a)   A tender
    (b)   An auction

7   A local authority bond is purchased direct from the Treasury Department of the authority.

8   A debenture (corporate bond) carries a higher risk than a gilt because there is less security. A gilt is a loan to the government; a debenture is a loan to a company.

Chapter 4

1   This is a life assurance policy which does not satisfy the rules contained in Schedule 15 Income and Corporation Taxes Act 1988. The proceeds of such a policy are not tax-free.

2   Pound cost averaging occurs when an investor contributes a regular monthly amount to a unitised savings scheme. Each month the contribution purchases a different number of units. If the price of the units rises, the contribution will purchase less and if the price falls the contribution will purchase more.

3   The maximum regular premium to a Friendly Society tax-exempt fund is £270 per annum, or £25 per month if premiums are paid monthly.

4   On maturity of a TEP, a basic rate taxpayer may pay tax as follows.

   (a) If the policy is a qualifying one, then the proceeds may be subject to capital gains tax.

   (b) If the policy is a non-qualifying one, then a chargeable event will occur and the gain may be subject to tax at 20% if the 'slice' pushes the investor into the higher rate tax bracket.

Chapter 5

1   Funds offered by an investment bond may typically include: managed, equity, cash, fixed-interest, international, Europe, North America, Japan, South East Asia, property.

2   An income bond made up of a temporary annuity and a deferred annuity would be most suitable for a non-taxpayer.

3   The letters MVR stand for Market Value Reduction. Such an adjustment may take place if an investor takes a partial or total surrender of a with profit bond at a time when there has been poor stock market performance.

4   Insurance companies are reluctant to offer intermediaries the opportunity to run broker funds because of restrictions placed on them by the FSA. The FSA insists that the insurance company satisfies itself as to the competence of the broker to run the fund and they must monitor his subsequent performance.

5   The charges on an offshore bond are generally higher than for an onshore bond because the insurance company is unable to offset expenses against income for tax purposes.

6   An annuity which is treated as a purchased life annuity has a capital content.

7   You would complete an R85 if you were a non-taxpayer and wished to receive the interest from a bank or building society (or similar) without deduction of tax.

8   The expression 'without proportion' means that on the death of an annuitant, the insurance company is not responsible for the balance of any payment. If the annuity is 'with proportion' and the annuitant dies (for example) midway between payments, 50% of the next payment is due to the estate.

9   The pension from a retirement annuity is taxed as earned income.

10   Two methods of creating a back-to-back arrangement are:

(a) A temporary annuity and an endowment policy

(b) A temporary annuity and an ISA (unit trust, investment trust, zero preference share)

11   If you used a back-to-back arrangement to mitigate inheritance tax, you would use a purchased life annuity and a whole of life policy.

Chapter 6

1   A unit trust tracker fund is a fund which mimics the performance of a selected index. It usually slightly under-performs the index because of the charges (which are low).

2   A unit trust is called an 'open ended fund' because new units can be created to meet demand.

3   The charge on a gilt and fixed interest unit trust is likely to be 3%.

4   A unit trust manager can employ historic or forward pricing.

5   A unit trust accumulation unit is one where the income is reinvested at each distribution and the price of the units rises accordingly.

6   An investment trust may issue: an ordinary share, a preference share, a capital share (split capital trust), an income share (split capital trust), an annuity share, a zero dividend share, debenture stock, stepped interest debenture stock, unsecured loan stock, convertible loan stock, warrants, subscription shares.

7   The unsecured loan stock is less secure and has a lower priority on the winding up of the trust.

8   A factor of 180 would suggest that the investment trust is highly geared.

9   An investment trust does not pay tax on capital gains on the sale of its investments so long as it is approved under the Income and Corporation Taxes Act 1988.

10   The letters 'NAV' refer to Net Asset Value.

Chapter 7

1   The letters 'SEAQ' stand for Stock Exchange Automated Quotation system.

2   The Panel of Takeover and Mergers Levy is £1 per deal (both purchases and sales) in excess of £10,000.

3   The letters 'CREST' stand for Certificateless Registration of Electronic Stock and Share Transfers.

4   A company may change its share capital by a rights issue, a split of shares or a scrip issue.

5   A preference share carries a lower risk than an ordinary share because it pays a fixed amount of dividend and ranks ahead of the ordinary share holders in the event of a liquidation.

6   A warrant is not a share: it carries no right to a dividend nor voting rights.

7    $\text{Gross yield} = \dfrac{\text{gross dividend per share}}{\text{share price}} \times 100$

8   A high dividend cover implies that the company should be able to maintain a similar dividend in the future.

9   (a) Participating preference share
     (b) Cumulative preference share
     (c) Redeemable preference share

10   The letters xr would appear after a share at a time when the share was subject to a rights
     issue. The letters would indicate that the purchaser would not be eligible for the rights
     issue.

11   The letter A after a share shows that the share carries limited or no voting rights.

12   £250.

Chapter 8

1   £7,000.

2   (a) Tax-free
     (b) 20% charge deducted at source
     (c) Tax-free (subject to tax only if more than £180 interest is withdrawn in a tax year)

3   Yes, it is possible to transfer existing PEPs between managers.

4   The minimum age is 16 for a cash mini-ISA and 18 for other ISAs.

Chapter 9

1   An FSA-recognised fund is an offshore pooled investment which is recognised under the
     Financial Services and Markets Act 2000.

2   Marketing restrictions are placed on non-recognised offshore funds. They cannot promote
     their funds directly in the UK. Prospectuses can only be forwarded to professionals such as
     stockbrokers or IFAs on request.

3   Recognised funds are most likely to be based in EU countries.

4   A non-taxpayer may find a fixed-interest offshore fund attractive because the dividends will
     be paid to him gross.

5   If an investor encashes an offshore holding with distributor status, any gain will be subject
     to UK capital gains tax.

     If an investor encashes an offshore holding with non-distributor status, any gain will be
     subject to income tax. This means that the investor cannot take advantage of
     indexation/taper relief for capital gains tax purposes or the annual exemption for capital
     gains tax purposes.

6   Two high risk types of offshore funds could be: commodities and currencies.

Chapter 10

1   London International Financial Futures and Options Exchange.

2   Over-the-counter.

3   The London Clearing House guarantees that goods or securities being traded on the various
     futures and options markets will be delivered to the buyer and that settlement will be
     forthcoming. The Clearing House takes the risk of one party defaulting.

4   The clearing house allows the market to run smoothly by taking on the risk of a party defaulting on a deal.

5   Derivatives can be used either to increase or to reduce risk.

6   A warrant is a right to buy an ordinary share of a company on a particular date or dates in the future at a fixed price.

Chapter 11

1   Indirect methods of investing in property are via a property unit trust or the property fund of an investment bond.

2   An investor in an Enterprise Zone property will receive 100% tax relief on the investment.

3   Under 'rent a room relief', rental income up to £4,250 is tax-free (2005/06).

4   The spot price is the price paid on a commodity deal for immediate delivery.

5   If the sale proceeds of the antique does not exceed £6,000 it will be exempt from capital gains tax. If it exceeds this amount, the maximum capital gain is 5/3 of the excess over £6,000.

6   The role of a managing agent at Lloyd's is to run the syndicate on behalf of the names.

7   Coffee, tea, oil, wheat (see the *Financial Times* for full listings).

Chapter 12

1   The rate of interest deducted from a building society net interest payment is 20%.

2   If the gross interest on the building society account in any one tax year is in excess of £100, it will be treated as the father's income and taxed accordingly.

3   The nil rate band for inheritance tax purposes is £275,000 (2005/06).

4   A deed of variation can be employed at any time up to two years after the death of an individual. It may be used to re-arrange the individual's will.

5   If you are using a back to back arrangement to provide funds to pay inheritance tax no-one knows when the life assured will die, so a temporary annuity is not suitable: it may well cease before the life assured dies and then there would be no further income to pay the premiums.

6   You can justify a gift out of normal expenditure for inheritance tax purposes if the donor makes the gift regularly and, having made the gift, is left with sufficient income to maintain his normal standard of living without having to resort to capital.

7   Three types of insurance based scheme for the mitigation of inheritance tax are:

   (a)   Conversion plan
   (b)   Gift and loan
   (c)   PETA plan

8   The small gifts exemption is £250.

Chapter 13

1   A person who has been self-employed all their working life will receive only the basic state pension.

2   12.5% of income (= 40% – 27.5%).

3   £105,600 (2005/06).

4   Guaranteed Minimum Pension. GMP no longer accrues from April 1997 but existing GMP is preserved.

5   A member of a final salary scheme is entitled to a percentage of his final earnings as a pension. By buying 'added years', the member can increase this percentage of final earnings and thus his pension.

6   33% tax would be paid on the refund.

7   The letters 'SIPP' stand for 'Self Invested Personal Pension'.

8   The annuity under a drawdown facility must be purchased by age 75.

9   If you wish to take an open market option to company A from a retirement annuity, you need an existing retirement annuity with company A. Alternatively, you can convert the retirement annuity into a personal pension and take the open market option from the personal pension.

Chapter 14

1   The items of personal information in a fact find are: name and address, date and place of birth, residence and domicile, marital status, health, hobbies and pastimes, children and other dependants.

2   An adviser needs to know about a client's state of health because part of the recommendation may include the use of a life assurance, permanent health, critical illness or private medical insurance products. If the client's state of health is poor this would be relevant to the advice given.

3   (a)   The adviser needs to know the client's total remuneration if he is trying to replace it in the event of death, illness or retirement.

    (b)   Benefits in kind can be taken into account when calculating the total amount which can be contributed to a personal pension or AVC.

4   (a)   Interest
    (b)   Dividends
    (c)   Rental income

5   (a)   State pension
    (b)   Child benefit
    (c)   Long-term incapacity benefit

6   It is important to know if a policy is written in trust because the benefits belong to someone other than the life assured.

7   (a)   Saving for a holiday
    (b)   Paying the next term's school fees

8   (a)   Saving for a daughter's wedding
    (b)   Saving for retirement

9   (a)   The client's attitude to risk
    (b)   The client's tax position
    (c)   The term of the investment

10 Statements which may appear in a report:

   (a) Statement of assets and liabilities
   (b) Statement of income and expenditure
   (c) Summary of investments

Chapter 15

1 If you want to inflation-proof the sum assured under a protection policy, you need the cover to increase each year in line with the RPI.

2 In order to obtain tax relief on premium payments, the life policy must be taken out as personal pension or AVC life cover.

3 If a policy is written under a MWPA trust, the proceeds pass immediately to the trustees without waiting for probate.

4 If you are repaying your mortgage by means of ISAs/PEPs, you will normally need level term assurance to repay the mortgage on early death.

5 The maximum permanent health cover you are likely to be able to obtain is 66.66% of earnings less a single person's basic state sickness benefit.

6 The benefit from an individual permanent health policy is tax-free.

7 Typically insurance companies limit the income protection cover on housepersons to, say, £10,000 pa.

8 A cash unit trust normally offers competitive interest rates for small investments. The reason is that they have large sums to place on the money market and obtain advantageous rates.

9 The main advantages of tracker funds are:

   (a) Low costs
   (b) The investor is not dependent upon the expertise (or otherwise) of a fund manager
   (c) Very few investment managers actually outperform the index

10 An investment trust may give a higher income than a unit trust if the income share of a split capital trust is used.

11 A form R85 needs to be completed to receive gross interest from a building society.

12 Waiver of premium is an option added to policies, or supplementary to policies in the case of personal pension plans begun after 5 April 2001, which allows premiums to continue even if the policyholder cannot work because of long-term illness or disability.

Answers to practice questions

PRACTICE QUESTION 1: PORTFOLIO

(a) (i) As John is relatively young, he needs to maintain the purchasing power of his inheritance for, say forty years.

(ii) If he invests this capital totally in deposit or fixed-interest investments, the underlying value of his capital will not increase in purchasing power.

(ii) The only long-term method of inflation-proofing the capital is to invest at least part of the portfolio in asset-backed investments such as equities or property. Property has been a poor performing investment in recent years, but in the past it has given a hedge against inflation.

Tutorial note

Seven marks are given for this part of the question. Two marks would be gained for each point listed above. The extra mark would be given to a student who demonstrated a thorough understanding of inflation and its effects.

(b) You should explain the following to John.

(i) The need to have a well spread portfolio in order to reduce risk. Although a property or an investment in a pooled property investment, such as a unit trust or an investment bond, could form part of a portfolio, to place the total investment into a property would be exposing the capital to a very high risk.

(ii) The illiquidity of property. A sale can only be made if a buyer can be found and this may take many months or years.

(iii) The costs of investing in property. The professional charges of surveyors and solicitors may be high. Once the property is owned an agent may be required to select tenants and oversee repairs.

(iv) Although property may produce a rising rental income, this is only possible if a suitable tenant can be found and maintained.

(v) Although property has proved a hedge against inflation in the past, it has been a poor performing investment over some periods, and house price falls are possible.

Tutorial note

Each point carries two points. In this question it is essential to demonstrate not only the disadvantages of property as an investment but also the importance of having a well spread portfolio and not having all your eggs in one basket.

(c) A portfolio for John may consist of the following.

(i) Cash on easy access in a building society account – perhaps some in an instant access account and some on, say, 90 day call in order to obtain a better interest rate. The amount will depend on how much he will need in 12 months time.

(ii) Investments for long-term growth. The portfolio should take advantage of all the tax-free investments which are available. Part of the portfolio could comprise:

(1) NS&I Savings Certificates (fixed and index linked)
(2) ISAs, perhaps with a corporate bond component to reduce risk

As John has indicated that he wishes to invest without undue risk, we should include in the portfolio investments which attempt to reduce risk by spreading. By this we mean pooled investments such as unit and investment trusts and investment bonds. The funds which could be selected within the pooled investment could, again, be chosen to spread and minimise risk, for example, managed funds or funds of funds.

(i) In this question you are asked to briefly explain how you would construct a portfolio. The emphasis is on the broad construction of the portfolio: the question is not looking for individual recommendations.

(ii) You would be expected to explain the method of keeping funds available on easy access with perhaps one or two examples of ways of achieving this.

(iii) You would also be expected to make reference to the use of tax-free funds with examples.

(iv) Finally you would need to tackle the matter of long-term growth. As John has indicated he is not prepared to take undue risk, reference should be made to pooled investments. You would receive marks for other methods of achieving long-term growth as long as the methods did not involve undue risk.

(d) If John's wife is a non-taxpayer then John must be asked if he is prepared to invest any or all of the capital in his wife's name. The aim of this would be to produce a gross income up to the level of Amy's personal allowance (£4,895 in 2005/06).

If John is agreeable, this may influence the construction of the portfolio. It would seem sensible for the easy access money to be placed in her name and the building society to be asked (after completion of an R85) to pay out gross interest. As the aim of the portfolio is for growth, it may be necessary to secure tax-free income in Amy's name and then reinvest to achieve the desired growth.

Tutorial notes

(a) In this part of the question, one mark would be earned for making the point that John must be asked how he feels about investing in Amy's name.

(b) You must show the importance of making use of Amy's personal allowance and achieving tax-free income up to this amount.

(c) You would receive marks for any suggested re-arrangement so long as it achieves a tax-free income or the ability to reclaim tax.

PRACTICE QUESTION 2: DEPOSITS

(a) **Current account**. A current account will give James instant access to his capital. He will also have chequebook, debit card and cashpoint facilities. The account may pay a nil or low rate of interest.

(b) **Onshore building society account**. If James uses a building society account, he has a greater choice of interest rates than with the current account. He could place the majority of the capital in an instant access account, possibly using a postal or internet account to obtain the best rates. The question implies that James will buy a cheaper house and retain the balance of the capital. Therefore, it may be possible to place a percentage in an account with a longer access period, say 90 days. This account may give a higher rate of interest. Unless he is prepared to tie up some of the money for, say, one year, the interest rates offered will be variable and paid to him net of 20% tax unless he is in a position to complete an R85.

(c) **Offshore building society account**. An offshore account will work in a similar way to an onshore account. Interest rates will be similar and variable. The only difference will be that the offshore building society will pay the interest to James gross.

(d) **Money market deposit**. As James has a large sum to invest, he could place this on the money market and receive a higher rate of interest than he could obtain from a bank or building society's normal accounts. The rate he would obtain would be fixed for the period of deposit, say one month or three. The interest would be added to the capital at the end of the fixed term. As the investment is in excess of £50,000 it may be possible to obtain the interest gross.

(e)   **Unit trust cash fund**. This is a unit trust where the assets are invested on the money market. Because of the size of the funds invested, advantageous rates can be obtained. The interest created is variable. Interest is paid to the investor net of 20% tax.

We will now run through each account saying whether it is suitable for James' needs.

(a)   **Current account**. This is not suitable because there is nil or very low interest. James can find an alternative account with access and interest.

(b)   **Onshore building society account**. This gives James the ability to spread his money between instant access and notice accounts to give him flexibility and better interest rates than a current account. However, it is unlikely that he will be able to complete an R85 if he has been in employment during the current tax year so he must receive interest net.

(c)   **Offshore building society account**. This is the most suitable account. James can split up the money so he has sufficient in an instant access account to buy a new house and the balance in a notice account. The interest from this latter account can be used to cover living expenses until a new job is found. The great advantage of the offshore accounts are that interest will be paid gross. This gives James greater flexibility, he may or may not have to pay tax on the interest depending on his circumstances. The longer he is unemployed, the more chance that no tax will need to be paid on the gross interest. In the meantime James has had the gross interest available to cover his living expenses. Tax may not need to be paid to HMRC (the former Inland Revenue) until he is back in employment.

(d)   **Money market deposit**. This is fine from the point of view that the interest rate is high and guaranteed, and it may be possible to obtain gross interest. However, the disadvantage is that the money is tied up for a fixed period and James does not know when he will find a suitable house.

(e)   **Unit trust cash fund**. Tax can be claimed back from the dividend/interest and the scheme is flexible. However it is felt that the offshore account has a slight edge as interest is paid gross.

The further information we may need is as follows.

(a)   How much of the available capital James intends to use to buy the new house.

(b)   Whether he intends to get a mortgage.

(c)   Whether he has a property in mind and how long it may be before he completes.

(d)   What level of income he requires to meet his basic outgoings. This information would help the adviser to recommend to James a split between capital for the house and capital to create income.

(e)   What are James' job prospects? Is he likely to obtain another job easily? And when he does get another job, will it pay him as well as his previous job and if not, will he need to supplement his income from his capital?

Tutorial notes

You should be aware of the time constraints and avoid verbosity in answering this question. Basic facts are all that is required in the definition of each type of account. Make reference to whether interest is fixed or variable and the tax situation on each account. Show that you have read the question properly and make some attempt to suggest a split of capital between instant access and notice accounts.

Four marks would be given for the explanation of each account and five marks for a reasoned argument for the use of one particular account. It does not have to be the offshore account, so long as the argument is sound.

In the last section of the question, marks will be given for reasonable questions but they should involve questions on access to capital and possible levels of income required.

PRACTICE QUESTION 3: FIXED INTEREST

(a)   Tom Downs could consider:

      (i)   Building society accounts

      (ii)   NS&I Savings Certificates

      (iii)   Capital Bonds

      (iv)   Cash mini-ISA

      (v)   Gilts

      (vi)   Local authority bonds

Tom needs complete security of his capital because he needs to use it to repay the mortgage. The most suitable investment is NS&I Savings Certificates because this will produce a secure tax-free return. All the other investments, except an ISA, will suffer tax on the interest produced and should only be considered if their net return is greater than the gross return from the NS&I Savings Certificates.

The NS&I Savings Certificates are a two or five year investment producing a tax-free return. There are fixed rate and index-linked issues. The fixed rate issue, as its name implies, offers a fixed rate over the term and the index-linked provides a return of a small percentage over inflation over the term. If James is unsure as to whether interest rates will rise or fall, he should split his capital 50/50 between the fixed rate and index-linked. If interest rates fall, the Fixed Rate Certificate will look attractive and if rates rise, so too may inflation and the value of the Index-Linked Certificate will rise.

The cash ISA would also produce a tax-free return. However, James could only invest a total of £3,000 in the current year.

(b)   (i)   Two investments which could be used by Mrs Watts are as follows.

            (1)   *Pensioners Bond.* Mrs Watts is over 60 so she could use the Pensioners Bond. This will give her a high rate of guaranteed income for a one, two or five year period. The income will be paid monthly. The income will be paid gross and Mrs Watts will be responsible for tax up to 40%.

            (2)   *Building society monthly income account.* This will have a variable rate and interest will be paid to Mrs Watts net of basic rate tax. She will have to pay higher rate tax.

        Alternatively, Mrs Watts could purchase a short-dated gilt if rates are competitive with those offered by the building society. However interest will only be paid half-yearly.

      (ii)   Investments suitable for the grandchildren are as follows.

            (1)   *NS&I Children's Bonus Bond.* This is a bond specifically for children. The maximum investment per child is currently £3,000. A fixed rate of interest is declared for five years and then a further rate for five years. The interest is tax-free. Children can hold the bond until age 21. The oldest age of entry is age 16.

            (2)   The balance of the available capital could be invested in *NS&I Savings Certificates*. This is a five year certificate giving a tax-free return. There are two varieties of certificate, fixed-rate and index-linked. The choice would depend upon Mrs Watts' attitude to interest rates. If she felt they were likely to fall she should select the fixed rate certificate. If, on the other hand, she felt they were going to rise, she should select the index-linked certificate. The certificates can be taken out in the name of the child.

Tutorial notes

(i) In part (b) of this question, there is freedom of choice of investment. However, the investments for the grandmother must produce a regular income, monthly if possible. The pensioners bond is an obvious choice because it gives a high level of guaranteed income.

(ii) The investments for the grandchildren can be tax-free and the Children's Bonus Bond is an obvious choice. For a second choice, you could suggest any investment that produces a gross income. As this is a gift from the grandmother, any income will be treated as the child's. The child will have a personal allowance and this could be used up with some gross interest.

PRACTICE QUESTION 4: PACKAGED INVESTMENTS

(a) (i) An endowment policy is a regular premium savings policy for a fixed term. The policy will incorporate a guaranteed death benefit and a lump sum benefit will be forthcoming at maturity.

So long as the term of the policy is ten years or more, premium payments are maintained throughout the term and no significant alterations take place, such a policy would be treated as a qualifying policy under Schedule 15 Income and Corporation Taxes Act 1988. As a qualifying policy, the proceeds will be free of all tax.

The premiums paid to such a policy can be invested in a with profits or a unit linked fund depending on the risk profile of the client.

If an endowment policy is used as a savings policy for a child, the policy will normally be taken out on the life of one or both parents in trust for the child. The parents will act as the trustees of the policy and the proceeds will be paid to them to distribute to the child. When commencing the policy the parents will select a term to coincide with, say, the child's 18th or 21st birthday.

As the policy is taken out on the life of one or both parents, in the event of the death of the life assured(s) prior to maturity the guaranteed death benefit will be paid to the beneficiary via the trustees.

As an alternative, it may be possible to write a policy in the name of a child. This is possible with Friends Provident (under a special Act of Parliament) for a child of any age. Other insurance companies can write a policy in the name of a child but in the event of death prior to age 16, only the premiums paid are returned as a death benefit.

(ii) The advantages of using an endowment policy as a savings scheme for a child are as follows.

(1) The parents can remain in control of the money by acting as trustees.

(2) A safe 'with profits' fund can be selected for the investment.

(3) A maturity date can be selected to coincide with a particular birthday.

(4) As the policy is written on the life of one or both parents, a lump sum death benefit will be available on the death of a parent even if only one premium has been paid.

The disadvantages of using an endowment policy as a savings scheme for a child are as follows.

(1) The policy is inflexible; it is for a fixed term.

(2) The charges levied on an endowment policy may be higher than on other forms of saving.

(3) The life fund suffers tax. Other investments such as NS&I Savings Certificates or Children's Bonus Bonds would produce a tax free return.

Tutorial notes

(i)   An endowment policy needs to be defined before the explanation of its use as a children's savings policy.

(ii)   When explaining about its use as a children's policy, you need to mention the two main methods of construction. The choice is a policy taken out on the life of the parent, or the child. You must then note the restriction on life cover with most insurance companies. The marks would be split, four marks for a good definition of an endowment assurance and four for the specific use.

(iii)   Advantages and disadvantages, one mark per point. Any alternative points which were significant would earn marks.

(b)   (i)   If an annuity is treated as a purchased life annuity, part of each income payment is treated as a return of capital and only the balance, the interest, is taxed.

The capital content is fixed at outset by reference to a mortality table agreed by the Inland Revenue. The amount of the capital content is dependent upon the annuitant's age when he takes out the policy. To ascertain the capital content, the purchase price is divided by the individual's life expectancy.

The annuitant must submit a form PLA1 to the Inland Revenue in order that the annuity can be treated as a purchased life annuity. If it is acceptable, the insurance company will pay out the annuity with 20% tax deducted only from the interest content. A higher rate taxpayer will be responsible for the balance of the tax to the Inland Revenue.

In certain circumstances, the insurance company can pay out the annuity gross. One such occasion is if the annuitant's income is below a certain level and the Inland Revenue have given approval. In certain circumstances, payments can be made gross to non-residents.

(ii)   Annuities which receive alternative tax treatment:

(1)   An annuity resulting from an occupational pension scheme, a personal pension scheme or a retirement annuity

(2)   An annuity certain

(3)   A deferred annuity

(4)   An annuity purchased under the terms of a will or a trust

(iii)   The annuity resulting from a personal pension will be taxed as earned income.

Tutorial notes

(i)   In answering part (b)(i) of this question, you would receive marks for explaining the concept of capital and interest content (2 marks). Further marks would be given for explaining how a capital content is decided (2 marks), the actual method of taxation, PLA1 etc (2 marks) and a final 2 marks for mentioning that some purchased life annuities can be paid out gross.

(ii)   In part (b)(ii), one mark is given for each type of annuity listed. The pension annuities may be listed separately and will score a mark.

(iii)   In part (b)(iii), you need only write one sentence stating the tax treatment of the selected type of annuity. As it is clear that only three marks can be scored only a short time should be spent on this section.

PRACTICE QUESTION 5: COLLECTIVE INVESTMENTS

(a)   Common features of a unit trust and an investment trust are as follows.

   (i)   Both types of investment are pooled or collective investments.

   (ii)   Both types of scheme offer their investors the choice of investing in a number of pools of shares (funds) in a wide range of geographical areas, eg UK, Europe, North America, Japan, Far East.

   Differences between unit trusts and investment trusts are as follows.

   (i)   A unit trust is a trust operated by trustees. An investment trust is a limited company quoted on the London Stock Exchange.

   (ii)   Unit trusts are open-ended funds: the manager can create or cancel units depending on supply and demand. Investment trusts are closed-end funds: the number of their shares is limited by the Articles of Association of the company.

   (iii) A unit trust manager must always buy back his units. The holder of an investment trust can only sell if a buyer can be found in the market.

   (iv)   At the time of a stockmarket crash, unit trust managers may have to sell securities to raise cash to pay out investors. This does not happen in an investment trust as shares will be traded independently of the actual trust investments.

   (v)   Investment trusts can borrow money. Unit trusts cannot do so for long term purposes.

   (vi)   Unit trusts are worth the value of the underlying investments. Investment trusts may not be. Investment trust shares are only worth what someone will pay for them, so sometimes the shares trade at a discount to net asset value and sometimes at a premium.

   (vii) The charges levied on unit trusts tend to be higher than for investment trusts. All unit trusts pay commission to introducers, IFAs and brokers. Some investment trusts pay no commission.

   (viii) Unit trusts can freely market their units. Investment trusts cannot advertise their existing shares direct to the public. (They can advertise new issues.)

   Tutorial note

   The answer given to this question above is in sentence form to remind you of the detail. However, this is a long question for eight marks. Read the question and, as directed, use notes in a list form. Marks will be given for two similarities and any six differences. The differences must include the fact that an investment trust is a company. If this fact is omitted, one mark will be deducted.

(b)   (i)   *Bob*. On encashment of the investment bond, a chargeable event will occur and a slice of £2,133.33 will be added to Bob's income in the year of encashment. The slice is calculated as follows:

          (Encashment value + Withdrawal – Original investment)/Years of investment

          £33,600 + £12,000 (£1,000 × 12) – £20,000 = £25,600. £25,600/12 = £2,133.33

          As Bob already has a taxable income in the higher rate of tax, the whole of the gain, £25,600 will be subject to tax at 40% – 20% = 20%. Tax will be £5,120.

          James

          The gain on the unit trust, £42,000 – £20,000 = £22,000 will be subject to capital gains tax. On the assumption that the client has not used any of his annual capital gains tax exemption, the tax will be 40% of (£22,000 – £8,500) = 40% of £13,500 = £5,400.

   (ii)   (1)   The only ways Bob could have avoided paying so much tax would be:

303

- Deferring encashment until he was a basic rate taxpayer

- Assigning the bond to his wife prior to encashment if she was a basic rate taxpayer

James could have avoided the high capital gains tax liability by transferring the units to his wife prior to encashment if she was a basic rate taxpayer, or determining encashment to benefit from maximum taper relief.

(2) The reasons why the investors received different amounts are as follows.

- The underlying life fund was taxed (investment bond) whereas the unit trust paid no capital gains tax on its investments.

- The charges levied on the bond were higher than the charges on the unit trust.

- In the early years or in years of poor performance, Bob may have been encashing capital in order to produce the 5% withdrawal from his bond. This in turn would reduce performance. James would simply have been receiving a dividend without affecting the value of his units.

Tutorial notes

(i) In calculating the tax, you should read the question carefully and see that the words 'taxable income' are used. This implies that this is the income after taking into account the personal allowance.

(ii) In this question, five marks each will be awarded for the correct calculation of the chargeable event and the capital gains, one mark each for methods of avoiding payment of so much tax and two marks each for suggesting two reasons why James and Bob received different amounts.

PRACTICE QUESTION 6: EQUITIES

(a) Current value of holdings:

Treasury 9.5% 2010 value £9,800

Sainsbury 25p shares value £38,100

(b) Interest yield on the Treasury stock is 9.69%, which is higher than the nominal yield of 9.5%. The interest yield is dependent upon the current price and is calculated as:

$$\frac{\text{Coupon}}{\text{Current price}} \times 100\%$$

Redemption yield of the Treasury stock is 10.37%. This yield takes into account the interest earned on the gilt plus the capital gain or loss. In this instance there is a small capital gain. The formula for calculating this is:

Interest yield + annualised capital gain or loss to redemption

Yield on the share is shown as 3.9% and has been calculated as follows:

$$\frac{\text{Dividend per share}}{\text{Share price}} \times 100$$

This yield will change with alterations in the share price and the dividend.

(c) The income received from the gilt is guaranteed at the interest yield applicable at the time of purchase. The interest will be paid gross. If Mrs Jones is a higher rate taxpayer she will be responsible for paying 40% tax on the interest.

The dividend from the share will be received net of 10%. A non-taxpayer may not reclaim tax and a higher rate taxpayer will be responsible for paying 22.5% to the Inland Revenue.

Tutorial notes

(a) You need to be able to show a knowledge of the information given in the extract from the Financial Times.

(b) In the answer to (b) you must explain the terms and reproduce the formula. You need to relate it to the information in the extract to earn full marks. (15 marks, 5 marks per explanation)

(c) Part (c) simply asks you to demonstrate a knowledge of the taxation of interest and dividends. (5 marks for the interest and 5 marks for the dividend explanation)

PRACTICE QUESTION 7: ISAS

(a) (i) An ISA will be an advantageous investment for a higher rate taxpayer because:

  (1) The fund rolls up free of tax

  (2) If the investor takes an income, it is tax-free (although tax credits on dividends cannot be reclaimed)

  (3) On encashment there is no charge to tax, even if the taxpayer has used their annual capital gains tax exemption (£8,500 in 2005/06)

 (ii) The maximum amount which the client and his wife can invest per tax year is £7,000 each.

 (iii) If a client is prepared to take medium to high risk with his investments, he has the following choices.

  (1) **Managed ISA**. This will be managed by a broker using individual shares. The client can indicate to the broker the level of risk he is prepared to take.

  (2) **Self-select ISA**. In this case the client could construct his own ISA portfolio, making his own choice of shares and concentrating on medium to high risk holdings.

  (3) **Pooled investment such as a unit trust or investment trust**. In this case, the client could select higher risk funds such as 'recovery' or smaller companies.

Tutorial notes

(i) Two marks each for mentioning the taxation of the fund and the individual taxation of income and capital growth.

(ii) You should have identified at least three different types of fund and be able to identify the risk level of each (two marks per type).

(b) Eligibility and subscription rules for an ISA.

  (i) Only authorised managers can run an ISA plan.

  (ii) The investor must be resident and ordinarily resident in the UK for tax purposes and must be over the age of 18 (16 for a cash mini-ISA).

  (iii) The investor may only invest in one maxi ISA or one of each of the two types of mini ISA per fiscal year. He may have a different provider for each mini ISA.

  (iv) Investment limits:

	Maxi	*Mini*
	£	£
Cash	3,000	3,000
Stocks and shares	7,000	4,000

(v)   Shares and bonds issued in any recognised exchange may be held in the stocks and shares component. AIM shares may not be held.

(vi)   Gilts may be directly held.

(vii)   From 6 April 2005, medium-term stakeholder products and life assurance products qualify for the stocks and shares component under the 5% test.

(viii)   There is no minimum period for holding an ISA investment.

PRACTICE QUESTION 8: OFFSHORE FUNDS

(a)   The letters UCITS stand for Undertakings for Collective Investments in Transferable Securities.

(b)   The main features of the European Directive on UCITS are as follows.

(i)   It has created a framework by which fund management groups domiciled within the member states can market their funds freely to investors in other member states.

(ii)   The investments which can be marketed in this way are known as UCITS.

(iii)   A member state cannot refuse permission for the manager of such an investment to market the fund in his country so long as it complies with local marketing requirements.

(c)   A unit trust can be marketed as a UCITS.

(d)   An investment trust cannot be marketed as a UCITS, as it is a closed-ended fund.

(e)   A currency fund may be the choice of a basic rate taxpayer who is prepared to take a risk. He cannot obtain access to such a fund onshore.

Tax position - will depend on whether the fund has distributor or non-distributor status.

Distributor. Dividends paid gross but subject to UK income tax gain on encashment subject to CGT.

Non-Distributor. Income tax paid on dividends and final encashment.

(f)   A fixed-interest fund with distributor status may be the choice of a non-taxpayer. The fund will roll up tax-free.

Tax position - Dividends paid gross, no further tax to pay. On encashment - no CGT liability because non-taxpayer.

(g)   A non-distributor fund may be useful for a higher rate taxpayer who may later become a basic rate taxpayer. The funds he may select if he wishes to take a higher risk are either currencies or commodities. He can encash when his tax rate has reduced and pay less tax having previously had his money rolling up in a tax-free fund.

Tutorial notes

(a)   This is a long question, so the use of notes is helpful.

(b)   In the answers to (e), (f) and (g), you must demonstrate a knowledge of the different funds available and their risk profile. You must also be able to distinguish between distributor and non-distributor status in order to earn full marks.

PRACTICE QUESTION 9: DERIVATIVES

(a)   A forward contract is an agreement for the purchase or sale of a commodity and its delivery at a certain date in the future. The price is fixed at the time of the contract.

A futures contract is the purchase or sale of the forward contract within an organised exchange market. The use of the futures contract is a method which allows the purchaser of the commodity through the forward contract to hedge against price changes.

(b)   The owner of an option has no obligation to exercise it. If he does not exercise the option, he loses his premium.

(c)   The main advantage of trading on an exchange rather than over the counter is the security offered by the clearing house which takes the risk of one party to the deal defaulting.

(d)   One type of swap which can be arranged is an interest rate swap. In this instance, A agrees to pay to B a fixed rate of interest on a loan of say £100,000. In return, B agrees to pay to A a variable rate on the same amount of loan.

(e)   Hedging is an action to reduce the uncertainty relating to the price of a commodity, security or currency. It is possible to reduce this risk by undertaking forward sales or purchases on the futures market or by taking out an option which limits exposure to price fluctuations.

PRACTICE QUESTION 10: OTHER INVESTMENTS

(a)   (i)   (1)   The investment in an Enterprise Investment Scheme is 100% unquoted shares.

(2)   The underlying investment of a VCT need only be 70% in the shares of unquoted companies, and half of that 70% can be in loan stock.

(ii)   The maximum amount which can be invested in a VCT in a tax year is £200,000 (2005/06).

(iii)   Losses on EIS shares can be offset against other taxable income or gains.

(iv)   Reinvestment relief occurs when an investor with a large capital gains tax liability from the sale of another asset invests the gains in an EIS and thereby defers payment of the tax.

CGT deferral relief was withdrawn for VCT shares issued after 5 April 2004.

(b)   (i)   *The workings of the Lloyd's market*

(1)   Lloyd's is a market of underwriters and brokers (Lloyd's brokers) who place the business on the market. Most of the Lloyd's business is now underwritten by corporate entities rather than individual 'names'.

(2)   The underwriters form themselves into syndicates, which may specialise in particular types of business.

(3)   Many of the individual underwriting 'names' do not work in the market. They provide the risk capital and share in the profit or loss of the syndicate. The amount of risk each name takes is his premium income level. The names have unlimited liability.

(4)   The day-to-day running of the syndicate is conducted by the managing agent and the interests of the names are looked after by a members agent.

(5)   Because of the length of time it takes for claims to be settled, each syndicate draws up annual accounts but these are left open for a further two years before all the claims are known.

(ii) The risk involved in being a Lloyd's name is that the names have unlimited liability. If a syndicate suffers heavy losses, a name could lose all his assets. The problems which have occurred in the past may have arisen because many of the names were ignorant of the risk they were taking and relied on others to guide them in the selection of a syndicate or syndicates. Many of them became involved in syndicates which were taking on high risk business. The names were not necessarily aware of this until it was too late and the losses arose. Some names did not have a sufficient spread of syndicates or had too high a premium income level.

(iii) Risks involved in investing in antiques:

(1) An antique can only be sold if a buyer can be found.

(2) There may be a problem with valuation on sale.

(3) Certain periods and types of antique go in and out of fashion for collectors, so an item can lose its value suddenly and without good reason.

(4) The investor is vulnerable to the unscrupulous expert.

PRACTICE QUESTION 11: TAX AND PENSIONS PLANNING

(a) (i) (1) Harry creates a trust and appoints trustees. £3,000 is given to the trust (a PET). Sarah, Harriet and James are the beneficiaries of the trust.

(2) Harry then makes an interest free loan to the trustees repayable on demand for an amount of £97,000.

(3) The trustees invest the £100,000 in one or more investment bonds and use the 5% withdrawal facility to repay the loan to the donor over a 20 year period.

(4) On death the outstanding loan is a debt to the estate but the remaining assets of the trust can pass to the beneficiaries free from inheritance tax.

(ii) The tax implications of this action are as follows.

(1) Harry has sold securities to the value of £100,000 so this may give rise to a charge to CGT.

(2) The initial gift to the trust is a potentially exempt gift (PET) for IHT purposes. However, if Harry has made no other gifts during the fiscal year this gift could use his annual exemption for IHT purposes.

(3) Whilst the bonds are in operation and the trustees do not exceed a 5% withdrawal, no income tax liability falls upon Harry.

(4) As mentioned above, on death any outstanding loan is a debt owing to the estate but the remainder of the trust assets are outside the estate and thus free of IHT.

(5) On death a chargeable event will occur on the bond or bonds and a charge to higher rate income tax could arise. This would be the liability of the donor, Harry. Whether tax needed to be paid would depend on the time in a fiscal year when Harry died. If he died early in a fiscal year, there would be little income in the year, so the gain on the bond would not bring him into the higher rate tax bands. However, death later in the year might have the opposite effect.

Tutorial notes

(i) You should be able to reproduce at least three relevant facts about the workings of the gift and loan scheme (two points each with one extra point for demonstrating a real understanding of the scheme).

(ii)   In answering the second part of the question, you need thoroughly to read the question and see the words 'all tax implications' The question calls for you to comment on the capital gains tax, inheritance tax and income tax situation.

(b)   (i)   You should explain to Jim the following points.

(1)   Jim can be a member of an occupational pension scheme and also contribute up to £3,600 pa to a personal pension scheme, if he has not been a controlling director since 5 April 2000, and if his earnings have been £30,000 or less in one of the years 2000/01 to 2005/06 (concurrency rules).

(2)   You should explain to him that the occupational scheme offers him a guaranteed pension based on his earnings near retirement. The pension achieved from the personal pension is totally dependent upon performance. In addition he is likely to receive death in service benefits if he joins the company scheme. If he continues the personal pension, the company will make no contributions to this.

(3)   He can cease paying contributions to the personal pension and make it paid-up. He may continue with the personal pension if it will just receive contracting out rebates of national insurance.

He may be able to continue to make contributions to the insurance company but as FSAVCs. However, with an FSAVC scheme there is no tax-free lump sum available on retirement.

He can ask the insurance company to quote a transfer value and move the money to the occupational scheme. The trustees of the occupational scheme would be able to give him an idea of the additional pension which the transfer value would purchase, possibly 'added years of service'.

(ii)   The information you would need on the existing scheme is as follows.

(1)   Name and address of the administrator so that you could write for full information.

(2)   Whether the scheme was a money purchase or final salary scheme.

(3)   The transfer value.

(4)   The date Jim left service and whether the paid-up pension is increasing in whole or part in deferment.

(5)   Whether Jim's service was treated as contracted-out of the State Second Pension/SERPS and if so, by what method.

(6)   The deferred benefits if the pension is not transferred including spouse's pensions and possible increases to pension in retirement.

(7)   If the pension is not transferred, the benefits which would be available to Jim's family if he died before retirement age.

(8)   Whether the scheme is in surplus and whether there are likely to be any improvements to benefits.

(9)   Whether Jim paid any AVCs and their value.

Tutorial notes

(i)   In answer to part (i), you need to remember to deal with the advantages of joining the occupational scheme and then the action that Jim may take with his existing personal pension. If you only tackle one aspect of the problem you will not score full marks (four marks are awarded for each aspect).

(ii)   In answer to part (ii) you should be able to produce at least seven points (one mark per point).

PRACTICE QUESTION 12: CLIENT INFORMATION

(a)   (i)   The information you would need on the shares, gilts and unit trusts is as follows.

        (1)   **Shares**: date of purchase, name of shares, type of share eg preference or ordinary, number of shares. current value.

        (2)   **Gilts**: date of purchase, name of gilt, nominal holding, current value.

        (3)   **Unit trusts**: date of purchase, name of fund, number of units (income or accumulation units, if applicable), current value.

   (ii) You need this information for the following purposes.

        (1)   To value the portfolio as part of the client's assets

        (2)   To be able to calculate any capital gains tax liability on the portfolio

        (3)   To be able to make comments on the suitability of the holdings to meet the client's financial aims and objectives

(b)   (i)   You would need to find out the following information.

        (1)   The existing lender
        (2)   The amount of the loan or the amount outstanding
        (3)   The method of repayment
        (4)   The current monthly mortgage repayment
        (5)   The current interest rate
        (6)   Whether any penalties apply to early repayment
        (7)   The client's and partner's current salaries

   (ii) You may be able to help him by suggesting that:

        (1)   He may wish to consider a remortgage if his income is sufficient

        (2)   The remortgage may be on a fixed rate

        (3)   The remortgage may be on a discounted rate for say the first 12 or 24 months

        (4)   The client may be able to take advantage of an offer giving a cash incentive payment or an incentive of payment of surveyor's and legal fees

PRACTICE QUESTION 13: CONSTRUCTION

(a)   Bill and Sally's financial aims are:

   (i)   To create an income from the money inherited
   (ii) To preserve the capital for the next generation

(b)   *Recommended portfolio*

Investment	Amount	Investor's name
Building Society instant access postal/online account	£10,000	Joint names
NS&I Pensioners' Bond	£20,000	Sally
NS&I Pensioners' Bond	£20,000	Bill
Unit Trust UK Equity Income	£7,000	Bill
Unit Trust UK Equity Income	£7,000	Sally
ISA corporate bond	£7,000	Bill
ISA corporate bond	£7,000	Sally
Unit Trust Tracker fund	£12,000	Joint names
NS&I Savings Certificates Index-linked	£10,000	Sally

The investments have been chosen for the following reasons.

(i) **Building Society**. Every client should have an emergency fund. This can be held in joint names so that there is always access to funds if one partner dies. A postal or online account has been selected because higher rates of interest are usually available.

(ii) **NS&I Pensioners' Bond**. This gives a high level of guaranteed income. It provides a monthly income. The income is paid gross. The investment has been split between Sally and Bill. The reason for this is that Sally only has a small state pension and she can use up the balance of her personal allowance with the gross income from the pensioners' bond. She will not need to pay tax on this.

(iii) **Corporate bond ISAs** have been used. These will give a high level of tax-free income with a small amount of risk to capital.

(iv) The **tracker unit trust** is used to produce some 'real' growth in the portfolio. Equity income unit trusts will provide a higher level of income plus some opportunity for capital growth.

(v) The **NS&I Index-linked Savings Certificates** are used to give a real rate of return on the capital.

(c) *Tax situation*

Building society account. Interest will be paid net of 20% tax. Initially Sally will be using up her personal allowance with her state pension and the income from the pensioner's bond. However, when she reaches age 65, her personal allowance will increase and she may be able to complete an R85 and have her part of the interest paid gross.

NS&I Pensioners' Bond. Interest will be paid gross. Sally will be able to pay no tax. Bill will be liable for tax on the income.

ISA. Income from the ISA will be paid tax-free. No capital gains tax will be paid on encashment.

Unit trust. The tracker trust selected is unlikely to produce income. Any gain could be subject to capital gains tax but is likely to fall well within the annual exemption for CGT. The Equity Income Unit Trust will have a tax credit of 10% and no further liability to tax on dividends will arise for basic rate tax payers although non tax payers will not be able to reclaim this.

NS&I Savings Certificates. The return from the certificates is tax-free.

Tutorial note

There is no single right answer to this question. You will be awarded marks so long as you construct a portfolio which meets the aims. You should make use of low to medium risk schemes and if at all possible make use of tax-free schemes. You should display knowledge of the maximum amounts which can be invested in various schemes.

PRACTICE QUESTION 14: RECOMMENDATIONS

(a)   *General strategy*

Anne's general strategy should be:

(i)   To invest for capital growth, she has no immediate need for income
(ii)   To maintain an emergency fund in case her temping work ceases for any period
(iii) To provide an income for herself if she is unable to work through sickness
(iv)   To provide for income in retirement
(v)   To aim to pass as much capital to her step-children as possible free of IHT

Long-term investment approach

Anne's long-term investment approach should be as follows.

(i)   Increase the value of her capital taking particular notice of the effects of inflation. To this end asset-backed investments, particularly equity funds, should be used.

(ii)   To employ a diversification of types of investment and terms, particularly as she may need access to capital at certain times to create income

(iii) To provide a certain level of liquidity of funds at all times

(iv)   To make maximum use of all tax incentives and tax-free investments

(b)   *Recommendations*

The recommended portfolio is as follows.

Type	Amount
Building society instant access postal account	£16,250
Single premium pension contributions	£7,500
Maxi ISA (UK Growth)	£7,000
NS&I Savings Certificates fixed-rate	£10,000
NS&I Savings Certificates index-linked	£10,000
Unit trusts/investment trusts	£70,250
With Profit Bond (no withdrawals)	£25,000

Income from unit trust/investment trust portfolio to be used to fund:

(i)   Regular personal pension premium £100 per month with waiver of premium
(ii)   Permanent health insurance
(iii) Personal pension term assurance £100,000, nominated beneficiaries stepchildren

Reasons for recommendations

Building society. An emergency fund is essential.

Pension. Anne should pay the maximum single premium towards a personal pension. She can contribute £3,600 gross per annum which is more than 20% of NRE. If she elects and makes the contribution by 31 January 2006, she can carry back contributions to 2004/05. She should now commence a regular premium personal pension with a separate waiver contract. The premium can be funded from the income from the unit trust/investment trust portfolio.

ISA. An equity ISA should be used to give a prospect of long-term real growth. She could sell her unit trusts in later years, use up her CGT exemptions and buy ISAs with the proceeds to ensure she is using her full ISA allowances.

NS&I Savings Certificates. These have been included to give diversification and tax-free growth without risk.

Unit trusts/investment trusts. A portfolio of unit trusts and investment trusts should be constructed to give long term growth. Some income is required to fund the policies mentioned. It is considered that the portfolio is too small for shares as insufficient spread could be achieved. Pooled investments will give exposure to equities, both UK and international, but reduce the risk encountered by direct investment into shares.

With profits bond. This investment is cautious risk and should provide Anne with capital growth through the addition of reversionary bonuses. When Anne needs to draw income she could take advantage of the cumulative 5% allowance. The bond could be written in trust to benefit her step children on death.

Income protection insurance. IPI cover is important to safeguard an income for Anne if she cannot work through long term illness. This would mean that the portfolio would not need to be touched because an income was being provided tax-free from the policy.

Personal pension term assurance. Anne has indicated that she wishes as much capital as possible to pass to the step-children without IHT. Currently the IHT liability will be in the region of £120,000. She could cover this liability by using pension term assurance, obtain tax relief on the premiums and nominate the step-children as potential beneficiaries. An amount of up to 10% of the contributions paid for retirement benefits may be paid towards life cover.

Tutorial note

Once again there is no single right answer to the question: any well reasoned answer is acceptable. However, recommendations must take into account the lack of pension and permanent health provision as well as the investment aspects. The investments chosen should be as tax efficient as possible.

PRACTICE EXAMINATION

PERSONAL INVESTMENT PLANNING

Time Limit: 3 Hours

You should base your answers to this paper on tax rates and rules applying to the 2005/06 tax year, and you can assume throughout that the English law and practice applies. You may use the Tax Tables provided in this Study Text.

All individuals should be assumed to be resident, ordinarily resident and domiciled in the UK, unless it is stated otherwise.

You may use a non-programmable calculator. You may not use any reference materials other than the tax tables.

You should attempt all the questions in parts A and B of this paper, and two of the three questions in part C. The time limit is 3 hours.

Section A carries 45 marks, and we suggest you spend about 40 minutes on it.

Section B carries 75 marks, and we suggest you spend about 70 minutes on it.

Section C carries 80 marks (40 each for each question), and we suggest you spend about 70 minutes on it.

You can answer the questions in any order you wish.

SECTION A

Answer all questions in this section, which carries 45 marks.

1	(a)	What is a fixed-interest security?	(2)
	(b)	Give three examples of fixed interest securities.	(3)
	(c)	What is a yield curve?	(2)
	(d)	Define yield to redemption.	(1)

2   (a)   A new unit trust is being advertised at a discount. What does this mean? (2)

      (b)   A friend mentions that a particular investment trust is trading at a discount. What does this mean? (2)

      (c)   If an investment trust is said to be 'heavily geared', what does that mean? (3)

      (d)   If interest rates rise and stock market values fall, what effect may this have on an investment trust which is heavily geared? (2)

3   What do the following expressions mean?

	(a)	cum div	(2)
	(b)	xr	(2)
	(c)	Dirty price	(2)
	(d)	Partly-paid shares	(2)

4   What are the following?

	(a)	A convertible loan stock	(2)
	(b)	A cumulative preference share	(2)
	(c)	A zero coupon bond	(2)
	(d)	A subscription share	(2)

5   What are the risks involved in purchasing the following?

	(a)	Unit trust	(3)
	(b)	A warrant	(3)
	(c)	A property bond	(3)
	(d)	A with profit bond	(3)

SECTION B

This question is compulsory and carries 75 marks.

6   A client telephones you, the adviser, to say that he is concerned about his sister's investments. Last year she sold a property and he believes that she was persuaded to invest the total proceeds into one investment. He does not have any details. He asks you to telephone the sister and then to visit her. On your visit, you discover the following information.

(a) Miss Jenkinson is aged 73 and in poor health.

(b) Miss Jenkinson was a teacher. She has a teacher's pension of £10,000 pa plus a full state pension. The teacher's pension is index-linked.

(c) She has a portfolio as shown below.

(d) Her brother was correct: last year she invested £60,000 in an investment bond (managed fund) with the Sleak Insurance Company. She is taking a 5% withdrawal.

(e) Miss Jenkinson owns her own property worth £75,000, with no mortgage.

(f) She says she would like a gross income of, say, £5,000 pa from her investments.

(g) She has written a will leaving a small bequest to a charity. The remainder of the estate goes to her two nieces.

(h) She says that, at her time of life, she does not wish to take too much risk, although she is prepared to take some risk to ensure that as much capital as possible passes on to the nieces.

Portfolio

Type	Holding	Mid-market price £	Valuation £	Gross yield
N/W Electrics	1,000	4.50	4,500	4.0%
Cheapshops plc	2,000	3.50	7,000	3.5%
Frostytravel	3,000	1.90	5,700	1.8%
Deadly Tobacco	3,000	2.10	6,300	1.5%
Tops Builders	2,500	4.60	11,500	2.0%
Greasy Oil	6,000	3.20	19,200	-
			54,200	
Exch. 2006 6%	10,000	104.00	10,400	
Building Society			1,500	4.0%
Sleak Insurance Co Bond	60,000	90.00	54,000	5.0%
Total assets			120,100	

(a) Comment on the portfolio and its suitability to meet Miss Jenkinson's needs.   (22)

(b) Calculate her current investment income, gross and net.   (10)

(c) Do you think an investment bond investment of this size is unsuitable? If so, why? (6)

(d) If you were to re-arrange the portfolio:

   (i) What further information might you need?   (3)

   (ii) What other aspects might you consider before proceeding?   (4)

   (iii) What costs might be involved in selling the shares and the bond?   (7)

   (iv) What, if anything could be done, to limit the cost?   (2)

(e) If it were possible to re-arrange the portfolio, briefly list the investments you would include, the amounts, the reasons and a rough indication of the income the portfolio would produce. (21)

Total marks for question: 75

SECTION C

Answer any TWO of the three questions in this section.

Each question carried 40 marks.

7   Mr Stephenson, aged 48, wants to retire at age 55. He has capital available to invest of £30,000. His current situation is as follows.

Mr Stephenson's earnings as managing director of Glowarm Electrics plc are £110,000 pa. His basic salary is £75,000 pa. The balance is made up of bonus.

He is a member of the non-contributory final salary pension scheme which provides a 1/60th accrual rate. By the time he reaches age 60 (normal retirement age) he will have earned 30 years service in the pension scheme. His company offers a money purchase AVC scheme linked to a building society investment.

He also has self-employed net relevant earnings from lecturing of £25,000. He has pensioned these earnings by use of a retirement annuity into which he pays £50 per month.

Mr Stephenson is keen to take some risk with his investment in order to maximise his pension at age 55.

(a) Mr Stephenson has heard that he can contribute up to 15% of his total earnings toward his pension. Can he therefore contribute up to £11,250 as an AVC? (2)

(b) If Mr Stephenson pays an AVC would it be better to contribute to the in-house AVC or a FSAVC? Explain the differences to him and which you think would be most suitable for his needs. (10)

(c) What is the maximum extra amount Mr Stephenson can contribute to his retirement annuity and is there any point in starting a new personal pension? (9)

(d) Explain carry forward relief. How might this help Mr Stephenson? (14)

(e) Mr Stephenson has also considered using an ISA. Would this be sensible? What are the advantages and disadvantages? (5)

Total marks for question: 40

8   Mr Williamson calls to see you and states that he is paying too much tax. He has already invested the maximum in pensions and wants to know what other schemes are available to him, which will give tax relief. (2)

(a) Describe the two UK-based schemes which will give him tax relief on amounts invested. (22)

(b) Explain the risks involved in these schemes. (4)

Mr Williamson also asks for more information about qualifying Maximum Investment Plans and tax-exempt Friendly Society plans as a means of regular saving. Explain the similarities and differences between these two types of plan with regard to:

(c) Tax treatment (6)

(d) Contribution limits (6)

Total marks for question: 40

9   A higher rate taxpayer says he is interested in buying a traded endowment policy.

    (a)   Advise him of the methods of purchase.   (9)

    (b)   Advise him of the methods of valuing such policies and the type of policy which will be most attractive.   (10)

    (c)   Advise the client of the tax implications.   (14)

    (d)   Advise the client of the risks involved.   (4)

    (e)   Might he be better advised to invest in the market via the purchase of shares in a traded endowment investment trust?   (3)

Total marks for question: 40

Answers to practice examination

SECTION A

Commentary. All the answers in this section call for you to have understood the meaning of various expressions and to be able to reproduce concise definitions. It is worthwhile memorising definitions rather than resorting to your own description, which may not be concise.

Question 2 requires a thorough knowledge of the workings of an investment trust and the consequences of gearing.

This section should be completed as quickly as possible. If you have learned definitions and the formulae for various yield calculations it should be easy to pick up full marks - a good start to the examination!

1   (a)   A fixed interest security gives a fixed rate of interest each year, normally paid half-yearly.

       (b)   Three examples of fixed-interest securities are gilts, corporate bonds (debentures) and local authority bonds.

       (c)   A yield curve is a graph of yields given by different gilts (or other securities) shown against the time they have left until maturity.

       (d)   Yield to redemption = Interest yield + Annualised capital gain or loss to redemption.

2   (a)   If a unit trust is being offered at a discount it means that the manager is reducing his bid/offer spread to attract business.

       (b)   If an investment value is trading at a discount it means that the market value of the shares is less than the net asset value of the company.

       (c)   If an investment trust is heavily geared it means that the manager has borrowed substantially.

       (d)   If interest rates rise and stockmarket values fall, the manager may have trouble in paying the interest on his outstanding borrowings and may have to sell assets to repay borrowings.

3   (a)   Cum div means that a share is purchased with the right to the next dividend.

       (b)   xr means that a share is purchased without the right to a rights issue.

       (c)   A dirty price is the price of a gilt plus the price of a few days of interest.

       (d)   Partly-paid shares are shares which are paid for in instalments and not all the instalments have been paid.

4   (a)   A convertible loan stock offers the investor a fixed rate of interest plus the opportunity to convert into the company's ordinary shares at a later date at a prearranged price.

       (b)   A cumulative preference share pays a fixed rate of dividend. The shareholder is entitled to arrears of dividends if none are paid for a particular year.

       (c)   A zero coupon bond pays no interest but gives a guaranteed return of capital at a set date.

       (d)   A subscription share is a type of warrant which earns a dividend.

5   (a)   The risk associated with a unit trust depends upon the type of trust selected. Equity trusts are more risky than cash funds. Funds in sterling will be less risky than unhedged foreign currency funds.

(b) The risk associated with a warrant is that the price at which the warrant can be exercised is above the market price. The warrant then becomes worthless.

(c) The risk associated with a property bond is that the value of the fund can fall and that the investor may be prevented from withdrawing his money when it is required. The manager has a right to withhold settlement for up to six months.

(d) The risk associated with a with profit bond is that the bonus rate will fall and that, on a full or partial encashment, the insurance company may impose a market level adjustment to the surrender value.

SECTION B

6   *Commentary.* You are asked to analyse certain information concerning a portfolio. In order to be able to do this effectively, it could help to have studied and understood the headings shown in a valuation and the column headings which appear in the Financial Times.

When commenting on the make-up of the portfolio, you should be able to break down the investments into types, eg equities, fixed interest and cash, and identify the percentages in each type. You should comment on spread and diversification. You should also comment on the level of risk in the portfolio and whether this complies with the client's attitude to risk.

You should also comment on the use or lack of tax efficient investments such as ISAs and NS&I Savings Certificates.

Part (b) calls for a simple calculation. Marks are given for remembering that the withdrawal from the bond will not be subject to immediate tax.

Part (c). You can argue either point of view, although you will have to be very convincing if you argue that the bond investment is not too large! The natural conclusion is that this is too large an investment and you should then set out the disadvantages of bonds.

Part (d). The further information required is sufficient information on the shares to be able to calculate the CGT liability and on the bond to be able to calculate the likely penalties.

When calculating the charges made by the broker, you are not expected to produce an accurate calculation but simply to state the type of charge that may be levied. You should remember to include the PTM levy and exclude stamp duty (payable on purchase, not on sale).

The costs may be reduced by the use of a share exchange. You should mention that share exchange can be used into ISAs, unit trusts and investment trusts.

Part (e). Any rearrangement of the portfolio would be acceptable, as long as there is a convincing argument. The new portfolio should, however, include a higher level of liquidity, the use of pooled investments rather than the individual shares, and some tax efficient investments such as an ISA. In order to gain the maximum marks, you should make reference to the fact that the revised portfolio meets the client's investment aims.

(a) *Comment on the portfolio*

    (i)   Over 50% of the portfolio is in equities. This is too high.

    (ii)   The spread in the portfolio is too low.

    (iii)   There appears to be no international diversification.

    (iv)   There is insufficient cash in the building society.

    (v)   There is too much capital in one investment bond.

    (vi)   Income is sufficient.

    (vii) There is no ISA.

    (viii) There are no unit trusts or investment trusts.

    (ix)   Only six shares is too few shares for a spread.

    (x)   The portfolio has a high risk profile.

(b) *Current investment income*

Type	Holding	Valuation £	Gross yield	Gross income £
N/W Electrics	1,000	4,500	4.0%	180
Cheapshops plc	2,000	7,000	3.5%	245
Frostytravel	3,000	5,700	1.8%	103
Deadly Tobacco	3,000	6,300	1.5%	94
Tops Builders	2,500	11,500	2.0%	230
Greasy Oil	6,000	19,200	-	
Exch. 2006 6%	10,000	10,400		600
Building Society		1,500	4.0%	60
Sleak Insurance Co Bond	60,000	54,000	5.0%	3,000
Total assets		120,100		4,512

Gross income = £4,512

Tax: the pensions put all the investment income (except the 5% bond withdrawals) into the basic rate band, where it will be taxed at 10%. Dividend tax = 10% × 852 = 85.20. Other tax = 20% × 660 = 132.

Net income = £4,512 – £217.20 = £4,294.80

(c) An investment bond of this size is unsuitable for the following reasons.

    (i)   There is too much capital in one investment, creating too high a level of risk.

    (ii)   The investment itself may not be the most suitable for Miss Jenkinson for the following reasons.

         (1)   Charges are high.

         (2)   The fund is taxed.

         (3)   She could lose her age allowance in a year of encashment.

         (4)   The 5% withdrawal could eat into capital if performance is not good.

(d) (i)   The further information needed is as follows.

         (1)   When were the shares purchased?

         (2)   What was the purchase price of the shares?

         (3)   A calculation of CGT liability using the information in (1) and (2) above.

    (ii)   The other aspects to consider are as follows.

         (1)   Performance history of the fund in which the investment bond is invested

         (2)   The penalties, if any, on withdrawing from the bond

         (3)   The potential tax liability on encashing the bond

         (4)   Whether the bond has gone down in value because of initial charges, poor performance or the 5% withdrawal

(iii) The costs in selling the shares would be broker's charges. If the total portfolio was sold the cost might be as follows.

Shares value £54,000

	£
£7,000 @ 1.5%	105
£8,000 @ 1.0%	80
£39,000 @ 0.5%	195
	380
PTM levy	1
Total costs	381

The cost of selling the bond would be the bid/offer spread plus penalties, if any.

(iv) The cost of the sale of the shares may be reduced by the use of a share exchange scheme to exchange the shares into unit trusts or investment trusts.

(e) *Re-arrangement of the portfolio*

Type	Amount	Reason	Gross income
	£		£
Building Society	12,000	More liquidity, especially as ill	480
Maxi ISA equity income	7,000	Tax-free	280
Gilt	12,400	Retain good income	1,252
Pensioners Income Bond	30,000	Monthly income	2,100
Investment Bond	25,000	Retain in part	0
Unit Trust/Investment Trusts	33,700	Better spread	842
	120,100		4,954

Comments

Building Society - this gives greater liquidity especially as the client is ill.

ISA- tax free returns. ISAs can be increased from unit trust portfolio, by cashing in the unit trusts and using the proceeds to fund next year's ISAs.

Gilt - is retained - good level of income. Extra £2,000 investment to create some more income.

Pensioners bond - used to create high level of guaranteed income.

Investment bond - this is reduced to a realistic amount. A partial surrender can be taken without tax charge as the value of the bond has reduced. As part is retained, any penalties have been reduced. No withdrawals taken to allow fund to build up.

Unit trust/investment trust - pooled investments give a better spread than individual shares. The shares could be sold over a number of tax years to minimise CGT liability.

Satisfying aims. The correct level of income has been achieved. The bond and unit trusts should achieve capital growth so that as much capital as possible can pass to the nieces.

SECTION C

7 *Commentary.* Part (a). The client can contribute 15% of the total earnings because he is a pre-1987 member and not subject to the earnings cap.

Part (b). When calculating the maximum contributions, you must remember to deduct the contribution currently being paid to the retirement annuity.

Part (c) calls for an understanding of carry forward relief. You would need to mention all the main points given in the answer to score full marks.

Part (d). In this answer you should draw attention to the comparison between the ISA and the personal pension/retirement annuity.

(a) He can in fact contribute £16,500, ie 15% of his total remuneration. The earnings cap does not apply because he is a pre-1987 member.

(b) If Mr Stephenson contributes to the in-house AVC, the situation will be as follows.

    (i) He has no investment choice: the money is invested in a building society.

    (ii) The in-house AVC will have a retirement age of 60, as for the main scheme. (It is now possible to draw down on the AVC fund separately of the main scheme but trustees have to approve this.)

    (iii) The charges on this scheme will be low.

    (iv) The contribution will be deducted through the PAYE system so he will receive immediate tax relief at his highest rate. With the FSAVC he can pay net of 22% tax but has to claim back the higher rate relief.

The FSAVC will offer the following.

    (i) Wider choice of investment

    (ii) Retirement age can be 55 (or as low as 50 if required and the link with the main scheme is broken)

    (iii) Charges will be higher

Choice: The FSAVC would appear preferable for the following reasons.

    (i) With a contribution of £16,500, a choice of funds is desirable.

    (ii) Mr Stephenson is funding for retirement at 55 which is possible with a FSAVC.

    (iii) As he is paying a single premium contribution, charges will not be too high.

(c) The maximum extra amount he can invest in a retirement annuity for the current fiscal year is 17.5% of £25,000 = £4,375 – £600 (monthly contribution) = £3,775.

The advantages of effecting a new personal pension would be as follows.

    (i) The ability to make a larger contribution in the current fiscal year, 25% of £25,000 = £6,250, *minus* contribution to retirement annuity £600 = £5,650.

    (ii) Mr Stephenson is considering retirement at age 55. This can be provided by a personal pension, but not by a retirement annuity. It may be sensible to set up a personal pension into which the retirement annuity benefits can be switched at age 55.

    (iii) The existing retirement annuity may not offer investment choice: it may simply be a with profit fund.

    (iv) The use of a personal pension is a means of spreading the investment. The disadvantage would be the cost of setting up a new scheme.

(d) Carry forward is a process whereby a person with a retirement annuity can carry forward unused relief for pension contributions.

The relief can be carried forward for a maximum of six years.

Before the carry forward relief can be employed, the claimant must first pay the maximum contribution in the current fiscal year. He then uses up reliefs starting with the oldest year.

The contributions which can be carried forward are calculated on the claimant's age in the particular year and his net relevant earnings in that year.

The reliefs carried forward are paid in the current fiscal year and relieved at the claimant's tax rate in the current fiscal year.

The amount which can be relieved cannot exceed the net relevant earnings in the current fiscal year, in this case £20,000.

Mr Stephenson could employ carry forward relief on his retirement annuity and this would save the cost of setting up a new personal pension plan. Unused relief from 1999/2000 onwards may be utilised by carry forward to 2005/06, and 2005/06 contributions can be carried back to 2004/05. Alternatively he may decide to use a personal pension. In that case, carry forward relief will not be available.

(e) The advantages of using an ISA are as follows.

(i) There is a facility to take a tax-free cash sum at retirement. There is no facility to take a tax-free lump sum from an AVC.

(ii) The funds are tax-exempt, as are pension funds. Tax credits on dividends cannot however be reclaimed by pension funds or in ISAs.

(iii) The tax-free lump sum can be withdrawn at any time. The scheme is not dependent on a retirement age.

(iv) The ISA fund can be retained after retirement age and a tax-free income withdrawn. The income from a pension is taxed as earned income at the marginal tax rate applying to the recipient at that time. The disadvantage is that there is no tax relief available on the contribution.

8 *Commentary.* You need to identify the two schemes, EIS and VCT, for (a) and (b), and then explain the features of both. Bullet points and notes will suffice.

The topics covered in parts (c) and (d) were examined in the April 2003 exam.

(a) The schemes currently available which will give the client tax relief on an investment are Enterprise Investment Schemes and Venture Capital Trusts.

The following are rules of an EIS scheme.

(i) The company must be unquoted but it need not be resident or incorporated in the UK.

(ii) Participation in these schemes is limited to companies with gross assets of less than £15 million before an investment and no more than £16 million after it.

(iii) The company must carry out a qualifying activity.

(iv) The investors must subscribe for new shares.

(v) The investor must not acquire more than 30% of the issued ordinary share capital in a particular company.

The tax reliefs available to a private investor in an EIS are as follows.

(i) The investor need not be a UK resident but he must be liable to UK tax.

(ii) The private investor can subscribe up to £200,000 (2005/06) for qualifying shares and obtain tax relief of 20%.

(iii) The shares must be retained for three years.

(iv) If a profit is made the investor will pay no capital gains tax.

(v) Losses on an EIS can be used to offset other taxable income or chargeable gains.

(vi)   The investor with large capital gains from the disposal of other assets can invest the gains in the EIS and defer the payment of the capital gains tax.

The rules of a VCT scheme are as follows.

(i)   The venture capital trust is similar to an investment trust but it must not be a close company.

(ii)   The company need not be resident in the UK but must be quoted on the London Stock Exchange.

(iii)   It must hold at least 70% of its investments in the shares of unquoted trading companies but not more than 15% in any one company. At least 50% of the qualifying holding must consist of ordinary share capital.

(iv)   The income of a VCT must be derived wholly from shares or securities and it must not retain more than 15% of its income derived from shares or securities.

(v)   VCTs may invest up to £1 million in any one qualifying unquoted trading company but the gross assets of the unquoted company must not exceed £15 million prior to the VCT investment.

(vi)   If the companies in which the trust invests are subsequently floated on the stockmarket, the trust can hold the shares within the portfolio for a further five years.

The tax reliefs available to a private investor in a VCT are as follows.

(i)   The investor will receive tax relief of 40% (2005/06) on any investment of up to £200,000 in a fiscal year provided the shares are held for three years.

(ii)   The investor pays no tax on dividends received.

(iii)   The investor pays no capital gains tax on encashment if a profit results.

(iv)   The investor cannot, however, offset losses on disposal against other income or chargeable gains.

(b)   The risks involved with these schemes are as follows.

    (i)   If the investments are realised within three years, the tax relief is lost.
    (ii)   There is a chance that it may be difficult to dispose of the assets after three years.
    (iii)   The value may go down.
    (iv)   They are high risk investments.

(c)   (i)   In both cases, the return is tax-free if the plan is held for at least 10 years, or three quarters of the term if sooner.

    (ii)   The investor may have to pay income tax on either type of plan if it is encashed within the earlier of 10 years or three quarters of the term.

    (iii)   A Maximum Investment Plan fund is subject to income tax and capital gains tax.

    (iv)   A Friendly Society is not subject to income tax or capital gains tax on investment returns.

    (v)   Neither type of product qualifies for tax relief on contributions.

    (vi)   For both types of product, the proceeds on maturity are tax-free.

    (vii)   A Friendly Society can no longer reclaim UK dividend tax credits of 10%.

(d) (i) Maximum Investment Plans (MIPs) generally have a higher minimum contribution than tax-exempt Friendly Society plans.

 (ii) Mr Williamson should be able to contribute £50 per month to an MIP whether this is on a single life or joint life basis.

 (iii) There is generally no maximum contribution to a MIP.

 (iv) The maximum contribution for a Friendly Society plan is £270 per annum, or £25 for monthly payments. The plans cannot be held jointly.

(e) The client has indicated that he wishes to 'hide' the money. For money laundering prevention purposes the adviser should first establish his identity, for example by seeing a birth certificate or passport, his address by reference to a utility bill and finally ask for evidence of the source of the capital to be invested.

9 *Commentary.* This question calls for a thorough knowledge of traded endowments, their features and taxation. Good marks would be scored if you could remember the taxation details, in particular the various points involved with a non-qualifying policy.

In part (e) you should be able to demonstrate that you understand the different tax treatment of the investment trust and the traded endowment policy.

(a) Endowment policies can be bought and sold via:

 (i) Market makers
 (ii) Brokers
 (iii) Auctioneers

 (i) The market maker buys policies and holds them on his books until a suitable buyer can be found. There will be no charges for the buyer to pay. The market maker will secure his profit on the difference between the buying and selling price of a particular policy.

 (ii) The broker approaches a number of market makers on behalf of a client. The idea is to achieve the best investment for the client who is buying.

 (iii) *Auctioneers.* This is the oldest method of buying policies. Auctions are held regularly. Fees of one-third of the excess over the insurance company's surrender value are charged to the seller. Sellers can decide to impose a reserve price below which they will not sell.

(b) (i) The policies bought and sold are with profit endowment policies which have normally been in force for five years and have varying maturity dates. The policies can be either qualifying or non-qualifying.

 (ii) The market value of a traded endowment policy will depend on the following.

 (1) The current surrender value quoted, maturity date of the policy and reversionary bonus to date.

 (2) The long-term outlook for bonus payout and in particular terminal bonus of the company in question and the financial strength of the company.

 (3) The purchaser of the endowment policy will need to calculate a possible maturity value based on current terminal and reversionary bonus rates. He then needs to see what effect there would be if the bonus rate changed. Most market makers will provide tables to assist the investor in this calculation.

 (4) The yields on those policies with less time to run until maturity will be less affected by falls in reversionary bonus. These are the policies which are attractive to the client.

(c)   The tax treatment of secondhand policies depends whether the policy purchased is a qualifying or non-qualifying policy.

   (i)   If it is a qualifying policy the situation is that at maturity or on the death of the life assured or the owner, the proceeds of a qualifying policy may be subject to capital gains tax. The calculation will be made taking the proceeds and deducting the purchase price, expenses, premiums paid and indexation.

   (ii)   If it is a non-qualifying policy the situation is that at maturity or the death of the life assured or owner a chargeable event will occur. The chargeable gain will be calculated by taking into account the proceeds less the premiums paid throughout the life of the policy by both the seller and buyer. Top-slicing relief will apply but if the gain once added to the purchaser's income pushes him into higher rates of tax then the gain will be subject to tax at 20% (from 6 April 2004).

   (iii)   In addition, the proceeds from the non-qualifying policy may be subject to capital gains tax. However, the taxable capital gain is reduced by any amount which is subject to income tax, so double taxation should not apply.

(d)   The risks associated with the purchase of a traded policy are as follows.

   (i)   The future reversionary bonus of the provider will not continue at current rates and may fall substantially due to market conditions.

   (ii)   The future reversionary bonus of the provider will not continue at current rates and may fall due to weakness in the financial strength of the insurance company.

   (iii)   The insurance company may be taken over and that this may have an adverse affect on long term bonus rates.

   (iv)   The terminal bonus paid on maturity may be substantially less than predicted.

(e)   The advantages of the client investing in a traded endowment investment trust are as follows.

   (i)   A spread of investments via the pool.

   (ii)   The ability to encash the investment at any time, not having to wait until the maturity date.

   (iii)   The taxation situation may be better for a higher rate tax payer. He can bed and breakfast his investment each year and therefore avoid a potential CGT liability. Tax cannot be avoided with the purchase of a single policy because the whole gain crystallises on a particular day and there is no flexibility.

Index

REVIEW FORM & FREE PRIZE DRAW

All original review forms from the entire BPP range, completed with genuine comments, will be entered into one of two draws on 31 January 2006 and 31 July 2006. The names on the first four forms picked out on each occasion will be sent a cheque for £50.

Name: _____   Address: _____

_____

Date: _____   _____

How have you used this Text?
(Tick one box only)

☐ home study (book only)

☐ on a course: at _____

☐ with 'correspondence' package

☐ other _____

Why did you decide to purchase this Text?
(Tick one box only)

☐ recommended by training department

☐ recommendation by friend/colleague

☐ recommendation by a lecturer at college

☐ saw advertising

☐ have used BPP Texts in the past

☐ other _____

Your ratings, comments and suggestions would be appreciated on the following areas.

	Very useful	Useful	Not useful
Introductory section	☐	☐	☐
Main text	☐	☐	☐
Questions in chapters	☐	☐	☐
Chapter roundups	☐	☐	☐
Quizzes at ends of chapters	☐	☐	☐
Practice examination	☐	☐	☐
Structure and presentation	☐	☐	☐
Availability of Updates on website	☐	☐	☐

	Excellent	Good	Adequate	Poor
Overall opinion of this Study Text	☐	☐	☐	☐

Do you intend to continue using BPP Study Texts?   ☐ Yes   ☐ No

Please note any further comments and suggestions below on the reverse of this page, or write by e-mail to fpqueries@bpp.com

Please return this form to: AFPC Range Manager, BPP Professional Education, FREEPOST, London, W12 8BR

REVIEW FORM & FREE PRIZE DRAW (continued)

Please note any further comments, suggestions and apparent errors below.

FREE PRIZE DRAW RULES

1   Closing date for 31 January 2006 draw is 31 December 2005. Closing date for 31 July 2006 draw is 30 June 2006.

2   Restricted to entries with UK and Eire addresses only. BPP employees, their families and business associates are excluded.

3   No purchase necessary. Entry forms are available upon request from BPP Publishing. No more than one entry per title, per person. Draw restricted to persons aged 16 and over.

4   Winners will be notified by post and receive their cheques not later than 6 weeks after the relevant draw date.

5   The decision of the promoter in all matters is final and binding. No correspondence will be entered into.

See overleaf for information on other
BPP products and how to order

AFPC® Order

To BPP Professional Education, Aldine Place, London W12 8AW

Tel: 020 8740 2211. Fax: 020 8740 1184

E-mail: Publishing@bpp.com Web:www.bpp.com

Mr/Mrs/Ms (Full name)

Daytime delivery address

Postcode

Daytime Tel

E-mail

	Study Text £39.95	i-Pass CD-ROM £29.95	Practice & Revision Kit £19.95
ADVANCED FINANCIAL PLANNING CERTIFICATE (7/05 editions, except H15)			
G10: Taxation and Trusts	☐	☐	☐
G20: Personal Investment Planning	☐	—	—
G30: Business Financial Planning	☐	—	—
G60: Pensions	☐	—	☐
G70: Investment Portfolio Management	☐	—	—
H15: Supervision and Sales Management	☐ (1/05)	—	—
H25: Holistic Financial Planning	☐	—	—
Half-credit subjects	£32.95		
K10: Retirement Options	☐	—	—
K20: Pension Investment Options	☐	—	—
SUBTOTAL	£	£	£

TOTAL FOR PRODUCTS £

POSTAGE & PACKING

	First	Each extra
Texts/Kits		
UK	£5.00	£2.00 £
Europe*	£6.00	£4.00 £
i-Pass		
UK	£2.00	£1.00 £
Europe*	£3.00	£2.00 £

TOTAL FOR POSTAGE & PACKING £

Reduced postage rates apply if you **order online** at www.bpp.com/afpc

Grand Total (Cheques to *BPP Professional Education*) I enclose a cheque for (incl. Postage)

Or charge to Access/Visa/Switch £

Card Number

Expiry date   Start Date

Issue Number (Switch Only)

Signature

We aim to deliver to all UK addresses inside 5 working days; a signature will be required. Orders to all EU addresses should be delivered within 6 working days. *Europe includes the Republic of Ireland and the Channel Islands. For delivery to the rest of the world, please call us on +44 (0)20 8740 2211. For information about BPP's study material for the new Certificate in Financial Planning, please call 020 8740 2211.